D0192867

A FIRESIDE BOOK

Published by
SIMON & SCHUSTER INC.

New York   London   Toronto
Sydney   Tokyo   Singapore

CULT
BASEBALL
PLAYERS

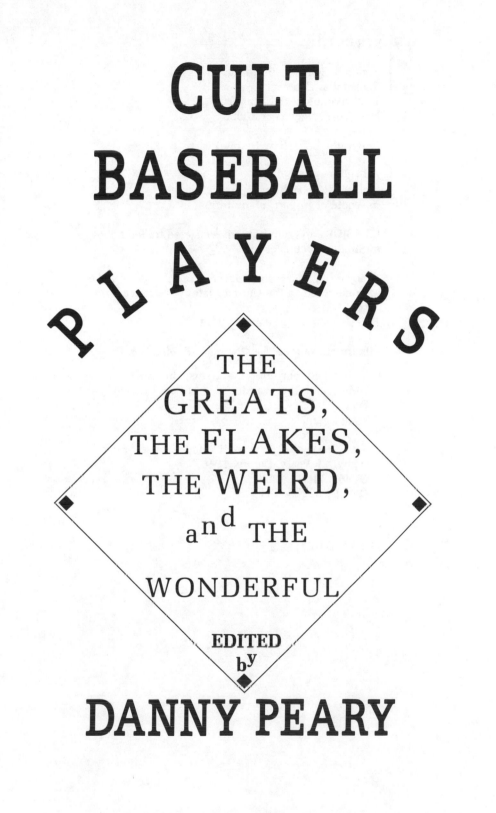

THE
GREATS,
THE FLAKES,
THE WEIRD,
and THE

WONDERFUL

EDITED
by

DANNY PEARY

F FIRESIDE

Simon & Schuster Building
Rockefeller Center
1230 Avenue of the Americas
New York, New York 10020

FIRESIDE and colophon are registered trademarks
of Simon & Schuster Inc.

Designed by Marysarah Quinn
Manufactured in the United States of America

10   9   8   7   6   5   4   3   2   1

Library of Congress Cataloging in Publication Data

Cult baseball players : the greats, the flakes, the
  weird, and the wonderful / edited by Danny
  Peary.
      p.   cm.
  "A Fireside book."
    1. Baseball   players—United   States—Biog-
raphy.   I. Peary, Danny, 1948–
GV865.A1C85 1990
796.357'092'2—dc20
[B]   89-27907
                                                 CIP

ISBN 0-671-67172-3

To my hero,
Victor Pellot Power,
for a childhood full of excitement.

Acknowledgments

I received a great deal of help and encouragement while assembling this anthology. I would especially like to thank my editor, Ed Walters, Hollie Manheimer, and Liz Cunningham for bringing order to chaos. I am also indebted to my agent, Chris Tomasino, the late Tim McGinnis, Sydny Weinberg-Miner, and Sol Skolnik for initiating this strange project. I thank Dan Farley, Jeff Neuman, copy editor Steven Boldt, production manager George Turianski, Laura Yorke, Pat Eisemann, Liza Wright, Stephanie Bowling, Ellen Pluta, Gary Shrader, Cathy Dorsey, Marysarah Quinn, Jackie Seow, Drew Hodges, Suzanne Donahue, and everyone else at Fireside.

I thank Vic Power.

I am eternally grateful to John Krich for putting me in contact with Vic Power. I also received special help from other authors: John Schulian, Mike Downey, Rebecca Stowe, Elinor Nauen, Max Manning, Lawrence S. Ritter, Roy Campanella II, Dan Shaughnessy, George Kimball, Gerald Peary, Tom Mortenson, Joan Mellen, Tom Sewell, and Cory Gann.

I sincerely appreciate the assistance of Pamela Jameson, Paul Brenner, Herb Gardner, Rhea Tabakin, Samuel Berg, Angela Owens, Leigh Brown, Meri McCall, Anne Kostick, Chick Foxgrover, Susan Cohen, Jim Bouton, Garry Trudeau, Donna Villani, Luis Alverez, Mimi Lupinski, Kurt Loder, Lanford Wilson, Roger Nygard, Jerry Izenberg, Dana Schreiber, Cheryl Bord, Tug McGraw, Ossie Davis, Larry Hogan, Bill Cooper, Jeanine Evert, Gary Van Allen, Chris Smith, Dale Long, Susan Smith, Roy Campanella, Annette Campanella, Skip Battin, Karin Freud, Loretta Farb, Mike Stephen, Larry Babcock, Susie Gharrity, Tyler Barnes, Connie Piotrowski, Thomas Treece, Wanda D. Taylor, Vicki Johnson, Michael J. Williams, Patty Waters, Gloria Follaci, Debbie Matson, Susan Selig, Maria Jacinto, Christine Urban, and Patricia Kelly, Dan Bennett, and Helen Kubis at the National Baseball Hall of Fame.

I am most appreciative to the National Baseball Hall of Fame, and those major league teams and individuals who supplied photos. Since baseball cards played such an important part in my childhood and those of a number of the authors, I thought it fitting to include some in this book—so I am most thankful to Topps Company, Inc. and Norman Liss of Liss Public Relations, Inc. for granting permission.

Finally I thank my parents, Joseph and Laura, and most of all, my wife, Suzanne, and daughter, Zoë.

Danny Peary

Contents

Introduction

Talk baseball and invariably certain players from the past will become part of the conversation. Mention their names, recall their nicknames, and waves of nostalgia flow through baseball fans. Stories are swapped, stats are offered, debates follow, legends grow. Of the thousands of players who are part of baseball history and lore, there are only a few for whom fans feel passion long after their careers have ended. Not all of this select group were stars on the field, but they all had a mysterious "star quality," an undeniable mystique that made them objects of cult adoration.

This anthology is a tribute to 59 of those special former players—the greats, the flakes, the weird, and the wonderful—whose distinct play (good and bad) and colorful personalities provided us with instant pleasures and precious memories and earned them our admiration, deep affection, and sincere gratitude. And it is equally an exploration of the attachments that baseball fans—be they youngsters or adults, sportswriters, broadcasters, or even teammates—develop for such players.

The essays in this collection were written by sports columnists from around the country, broadcasters, and former players, as well as actors, directors, and an assortment of writers who have a deep love of baseball. With the exception of a few sportswriters who selected the most memorable players they have covered while on the job, the contributors elected to write about their all-time favorite players or, in a few cases, those players who had even more lasting impact. Since I found my lifelong baseball idol, Vic Power, before I entered grammar school, I expected almost all of the writers to choose players they discovered at a similar age. I was pleasantly surprised that they came upon their special players at all ages, even as adults. Just as their subjects range from the sport's most famous players to relatively obscure figures, the authors are a varied lot who approach their subjects differently. Yet I think they all touch on the distinctive bond they have with their subjects, be it simple appreciation for their talents and contributions to baseball history or deep emotional attachment. Some pieces are quite personal, while some (but not all) penned by sportswriters exhibit the detachment of the professional. If there is a common thread to at least a majority of the essays, it is that the writers are unabashedly protective of their players, giving even all-time greats underdog status and defending them against any still-flying slings and arrows of unappreciative fans, owners, and sportswriters.

Why do individuals become attracted to particular players? It could be the player's swing, batting stance, fielding ability or inability, hustle, class, attitude, behavior, looks, or a combination of these traits. It could be one game-winning homer, the way he argued with umpires, or just an exciting baseball card. Or it may be something deeper. Individuals may adopt a player who they feel is under attack from the media, fans, and ownership and needs a defender and a friend. In turn, a player could be the answer to a person's loneliness—he becomes both his loyal friend and, with bat swinging, his champion. He might well become like a member of the family: It's quite ironic that a boy and girl can look in the sports pages and know exactly what and how well their favorite players did at work the day before, yet have no idea what their own father did at his job or how well he did it.

As the essays illustrate, ballplayers have the uncanny ability to become integral to the lives of individuals, even complete strangers. The players in this book have not only contributed excitement and entertainment to their sport, but have also enriched many lives. Isn't it scary to think how baseball and our memories would have been diminished if just those 59 players written about in this book, of all the men who ever played professional baseball, had opted for tennis? But they were drawn to baseball, just as we are drawn to them.

CULT
BASEBALL
PLAYERS

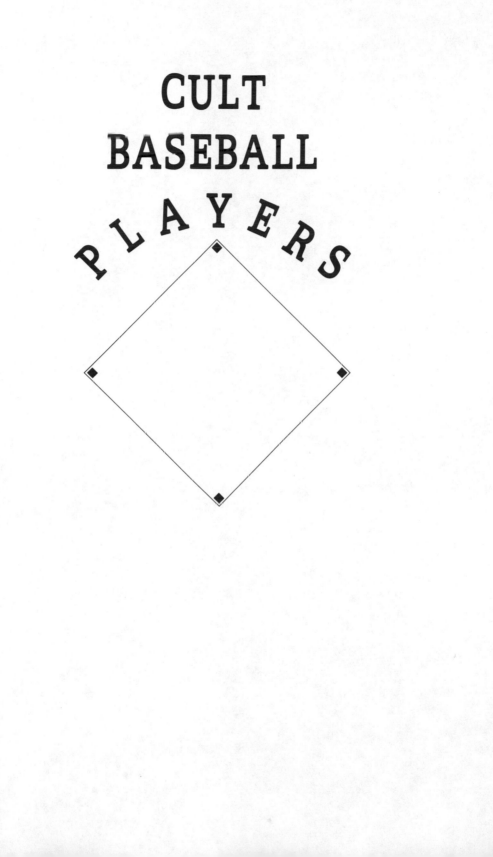

RON SHELTON on
STEVE DALKOWSKI

It was a groundskeeper in Stockton who first told me about Steve Dalkowski, the fastest pitcher of all time. Dalko once threw the ball through the wooden boards of the right-field fence, he said. The groundskeeper studied the broken boards, maintained like a shrine, and the Dalkowski stories started flowing. In minor league ballparks all over the country, they still talk about the hardest thrower of them all.

He's not big, they always say. Little guy, glasses, doesn't say much. Just to look at him you'd never guess who he was, but then most people never heard of him anyway. A cop in Bakersfield still keeps an eye on him, makes sure his rent is paid, picks him out of the gutter. His arrest record is fourteen feet long, the cop says, all drunk and disorderly. A bar in Oildale, another fight with some unemployed oil rigger, a fight about nothing, about everything.

The cop says, "Don't try to be a hero, don't try to help him, he's gettin' by. Some woman fell for him again, is trying to clean him up. It won't work, never has, every five years some decent broad tries to clean him up. Fails. Leave it to the broads. Nothin' can be done."

Summer nights in Bakersfield he can still be found, standing in the oven heat down the right-field line near the bullpen, watching the minor league pitchers loosen up. Every few years a sportswriter from the East flies in to do a piece about him for a big magazine, but the little guy never shows up for the interview. Except for that, and the cops and the groundskeepers, nobody knows who he is.

To the ballplayers in the bullpen he's just another drunk. It matters not that he used to pitch in that very ballpark, that he used to be the greatest pitching prospect of all time. From a prospect to a suspect, they used to say. And if you don't believe the groundskeepers and the cops, ask the veterans.

The fastest pitcher I ever saw? Easy. Dalkowski. Dalko, we called him. Little guy, glasses. Drank like a fish. Had unbelievable heat. Blew it by Ted Williams in spring training. "Fastest ever," Ted said. "I never want to face him again." Harry "The Cat" Brecheen called it "the best arm in the history of baseball." Cal Ripken, Sr., his catcher in the minors, said, "Nobody else was close." And the stories are endless.

In the days before radar guns, the Baltimore organization sent him out to the Aberdeen Proving Grounds the night after throwing a complete game. They set up a tubelike device on a tripod above home plate that could measure the speed of an object in flight. The problem was, of course, Dalko couldn't hit the damn thing. He threw for forty minutes before sneaking a fastball down the tube: 98.6 miles an hour—without a mound. A fresh, sober Bob Feller threw 5 miles an hour slower through the same machine. Some say Dalko would've stopped a radar gun at 120 mph.

In Wilson, North Carolina, he threw a wild pitch through the welded mesh screen sixty feet behind the catcher. Thirty years later the hole in the screen is still there.

He stood in front of the center-field clubhouse in Stockton, 430 feet from home plate, watching his teammates place bets to see if any of them could throw a ball to home plate on a single bounce. One of them did. His curiosity aroused, Dalko picked up a ball. Without warming up, still in street clothes, he threw it over home plate. Over the backstop. It landed in the press box somewhere.

There was the time his catcher couldn't get the glove up fast enough and a rising fastball hit the umpire in the mask, shattering it in three places. The ump got off easy, people say, compared to the guy who had his ear ripped off by one of Dalko's 0-and-2 pitches. It was a clean tear, they said. Sewed back on real easy.

They sent him to Florida to play under the steady influence of a veteran manager and just maybe, shake his love of drinking and partying. They wanted him to mature. Instead, he became pals with Bo Belinsky. The manager had a heart attack.

And if the stories can be challenged, the numbers can't. In the end, that's what baseball reduces to after all—stories and numbers. That's what's wonderful and terrifying about the game. A broken-bat hit looks like a line drive in the box score. And a line drive to

short is just another 0 for 1. In the history of professional baseball, there are no numbers like Dalko's.

In a nine-year career, he average 13 strikeouts for every 9 innings. He also averaged 13 walks.

He struck out 262 in 170 innings in Stockton in 1960. He walked 262 the same year.

He threw 283 pitches in a complete game at Aberdeen one night, but a few days later 120 pitches only got him into the second inning.

There was the game he walked 21, struck out 18, and threw a no-hitter.

The Appalachian League, the South Atlantic League, the Carolina League, the Northern League . . . nine leagues in nine years. Every league but the one that matters. With the best minds in baseball trying to teach him control. Paul Richards, Earl Weaver, Billy De Mars, Harry Dunlop—these were the great Oriole years when a base-ball empire was built on fundamentals—none of them could help Dalko get the ball over the plate.

And then, in '63, something happened in Elmira. Suddenly Dalko was throwing strikes. His strikeout numbers stayed high, his bases on balls dropped dramatically. He changed, they said, maybe because he'd met a woman. More likely because he hadn't. Koufax had been wild in his early years until, magically almost, he took a little off the ball and began throwing strikes. Koufax had been letting up? It's a frightening thought, but maybe that's what Dalko needed. Tame the thunderbolt—it's still a thunderbolt. His ERA dropped under three—there were years it had been over twelve—and he started winning.

Dalko went to spring training with the Orioles where the big leaguers gathered around the cage to see firsthand the arm they'd been hearing about. That's where he blew it past Ted Williams. Where he struck out the side in two appearances. His wandering in the wilderness was going to be worth it. Dalko would be the greatest short reliever in history—come in with the bases loaded and throw 120 mph strikes to close out the game. All the bus rides and drunken binges and seasons in mildewed motels in places like Pensacola, Stockton, Kennewick, were leading to New York, Chicago, Los Angeles, after all. . . .

Jim Bouton was the batter, of all people, in the spring training game. There was a runner on first when Bouton laid down a sacrifice bunt. Dalko jumped on the bunt, whirled, threw to first. And his arm went dead. It was nothing dramatic, nobody even knew at first. Bouton barely remembers the moment, but the indestructible left arm of Steve Dalkowski, abused, alcohol sodden, able to throw baseballs through wooden fences—was gone like that. Zeus quietly took back his thunderbolt, and Dalko returned to the minors to wander around for a couple more years.

He threw his last pitch in the Mexican leagues, drifted back to Stockton, got married, divorced, and lost a dozen jobs. A bartender, a forklift driver, a ditchdigger—he even worked in his mother-in-law's pet shop, but he couldn't hold that job either. Up and down Highway 99 in the San Joaquin Valley, another marriage, another divorce, a couple kids along the way, hitting all the bars in all the farm towns, he found at last the one job that required neither a resume nor a reference. Dalko began picking cotton in the towns where he once pitched.

Twenty years later, he's still standing down the right-field line in Bakersfield, still watching the games, still drinking. On this night the woman finds him and takes him home. Or maybe it's the cop. In either case it's a night he won't end up in jail.

At dawn, he's in the back of a truck filled with Mexican farmworkers. He rides silently to the fields. Certainly he's the only Polish grapepicker in Kern County, the only migrant farmworker from New Britain, Connecticut, and the only man on that truck who ever terrified Ted Williams.

And whether the gift of his left arm was an act of grace or just a cruel trick, and whether or not any strong woman ever dries him out, and whether he lives out his life in peace or shows up some

4   CULT BASEBALL PLAYERS

morning in the Bakersfield morgue—just another drunken brawl—
he takes something to the fields of Delano no one else can claim.

Dalko, the little guy with glasses, the guy who drank like a fish,
was the hardest thrower of them all. It's in the numbers and it's in
the stories. And in baseball, at least, that's enough.

Ron Shelton is a former minor league player who directed and cowrote
the award-winning script for *Bull Durham,* a film about minor league
baseball, and *Blaze.* He wrote the screenplay for *The Best of Times.*

JOHN SAYLES
on
DICK STUART

I once did an experiment in Biology in which we imprinted baby chicks just out of the shell on something other than their mothers. The first thing they saw moving and making noise became their mother figures and role models. It could have been a lab assistant or windup toy or a vacuum cleaner (though the latter tends to be dangerous when chicks are very little). There is a similar sensitive period in the life of a baseball fan, usually coming between the ages of five and ten, when he imprints on a certain team and certain player. I was vaguely entering the age of reason when I became aware that you were supposed to have a "favorite team." There was much playground discussion around these decisions, and a certain amount of violence. A kid in my first grade hit another in the face with a gooey stick (a branch with sap still running out of it—a favored weapon in class wars) because the other kid wouldn't agree that the Cubs were going to win the World Serious. That the Cubs weren't going to *play* in the World Serious didn't seem to matter.

At this point, I'd never really sat down and watched a whole professional ball game on TV, but there was a big hayfield across the street where, every day the weather permitted, you played baseball. If you were a boy kid, that's what you *did*, like cows gave milk and Davy Crockett shot at bad guys. I was tall for my age and wouldn't go away, so I got to play with kids two, three, sometimes four years older, quantum leaps for a first-grader. This caused even more pressure to have opinions on teams and players. My brother liked the Yankees, so that was out, the Dodgers and Giants had already split

CULT BASEBALL PLAYERS

for California, and the Mets hadn't made the scene yet. I chose the Pirates, I think because I liked their uniforms in the baseball-card pictures. Being a Pirates fan in upper New York State in the fifties wasn't as sociopathic as being a Cubs fan there (or being a Cubs fan anywhere), but it was unusual.

So one day I turned on the TV and there was my favorite team, the Pittsburgh Pirates, in the uniforms I thought were so neat. I don't know whom they were playing or where, but it was late in the game when this big guy gets up and WHAM (!) wins it with a shot over the center-field wall. *Way* over. There was no instant replay in those days, but I feel like I saw it over and over again. And that was it—I was imprinted on Dick Stuart.

Stuart was one of a crop of big bangers that operated in the late fifties and early sixties. Big guys (Stuart was 6'4") can't field much maybe, can't run much, strike out a lot, but when they got hold of one—forget it. Downtown. Frank Howard was in business then, and Ted Kluszewski, Joe Adcock, and Walt Dropo still, and Cash, Long, Colavito, Killebrew, Gentile, Gordy Coleman—mostly white guys with muscles who they'd stick at first base or bury in the corners of the outfield. When they came up with men on, it was always exciting.

Stuart had the misfortune of playing the meat of his career in

Courtesy of Pittsburgh Pirates

spacious Forbes Field, where the fences were high and far, far away. He hit a lot of doubles and long outs while he was there from 1958 through 1962. How he would have hit playing half his games in a smaller park is one of the eternal what-ifs of baseball. Ask Ralph Kiner, who was before my time but must have been some piece of work to have put as many out of Forbes as he did. But one of Dick Stuart's charms was that he was not with the program. A power hitter with a slash-and-run team in a slash-and-run ballpark, a guy who had one of his worst years in 1960 when the Pirates won the pennant and just three singles and no RBIs when they beat the Yankees in the Series, an intensely bad fielder on a club with gloves like Groat, Mazeroski, Virdon, and Clemente.

What he did have was muscle and an implacable ability to do one thing well and nothing else. He could hit. Boys are obsessed with muscles, with who can "take" whom, who can throw the hardest and hit the farthest. The subtleties of baseball come later. Though watching Roberto Clemente was always thrilling, trying to play like him never quite worked out—all I could manage was the *swinging* at bad pitches. And though I could hit line drives steadily, my feet at that age were obscenely big and hard to move—I knew Roberto had never been thrown out at first on a clean single to right.

What big leaguer was that slow?

Dick Stuart, who stole only two bases in ten years of major league ball (and with those the element of surprise must have helped).

For some reason the first glove I owned weighed more than my head and had fingers as thick as my wrist. I couldn't hold the thing up, much less field grounders with it.

What big leaguer could mangle an easy roller like me?

Dr. Strangeglove, the man who once got an ovation in Fenway for successfully picking up a hot dog wrapper that had blown onto the field. The awfulness of Stuart's fielding has not been exaggerated. In his first seven seasons he led his league's first basemen in errors five times outright and was coleader the other two years despite playing just 64 and 101 games in the field. His 29 errors in 1963 almost tripled that of his nearest competitor.

Who just didn't have it some days, who never quite became the next Kiner, much less the next Ruth? Me and Dick Stuart.

The lure of Dick Stuart was the lure of potentional, the lure of all long-ball hitters. Couple men on base and just one swing—just one fat pitch—just one good year in a ballpark with friendly fences and you're in the history books. When you're seven years old, everything is potential, and I wasn't the only one who thought he'd explode one of those years.

Stuart got a trade made in heaven in '63, going to the Red Sox of Fenway Park, where punch hitters like Felix Mantilla would end up before retirement and poke twenty or more balls over the left-field wall. The Green Monster beckoned and Stuart answered with 42 homers (and a league-leading 118 RBIs) and 33 homers (and 114 RBIs) in two seasons. Boston was a pretty sad team then, usually so far out of the race that Stuart's fielding was more entertaining than frustrating, and he was popular there. If he was a disappointment to the fans, he wasn't the *special* disappointment he'd been to Pirate fans, who'd been fed on the rumor that he'd hit 66 homers one season in the minors. Red Sox fans *breathe* disappointment, so Stuart was nothing new.

He was human, so clearly human in a game that works hard to create heroes, and I think that's why the early imprinting with me survived the trades. As life got more complicated, as baseball rules and teams began to change, it was comforting to know that someone out there was still going for the fence every time up, trying to win it all with one good shot. He hit 228 homers for the Pirates, Red Sox, Phillies (in 1965 for his final full season), Mets, Dodgers, and Angels (with whom he attempted a comeback in 1969) while averaging over 100 strikeouts for every full season. He couldn't field. He couldn't run. But every couple days, boy, runners on base and Dick Stuart at bat, and WHAM!

Forget it.

Downtown.

John Sayles wrote and directed the films *Eight Men Out*, about the Chicago Black Sox scandal, *Return of the Secaucus 7, Lianna, Baby, It's You, The Brother from Another Planet*, and *Matewan*. He is the author of *Pride of the Bimbos, The Anarchists Convention, Union Dues: A Novel*, and *Thinking in Pictures: The Making of the Movie Matewan*.

BUD COLLINS
on
BUDDY ROSAR

Warren Vincent Rosar as a god? Miscast, maybe, but that's the way it was in my adolescent circle in 1944. Our gods didn't have wings on their heels or omnipotence or omniscience on their brains. They had spiked feet, billed headwear, raiment of flannel that was emblazoned INDIANS, and a fifth-place mission.

They were a Lake Erie neighborhood godsquad entitled Cleveland Indians, based at a shabby Olympus of brick, timber, concrete, and iron—League Park. Beloved League Park has gone the way of *Citizen Kane's* Rosebud, a place where, clinching the 1946 pennant for the Red Sox, Ted Williams hit his shabbiest home run. A roller it was, along the third baseline, countering an overshifted defense. Can you picture that ball trickling tantalizingly into empty left field, a mischievous runaway, as Williams—no candidate for *Chariots of Fire*—galloped the bases and giggled, his baggy gray uniform flapping? All the while Cleveland infielders and outfielders, positioned on the right-field side in manager Lou Boudreau's celebrated "Williams Shift," were scrambling madly, hares who knew they'd been had by the tortoise.

You had to be there. Only Buck Rogers had TV then.

You could worship from afar, of course, taking the daily scripture in the paper, or listening to games on the radio, whose bullfrog voice, former Indian Jack Graney, took a few liberties in those untelevised days. A few? Very little was routine that happened before the eyes of the imaginative and histrionic Graney, who had been an outfield extra for the 1920 champions.

The only way to see the gods of baseball, reasonably lively and in color, was at the ballpark. For my friends and me, living in a small town amid farmland to the southwest of Cleveland, it meant a pilgrimage, gladly made, to the city's East Side. Two hours by bus and streetcar to East 55th and Lexington, where League Park stood, a pleasure dome (despite its decrepitude) in dusky green. Though a little smaller in seating capacity, it was a sort of Fenway Park reversed—up-close right-field wall, topped by screen, and deep left and center, a meadow where I first saw the illustrious enemies camped, Ted Williams and Joe DiMaggio.

I also saw a god named Bob Feller, a young, steam-throwing pitcher for the Indians. Feller was the first ballplayer I ever spoke to—so to speak—a conversation that took some of the luster off his godliness. Waiting outside the players' entrance with other kids, I accosted Feller on his way to his car, parked at the curb.

Extending my scorebook: "May I please have your autograph, Mr. Feller?"

Opening the car door: "Get the hell out of the way, kid, or I'll run you over."

Later, in the line of duty, I would have some less pleasant conversations with ballplayers, as well as some very good ones. But nothing could diminish, or even improve on, the very first day at the ballpark. Who can forget his own big league debut as witness? As a fifth-grader, hyped by anticipation, I ran headlong up drooping and echoing staircases to League Park's upper deck, then sprinted along a gangway and through an entry to be struck in the face by a green flash. Dazzled, I beheld the field. No grass had ever looked greener. It even grew, carefully groomed, riven by basepaths, in the infield. I had only seen skin diamonds, entirely dirt.

The grass was spattered with gray—the Washington Senators in their pregame workout. Lowly Washington was always the team you got with the tickets the Indians sent around to schools. With such tickets, upon payment of twenty-five cents, you were admitted.

It didn't matter. Washington . . . anybody . . . it was a big league game. A jolly-looking Washington outfielder named Bobby Estalella smiled up at us screechers, and waved, that day. His demeanor helped soften the fact that he was in on beating our Indians.

One of those bus-and-streetcar journeys, five years later, was how I met our particular god of 1944, Warren Rosar. Better known as Buddy, he was a thirty-year-old catcher for the Indians who had done his bit for the pennant-winning Yankees in 1941–42. World War II was on, and the figures more important to a ballplayer than batting average or ERA were his draft classification. I can't remember whether Rosar had the magic number, 4-F (physically incapable of bearing arms), but another god, Lou Boudreau, did. In spite of gimpy ankles, Boudreau led the league in batting at .327. He had become the "boy manager" of the Indians two years before at twenty-five, all the while a practicing shortstop, and was on his way to the Hall of Fame.

Even though quality ballplayers were in as short supply as silk stockings, rubber tires, and gasoline, my friends and I were nonetheless enthusiastic about whatever overage or somewhat infirm leftovers the Indians put on display. A big leaguer was a big leaguer whether he was one-eyed outfielder Paul O'Dea of the Indians, one-armed outfielder Pete Gray of the Browns, or big-bellied thirty-eight-year-old ex-shortstop Joe Cronin, closing out his Hall of Fame career at first base for the Red Sox.

Buddy Rosar was a communal god, our team's namesake. In the kids' league we played in, Class F (a forerunner of Little League, organized jointly by the *Cleveland News* and a grocery-store chain), teams were named for big leaguers. Preferably Indians.

I suppose we wanted to be the Boudreaus, but somebody else in our division beat us to it. So we wholeheartedly became the Rosars, following his every move, hoping he'd go on a hitting rampage, which he never did.

There was more to our adoption of Buddy Rosar as household god than that. Our mothers had a lot to do with it. Practical women that they were, they immediately vetoed the candidates of our pitcher, a Polish kid named Mousie Janowick: Casimir Kwietniewski, a White Sox infielder, and Hank Ruszkowski, another Indians catcher.

"Nothing against Poles, Mousie," my mother said. "One of my best grandfathers was Polish. I am also a great admirer of the piano player, Ignacy Paderewski, which would be a ludicrous name for the team because you all have bad hands. But do you realize how many letters are in those names?"

The problem was effort, not ethnic. Among innumerable maternal chores was baseball seamstressing, the cutting of letters of navy-blue felt and affixing them to uniforms. Could you blame a mother for rooting for a god with a short name?

"If it's Ruszkowski, I'm just doing one letter—R!" announced Mrs. Brady.

Mrs. Nock was pleased because her kid's team was five letters, the O'Deas, honoring the half-sighted Indian, Paul O'Dea.

"What about Mel Ott?" she said to my mother. "The Otts."

"Perfect. But they turned it down. Apparently Mel Ott is an alien god because he plays for the New York Giants."

Mother suggested Poats. But Ray Poat was a pitcher of little charisma, and the name, as our center fielder, Ned Livengood, said, was "kind of weird."

The mothers turned down Roy Cullenbine, an outfielder, and I think it was Mrs. Curtis who suggested Rosar as a compromise.

All right, Buddy Rosar was our man, a .263 hitter with zero home runs that summer who wound up his career in 1951 with the Red Sox. With ROSARS illuminating our proud and concave chests, we won our division, and my father got a sportswriter he knew to arrange an introduction to the god himself.

League Park, rusting and rotting, was by then used only part-time by the Indians, who had begun to play night games and Sundays at their present downtown homestead, cavernous Municipal Stadium. But could a papal audience at the Vatican compare to meeting Buddy Rosar at League Park? The whole team couldn't be included, the sportswriter, Dan Taylor of the *Press*, told us. Just three or four. On the appointed day, we delegates nervously stood at a railing near the Indians dugout from which the god would emerge.

Gods, as you know, come in all forms. The one called Rosar was burly and rumpled. "He looks hung over," Mousie whispered. A chaw puffed one cheek, evidence of which could be seen on his shirtfront. He seemed nice enough, shook hands, and said a few words like "Good luck," and ambled back to work to take batting practice. We did not exactly feel in a state of grace. But if Rosar was just another god, he was our god.

My mother wasn't impressed, hearing about the tobacco stains on the holy letters INDIANS.

"He wouldn't get away with that if his mother had to sew them the way I did, and keep the uniforms washed. She'd straighten him out," said my mother. "Maybe we were wrong in turning down Ruszkowski."

Bud Collins is a tennis broadcaster with NBC and sports columnist for the *Boston Globe.* He is the author of *My Life with the Pros,* and coauthor of Rod Laver's *The Education of a Tennis Player* and Evonne Goolagong's *Evonne: On the Move.*

ELMORE
LEONARD
on

GEORGE KELL

A scene in the final chapter of a 1969 novel of mine called *The Big Bounce* begins:

He cut across the vacant frontage then and approached the side of the house, hearing the TV and recognizing the announcer's voice—George Kell, with the faintly down-home Arkansas drawl—before he reached the window and saw the picture and Mr. Majestyk watching it, his short legs stretched out on the fold-out ottoman.

Boston was at bat. McLain was pitching, looking in and taking his windup and coming in with a hard overhand fastball, grooving it past the hitter before he could swing. George Kell, sounding pretty relaxed, said it was McLain's fourth strikeout in three innings. He said boy, when this youngster was on, you just didn't hit him. Ryan watched the Tigers go out one two three in the fourth. With Boston coming to bat and McLain taking his warm-up throws, he decided, what the hell, sit down for maybe a couple of innings. There wasn't any rush.

A cutaway scene follows that sets up another scene in which a friend of Ryan's walks into a house and is shot dead. The young lady who does it thinks she's shooting Ryan. So watching the ball game saves his life. Now back to the scene in front of the TV set.

"Two away, a man on second, the tying run at the plate," Mr. Majestyk said. "How would you pitch this guy?"

"Probably something breaking. Low and away."

"He's not going to hit it," Mr. Majestyk said.

Ryan kept his eyes on the set. "I don't know. That short left field wall, you lay a fly ball up there, you got two bases."

And George Kell, a voice coming out of the TV set, said, "You got to pitch to everybody in this ballpark."

"In tight on the hands," Mr. Majestyk said. "Back the son of a bitch away. If he swings, he hits it on the handle."

"He better keep it low," Ryan said.

When the batter bounced out to the second baseman, Mr. Majestyk said, "I told you."

George Kell said, "Going into the sixth with a two-run lead, let's see if the Tigers can put some hits together and get something going. I imagine Denny McLain wouldn't mind that about now."

"He's good," Mr. Majestyk said. "You know?"

"Kell," Ryan said. "He was a good ballplayer."

"You know, he got over two thousand base hits while he was in the Majors?"

"Two thousand fifty-four," Ryan said.

"Did you know they had a sign outside his hometown? Swifton, Arkansas. You're coming in the sign says 'Swifton, Arkansas—The Home of George Kell.' "

Ryan took a sip of beer. "I don't know if I'd want a sign like that. Some guy comes along, he knows you're away playing ball, nobody home, he goes in takes anything he wants. Or you're in a slump and some nut fan throws rocks at your windows."

"That could happen," Mr. Majestyk said. "But when a guy is good, like Kell, you got to be able to take a lot of crap and not let it bother you. So a guy throws a rock. So you get the window fixed. Listen, you hit three thirty, three forty like Kell, the pitchers are throwing crap and junk at you all the time and it's worse than any rocks because it's your living, it's what you *do*. You stand in there, that's all. When they come in with a good one you belt it."

George Kell was that kind of bear-down ballplayer. From the time I started watching him, when Kell was with Detroit from 1946 through the '51 season, I considered him not only the best third

baseman I'd ever seen, but the best all-around baseball player. He was an All-Star five of those six years.

In 1949, Kell beat out Ted Williams for the batting crown by .0002 percentage points, .3429 to .3427. Kell came to bat that year 522 times. You know how many times he struck out? Thirteen. Something like once every two weeks. During the middle part of that season he was knocked down fifteen times. Kell said, "Somebody is going to get hurt . . ."

The next year he struck out 18 times in 641 at-bats. You believe it? He hit .340 and almost won the batting crown again. Billy Goodman, with 217 fewer times at bat, beat him by .014 percentage points, while Kell led the league in base hits, 218, and doubles, 56.

When Kell began his career with the Philadelphia A's in '43, Mr. Connie Mack liked his glove but said he would never be a hitter. So Kell bore down and taught himself how to hit by studying pitchers and moving around in the box. "You never stop watching and you never stop learning." He used a light 32-ounce bat and sprayed line drives to all fields. One out of four of his 2,054 hits were for extra bases. Nine of his fourteen years in the Majors he hit over .300 for a lifetime .306 average.

And seven of those years Kell led AL third baseman in fielding percentage, playing at five-nine, 180 pounds, and bearing down with every pitch: taking shots off his chest if he had to, or other parts of him. At Yankee Stadium in '48, The Great DiMaggio hit a rocket at Kell that took a bad hop and caught him in the face. Kell picked up the ball and made the play, with a broken jaw.

Detroit opened its 1952 season by losing 10 of its first 13 games (they would go on to finish 50-104, the worst season in the team's history), knew they had to rebuild, and sent Kell to the Red Sox in a dreadful nine-player swap. Kell hit .311 that year in Boston. With the White Sox in '55 he hit .312; and finally with Baltimore in '57, he managed to hit .297 despite a bad back that would end his career that season. Before leaving the game, though, Kell showed Brooks Robinson how to play third. So there you are.

In '49, the year Kell won the batting title, he went into the last game of the season two percentage points behind Ted Williams. That day against the Yanks, Williams walked twice, went 0 for 2, and the Yanks beat Boston for the pennant. Meanwhile, Detroit was playing Cleveland at home, with nothing at stake. Kell singled and doubled off Bob Lemon his first two times up and struck out his third trip with Bob Feller in to relieve. He was due up again in the bottom of the ninth when word reached the dugout that Williams had gone hitless in New York. It meant that Kell, with his two hits, was now two ten-thousandths of a percentage point ahead of Williams, as of this moment the batting champ. . . . But wait a minute. He could be up again in the ninth, and if he didn't get a hit, a walk, or a sacrifice, Williams would move back into the lead and take the crown.

Courtesy Detroit Tigers

Red Rolfe, the Tigers manager, said to Kell, "If you don't bat, you win it," ready to take him out.

It gave George Kell a lot to think about in a hurry. The game didn't mean anything, the Tigers were out of it, the season would be over at the end of this inning. But Kell would win it straight if he was to win it at all. He moved into the on-deck circle with one out and a man on first, Eddie Lake at the plate.

Those must have been the longest moments of George Kell's career: watching Eddie Lake take his cuts . . . watching Eddie Lake ground into a double play, abruptly ending the game. Kell let out a yell that had a chance of bringing every razorback in Arkansas up to Detroit and threw his bat fifty feet in the air.

Who wouldn't?

He's in the Hall of Fame now, respected as one of those rare players who did not have to be "managed." But do you know what he considers the highest honor ever paid him?

It was Mr. Mack saying, simply, "George Kell knows how to play the game."

Elmore Leonard has written twenty-eight novels, including *Killshot, Freaky Deaky, Valdez Is Coming, Glitz, Fifty-Two Pickup, Mr. Majestyk, The Big Bounce,* and *Stick.* He wrote the screenplay for *The Rosary Murders.*

PAUL BUHLE
on

WILLIE MAYS

Fall, 1954. I was playing sick in order to listen to the World Series on the radio. With both parents at work and my sisters in school, I sat alone listening (or pretending to bat and to pitch) while the New York Giants took game after game from the Cleveland Indians. My friends had a little trouble understanding the extreme measures. The middle of Illinois was Cardinals or, to the truly devoted, Cubs country. A White Sox fan could be found, occasionally; Giants fans remained unknown. But to me, the ultimate in sports apotheosis had been reached during the first game, when Willie Mays raced back to dead center in the Polo Grounds to catch Vic Wertz's line drive over his shoulder, and spun around (his hat flying off) to throw (before landing on his outstretched arms) a strike to second base to keep two runners in check. *Sport* magazine ran four full-page photos of that continuous motion, and I Scotch-taped them to my bedroom wall, where they remained for years objects of my rapt contemplation.

I saw Mays in action only twice, at Wrigley Field and Sportsman's Park (before it became Busch Stadium), until some years later. But I scrutinized all the newspaper and magazine reports on him that I could lay hands on, the *Baseball Digest*, *Sport*, and the *Sporting*

WILLIE MAYS   outfield NEW YORK GIANTS

News in particular. There was plenty of journalism about Mays to choose from, especially in those years everyone participated in the Mays vs. Mantle "best player" debate. Sportswriters told endless stories about the instinctive and unique jump he got on line drives to the outfield, about the speed—up to a hundred miles per hour— with which he returned the ball to infielders and catchers, about his strength at the plate, and even about the innovation he made by wearing an outsize glove that he operated with his fingertips. Most of all, they wrote about the excitement that he continually introduced, with the threat of clutch hits in late innings or his cap flying off as he raced around the bases or toward some critical catch.

The Giants did not continually break their own away-from-home attendance records just because Mays put up big numbers or the team won games. Rather, fans of all descriptions found him, as I did, immensely exciting in almost everything he did. Of course I was impressed by his line in the daily box scores and statistics that would guarantee him the status, at his enshrinement into the Hall of Fame in 1979, of getting more votes than any previous candidate in the history of the balloting. Yet my major impressions centered on Willie as a pure athlete, gifted with such talents and grace, and concentrated so single-mindedly upon the game that he became the perfect hero.

Race inevitably came into the picture, and Willie Mays was practically my introduction to the locus of the central contradictions in American life. Debuting early in the 1951 season (after hitting nearly .500 for six weeks at Minneapolis of the American Association), just in time to help the Giants win the pennant and earn himself the Rookie-of-the-Year award, Mays followed the early breakthroughs of the political-social battle for sports integration. He was spared the meanest treatments dished out to the likes of Jackie Robinson, if not the final era of southern segregation or baseball's tenacious residual racism. Willie's sports purity played strangely into the equation. I remember being moved by a recounting of a conversation between Mays and Giants owner Horace Stoneham about a contract renewal. What was the new price tag? Willie didn't look at it. How much should he receive? "Whatever you think, Mr. Stoneham," was the way the press reported Willie's answer.

I'm not sure how we should interpret this today. "The man is so complex," Mays's wife Mae said later, in response to some hurtful journalistic stereotypes of Willie as the one-dimensional black athlete. Willie spoke little about himself, ever. But what might be taken later as acceptance of paternalism could also be seen as indifference. The paycheck was not Willie's main concern. Even when, in later decades, he briefly reigned as the highest-paid player in baseball, the older image of purity remained. Branch Rickey, who sponsored baseball integration, argued that Mays had more power and speed in his swing than any player in the history of the game. But what made him great was something different: "The secret weapon . . . is the frivolity in his bloodstream . . . Willie Mays has doubled his strength with laughter." The "Say Hey Kid," a moniker he acquired from his persistent greeting to friends and strangers in the early years, epitomized supple youth, freedom of motion, love of life.

His family saga tends to confirm young Mays as the result and vehicle of rising black expectations. His grandfather Walter Mays, a sharecropper in Alabama, had been a noted amateur pitcher in the early years of the century. He raised a son—Willie Howard, named after President Taft—who was known as Kitty Kat, for his speed as a basestealer and grace in the outfield, on the Birmingham steel company team and the semipro Gray Sox. Willie Howard and his wife, Anna Sattlewhite Mays, meanwhile set themselves upon hard work and a better life for their children. Young Willie's family got a hefty bonus for his signing with the Giants (so did the Birmingham Black Barons for giving him up). He was dispatched for brief seasoning in the minor leagues. But I like to think that by the time the young Willie got to the big leagues he had been ready, so to speak, for generations.

I had been waiting generations, too, in a similar sense, for his appearance at the center of American popular life. My great-grandfather had been an Abolitionist, and my mother, scarcely conscious of politics, looked back upon her New York years as a settlement-house worker, living on 125th Street, as the most fulfilling of her career, perhaps even the happiest in her troubled life. My paternal grandfather, on the other hand, had passed through the Ku Klux Klan in Illinois before leaving family and a failed business to work as a pattern-maker in West Coast defense plants. He had the reputation of a sports enthusiast, wrestling in particular. My father, a typical midwestern Congregationalist (i.e., a semiliberal Republican) and minor civil servant, was the original Giants' fan, from his 1930s New York days. I think he admired the Giants for the same reason that he, a noninvestor, admired the *Wall Street Journal*: the Giants projected the image of a deeply conservative organization that Wall Street had supported for generations. As he introduced me to the Giants, he shared my enthusiasm for Mays, even while he remained uneasy about the intermixing of black and white off the playing fields, in our house for instance.

Events that flowed (for me) out of Mays's personal triumph, as out of the concurrent civil rights movements, therefore introduced generational warfare to my family. What started with Alabama and my ceaseless discussion of American racism ended up with Vietnam, provoking emotional scenes to be reenacted again and again over meals of typically midwestern overcooked food. Our life improved somewhat with the addition of a television set and TV tables: we only stared at each other over Sunday dinner.

My father, had he been more vindictive and less convinced that I was "going through a stage," would have blamed my warped development on my personal failure in baseball—and he would not have been entirely wrong. Slow afoot, I promised myself a shot at the minor leagues as a pitcher. I threw a Little League no-hitter at age eleven. But I lacked the strength to fire real fastballs, and my desperate attempt at curves gave me a permanent sore arm. Exiled to the outfield—where I was no Willie Mays, to say the least—I was quickly cut from a Jaycees squad. My sports fantasies turned for a few years to intense study of statistics (beginning no doubt with Willie's), to examination of minor league prospects (via the *Sporting News* columns), historical archeology of past Giant players and teams (after sending away for a volume titled *The Encyclopedia of Baseball*, I circled the record of every Giant, to the most brief and obscure), and to prospects for management. There, in the *Sporting News*, which defended the Reserve Clause as the essence of the American way, I found a desperation plan to save the collapsing minor leagues: the old socialist program of municipal ownership. That was the subject of my first serious research paper, at age fourteen. If anyone had asked, I would still have recorded myself a Republican.

Meanwhile, my adulation of Mays had passed to other black athletes, national and local, to black musicians and singers, and to heroes of America's unfolding political drama. To my ears, Little Richard (or his more obscure rhythm 'n' blues counterparts, heard, late at night, from Nashville radio stations), in the purity and unadulterated perfection of tone of "Keep a Knockin'" or "Tutti Frutti," was a Willie Mays of music. Martin Luther King, Jr., whose *Stride Toward Freedom: The Montgomery Story* I had plucked randomly off a drugstore rack, seemed the Mays of social movements. King had come, in his great personal courage but also profound awareness of his destiny, to set me free, from what I could not have articulated.

At the same time, Mays's real sociopolitical reputation was catching up with me. He surely earned the "Player of the Decade" award from the *Sporting News,* but the 1960s was a curious decade for such a choice. Jackie Robinson would bitterly comment that Mays and Maury Wills had been the most prominent black stars who *refused* to make the struggle for black rights public. Whether Mays saw himself as a unique athletic giant rather than a black man playing baseball—as Curt Flood would charge—or he merely believed too intensely in the privacy of his conscience, we will likely never know. But Mays seemed, to the go-slow logic of contemporary white conservatives and many liberals, to be what an athlete should be, and what black radicals patently refused to be. His vaunted purity took on a different light.

I had also, as part of my disillusionment with baseball because of its unending racism and race for profits, begun to see the Giants as they really were. Something in the bowdlerized calypso music of the day (in defense, one could also say that Harry Belafonte's "Banana Boat Song" was the equivalent of Tennesee Ernie Ford's "Sixteen Tons": mainstreamed work music) had introduced the idea of the Caribbean to me. From that land came a battalion of brilliant athletes to the now San Francisco Giants, including Juan Marichal, Orlando Cepeda, and three Alou brothers. It was, I thought, an opportunity of enormous value for all concerned. The Giants blew it. Manager Alvin Dark, hemmed in mentally by his southern-white background, regarded tired Caribbean players—who had been on the field for more than six months by July—as typically lazy blacks. Mays personally talked the team down from outright revolt against Dark, his former teammate. A few of the Caribbeans went on to great heights with the Giants, but the élan disappeared on the

CULT BASEBALL PLAYERS

perennially listless, infighting team. Meanwhile, I joined the civil rights movement.

Willie Mays himself failed to receive the sort of San Francisco fan appreciation that his extraordinary play had earned him. Charles Einstein, who wrote Mays's 1954 "as told to" autobiography, *Born to Play Ball*, and the later ruminative *Willie's Time: A Memoir* (1979), blames San Francisco. Clearly, New York fans regarded Willie as their own, his adoptive status confirmed in stickball games with Harlem kids. San Francisco fans had their nostalgia for Joe DiMaggio, their centerfielder in decades past, as they looked upon the misconceived Candlestick Park as a poor substitute for a picturesque old favorite, Seals Stadium. Besides, they had a contemporary hero free of New York connections: Willie McCovey, archetype of the slugger. Local sportswriters, keenly in tune with the liberal (and sometimes radical) traditions and moods of the city, turned iconoclastic toward the Giants' doughty front-office and extended their iconoclasm toward the national idealization of Mays.

In time, San Franciscans, including the writers, warmed to Willie. He kept playing, with style and brilliance, into early middle age, eventually surpassing 600 homers, 2,000 runs scored, and 1,900 RBIs. In 1971, by this time forty, he led the Giants' march into the Western Division playoffs, where they lost to the Pirates. Sold to the Mets the next season (in order to free up his salary to a cash-desperate Giants' management), he fittingly epitomized (as had Casey Stengel) New York baseball nostalgia. The mediocre Mets led the league in attendance. The next year, when the secretaries in an office where I used to work mounted a large sign that read "If the Mets Can Win the Pennant, the US Can Get Out of Vietnam," an aching and weary Willie added a few clutch hits, including a decisive one in the twelfth inning of the second game of the World Series against the A's. He'd announced his retirement in midseason. But for me, what Willie Mays had been, and meant, had already passed with the 1950s. If I had known about ex-manager Herman Franks's late 1960s effort to buy the Giants, and install Mays as the first black manager, I might have felt another twinge for Willie. His personal strategy would have worked to the greatest good. Franks's plan fell through like so many other liberal hopes and promises in those harsh days.

The last time I focused clearly on Mays, I remember, was the 1962 World Series between the Giants and Yankees, the first time I had watched television continuously since the Cuban missile crisis a year earlier. Baseball no longer had anything like the same meaning to me. The next summer, I set out on a bohemian escape from college to San Francisco, and at the end of the summer, a few days before my return to Illinois and to dull reality, I went to see a Giants game. By the seventh inning—Willie notwithstanding—my girlfriend and I couldn't think of anything but sex. We caught an early bus back to our dark apartment, just off Fillmore, where a few weeks earlier we had been chewing morning-glory seeds, a low-level LSD-like hallucinogen. No, things had changed.

Around 1968, I discovered my chief intellectual mentor in the person of a Trinidadian-born scholar and politico, C.L.R. James, who made his name as a cricket reporter and wrote *Beyond a Boundary*, the finest sports history in the English language. It was through James that my feelings about Mays and baseball were strangely awakened. He had, he told me, been one of Willie Mays's most enthusiastic fans in 1951, watching Willie at the Polo Grounds and listening to games on the radio. Like Garfield Sobers, the greatest of West Indian cricketers, or like football player-singer-actor Paul Robeson in another era, Mays was to James the decisive disproof of white superiority. But also much more than that.

James, who as a young cricketer and cricket critic began to see the discrimination against black players as the essence of Imperial blindness, viewed the triumph over that discrimination, and the grace of the accomplishment, as the promise of a new world aborning. The Western world had nearly destroyed itself and all civilization in the wars of the twentieth century. But—as mundane as the evidence may sound—the warmth of popular response toward athletes of color proved regeneration to be possible. For that regeneration to take place, the pastimes and the heroes of common people had to be recognized as manifestations of untapped democratic potential. America never quite got the point, and Mays couldn't articulate it, either. Nevertheless, when he played ball, Willie Mays, as Bill Cosby once put it, stood in for every black American. In his physical perfection and movement, he had been a new phase of sports and social life.

Paul Buhle is the author of *Marxism in the United States: Remapping the History of the American Left* and *C.L.R. James: The Artist as Revolutionary;* and editor of *The Encyclopedia of the American Left, Popular Culture in America, Madison: Encounters in Exile,* and *C.L.R. James: His Life and His Work.* He teaches U.S. history at the Rhode Island School of Design.

CULT BASEBALL PLAYERS

TONY KUBEK
on

MICKEY MANTLE

1954 Bowman: Copyright © The Topps Company, Inc.

I could start talking about Mickey Mantle by saying he was the greatest ballplayer I have ever seen.

I could start by saying he had Willie Wilson's speed or better. The scouts timed him at 2.9 seconds going down to first base on a bunt. No one, not Wilson, not Lou Brock, nor anyone else was ever clocked at better than 3.1 seconds. No one but Mickey.

I could start by mentioning that he is credited with hitting the longest home run in baseball history, 565 feet off Washington's Chuck Stobbs. I suppose it's open to debate, but I'm convinced that Mickey hit more long home runs than anyone. In addition to broadcasting the *Game of the Week* on NBC, I have been doing some television work for Toronto, and the Blue Jay players are probably sick of my pointing to a spot in the upper deck, about 500 feet away, of some park and saying, "Up there, that's where I saw Mickey hit one."

I could start by telling how he'd hit the ball off the fists or off the end of the bat, figure that he'd popped up, and then disgustedly whack the bat on home plate, breaking it in half. But then Mickey would look up just in time to see the ball go out of the park. I have three distinct memories of Mickey Mantle hitting broken-bat homers.

I could say that he was the greatest switch-hitter of all time, that he played a tremendous center field and could have stolen 50 bases a year if his legs didn't hurt and if Manager Casey Stengel had let a young Mickey Mantle loose on the bases. But Mickey Mantle stole a base only when it meant something to the team, not to his stats.

I could even reminisce about his knuckleball. It was as good as any I've seen. No one wanted to play catch with him if he was going to throw it, because you were afraid you'd end up with a fractured skull. Just ask Jake Gibbs. He was a rookie catcher fresh out of Ole Miss and Mickey was playing catch with him. He threw Jake a couple of soft knucklers and then told Jake to get his mask because he was going to show Jake the real thing. Jake was also a football star at Ole Miss and figured he was tough enough to catch Mickey's knuckler without a mask. He figured wrong because Mickey cut loose with one that broke so much that it broke Jake's nose. Mickey used to beg Casey Stengel and Ralph Houk to let him pitch in a blowout, so he could show off the knuckler, but they never did. The last thing any manager wanted was Mickey Mantle's hurting himself while messing around in a game that was 14–1.

All of those things are worth talking about and you can do it for hours, but there was more to Mickey than that. It was my old Yankee teammate Jack Reed who said something that stuck with me: "The first time I saw Mickey, I said, 'Good night, ole Moses, there is one fine-looking ballplayer. He was so young, so strong, and he looked immaculate in that white Yankee uniform, like he was born to wear it. And another thing about Mickey, it always seemed like he could run as fast as he wanted. He could do almost anything he wanted."

This really is the heart of the matter. To those who played with Mickey in the 1950s and 1960s, and I suppose to the fans, Mickey *was* the Yankees. That's why guys such as Jack Reed who were in the clubhouse with him, or fans such as Bob Costas who simply watched him, almost idolize Mickey. He wasn't "a kid in bad need of a haircut whose sport coat barely covered his wrists," as veteran sportswriter Dan Daniel described him. Or "a hillbilly in a velvet suit," according to Joe Trimble, a writer who had no reason to talk since his wardrobe usually looked like an unmade bed. Mickey wasn't a hick, he wasn't sullen, moody, or inarticulate, as other writers were to label him over the years.

The first time I met Mickey Mantle was at Casey Stengel's acceleration camp in 1953, which was really a forerunner to the winter instructional leagues of today. All of the Yankees best minor league prospects were there, and Mickey showed up one day to watch. He made a point to introduce himself to all of us, and that meant something because he was already a star and we were just kids—many of us had never even seen Yankee Stadium. Yet, there was Mantle saying hello and there we were looking at him almost in disbelief. I wouldn't be surprised if some of us wanted to ask him for an autograph.

Mickey went out of his way to be nice to me. When I first joined the Yankees, clubhouse man Pete Sheehy wanted to give me number 34, but Mickey stepped in and said, "No, Pete, give Tony a lower number. He's gonna be around here for a long time." That's how I ended up wearing number 10 with the Yankees.

Mickey may not always have known the right thing to say to the press, but he did to the players. We had heard the stories about how Joe DiMaggio was apparently very aloof to Mickey during Mickey's rookie year, and that always bothered him. On the field, the writers were comparing him to DiMaggio. Some of the fans were even booing him because he wasn't DiMaggio, but he was someone very special to us. Mickey Mantle was a ballplayer who was first loved by the ballplayers, then by the fans.

His relationship with Roger Maris in 1961 was a tremendous example of what Mickey meant to the Yankees. While some writers were trying to create a feud between Mickey and Roger as they both tried to break Babe Ruth's record of 60 homers, Roger and Mickey were living together in an apartment in Queens. Roger used to cook breakfast for Mickey and Bob Cerv. I think that 1961 was a key year

Courtesy New York Yankees

for Mickey. He didn't break Ruth's record, but Maris did. No doubt Mickey wanted it and I know that we wanted the record for him, but I also remember Mickey standing on the top step of the dugout, yelling encouragement to Roger when he was at bat. In fact, we all heard Mickey from the dugout, pulling for us. It was 1961 when the fans finally stopped booing Mickey because he wasn't DiMaggio and started cheering Mickey for being Mickey. Of course, some of them made Roger their whipping boy because he wasn't Ruth.

I think what Mickey always wanted was to be accepted as Mickey Mantle, a man with his incredible talent and his flaws. Mickey is one of our most human heroes. On the field, he did amazing things, but he would also become frustrated and you'd see it—he'd break bats, he'd occasionally not run out a pop-up, and he played in pain.

That is what many people remember about Mickey—the pain.

We'd get a cab and go to dinner, but when we arrived at the restaurant, Mickey would need help getting out of the back of the cab. His legs just wouldn't work. There were moments in a game when he would be running and then his knee would just buckle and he'd go down. We'd hold our breath because we were worried; we thought maybe this was the time that he went down and didn't get up again.

Of course, there was Mickey's family history, where nearly all the males died before the age of forty because of Parkinson's disease, and Mickey was convinced that he'd never see forty. One of the reasons the Yankees brought me to the majors in 1957 at the age of twenty and used me in the outfield was that they were worried about Mickey—his legs, his health in general. It was always as though the clock were ticking down on Mickey's career. But Mickey played when his legs were killing him, he played after long nights on the town, and he played so hard and he played so well.

Only now does Mickey feel fully appreciated. Mickey once mentioned to me that he was even booed at some old-timers games and that bothered him. "I'm not even playing anymore and I got booed," he once said with kind of a bemused smile. Mickey also went through a period of some financial difficulties, and his son had a serious battle with cancer, so he was out of the public eye. But now he has had a book that was a best-seller, he has more invitations to speak and make appearances than he can ever handle, and everywhere he goes, the fans are there just to see him and he really feels that the people love him as we did when we played with him. He has lived longer than he thought he would, done more than he imagined, and now he means more to the fans than he ever did as a player. To me and Mickey, that's the ultimate irony—he had to step back from the public eye before they really got to know him.

Tony Kubek is the broadcaster for the New York Yankees and was a longtime broadcaster for the Toronto Blue Jays and NBC's *Game of the Week*. He is the author of *Sixty-one* (with Terry Pluto). He played shortstop for the Yankees from 1957 to 1965.

DAVID
HINCKLEY
on

DUKE SNIDER

Duke Snider has been in the Hall of Fame for ten years. There are still nights, bad nights, when I'll be running through all the things that are not right in my life, or the world, and this thought, too, will flash by: Did they vote him in only because of the song? Because Willie and Mickey were there, so they figured they might as well round it out with The Duke?

Rationally, of course, I know different. Duke Snider was voted into Cooperstown in 1980 for his baseball achievements, and besides, Terry Cashman's "Talkin' Baseball (Willie, Mickey and The Duke)" wasn't released until 1981. Still, my scenario underscores the two salient facts about being a Duke Snider fan: (1) It's not easy work even though (2) you've got the goods.

I suppose that's not a bad synopsis of life, either. But what first drew me to Duke Snider, if I can do some psychological extrapolating to re-create the reasoning process of a seven-year-old, was a little more visceral. He was everything I wasn't (left-handed and physically skilled); he had a great nickname; and he had a job that enabled him to play baseball whenever he wanted.

It was only later that I began to understand why he was such a good choice for My Favorite Player Ever. That's a designation that has nothing to do with the sort of life he has led, though it seems to have been exemplary, or with his baseball statistics, although those are also first-rate: 407 home runs, 2,116 hits, .295 batting average, .540 slugging percentage, 11 World Series home runs, .985 fielding average.

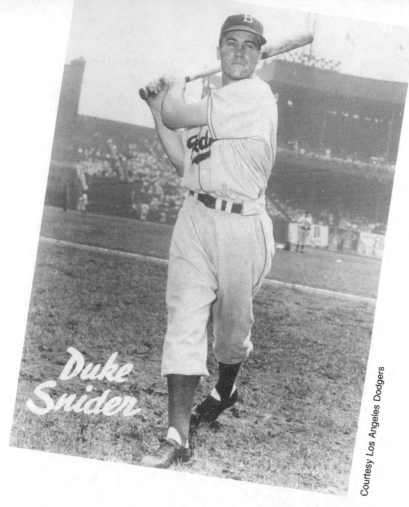

Courtesy Los Angeles Dodgers

What's so intriguing, rather, is the thread of frustration woven through his career. When he hit 40 home runs, it bothered him that he also had 90 strikeouts. However good he became, he felt he should be better.

Now picking one example of frustration from the 1947–56 Brooklyn Dodgers is like picking a single apple from an orchard and saying, "Hey, this one's red." This is the team, remember, that won six pennants and lost five World Series. It lost two other pennants in the last inning of the last game of the regular season. Frustration was God's price for putting those teams on earth—Duke, Skoonj, Gil, Pee Wee, Campy, Newk, Oisk, Jackie—and His price for lifting the curse in 1955 was that He removed them from Brooklyn three years later. Nathaniel Hawthorne once wrote a story about a girl who was perfect save for a birthmark; her lover insisted she have it removed, and when she did, she died. That's the Brooklyn Dodgers.

Even in this world, though, Snider's personal frustration stood out, for it was periodically read as a sign of indifference. A 1956 *Collier's* article, under the byline of Duke and Roger Kahn, was headlined "I Play Baseball for Money, Not for Fun"—which Duke denied saying—and then some years later, Kahn suggested in *The Boys of Summer* that Snider settled for good when he could have been great. When he drew a walk, wrote Kahn, he threw aside his bat as if he were relieved, as if a time at bat and by extension baseball itself were an ordeal rather than a opportunity.

I never got that feeling. But then, I never had Kahn's close-up view, and sometimes the fan is the last to know. How could Giants fans know that off the field, Willie could be sullen and moody? How many Yankee fans knew that Mickey didn't always take the best care of himself? So this disturbing thought—that baseball might be more important to me, who would have wrestled pit bulls to play it, than it was to a man who played it so well—became another voice that whispered to me on bad nights. It didn't go away, in fact, until the publication of Duke's autobiography in 1988.

Carl Erskine addressed that precise point, I suspect not by coincidence, right in his introduction. "No one," wrote Oisk, "agonized more about not doing well." More important, however, was Duke's own recollection of keeping a dinner date with his parents the terrible night of the Bobby Thomson home run. Snider recalls being quiet through most of the dinner, until his mother asked, "What's the matter?"

"I wasn't very cordial," he writes. " 'We just lost the National League pennant—that's what's the matter with me.' It wasn't a nice way for a son to address his mother, regardless of the circumstances."

Maybe not. But to me, it was poetry. Everyone who has felt a bad loss, at any level of competition, knows that dinner, that question, and that reply—which would not come so instinctively if Duke were at heart indifferent. It's the reaction of a man whose tragic flaw, if you will, was having his skills fail in a game where on the best of days there can be failure.

Perhaps that's why, with Duke Snider, there's always a periodic urge to look for reassurance in the numbers, the home runs, the strong anchoring presence in center field. Why there's almost a tangible sense of relief to open Bill James's *Historical Baseball Abstract* and see that under "Peak Value" Duke Snider is listed as the sixth-best center fielder of all time—behind Mantle, Cobb, Mays, DiMaggio, and Speaker, which is the approximate equivalent of finishing behind Einstein and Newton on your physics final.

The stats argue that the placement is legit. From 1950 to 1957,

Snider averaged more than 35 home runs, 75 walks, 110 runs batted in, 100 runs scored, a .300 batting average, and almost a .400 on-base percentage. Yeah, he was the only lefty in a right-handed lineup, so he saw a lot of righty pitchers, and that may have helped. So what? He didn't get those numbers off a batting tee, and they yield nothing to Willie or Mickey. It's not incidental that during those eight years, Brooklyn was the best team in the National League.

For Snider maybe more than others, though, the bad shadowed the good. His eleventh-inning double won the fifth game of the 1952 Series, one of the most dramatic in postseason history; two days later, with the bases loaded and one out in the seventh inning of the seventh game, Brooklyn trailing 4–2, he popped up. He singled in the winning run in the last game of the '49 season, giving Brooklyn the pennant, but when he seemed to have done the same thing in '50, Cal Abrams got thrown out at the plate and the Dodgers lost by a game to the Phillies. He made an all-time great catch at Philadelphia in mid-'54 off Puddin' Head Jones, saving a victory, but in 1951 against the Giants he was running over to play the carom on Thomson's shot when it went into the stands.

I probably should mention here that I didn't see that game. In fact, I didn't know major league baseball existed until late 1955—a few months after the World Series victory, which always struck me as perfect timing for a Brooklyn Dodgers fan. Even then, since I lived in central Connecticut, Ebbets Field might as well have been in Pocatello.

But through TV, newspapers, magazines, and baseball cards I got my images of Duke, and while those images today may be blurry and possibly even apocryphal, I don't think they're wrong, because the prime element I see, both in the swing and in the field, is grace. I remember being surprised when his baseball card listed him at 6', 180 pounds; I thought he was bigger because he looked so strong. But the grace would explain it. That he could be that powerful and that smooth—while swinging left-handed —was a rare and wonderful mystery to me.

It was also one I tried to solve. In the summers of 1956 and 1957, I created a facsimile diamond in my backyard and acted out Dodgers games along with the radio broadcasts. I would start out as the Dodger batter or pitcher, then become whoever had the most interesting part of the play.

This developed in me, among other things, a lifelong love of sliding. But my favorite parts were Duke's at-bats, and once the real game was over, I would play my own game to "correct" anything that had gone wrong. If the Dodgers lost their game, they'd win mine, of course, but more to the point, Duke Snider batted about .900. He also ran every at-bat to a 3-2 count while at least two teammates waited patiently for him to drive them in, which he always did.

I still sometimes wonder why I wasn't more wounded when the Dodgers left Brooklyn. Looking back, I suspect two years of the Dodgers and Duke was just about right; it cemented the relationship without giving it so much history that I would feel the deep, cold fury of betrayal.

But again, my reaction at the time was more instinctive, beginning with shock. They can't do this, can they? Just take a kid's team away, so far away he can't even hear their games on the radio anymore? Then I was puzzled. Yes, they did it. Finally, I was sad. I still am. But I never held it against the Dodgers, in whom I remain fiercely invested to this day. As I wear out my videotape of Kirk Gibson's depositing Dennis Eckersley's slider into the right-field seats in 1988, I often think this is God, at last, starting to balance the books.

Nor did I ever hold the departure against The Duke. Whenever I had a choice during my own slow-pitch softball career, I wore jersey number 4—though the only chance it could have been retired in my case was if the team had found a way to do so with me in it.

In any event, I followed Duke right up to his last at-bat in September 1964. He wore a San Francisco Giants uniform by then, and he singled. When that season ended, I sat down and calculated that when he left the Dodgers at the end of 1962, his career average was almost exactly .300. If he'd retired then, there would have been an appealing tidiness to it: .300 average, career Dodger (he started at Brooklyn's Class B Newport News farm team in 1944, reaching the majors in 1947). On the other hand, had he not played 1963 with the Mets and 1964 with the Giants, he wouldn't have reached 2,000 hits or 400 home runs. Then the Hall could really have been a stretch, though those two seasons added nothing more than numbers to what he did.

I told you this wasn't easy.

The one time I saw Duke Snider play live in a Brooklyn Dodger uniform was August 1957, when I convinced my father—who cared about baseball only slightly more than he cared about the seeding patterns of wild celery—to take me to Ebbets Field for a weekday afternoon game against Cincinnati.

The Dodgers won, 8–0, with Don Newcombe throwing a 5-hitter and Gino Cimoli hitting a 3-run homer. Duke walked once while going 0 for 3, which surprised me insofar as I was certain he would hit at least one home run and quite possibly more.

In fact, I was so certain, I brought my glove to catch one of them, not even realizing there were no seats in right field in fair territory. No matter. Something far more profound was at work here—the whole reason little boys always bring gloves to baseball games, and old boys never do: because through baseball, they have learned what they can reasonably expect from life.

Myself, I'd settle for Duke's stats. In fact, if you'll throw in just one chorus of his song, I might even settle for my own.

David Hinckley is the Critic-at-Large for the New York *Daily News.*

LARRY KING
on
BILLY COX

Billy Cox was flat-out-hands-down-no-doubt-about-it my favorite all-time ballplayer. I saw better players than Cox at bat. Stan Musial was an artist with the wood. I saw better all-around players than Cox. Willie Mays was not only in a class by himself, he had the whole school. But for me, for my taste in baseball, no one touched my heart more than the dimunitive third baseman, the best ever to field that position.

I became a Dodger fan at the age of ten in 1944, living in Brooklyn, New York. Cox became a Dodger in 1948, arriving from Pittsburgh along with pitcher Preacher Roe in one of the great one-sided deals of all-time. Gene Mauch, believe it or not, was also included in that arrangement, and Brooklyn sent Dixie Walker and pitchers Hal Gregg and Vic Lombardi to the Bucs. Had not Walker been such a vocal opponent of Jackie Robinson's color, the deal would never have come off. Later Dixie would tell me how much he regretted his own thinking; but I would thank him for giving me the joy of seeing Billy Cox play third on a daily basis.

He was originally a shortstop, but Pee Wee Reese owned short so manager Leo Durocher and then Burt Shotten, who came in as manager when Leo was suspended, put Cox on third. And magic happened. I mean it, absolute magic. He would hold his beat-up old Davega-type mitt, which couldn't have cost twenty bucks, in his right hand before each pitch was delivered. He would slip it slowly on his left hand as the ball came to the plate. He never crouched down in that typical infielder stance. He stood, almost casually, awaiting whatever was to happen. When the ball came to third, he invariably caught it. To his left, a master. To his right, like no one before or since. And that arm. That incredible, unbelievable arm. He threw the ball sidearm like a whiplash. Often he would hold it awhile before pegging it over to first just to keep things interesting.

He could hit in the clutch, batting a career .262; he hit .291 on the 1953 Dodgers, with 10 home runs.

But statistics are not the Billy Cox story. You had to see him, folks. I can still see Cox coming in on a bunt and that whiplike throw, literally in one motion. I've never seen anyone do it with that fluid grace. He would backhand a shot over third, then literally read the baseball before throwing. I can't remember an error.

I remember being at a spring training game in Miami in 1964. The Mets were playing the Orioles, and before the game Met manager Casey Stengel was holding forth in the dugout. Brooks Robinson came strolling by to get a bat and go up to take some batting practice. Casey yelled out, "You are the second-greatest third baseman who ever lived."

Brooks stopped in his tracks and walked over the the Met dugout. "Who's the best?" he asked.

Casey said quickly, "Number three. Used to play in Brooklyn. He had a better arm than you, Brooksie, a better arm. There was nobody like him. But don't feel badly. You're the second-best and he was in a world all his own."

In my humble, childlike way, I tried to be Billy Cox. I wore number 3 whenever I had the chance. I tried to ape the way he walked. I knew he was a sullen, noncommunicative type, caused by malaria during World War II, so I never approached him for an autograph. I was scared. I was in awe. I still am. Just the mention of his name brings chills up and down my spine. Billy Cox. Third base. I was there—and you can look it up. . . .

Larry King is the Peabody Award–winning host of Mutual's *Larry King Show*. He is the two-time Ace Award–winning host of CNN's *Larry King Live*. He writes a weekly column for *USA Today* and is the author of *Larry King* (with Emily Yoffe) and *Tell It to the King* (with Peter Occhiogrosso).

PETE HAMILL
on
EDDIE STANKY

The war was still raging in Europe the first time I saw Eddie Stanky play baseball, on a chilly April afternoon in Ebbets Field. The Brooklyn Dodgers were playing the Boston Braves. I was almost ten years old and had been taken to the great ballpark by my father and some of his friends from the war plant.

"Watch this little guy," said my father as Stanky came to bat in the last of the first. "He's a real ballplayer."

That was a high compliment; wartime baseball was considered a sham by most of the fans, including my father. So I watched Stanky. He fouled off a pitch, then took a ball. He was crouched over the plate and was choking up on the bat. He fouled off two more pitches, then took another ball. Two and two. He fouled off another pitch. And another. Then a third. Then took another ball, which seemed to me to be a strike. The count was three and two now. The fans started to cheer. He fouled off another pitch, then another, then two more. Until at last he got what he wanted: ball four.

"He'll drive you nuts, that little guy," my father said. His friend Big John Mullins laughed. "No, he drives *them* nuts!" Another man reminded us that a walk was as good as a single. Stanky then stole second. "Or a double!"

I don't remember much more about that game, except that the Dodgers won and Stanky scored twice. I remember it only because my father so loved Stanky. I wasn't as sure. I wanted to see home runs. Or even better, because so much more difficult to do, triples. With all my friends, I was waiting for the *real* Dodgers to come home from the war, players we'd never even seen (in those years before television): Pete Reiser and Pee Wee Reese and Dolph Camilli. Everybody knew that the wartime teams were dreadful, full of old guys and high school players and men who were 4-F.

Still, there was Stanky. He was small, but he was compact. He obviously had great eyes. And he played with intensity. And as the season moved on, I saw that he was leading the league in bases on balls, and my father kept reminding me about his skills. One afternoon, I read a column about Stanky in the *Brooklyn Eagle* and understood his attraction even more. Stanky had once been a soccer player. My father had been a soccer player, too, first in Belfast where he was born, later in the immigrant leagues around New York. Soccer, in fact, had cost him his left leg. At a tough Saturday game against a German team in Brooklyn in 1928, he had been kicked viciously, his lower leg broken in three places; by the time they got him to the hospital, gangrene had set in and the doctors were forced to amputate.

When my father got home the next morning (he worked nights at the war plant), I showed him the column about Stanky. He read it in silence. Then sipped his tea.

"I told you he was good," he said. And never used the word "soccer."

Stanky was indeed a very good soccer player at Northeast High School in Philadelphia, where he grew up in a tight, tough Polish family. He played on the baseball team, too, but in his senior year in 1934, he hit only .234. He graduated as the United States was deep into the Depression. Jobs were scarce. Even FDR's splendid oratory didn't help the many millions who were still out of work. Stanky started playing baseball for a semipro team, bringing home a few dollars a game. He still wasn't much of a hitter, but he played with great intensity and desire. so much so that a scout for Connie Mack's Philadelphia Athletics signed him up.

He was paid $125 a month (good money during the Depression) and sent to the A's Class C team in Greenville, Mississippi. After a few weeks, surrounded by the usual minor league assortment of raw kids, mediocrities, and fading rummies, he wanted out. He wrote home to his mother, begging for carfare. She refused, sending back a letter that Stanky talked about for the rest of his career. It ended with the admonition:

"Edward, I have tears in my eyes while I'm telling you this, but if you do come home, please do not come to 951 East Russell Street. We do not want quitters in this family. Your mother."

The 1947 Brooklyn Dodgers infield (left to right): Spider Jorgensen (3B), Pee Wee Reese (SS), Eddie Stanky (2B), and Jackie Robinson (1B).

Courtesy Los Angeles Dodgers

Stanky said later that he had cried for hours after receiving the letter, then decided he had no choice: He was going to become a professional ballplayer. And so he did. For the next eight years, he kicked around the minors. He hit over .300 in his first two seasons in Greenville, then dropped off in the next three. When the Athletics finally gave up on him, he was hitting .216 for Portsmouth in the Piedmont League. For a moment, his career seemed over; he might have to go back to the steel plants in Pennsylvania, where he sometimes worked in the off-season (and played soccer in the industrial leagues). And then he was picked up by the Macon team in the Sally League.

The Macon Peaches were managed by a man named Milton Stock, who had played for the Dodgers, Phillies, and Cardinals. Stock changed Stanky's life. He made him a leadoff man, taught him all the small things that a true professional must know about his craft, drove him hard, stoked Stanky's natural competitive fires. His guidance paid off: Stanky hit .305 in 123 games in 1939, .302 in 1940, .315 in 1941. That winter, the United States got into the war, but Stanky, who lost the hearing in his left ear after three separate beanings, was declared 4-F. In 1942, he married Stock's daughter, and his father-in-law made the move that would send Stanky to the majors. He sold his new son-in-law's contract to Milwaukee, a Triple-A team in the American Association, a farm club of the Chicago

Cubs. In 1942, playing at Milwaukee for Bill Veeck and Charlie Grimm, Stanky tore up the league. He hit .342, with 56 doubles, 124 runs scored, and was voted the league's Most Valuable Player. In '43, Grimm moved up to manage the Cubs and brought Stanky with him.

It didn't work out. In the 1943 season, with all the good ball-players away in the service, Stanky hit only .245. Grimm obviously lost faith in him. Some ballplayers stay too long in the minors, like prizefighters who spend too many years in the amateurs, and Stanky appeared to be one of them. He wasn't. But Stanky didn't play much in the early part of the 1944 season and finally went to see Grimm. He later remembered what he told the manager:

"If you can't play me, trade me. And if you can't trade me, send me back to Milwaukee. Just so long as I can play every day."

On June 8, 1944, two days after D-Day in Normandy, Edward Raymond Stanky was traded to the Dodgers.

He only had three full seasons with the Dodgers, but in memory, I always think of him as part of that splendid team. He played tough, driven, fierce National League baseball. He risked beanings by crouching over the plate. He slid hard into second to break up double plays, knowing that as the Dodger second baseman he could be run over by some of the bigger men on the other teams. He had no huge talent, but he had a hundred small talents, all of which he had mastered with intelligence and tenacity. Leo Durocher, who managed Stanky for two different teams, had such confidence in him that during the Dodgers' great playoff series with the Cardinals in 1946, he had Stanky execute the suicide squeeze five times.

"He can't run fast," Durocher once said of him, "he doesn't hit much, and he isn't really a very good fielder. But I wouldn't trade him for any second baseman in the National League."

Stanky's skills were described elsewhere by Durocher as "his intangibles." Billy Martin supplied the intangibles to the great Yankee teams of the 1950s, Ray Knight to the '86 Mets. They included spirit, fire, character. You don't recognize their value until the player is gone. But in the spring of '48, Branch Rickey traded Stanky to the Braves. There were two reasons. One was money. Stanky had bargained hard with the Dodger general manager that winter and ended up with a contract for $19,000—huge by Dodger standards. The other reason was more honorable. Rickey and Durocher had another second baseman on the team, a man possessed of all the intangibles of fire and leadership, but also blazingly fast on the bases and a great natural hitter. His name was Jackie Robinson.

I lost track of Stanky while he played for Boston, but then in 1950, he was back in New York, this time with the hated Giants, who were now managed by Durocher, considered by all of us in Brooklyn as the world's leading turncoat. That first year as a Giant, Stanky hit an even .300, somehow managed 8 home runs, drove in 51 runs, got 158 hits, and walked 144 times. It was his best year in the majors, and as much as I despised the Giants, I was happy for Stanky. So was my father.

"He's not as good as Robinson," my father said in some Irish variation of a Yogi Berra line, "but he's just as good."

The following year, *that* year, the year of Thomson's Home Run, the most heartbreaking year in the history of Brooklyn (except the last year of the team's golden presence), Stanky's average dropped 53 points. He still got 127 hits and 127 bases on balls. But at the end of the season, when the Cardinals asked him to come to St. Louis as a manager, he went. It's for others to judge his abilities as a manager for St. Louis and later for the White Sox; I remember hearing that he fell victim to the generation gap of the 1960s, unable to understand why young men of enormous natural talents wouldn't play as hard as he had, when he was scrambling through the Sally League, for $125 a month, learning how to hit behind the runner, to distract the batter, to do anything necessary to win baseball games.

But sometimes late at night, when I'm drifting off to sleep, I am with my father again in Ebbets Field. He is telling me to watch the little guy. And I watch Eddie Stanky as he fouls off a pitch, and then another, and then another, fouling them off forever in the green glade that is part of the lost city where I was young.

Pete Hamill is a columnist for *Esquire* and the *New York Post.* He is the author of *Loving Women: A Novel of the Fifties, Flesh and Blood, Irrational Ravings, The Gift,* and *Fighters.*

LARRY
COLTON
on

DALE LONG

In the spring of 1954, my mother was on the radio show *Queen for a Day*. That was the program where four women with financial woes were chosen from the studio audience and given three minutes to explain why they should be granted their material desires. Since we were as middle class as you could get, I don't know why my mother was selected to be on the show. Usually, the contestants told tear-jerking stories about how they needed a new reading light for little Johnny's iron lung or an apron for their blind grandmother living in an appliance crate under the bridge. My mother asked for a new television. She explained that we were just about the last family in Los Angeles without one, and it would be nice if her husband and son could watch the opening game of the Pacific Coast League season between the Hollywood Stars and the Los Angeles Angels on KTTV.

When it came time for the audience to choose the winner, the applause meter didn't even budge when host Jack Bailey put his hand over my mom. Her sister, sitting in the front row, didn't even clap for her.

I was one crestfallen eleven-year-old. My heroes were the Hollywood Stars, and my hero of heroes was Dale Long, the team's slugging first baseman. The year before, Long was the league's MVP, with 35 homers, 135 RBIs, and a .289 average for the pennant-winning Stars. Sure, I loved Mickey Mantle, too, but he was almost illusionary, playing in a league far, far away, appearing only in box scores and pictures in the L.A. *Times* that used dotted arrows to show the flight of his homer in Yankee Stadium against the Dodgers in the Series. Dale Long was real. As far as I was concerned, the Pacific Coast League *was* the major leagues.

Courtesy Pittsburgh Pirates

The highlights of my summers in 1953 and 1954 were the days my dad took me to Gilmore Stadium to watch Long and the Stars play. Gilmore was a cozy, venerable, wooden ballpark next to the Farmers Market on Fairfax Avenue, across the street from CBS's Television City. We sat in box seats behind first base, close enough to see the hair on his forearms. My dad pointed out that Milton Berle and Gordon McCrea were sitting two rows in front of us, but I couldn't have cared less. I was there to see the real Stars, players like Lee Walls, Carlos Bernier, Red Munger, and of course, Dale Richard Long.

I knew all his stats, all his personal data. He was born February 6, 1926, in Springfield, Missouri; he grew up in Adams, Massachusetts; he was 6'4", 210; he had a wife and an infant son; he swung a 35", 34-ounce Louisville Slugger from the port side. When his picture was in the paper with Debbie Reynolds as the cochairmen for muscular dystrophy, I clipped it and put it dead central on my bulletin board. I looked up his name in the phone book, and when I found a Dale Long listed in Pasadena, I begged my dad to drive me by his house. I about had a fit when he wouldn't do it. (Long actually lived in the San Fernando Valley.)

One Sunday my dad took me to a doubleheader between the Stars and the Angels, the dreaded crosstown rivals. I hated the Angels, especially their feisty little second baseman Gene Mauch. In the first game, Frank Kelleher and Long took Lefty Joe Hatton deep. I swear Long's clout went halfway to Azusa. Angel outfielder Bob Speake didn't even bother to move. The next time Kelleher was up, Hatton drilled him in the ribs. Within seconds, both benches charged the field in one of the biggest brawls in baseball history. *Life* ran pictures of it. The fight lasted longer than Archie Moore versus Carl Bobo Olson. The riot police were called. During the melee, I kept my eyes zeroed in on Long and prayed that nobody would coldcock him. When he and Mauch got close to each other near the back of the mound, I rooted for him to throw an Argentina Rocca headlock on the little twerp and grind his face into the dirt. After it was all over— and he and Mauch had survived in one piece—the game resumed with eight cops sitting on each bench.

Long was called up to Pittsburgh the next season, hitting a very respectable .291 with 16 taters and 79 ribbies for the woeful last-place Pirates. He also did something that year that will likely never be duplicated as long as there are balls and bats. He tied for the National League lead in triples with Willie Mays (13), while not stealing a single base.

"It was because Forbes Field was so huge in the alleys and in straightaway center," Long told me thirty-three years later, sitting in the living room of his home in Palm Coast, Florida. "It was 465 to center. Hell, it was so big that they even stored the batting cage out there, right on the field."

After retiring as a player in 1963, Long tried his hand at sales before getting back into the game as . . . boo . . . an ump. He made it as high as Triple A, working in the International League. But he found that advancing up the ump ladder of success, like just about everything else, involved a lot of politics, or at least too much for him—he had always been known as someone who told it like he saw it. He hung up his chest protector and went back into sales. But in 1982 he got a call from commissioner Bowie Kuhn's office, offering him a job as a field rep in charge of evaluating minor league operations east of the Mississippi. Since then, he has spent his summers traveling to minor league cities in the East, checking out everything from the quality of the light towers in Buffalo to the sale of souvenirs in Durham.

In 1987 his name resurfaced with the national media when the record that he set in 1956 for hitting a home run in eight consecutive games was equaled by Don Mattingly of the Yankees. It had been one of those records, like Joe DiMaggio's 56-game hitting streak and Don Drysdale's 58⅔ scoreless innings (since broken by Orel Hershiser), that seemed like it would stand forever.

"Those streaks were much tougher than mine," he observes. "They lasted over a longer period of time; their pressure was greater because the media had more time to hound them. In eight games, there wasn't enough time for the pressure of the media to build."

He's being a tad modest, downplaying the scope of his accomplishment. His eight homers, hit between May 21 and May 28, didn't exactly all come off a corp of cunny-thumbers. The list of victims included Warren Spahn, Curt Simmons, Lindy McDaniel, and Carl Erskine. Nor were the hits cheapo dingers down the line. Seven of the eight blasts were 400-footers plus. The fourth homer in the streak was off Herman Wehmeier of St. Louis, landing against a girder in the second tier in right field in Pittsburgh. Stan Musial said it was the longest ball he'd ever seen hit at Forbes. The next night Long crushed one off McDaniel that jetted over the 436-foot sign in right-center, the first ball ever to clear that spot in the forty-seven years Forbes Field had been in business.

He hit homer number six off Simmons in Philadelphia. After the game, while Long was still in the clubhouse talking to reporters, the team bus started to leave to take the players back to the Warwick Hotel. Nelson King, the winning pitcher that night, jumped off the bus and threw himself down in front of it.

"This bus doesn't move until our meal ticket gets on," he yelled. The bus waited.

The record for consecutive home-run games at that time was six, held by Ken Williams and a guy by the name of Lou Gehrig. As Long went for the record in game seven, the *pressure* was on. *Sports Illustrated* sent a crew to Connie Mack Stadium to cover the game. Pirate manager Bobby Bragan, sensing the drama, moved him from fourth up to third in the batting order to possibly give him an extra at-bat. In his first time up against Stu Miller, he nailed a high drive to right. Back, back, back. It hit a foot from the top of the wall and caromed off for a double. His next two times up, he lined out. He was down to his last chance. Ben Flowers was on the mound for the Phils. His first pitch was a ball. Then Long whiffed a curve. Then ball two, then another curve for a strike. Long stepped out of the box as Flowers looked in for the 2-and-2 sign. It was a knuckle ball. Long timed it perfectly, launching it over the light tower in right. He had the record. The ball was retrieved and sent to Cooperstown. *Sports Illustrated* ran a five-page pictorial spread, capturing the historic swing and the celebration at home plate.

When he had signed his contract the previous winter, Long had brashly promised General Manager Joe Brown that he would lead the Pirates out of the cellar. He had asked Brown if he could get a raise if he actually pulled it off. "If you do it," said Brown, "I'll come

Dale Long hits his record-setting seventh home run in seven games off Ben Flowers of the Phillies.

to you." In those days, the word "renegotiation" wasn't part of the baseball vocabulary. But after the seventh homer, Brown lived up to his word, calling him on the phone and raising his salary from $14,000 to $16,500.

But Long wasn't through. Two days later, after the last game in Philadelphia was rained out, he connected for number eight in the fourth inning of a 3–2 win over the Dodgers in Pittsburgh. It was off Carl Erskine. The 32,221 fans, the largest night crowd in six years, gave him a thunderous ovation as he Cadillac'd it around the bases. When he disappeared into the dugout, the cheering grew even louder. It did not stop until Long reappeared on the top step of the dugout and tipped his cap. As far as anybody could remember, it was the first curtain call in major league history.

The streak was stopped the next night, May 29, when he was horse-collared by big Don Newcombe. At that point in the season, he was hitting .405 with 14 homers. He had hit safely in 28 of 30 games. He was the toast of baseball.

"I give Joe Gordon a lot of the credit," says Long. "He was the hitting coach for Detroit that year and we were traveling north with the Tigers after spring training. Joe told me to watch Al Kaline's swing and how he had his arms extended, rolling over his wrists at contact, hitting the ball out in front. I paid attention. In our opening game against the Giants, I hit two homers off Johnny Antonelli in the Polo Grounds."

Two weeks after his homer binge, Long fouled two consecutive pitches off his ankle. The next day it looked like a rotten eggplant, but those were the days when players were told to rub a little dirt on it and gut it out. That's what he did. Then he went out and got one hit in his next fifty at-bats. He limped through the rest of the season, finishing with a respectable .263 average, 27 homers, and 91 RBIs. But his relationship with Joe Brown went down the tubes.

"Brown was the kind of guy who came into the clubhouse and was buddy-buddy if we won," recalls Long. "Or if a guy was going good, he was his pal. But if we lost, he stayed away. Or if a guy was in a slump, he treated him like dirt. I didn't like that and I told him so. As soon as I opened my mouth, I was sorry I did."

When Long started off the 1957 season hitting .182 after seven games, Brown dispatched him posthaste to the Cubs. He responded with one of the best seasons of his ten-year major league career, hitting .298, with 21 HRs. Take that, Mr. Brown.

The next season, he hit a tidy 20 homers and batted .271. It was his defensive work that year, however, that earned him another spot in the record books. He became the first left-hander since Homer Hillebrand in 1905 to catch in a major league game. The Cubs' two regular catchers, Sammy Taylor and Cal Neeman, were out of the game. In desperation, manager Bob Scheffing inserted Long behind the plate. The big firstsacker wasn't totally unprepared—when Long was in the minor leagues, Branch Rickey had toyed with the idea of trying him at catcher, going so far as to special-order two catcher's mitts for him. He tried them out catching batting practice on several occasions. In 1954, he even caught one inning with the Hollywood Stars during a game in which he played all nine positions. But when he reached the big leagues, the only thing he used his catcher's mitt for was as a cushion on the bench. When Scheffing waved him in, he went with his first baseman's glove. And how did he do?

"Not bad, I picked a runner off first," he responds. "Actually, I've never figured out any reason why a lefty couldn't play short or third either."

In 1959, he tied a record by hitting two consecutive home runs as a pinch hitter for the Cubs. In 1960, he was traded to San Francisco, but after only 37 games and a .167 average, he was traded again to the Yankees, where he hit a cool .366 in 26 games. In the World Series that year, he went 1 for 3 in a pinch-hitting role against his old team, the Pirates. He was voted a two-thirds share of $3,476.43. Today, World Series winners each receive over $100,000.

Back in 1956 following his homer streak, Long was asked by the *Sporting News* what the difference was between the majors and the minors. He replied, "You dress differently, eat differently. You're on TV. People recognize you on the streets. You're important, even with a last-place team. You can set records in the major leagues that last a lifetime. In the minors, there's hardly such a thing. Whoever remembers a minor league record?"

Whoa there, Mr. ex-Bucco. There was an eleven-year-old boy back when you were Mr. MVP Hollywood Star who still remembers your minor league stats. Sure, I know about your career .267 average and your 132 roundtrippers in The Show. And I know that you were the first guy to hit homers in eight consecutive games, the first lefthander to catch in ages, the first guy to take a curtain call, the first guy to lead the league in triples and not steal a base. But to me, what is more important is that you were there at Gilmore Stadium, bigger than the big leagues, when I was a boy sitting behind first base with my dad, cheering like crazy for you to slug that ball and whip those dirty Angels and their feisty second baseman. You were my King for the Day.

Larry Colton is the author of *Idol Time*, about the Portland Trailblazers, and the forthcoming nonfiction book *The Goat Brothers*. He pitched two innings for the Philadelphia Phillies in 1968, when their manager was Gene Mauch.

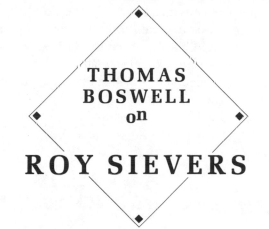

THOMAS BOSWELL
on
ROY SIEVERS

A baseball hero is a toy of childhood. Electric trains, cowboy guns, and plastic soldiers are the same kind. But with a baseball hero a youngster reaches out, for one of the first times, into the world outside the family. That connection with a big, mysterious environment gives a certain sense of power; a child discovers that it can invest its affections and actually get something special back in return. However, hero worship also brings with it the first morsels of the sort of pain and fear that wo come to associate with the word "reality." We begin to learn about adult disappointments and the profound uncontrollableness of nature.

I was fortunate. I got a wonderful hero. When I was eight years old in the spring of 1956, somebody gave me my first pack of baseball cards. Pathetic as it sounds, I can still remember where I was standing when I opened them—beside a coffee table in the living room. In that pack was only one player from my home-town team, the Washington Senators. I'm convinced that, by the luck of the draw, the player on that card was destined to be my first (and as it's turned out, only) hero. It could have been Pedro Ramos, who liked to pack a six-shooter and sometimes kept the vice squad busy. It could have been Herb Plews, who made four errors in one inning or Chuck Stobbs who lost thirteen games in a row.

But it was Roy Sievers.

1956 Topps: Copyright © The Topps Company, Inc.

At that time, he wasn't the best player on those bad Nat teams. Mickey Vernon was. Sievers, however, was about to blossom into the best home run hitter in the American League. And I had "spotted" him—that is, stumbled on him, a year before it happened. Maybe that's why, to this day, I'm still childishly certain that I have a special lucky relationship with baseball.

At the ages of nine and ten, I felt intimately connected with the most mythic public performer in my town—a man who hit 42 home runs in 1957 and then 39 in 1958. That doesn't sound like so many, but for that sliver of time (so symbolic to me), it was more than anybody in baseball except Ernie Banks. Yes, more than Mickey Mantle or Ted Williams, Hank Aaron or Willie Mays.

CULT BASEBALL PLAYERS

Sievers never failed me. In the pulp magazines and sports pages of the time, he was portrayed as modest to the point of shyness, as well as unselfish and charitable. On his home runs, he always trotted the bases with his head down as though embarrassed and anxious to get back into the dugout. Every story discussed the wide respect he'd earned by making "a dramatic comeback" after a shoulder injury nearly ended a promising career that had begun with a Rookie of the Year Award in 1949.

When I finally met him, he surpassed all expectations. One night in 1958, when he was at the height of his fame and I was ten years old, my mother took me to Hecht's department store where Sievers was giving autographs. Not selling them. Not hawking an autobiography. For all I know, maybe not even getting a fee from the store. Just giving autographs.

I got lost. Thought I knew better than my mother where he would be. So, I took off on my own. As the store closed down and I knew he had to leave, I cried with a frustration perhaps only children know.

Finally, my mother found me. Sievers should have left a half hour before. But he was waiting. Alone. For the mother and the lost little boy to come back.

My only memory is that he was big. But the picture, "To Tommy from Roy Sievers," in big, handsome, looping script, can still be unearthed, in mint condition, in a pinch. There was another picture, too, a standard-issue "Roy Sievers" that my mother had taken in case she couldn't find me in time. That one went on the bedroom wall and had darts and insults thrown at it after many an exasperating strikeout or pop fly came over the radio.

I watched Sievers play many times in Griffith Stadium and on TV. But what I remember much more clearly is reading about him, keeping scrapbooks of box scores and statistics, and above all, listening to absolutely every game on the radio. Or should I say praying on the radio. The incredible power of that daily connection is the unique hold that baseball has on its fans.

Listening to that radio under the covers long after bedtime, I learned that heroes fail, even my hero, that they fall from public favor while they are still in yours, that ultimately there is a world that does not care that you are listening in.

In his prime, before injuries and Harmon Killebrew pushed him out of the headlines, Sievers was given a "night." Not the kind that Ted Williams and Stan Musial got, with fancy cars, but a night with plenty of speeches and a station wagon. Vice President Richard

Nixon did the talking, and Sievers hung his head and cried when Nixon shook his hand. That required a breakfast-table explanation.

In 1959, Sievers's play went downhill; there was trade talk. I wrote in protest to Calvin Griffith—an eleven-year-old's letter. Griffith wrote back—a club-owner's letter. With fans like me, Sievers would never be traded. There was nothing to worry about. And would my family and I be interested in season tickets?

Before the next season, Sievers was traded. By that time I was too old to cry . . . much. After that, his name was no longer a constant part of my thoughts. When I was seventeen, Sievers was traded back to the expansion Senators from the Phillies in midseason of 1964. I barely noticed. At the time, it never crossed my mind that he escaped The Fold. (Or perhaps, missed his chance to prevent it.) I had my own high school games to play, and besides, I wore Ted Williams's number.

Still, for years when the name would sneak up on me on a TV sportscast, it would give a little private shock, like certain girls' names when you don't expect to hear them.

A couple of years after college, when I was working as a copy aide in the sports department of the *Washington Post*—fetching coffee, covering high school sports, and trying to find a way to get a story longer than six paragraphs in the paper under my byline—I decided to search for Sievers.

CULT BASEBALL PLAYERS

There he was, in his hometown St. Louis phone book, living in a placed called Spanish Lake. And there he was, again, picking up the phone and chatting with me for an hour as if it were nothing. Answering personal questions about how the A's had fired him as a minor league manager ("too nice") and how his son Robin was getting scant encouragement from the Cardinals in the minors.

He sounded relaxed and fairly happy, like a man who didn't require much to be content, certainly nothing as grand as hitting 318 home runs in the major leagues. Working as a salesman for the Yellow Freight Company and raising three kids was okay by him. "I'm set up fine here," he said, although he couldn't keep a certain gentle bewilderment out of his voice when he talked about how Eddie Yost was still in the major leagues, as a coach with the Mets. How do you do that?

The night I called him, Watergate was near its height. Not too far away, Woodward and Bernstein were probably digging. I asked my childhood hero what his fondest memory had been. Roy Sievers said it was the night Richard Nixon shook his hand at home plate. "I'm sentimental. That was really touching . . . in Washington I got to meet four presidents and have lunch with two. That's wonderful for a kid from St. Louis."

Then, Sievers's wife, Jo, called him to dinner in Spanish Lake.

"Tell [baseball writer] Bob Addie I miss him," said Sievers.

From the day I got his baseball card to the day I interviewed him (and got my first decent story in the *Post* sports pages) was sixteen years. Then, I didn't hear of Sievers again for sixteen more years. His name vanished from baseball so completely that, even to a writer on the baseball beat like me, he was nonexistent.

Finally, one day in 1988, a friend asked if I'd seen that TV commercial for the Maryland lottery. The funny one with the two old Senators ballplayers talking about how small salaries were in the fifties and how much money you could win now in the lottery.

I watched with trepidation. Sievers would be sixty-two years old.

In the commercial, Sievers looked young, handsome, and happy, with a great smile. At least that's how he looked on my TV.

Thomas Boswell is a sports columnist for the *Washington Post.* He is the author of *The Heart of the Order, Strokes of Genius, How Life Imitates the World Series: An Inquiry into the Game,* and *Why Time Begins on Opening Day.*

ROCKY COLAVITO

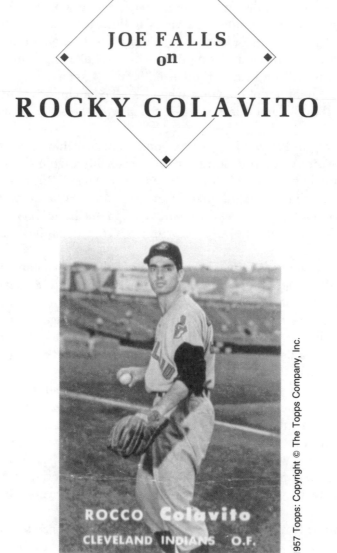

1957 Topps: Copyright © The Topps Company, Inc.

Dick Ferrell looked like he'd seen a ghost. It was Easter Sunday. The place was Lakeland, Florida. The year was 1960. The Tigers were playing their final exhibition game of the spring—

a humdrum affair against the Chicago White Sox—when Ferrell, who was the general manager of the Tigers in those days, came into the press box atop the roof at Henley Field and leaned over to where the Detroit writers were sitting, and started whispering to them.

His voice was barely audible. "We've got an announcement to make," Ferrell murmured. I thought he was going to tell us somebody had died. "We're sending Harvey Kuenn to Cleveland for Rocky Colavito."

With that, the last bit of blood drained from Rick's face and he backed away in silence.

Kuenn for Colavito?

A blockbuster.

It didn't take much to understand the impact of this one—the batting champion for the home run champion. Detroit's leading hitter for . . . well, for a man who was idolized and adored by all of Cleveland. Oh, my. What would they think of this deal? There could be panic in the streets.

Rocky Colavito.

Rocco Domenico Colavito.

The man who wrapped his muscular arms around his bat and pressed it tightly against his back in the on-deck circle. The man with all the mannerisms at the plate. The man who stretched and strained, twitched and turned, as he got set in the batter's box. He was an idol in Cleveland. How do you trade idols? Why do you trade idols? Idols are hard to come by. Harvey Kuenn was a ballplayer. Pure and simple. He cussed, drank, chewed tobacco, and could hit to all fields. You could count on one or two line drives a game. He didn't field all that well and didn't have much power, but he was a steady player.

Rocky Colavito, meanwhile, was a god in Cleveland. A matinee idol. A hero to young and old alike. He was good to his parents and he loved his family and he liked small children and he hit those long, looping drives into the left-field seats. They loved him dearly—embraced his every move—and now he was gone, wrenched from their grasp. What would they think? What would they do? Cleveland was his town.

Don't Knock The Rock.

How could they do such a thing to him?

I remember talking to Harvey in the clubhouse. He was smoking a cigar and didn't seem all that bothered by the trade. He didn't have a lot to say. He said it was one of those things that happen in life. Hey, is there any beer left in the cooler?

I thought of what was going on wherever the Indians were playing that day. It was out west, somewhere in Arizona, and I could envision the look on Colavito's face when they told him about it. I saw a face that was angry, a face that fell to disbelief—a face that would soon look like that of a dying warrior.

Even from a distance. The Rock could do that to you.

Frank Lane, the wheeling-and-dealing general manager of the Indians, had made the deal with Bill DeWitt, the wheeling-and-dealing general manager of the Tigers. Everyne knew Lane was a bold one. An outrageous operator. Trader Lane, they called him. He'd swap his mother for two aunts and an uncle to be named at a later date if it would help him. Or he might make the deal just to have something to do. Maybe it was a dull day and he was getting bored.

But: Rocky Colavito for Harvey Kuenn?

What made it so fascinating is that the Tigers were to fly to Cleveland that night to open the season against the Indians on the following Tuesday in Municipal Stadium.

The baseball world would get a head-to-head confrontation right away.

As I remember, Kuenn flew with us to Cleveland, then parted ways when we got to the airport. I felt for him. He was a good guy—a part of the scene in Detroit. But even more, I kept wondering how the city of Cleveland would take the trade of the beloved Rocco Domenico Colavito.

Cleveland was taking it badly.

The story was bannerlined in the papers the next day in bold, black headlines. The phones started ringing almost immediately. Lane was castigated by everyone, especially by teenage girls throughout the greater Cleveland area. Calls came in from all over, and Lane was called every conceivable name in the book. They threatened physical violence upon him if he dared show his face anywhere in the ballpark on opening day.

Some actually looked for rope in the basement and threatened to take it to the stadium with them.

Lane chortled. He loved the attention. It was exactly what he wanted. The town was suddenly talking about his team. Even better, they were talking about him.

"What's the problem?" Lane smirked. "All I did was trade a hamburger for a steak."

That did it. The ropes came up from the basement. They would string him on the nearest lamppost. He couldn't do this to their man. Not to Rocco Domenico Colavito.

On Tuesday, there were long lines outside of Municipal Stadium. Most of the early arrivals were teenagers. They came out with their signs and banners and hung them all over right field.

"We love you, Rocky."

"You'll always be ours, Rocky."

"Forever and ever, Rocky."

They got as close to their man as they could get, squealing in delight at the very sight of him, even if he was in the uniform of the enemy. At least they were close to him. He would be theirs, if only for a short period of time.

They played fourteen innings that day. The game seemed to go on forever. The Tigers finally won it on Al Kaline's single into center field. It was dark and cold by the time the game was over. The stands were almost empty. Rocky Colavito went to the plate six times against his old team. He struck out four times, popped up, and hit into a double play, and the signs and the banners and most of the teeny-boppers were long gone from the stadium. It was a day of defeat for them. A day of despair for the whole city of Cleveland. We love you, Rock. Good-bye, Rock. We can't stand it anymore. We have to go.

That's when my troubles started with this man.

Despite having the strongest arm in the league, Colavito was switched from right field (Kaline's domain) to left field by the Tigers, and at the suggestion of Larry Middlemas of the *Detroit News*, I wrote, "The Tigers are putting Colavito into left field because he has the feet for it."

Wrong, Joe.

He had flat feet, but you never criticized Rocco Domenico Colavito for anything, especially birth defects.

Don't Knock The Rock.

What did I know?

I thought he was a ballplayer like the rest of them.

How was I to know he was a self-ordained diety?

Things quickly went from bad to worse. Colavito struggled in Detroit. He did not get the same warm reception in my town that he got in Cleveland. They cheered him but they also booed him, depending on how he was playing. It was a whole new experience for him.

I didn't help matters by printing his RNBIs in my newspaper.

RNBIs are runs *not* batted in. It was a statistic I made up. I made it up just for Rocky. I noticed he was popping up an awful lot with runners on second and third and decided to go back in my scorebook and see how many runners he was leaving out there.

Wrong again, Joe Baby.

I was holding him up to public ridicule and you never do that with Rocco Domenico Colavito.

I thought I was providing a service to my readers—plus slipping the needle in—by letting them know where The Rock succeeded and where he failed.

Colavito never said a word to me, but as I learned later, the RNBIs grated at him. It turned out that they tore at his insides. He did not like to be criticized. He did not like being considered a failure.

It got worse.

A year later, the Tigers went to the West Coast. They were in first place at the time. It was May and the first stop was in Los Angeles where they would play the Angels in Wrigley Field.

Bill Rigney was the manager and he was a good guy—friendly and fun to talk to. No sooner did we go over to talk to him, Sam Greene of the *Detroit News* and myself (I was with the *Free Press* in those days), than Rigney started kidding us about the Tigers.

"First place, eh? You're going to win it all, eh? Run away with the whole race, eh?" He knew the Yankees were still in the league and the Yankees were a team that boasted the likes of Mantle, Maris, Berra, Howard, Skowron, Richardson, Kubek, and Ford, and Rigney knew it would only be a matter of time until they made their presence felt. After all, Roger Maris was on his way to a 61-home-run season. The year was 1961.

"So, you expect to win it in a breeze," said Rigney.

"I'm not so sure of that," I said, not wanting to be sucked into his trap.

"Really," said Rigney. "What's wrong with this great team of yours?"

I told him catching was a question mark—Dick Brown was doing a fine job but could he hold up? Jake Wood was doing a good job at second base but he was striking out a lot—and I wasn't sure if Steve Boros could keep up such a hot pace at third base.

"And there's always Colavito in left field . . . ," came the voice from my good friend Sam Greene. He was putting in his two cents from behind the nub-end of a short cigar.

Rigney laughed.

I went on to tell Rigney all the things I liked about the Tigers— Frank Lary's pitching, Al Kaline's hitting, Norm Cash's hitting, and the power of Rocky Colavito. What we didn't know is that a local baseball writer by the name of John Hall was standing nearby listening to this whole conversation. He never said a word but went back to the press box or his office and wrote a whole column about how this reporter from Detroit had all these nasty things to say about the Tigers.

He never mentioned the good stuff, only the bad stuff, and injected the telltale line: "And there's always Colavito in left field." He gave me full credit for the line.

I could not believe my eyes when I read the paper the next day. I could not believe another writer could eavesdrop on a conversation—which was mostly a kidding conversation—and choose to write about it, using only selected excerpts to make the article more sensational.

I knew I was in hot water with the team, so I went to manager Bob Scheffing to explain my predicament. I told him he had to explain to the team exactly what had happened. He said he would. He said he'd call a special meeting and set the whole thing straight.

He never did.

And from that day on, Rocco Domenico Colavito stared daggers at me.

But wait. There is more.

Having hit 45 homers and driven in 140 runs, Colavito held out the following spring. He wanted more dough than the Tigers were paying Kaline. Kaline was getting $57,000. Colavito wanted $57,500 to prove a point. The Tigers wouldn't go for it. General manager Jim Campbell stood firm in his offer of $52,000 to The Rock.

For the first and only time in his tenure as boss of the Tigers, Campbell had a holdout on his hands.

Colavito went to spring training but wouldn't sign, which meant he wasn't allowed to work out with the team. So he tried to get into shape back at his motel.

Guess who went over there with a photographer and got pictures of his "secret" camp?

All he was doing was playing catch with Norm Cash, but when The Rock saw the layout in the papers—especially the picture of me looking at him from the tall grass through binoculars—he went off the pad. He threatened to get me if it was the last thing he ever did.

And there is still more.

Later that season, the Tigers were playing the Baltimore Orioles in Tiger Stadium, and I was the official scorer. Colavito hit an easy fly to right field. Sam Bowens, the Baltimore right fielder, lost the ball and ran right under it and it landed behind him. I figured he lost it in the sun and was ready to give Colavito a hit. Jerry Green, no relation to Sam but again of the *Detroit News*, was sitting next to

Colavito as an Indian's coach in 1978.

Courtesy Cleveland Indians

me and said, "Why isn't that an error?" I had no answer for him. "He should have caught it, so it's an error," Jerry said. I picked up the microphone at my side and announced, "E, nine."

How can I put this? When I went in to see manager Charlie Dressen after the game, Colavito came storming into Dressen's office. He called me some names and I knew he meant it. I could see the anger in his eyes. I could surely hear it in his voice. He spluttered, "How could you take a hit away from me! You're trying to ruin my career!"

I knew he was serious.

He grabbed me around the throat and held me against the wall. I didn't mind that so much except my feet were an inch off the floor. Dressen kept tugging at him, telling him he should put me down. Dressen finally pulled him away and Colavito stormed back into the clubhouse.

Colavito's time in Detroit wasn't long. He lasted just four years. It seemed a lot longer. He became something of a fixture in my town. He hit 139 homers and drove in 430 runs and was a pretty popular player, but never what he was in Cleveland. He was traded to Kansas City in 1963 and later wound up back in Cleveland, but it was never the same for him again. The little girls had grown up and had other things on their minds.

We didn't speak for more than ten years, until the day he came to town as a coach with the Indians. The Indians were staying at the old Book Cadillac, and I picked up the telephone in my office on an impulse and dialed the hotel and asked for the room of Rocky Colavito.

He answered. "Hello."

"Colavito, you're finished. I'm coming over and I'm going to beat the hell out of you."

He said, "Who is this?"

"I'm going to mop the floor with you."

"Who is this?"

"Joe Falls. You better be ready. I'll be there in ten minutes."

"Come right ahead," he said.

I knocked on his door and he threw it open. We stood there and looked at each other. Then we embraced, two old geezers hugging in the doorway of a hotel room.

"Weren't we bad?" Colavito said.

"We were bad."

We shook hands and sat down and talked for a couple of hours. It's like I've been trying to tell you: Don't Knock The Rock.

Joe Falls is the sports editor for the *Detroit News* and was a longtime columnist for the *Sporting News*. His five books include *The Detroit Tigers—An Illustrated History, So You Think You're a Die-Hard Tiger Fan*, and *The Boston Marathon*.

MARTY APPEL
on
THURMAN MUNSON

Each day during the baseball season, early arrivals at Yankee Stadium are entertained by a video spectacular on the huge Diamond Vision scoreboard beyond the bleachers. The legendary names in the team's rich history pass by, and what team can evoke more awe than this one? You begin with Ruth, Gehrig, DiMaggio, and Mantle, and wonder whether these are the four athletes most imbedded on our national consciousness.

But wait. Suddenly there appears the scruffy figure of a battle-worn catcher. Like a fallen soldier, he crawls, then hobbles, attempting to rise from the ground. The pain of his profession is evident. The charm of Ruth, the strength of Gehrig, the grace of DiMaggio, the glamour of Mantle, are nowhere to be seen. Gallantly, he gets his footing and returns to battle, putting aside the pain. He ignores the onrushing trainer. The umpire looks on admiringly. And suddenly, the live crowd in Yankee Stadium becomes part of the video presentation, rising as one to cheer the image of the heroic leader. Even now, more than a decade after his demise, the pictures evoke tears of love. Recalled is that emotion-filled evening in the summer of 1979, when Yankee Stadium cried for the loss of the Yankee captain, Thurman Munson. For Munson are saved the biggest cheers, the greatest outpouring that the video will produce.

Thurman's endearing relationship with the fans was always a source of wonder, even before he crashed his jet while practicing landings during an off-day in Canton, Ohio. He was, after all, a rather well-known grouch, noncommunicative with most of the media and thus, seldom quoted, seldom heard by the fans. What they came to

CULT BASEBALL PLAYERS

love, instead, was not the glib "we can win this" that one expects from team captains, but rather, a day-after-day performance without quotation marks, in which his effort on the field provided all the punctuation he needed.

In 1977, after he had won the American League's Most Valuable Player award (as voted by the despised sportswriters), I approached him about collaborating on an autobiography. I had been, up through that year, the Yankees' public relations director throughout Thurman's career. I had reasoned that the book was a marketable one, and that since he had no sportswriters with whom he could collaborate (as he would have to speak to his coauthor), I might be a logical partner.

He wasn't impressed with the idea.

"I'm only thirty years old," he said "That's too young for an autobiography. Who'd want to read it anyway?"

I explained that thirty was not that young in sports, and many people did find a certain fascination with athletes. But what really sold him on the idea was my logical explanation of the way of the world.

"Look," I ventured, "when you play in New York, when you win an MVP Award, when you star in a World Series, feud with Reggie Jackson, fight with George Steinbrenner, and hate Carlton Fisk, someone is going to write a book about you. It will be an unauthorized biography, based on newsclips and conversations with other people. You will have no say in it, you will make no money from it, and it will live forever in libraries as the definitive story of Thurman Munson. If you write your own story, you can look at it as an insurance policy. Once word gets out that you're doing it, no publisher will do a biography to compete with it. You can make sure it all comes out just the way you want it."

This made sense to Munson. And so we spent ten weeks in the summer of 1977 engaged in conversation at his New Jersey summer home, a tape recorder between us, three small children scampering about, and a life story told. Almost.

Much of what was left out had to do with his father. It was a subject Thurman skirted over in the telling of his life story.

"My father was a long-distance truck driver," he explained. "He wasn't around a lot."

There was much more to the story. Thurman's wife, Diana, would fill me in, but if Thurman didn't want it in his autobiography, that was clearly his choice to make.

We learn something of Darrell Munson from the day on which Lee MacPhail visited the Munson home in Canton in 1968. Lee was the Yankees' general manager. Thurman had just been New York's number one draft choice, an All-American catcher out of Kent State University. The visit by MacPhail, along with Yankee scout Gene Woodling, was a big day in the Munson home. Thurman's mother made the place sparkle. Diana, then the girlfriend, was present, as were Thurman's brother and two sisters, all in their Sunday bests. The formality of the contract signing would take place at the dining room table.

Rolled out on the family sofa was Thurman's father. He was dressed in an undershirt and work pants. He didn't rise to greet the visitors. He said nothing, until suddenly, from across the room, he mumbled something to the effect of "he ain't too good on pop fouls, you know."

It didn't blow the deal. Still, the next time Yankee folks saw Darrell Munson was at Thurman's funeral eleven years later. The talk at the Munson home the night before was very much about Darrell. He had been a missing person for some time. After Thurman's mother suffered a stroke, his father bolted. He hadn't been heard from for years. It must have pained Thurman deeply, yet he never raised the point in his autobiography.

What it did was draw Munson close to his family of in-laws. His devotion to his wife and children was unusually strong. He sought to spend as much time with them as possible, and when he acquired sufficient wealth, he purchased a plane to make it possible to fly home often to be with them. When he mastered the plane, he bought a jet. It was his way. But the jet was too much plane for Munson, and it was a tragedy waiting to happen.

Amidst the incredible grief surrounding the funeral in Canton, Ohio, Darrell Munson did in fact appear. It was not a fact warmly received by the family. Darrell seized the moment to call a spontaneous press conference.

"I was," he told the assembled members of the media, "a better player than Thurman. I never had the breaks he did, but I was a better player."

He was wearing a sort of Mexican sombrero as he spoke, a rather odd outfit for the occasion, and he had apparently been living in the New Mexico area, to which he returned later that day, not to be heard from again. No wonder Thurman had found this all a source of embarrassment.

Munson could be an enigma. He pretended to be unimpressed by the trappings of New York Yankees history, but he was secretly caught up by them. He made it seem that it was "no big deal" to be named captain of the team—the first one since Lou Gehrig—but he had his best season when he received that honor and did indeed play the role of field leader, never permitting a teammate to accept defeat.

At the 1976 Old-timers' Day gathering in Yankee Stadium, an opportunity arose for a rare group portrait of the legendary Yankee catchers—Bill Dickey, Yogi Berra, Elston Howard, and Munson. Thurman, true to form, proved to be the most difficult to secure for the photo. He acted as though it were a waste of his time.

When I arrived at his home in Canton three years later, a sixteen-by-twenty of the picture hung in his den.

Everyone knew that Munson truly despised Carlton Fisk, but no one was sure why. I know he resented the accolades heaped on Fisk, many of which he thought were generated by Curt Gowdy on NBC. Gowdy, of course, was also the Red Sox announcer. Thurman said, "Fisk's always injured—he gets the credit. I don't and I'm out there every day." Thurman was the only catcher to have the stats to match Fisk's, but Fisk had the looks and the glamour. Thurman was probably jealous.

One of the jobs of a public relations director is to ask players to shake some hands or pose for some photos with sponsors, guests of

Steve Garvey collides with an immovable force, Munson, in the 1977 World Series.

the owner, contest winners, what have you. Thurman was at his best in this department. Other players would promise to be there in five minutes. You'd wait, go back to look for them, find them undressed, go back and make apologies, and wait some more. It was one of the least-pleasant assignments we had.

Thurman could make it a pleasure. You'd ask him to pose for the picture, he'd tell you to go to hell (or something less polite), and you'd get someone else. You always knew where you stood, which was better than Choice A.

He was a player's player. With the exception of Carlton Fisk, he was liked and admired by all teammates and opponents. It was apparent from the day he arrived on the scene that he would never accept .500 baseball, second place, or less than 100 percent effort from a teammate. He didn't have to spell it out for anyone, nor did he have to explain that he was going to become the team's regular catcher. He simply arrived and took over the job.

He has not fared very well in Hall of Fame voting, and it thus appears doubtful that he will ever make it. But one could certainly make an argument on his behalf by filling in a plaque with things like "Captain of three consecutive New York Yankee pennant-winning teams . . . First catcher to be named Rookie of the Year in the American League . . . Most Valuable Player, 1976 . . . Three-time Gold Glove winner . . . Batted over .300 five times in ten-year career . . . Made only one error, 1971 season, and that on a play in which he was knocked unconscious . . . Batted .529 in 1976 World Series, highest ever by a player on a losing team . . . Lifetime average in postseason play was .357 . . . First American Leaguer in a quarter century to bat over .300 and drive in over 100 runs in three consecutive seasons . . . Seven-time All-Star."

My favorite memory of Munson relates to his telling me of the times he would wander up to George Steinbrenners's office after batting practice to talk a little business. Said Thurman, "I loved to put my feet up on his desk while we spoke. It annoyed the hell out of him, but he never told me to knock it off."

When Munson died, I watched George Steinbrenner speak on television. "I remember," he said, "how he'd come up to my office and put his feet on my desk. We were very close."

In fact, none were as close as they would have liked to have been. But the fans, who still cheer that dirty uniform and fighting spirit, knew him better than they thought.

Marty Appel is the executive producer of Yankee baseball on WPIX-TV in New York. He is the coauthor of *Thurman Munson: An Autobiography*.

MOSS KLEIN
on
SANDY KOUFAX

The Dodgers had been my team since the day in October of 1955 when I came home from school, the afternoon kindergarten session at Chancellor Avenue, in time to see my older brother kick the red rocking chair in our living room, grab his foot in pain, and run upstairs.

I didn't know what had happened on the TV to set him off, but my mother explained that the Dodgers had just defeated the Yankees in the World Series. Immediately, a bond was formed. In my relatively short period of baseball awareness, I had already grown tired of hearing my brother talk about Mickey, Yogi, and Whitey, and those Yankees. Maybe if he had been more willing that summer to pitch to me out front at our summer house in Bradley Beach, New Jersey, I would've swung over to the Yankee side. But many afternoons, when I was waiting to play, he would say he had to listen to the Yankees on radio, and he would come out a couple hours later, talking about Mickey, Yogi, and Whitey.

And so, any team that could beat those Yankees, and provoke that temporary damage to his foot, was going to be my team.

The courtship with the Dodgers took another important step a few months later when my father, then a sportswriter for the *Newark Star-Ledger*, was assigned to cover the Dodgers in spring training for two weeks. My brother, mother, and I went along to Dodgertown, Vero Beach. I remember orange juice, palm trees, and a huge drugstore called Webbs' City where I caused a minor fuss. There were two water fountains, one marked COLORED, and I wanted to drink

SANDY KOUFAX

Courtesy Los Angeles Dodgers

colored water. My mother stopped me, and I learned about the world that no longer existed back in New Jersey.

But being in that bright, sunny world of spring training, seeing the team that had defeated the Yankees, made the attraction more complete. And anyway, I needed a team to call my own. I was in the first grade and most of my friends, brainwashed by local rooting and older brothers, were Yankee fans. The Dodgers would be mine.

But that, of course, was just the formative stage of rooting. A year later, back in spring training for another two-week fling, I discovered Sandy Koufax. At least I was the first kid from Chancellor Avenue School, of Mrs. Duchin's second-grade class, to discover him. And that was all that mattered.

I heard my father talking to my mother one night, telling her about this young Jewish pitcher named Koufax. My mother, despite having traveled extensively with my father when he was covering the International League's Newark Bears in the late 1930s and early 1940s, knew nothing about baseball. At one crucial Bears' game, she fell asleep, leaning on the shoulder of Irene Vitt, wife of the Newark manager, Oscar Vitt.

But she seemed intrigued by the presence in Dodgertown of a Jewish pitcher. My father repeated the name to her. And when I returned to school, I proudly told Andy Leiter, Roger Chlowitz, Dave

Haber, and the other guys in Mrs. Duchin's: This guy Koufax, he's going to be great.

And he would be, of course. But first he had to learn to control his fastball, develop his curve. My father told me stories about how they would make him throw on a different field in those early days, because he was so wild, and threw so hard, that hitters didn't want to face him in batting practice.

After the 1957 season, the Dodgers moved from Brooklyn to Los Angeles, a shift that provoked angry reaction in our area but didn't bother me at all. In fact, as it turned out, the distance made my affair with Koufax and the Dodgers even stronger. I was too young to have built up any feelings about Brooklyn or Ebbets Field or any of that tradition. I liked the idea of my team being more challenging to follow. I would prove my devotion.

I stayed up late, secretly most of the time, listening for the West Coast scores. Everyone knew what the Yankees did when we were in school the next morning, but I was the one who knew about the Dodgers. There was no ESPN or CNN in those days, and those West Coast scores didn't usually make the morning papers.

My father, who by now had settled into an editor's role at the *Star-Ledger*, working until the early-morning hours, would often bring home the wire-service account of the Dodgers' games, which didn't make most editions. So I not only knew the score, I could tell everyone what happened. And when Koufax pitched, I'd wake up to find not only the wire-service story but often a photo, from an early inning, lying next to my bed. That always amazed me—while I was sleeping in the house on Goldsmith Avenue in Newark, Koufax had made that particular pitch out in L.A. And here I was, waking up and seeing the picture.

And as I progressed through grammar school, Koufax was on the rise, too. By 1961, when I was in fifth grade, he won 18 games and led the league in strikeouts. He was still erratic, but the awesome ability was emerging. Now my friends were talking about him. In the mostly Jewish neighborhood of the Weequahic section of Newark in the early 1960s, a Jewish pitcher of Koufax's rising fame was a predictable topic of conversation.

Once, when I was walking down Hobson Street, around the corner from our house, I even heard the group of yentas, the women who sat on the stoop in the spring and summer in their flowery house-dresses and talked about everyone and everything, talking about Koufax. I beamed with pride. Koufax had made it into the Hobson Street gossip mill. I wanted to tell them, Hey, he was my discovery.

By the time 1963 rolled around, me and Koufax were ready for a big year. He was seemingly ready to emerge in 1962, but his season was cut short by an injury, and the Giants rallied to beat the Dodgers, winning the pennant in a playoff series.

But in 1963, there'd be no stopping Koufax and the Dodgers. I turned thirteen that summer, had my bar mitzvah, and had already accepted that I wouldn't be another Koufax. I was a chubby second baseman, decent power, no speed. My pitching career went downhill after a softball game, when I bare-handed a line drive by big Butch Zawacki. My index finger and middle finger split open, and there was blood on the white softball when I picked it up. But I completed the play, getting him at first, and shifting back to second base.

But in 1963, I was already known as the Dodger specialist, and the Koufax expert. And what a year we had. Koufax was 25–5, the first of four consecutive dominating seasons that would make him an automatic, first-ballot Hall of Famer. The Dodgers won the National League pennant. The Yankees won the American League pennant. It was showdown time, Dodgers against the Yankees for the first time since 1956, and me against the gang of Yankee fans, who joined forces days in advance to argue with me.

We made our first bets, mostly for a quarter or fifty cents. I handled all the Dodger action. This was the big time, bigger than the showdown stickball games we played at the empty lot across from Bernheim's Funeral Parlor.

Game one, Koufax against Ford at Yankee Stadium. Transistor radios securely in place in the flip-top desks in the eighth-grade class of Mr. Kaplowitz. Koufax was striking out one after another, and the Dodgers had an early 5–0 lead. I was motioning to my friends, who were ignoring me. But Mr. Kaplowitz spotted me. He came over to my desk, the large man who was known to poke students in the chest with his incredibly strong fingers when making a point. And a few times, he even grabbed guys around the neck, a predicament I experienced too often.

"Is there a problem, Mr. Klein?" he asked.

I mumbled, and he repeated the question. I figured what the heck, and to the amazement of my friends I said, "No problem, I'm just listening to Koufax beat the Yankees."

Mr. Kaplowitz looked at me, but before I flinched, he said, "What's the score?" I said, "Five nothing, Dodgers." And Mr. Kaplowitz actually smiled. "He's got them," he said. And, I would find out later, Mr. Kaplowitz, the man with the stern hands, was a Koufax fan, too.

Koufax won the game, 5–2, striking out a then-record 15 batters. The Dodgers won the next two games. That third game, we gathered at the Hobson Street house of David Felzenberg, a die-hard Yankee fan. My friends knew this was the big one. Drysdale beat the Yankees, 1–0. My friends were quiet. I skipped home.

The next day, a Sunday afternoon, the Series ended, as Koufax beat Ford, 2–1. Mantle hit a mammoth homer, but that was okay. I was sky-high, a four-game sweep, so I didn't begrudge Mantle that one moment.

Nothing would top that '63 season from my standpoint as a Koufax fan and Dodger rooter. But there would be many more moments the next three years, as Koufax settled in for his brief reign as baseball's legendary pitcher.

Watching Koufax pitch was made more special because the opportunities were so rare. On TV, I saw him against the Mets—who were hardly a challenge for him in those days—or during the World Series. Also, there were those occasional examples of perfect timing, when the *Game of the Week* on Saturday afternoons had the Dodgers when it was Koufax's turn. Those days, of course, were plotted well in advance on my schedule.

I saw Koufax pitch in person four times, three times at Shea Stadium, once at old Connie Mack Stadium in Philadelphia. Maybe I imagined it, but there seemed to be a certain atmosphere when he was pitching, as though the fans were generally more respectful, quieter. Seeing Koufax in person, on his stage, the pitcher's mound, was like watching Sinatra. You knew you were seeing a master, and that what he was doing was the best it could be done.

In person, I was surprised at how broad his back and shoulders were. I had seen so many pictures of him with Drysdale that I imagined him to be smaller, forgetting the size of the hulking Drysdale. Koufax was a free-and-easy type of pitcher. He worked hard. The strain and effort in each pitch was apparent. I was always amazed by—and proud of—how hard he threw, but the best feeling was watching the reactions of the batters, their late swings at the overpowering fastballs, the frozen looks when he broke off his curveball, which also happened to be among the best of all time.

I would try to guess his approach, calling for him to "blow away this guy" or occasionally "trick that guy" with the curve.

And the infrequent hits? They were simply mistakes, or lucky hitting. And they didn't happen often.

I moved ahead to high school, Weequahic High. The neighborhood was changing. The playground across the street from our house, where I had spent most of my free time during grammar school, became a site of black-white confrontations. Friends were moving out to the suburbs, but my closest buddies, like me, convinced our parents to stay. We didn't know that by the summer of '67, after our junior year, there would be full-scale riots in Newark, and our senior year would become an uneasy period.

But it was always sunny and pleasant when Koufax was pitching in L.A., or so it seemed to me, in those pre-riot days. Koufax was 19-5 in 1964, his season cut short again by an injury. In 1965, he was 26-8, and the Dodgers won another pennant.

During the World Series, my father was hospitalized because of a gall-bladder attack. He had surgery the day Koufax was pitching the seventh game against the Minnesota Twins. After school, I rushed over to Beth Israel Hospital. I was assured everything was fine. My father was drugged, and groggy. But he insisted I put on the game. Koufax, pitching on two days' rest, had a 2–0 lead in the eighth. We watched, and Koufax held the lead, winning the Series finale again.

1966 was Koufax's final season. Nobody knew it when the year was progressing, because nobody realized exactly how much pain Koufax's arm caused him. Everyone knew about the injuries, and the cortisone shots, and the worsening condition, but only Koufax lived with the pain.

Certainly nobody could tell from the way he pitched. He was 27-9, leading the league in earned-run average for the fifth straight year, leading in strikeouts for the third time in four years.

By 1966, naturally, girls had weaved their way into the lives of my group, and waiting for driver's licenses was the endless ordeal, the ticket to a new life in the fast lane of social activity.

But baseball still mattered to us, and Koufax still mattered to me. The Dodgers won the '66 pennant, but this time they lost to the Orioles in the World Series. Koufax's final game was a nightmare, a 6–0 loss to young Jim Palmer, ruined by usually outstanding centerfielder Willie Davis, who made three errors in one inning.

By the time Koufax made his announcement in November that he was retiring, I was prepared for it. There had been some speculation after the World Series that he might retire, even though he wouldn't turn thirty-one until December. Koufax, from what I avidly read, didn't want to take a chance on ruining his arm. And also, he had never been crazy about the nomadic life of professional baseball. He was pretty much of a loner, not one of the good-time boys on the road trips, and he had a life after baseball he wanted to get started on.

I didn't mind that Koufax would no longer be pitching, strange as that seems. I was glad he wouldn't be injuring his arm, and I was especially pleased with the idea that he was going out on top, the best in his business, like some undefeated heavyweight champ hanging up the gloves.

What I didn't know was that there would never be another hero like Koufax, because my days of having a baseball hero would never be the same. I followed eventually in the footsteps of my father and oldest brother, going into the sportswriting business. And in a nice touch of irony, I wound up as the beat writer covering the Yankees, beginning in 1976, a job I still hold.

The baseball world has become my world, from the inside. I've made hundreds of friends in my years in the business, admired and respected many baseball people, never lost my love for the greatest game. But there has never been another hero. Koufax was the one and only.

I went to see him, by the way, back in August of 1972. He was being inducted into the Hall of Fame, at Cooperstown. It was the summer after my senior year in college. I was working at a racetrack, killing time before beginning a brief fling at law school in Miami. But with Koufax reaching the heights I always knew he would, I felt I should be there. I was introduced to him before the induction ceremonies, by a baseball writer who was a friend of my father's. We shook hands, but I didn't tell him what he had meant to me as a kid. He was polite, seemed nervous, and our exchange ended quickly.

Years later, when I was covering the Yankees, I met Koufax again, back at Dodgertown, where the whole affair had started so many years ago. He was a spring-training instructor for the Dodgers, and he stopped in the pressroom after the game to visit with some friends. One of the veteran writers introduced us, but I made no attempt at pursuing a conversation. I was comfortable with superstars and celebrities by then, I moved in their circles during the baseball season, but Koufax was different. And I guess a part of me didn't want to take a chance on being disillusioned. I knew enough about other stars to know I wasn't going to take a chance on finding out that Koufax was less than perfect.

All these years later, I still take pride in hearing about Koufax, about his dominance. When I talk to ex-players from his era, now managers or coaches or broadcasters, I occasionally swing the conversation around to Koufax. And I know the person I'm talking to will sit back, shake his head, and say something filled with superlatives.

Koufax gained a special level. In *One Flew Over the Cuckoo's Nest*, watch the scene where Jack Nicholson does the fake narration of a Yankee-Dodger game, and he'll mention Koufax. In *Dirty Dancing*, when the family arrives at the hotel, there's talk of Koufax in the background.

And just recently, I heard my twenty-four-year-old nephew telling his friends that he saw Koufax pitch. One of the sharper guys in his group questioned him, because he was only two when Koufax retired. But my nephew tells the story of how I held him up in front of the TV, back on Goldsmith Avenue in Newark, and told him to look at Koufax, pitching against the Mets.

I remember saying to my nephew at the time, "Years from now, you'll be able to tell your friends you saw Koufax. None of them will be able to say that."

After all, I discovered him, didn't I?

Moss Klein is a sports columnist for the *Newark Star-Ledger* and the *Sporting News.*

REBECCA STOWE on

WILLIE HORTON

Tiger Stadium, 1972: I'm sitting in the left-field seats with my husband and some friends. It's my first game at Tiger Stadium in ten years—I'd been too busy being a Beatlemaniac during high school to pay much attention to baseball. But I'm older now, more mature, a college student, practically a *matron*. The opposing team is up and the batter hits a fly ball to left field. Willie lumbers after it, but he's not in time; it drops in, base hit, the crowd boos. I'm furious—how *dare* they? A group of drunks behind us starts chanting, "Trade 'im." "Booooo," hisses my husband, a mere *hockey* fan. "Don't listen to them," I shout to poor Willie, who's practically slumping inside himself he's so hurt and upset. "You just go up there and hit a home run. You'll show them!" And next at bat, he does—he sends one flying and the crowd roars. And cheers. And screams. And Willie, God love him, comes running around the bases, beaming and happy and forgiving as a child. That does it; I'm hooked. Back in love with baseball. Willie was "my" Tiger.

I grew up in a home where the radio was permanently set on WJR; I thought George-Kell-and-Ernie-Harwell was one word. I'd fall asleep listening to my parents discussing the merits and flaws of various Detroit players, and by the time I was twelve I wanted one of my own, a Tiger, my very own player to root for and adore. In 1962, my goals in life were to be the first woman governor of Michigan and to marry Rocky Colavito. I was crazy about him, in love the way only a twelve-year-old who knows nothing about it can be. It was my love for him, rather than baseball, that led me to my first game at Tiger Stadium—that 22-inning, 7-hour marathon with the Yan-

kees, which the Tigers lost despite Rocky's heroic 7 hits in 10 at-bats: more than Maris, Mantle, and Berra combined. Seven hours was a long time for a preteen whose only interest in baseball was Rocky Colavito, but was I weary? Never. During the "boring parts" (i.e., when the Yankees were at bat), I sat happily carving ROCKY in the chest of a stuffed Tiger my father bought me to keep me quiet.

Seasons passed. Rocky went back to Cleveland and the Beatles replaced baseball as my passion, even though my mother tried valiantly to keep my interest alive. "You need a new Tiger," she'd say hopefully. "What about Al Kaline?" Oh, pul-eeeze. Everybody loved Al Kaline. *She* loved Al Kaline. I wouldn't be caught *dead* loving the same Tiger my *mother* loved! My mangy old stuffed Tiger got tossed in the closet with the rest of my childhood. I still followed the Tigers and rooted for them faithfully, but it was mostly out of regional loyalty, during a time when practically the whole country was happily Detroit-bashing, calling it the Murder Capital of the U.S. and making other snide remarks. I secretly adored Al, and of course, I liked Stormin' Norman Cash . . . and I was kind of interested in this new Tiger, this local kid everybody kept comparing to some "Campy" guy. Willie Horton; Willie the Wonder. I thought it was great he hit so many home runs, but what was a "ribby"?

It wasn't love yet, it was more like a flirtation. I liked him because he was a ghetto kid, the son of a coal miner and the youngest of nineteen children. He was so poor when he was growing up he almost had to drop out of school because he didn't have shoes. When he signed with the Tigers, the first thing he did was buy a house for his parents. The guy had class.

Being sentimental, I liked that before his first All-Star Game, he ran around the field collecting his heroes' autographs. I also took note that he gave cookouts for the Tigers' grounds crew. I thought it was amusing when he showed up at spring training overweight and said, "I only eat two meals a day. I just like snacks." When he took off twenty-two pounds and Tiger manager Charlie Dressen presented him with a twenty-two-pound ham and told him not to eat it all at once, I could identify. It was the sixties, and while I was no radical, my consciousness was getting raised. So I liked that he donated time to work with ghetto kids, "kids who don't know what middle class means." Right on, Willie. And besides, he swung a mean bat.

I went off to college and got married, but not to Rocky. All anyone could talk about was Denny McLain and his damn organ. Willie the Wonder, meanwhile, was falling out of favor with the press and the fickle, fickle fans. The first time they booed him he got so upset he didn't show up the next day. Everyone was outraged, but I just grew more fond of him. The more they dumped on Willie, the more I liked him—how, I asked, can you not like someone who has two sons with the same first name? (Actually, one son spelled his name D-A-R-R-Y-L, the other D-E-R-Y-L.)

Just about then, I went to that fateful game. When we got home, I called my mother with the good news that I'd found my Tiger. "Who?" she asked. "Willie!" I said joyfully. "Oh," she said after a pause. "That big baby?"

Yes, that big baby. Because of him I fell back in love with baseball. In learning about Willie, I learned about the game, something he, being an inveterate fan, would appreciate. I also learned a kind of pidgin baseballese. "His stats are solid," I'd say. "He's horribly underrated as a fielder." "Have you forgotten that game in '69 when he tied the AL record for outfielders with eleven putouts?" "And what about that perfect throw in game five of the '68 World Series when he nipped Lou Brock at the plate?"

No one quarreled with Willie's power. In the five seasons he played more than 140 games for the Tigers, he hit between 25 and 36 homers. Pitchers were terrified of him. Third basemen backed up. He was known as both a power hitter and a power squeezer. "My ribs still hurt," New York manager Ralph Houk complained after Willie grabbed him during a Yankee-Tiger brawl, to which Willie replied, "He was lucky I just squeezed him." Willie was a one-man gang in brawls. After watching him in action, umpire Marty Springstead contended, "Willie is the strongest man in the league. Willie is the strongest man in *any* league."

It was true that he was injury-prone and rarely made it through an entire season. He invariably began the year leading in something—home runs or runs batted in (so *that's* a "ribby"!)—but he would pull a hamstring or tear a ligament or get hit in the head. Detractors squawked "Hypochondriac!" but how do you fake knee surgery? If he could play, he'd play—this is the man who got *hit by a car* while chasing the team bus and got up, grabbed a cab, went out to the stadium, and played!

But did the fans appreciate him? NO! On opening day in '73, forty-some-odd thousand fans cheered the Tigers as they were introduced—all except Willie, who got some jeers. Detractors called him moody, but how would *they* feel if they went into their offices and found forty-some-odd thousand hissing former fans stuffed into their cubicles?

He was human, but I liked those feet of clay. Every year at spring training, he'd arrive early and fat, using the "I just like snacks" routine, and when that didn't work, he'd say he couldn't help it, he had heavy muscles. (He did; he was going to be a boxer until his father saw him get beat up on TV and nixed that career.) He'd get upset when he didn't get to play and skulk off to the clubhouse, but he'd always get over it and end up back on the bench, cheering more heartily than the most vehement fan. Yes, he tended to sulk, but he'd always bounce right back and with boundless enthusiasm, come to the park five hours before anyone else, to work out with weights and practice his swing with a broom handle. (As a rookie, he'd show up for the team bus an hour and a half early to make sure it wouldn't leave without him.) When he became a DH in 1975, he'd spend his bench time pretending he was out in left field, thinking about how he'd field the ball. "I just want to play," he said. "I don't care if I have to play in the street."

The man loved baseball.

"The Tigers are my family," he said over and over, and even when they traded him in 1977, after all those years of loyal service, he still proclaimed, "I'll always be a Tiger." Yes, he was sentimental, but what's wrong with that? He had cried when the Tigers traded Mickey Lolich, but so did a lot of other people I knew.

I kept an eye on Willie after he got traded, and I was very proud when the *Sporting News* named him the American League's Comeback Player of the Year in 1979. As the DH in all 162 games for the Seattle Mariners, he hit 29 homers and had 106 RBIs, showing exactly what he could do if he played every day.

He went back down to the minors after another season in Seattle, his eighteen-year major league career over, and I didn't hear anything about him again until 1985, when I was out at Yankee Stadium cheering my newest Tiger, Chet Lemon. "Horton?" I asked while glancing at the Yankee roster. "Could that be Horton as in *Willie*?" Sure enough; Billy Martin, the man who, when managing the Tigers, had challenged Willie to a fistfight, had brought him to the Yanks as something called a "tranquillity coach."

Tranquillity and Willie didn't go together. I did remember his once saying, "I just judge everybody as a human being—even umpires," but that hardly qualified him for Buddhahood. Unless the TC was just a euphemism for the guy who sits on the players when they get out of line, it made no sense at all. Unless it was a joke, it wasn't funny.

Willie was a Tiger, not a Yankee. Willie was tempestuous, not serene. It was his perturbability that made Willie so wonderful—he was human and real, not a baseball card. If Willie wasn't Willie, who was I? I longed to see him come charging out of the dugout to toss a few umpires around, or at least to pout and stomp, but nothing happened. Even Billy Martin was restrained.

The Tigers won and Chet got a hit, but I found myself pouting and stomping and wishing I could toss a few umpires around. Somebody had to be disappointed and petulant. Somebody had to be Willie.

Rebecca Stowe has written for *Baseball Diary* and fiction for the *Florida Review, Farmer's Market, Cottonwood,* and other literary magazines. She is a recent recipient of an Artists' Fellowship grant from the New York Foundation for the Arts, for fiction.

JOHN SCHULIAN on

STEVE BILKO

In that summer I fell in love with baseball, I celebrated by practicing a form of heresy then common to boys throughout Los Angeles: I ignored the triple crown that Mickey Mantle was fashioning for himself. It was surprisingly easy to do. New York and Yankee Stadium seemed too far away to fathom; indeed, for many of us who were blissfully ignorant of Walter O'Malley's lust for the West Coast, the very idea of the major leagues was exotic, remote, maybe even unnecessary. After all, we had the L.A. Angels and the Hollywood Stars of the Pacific Coast League.

He was the first fat guy my friends and I ever had for a hero, the first fat guy we ever wanted to grow up to be. If he had been some anonymous tub of guts loaded down with beer and salami at the grocery story, we would have snickered behind his back. If he had been one of those unfortunate fifth-grade blimps, we would have made his days a nightmare. Unless the poor kid could hit like Stout Steve of the Angels. And Stout Steve hit what he must have weighed—a ton.

The 55 home runs, those 164 runs batted in, that .360 batting average. Mantle couldn't match any of them. Of course, less impressionable observers would have conceded that Bilko beat up on minor league cunny-thumbers in Wrigley Field, L.A.'s bandbox replica of the home of the Cubs. But that meant nothing to the kids who marveled at his power, and it probably meant even less to Bilko. For here was a coal miner's son who hit 21 homers in his rookie season with the St. Louis Cardinals, only to be chased off first base the following year by Joe Cunningham. Here was a vagabond slugger who couldn't earn steady employment with the perpetually forlorn Cubs and actually asked to be demoted to L.A. And now he was the biggest man in town in a way that had nothing to do with the Angels' plea that he tip the scales at no more than 230 pounds—fat chance— or the headline that claimed "NOT EVEN MRS. BILKO KNOWS HIS WEIGHT." He was bigger than John Wayne, bigger than Jimmy Stewart, bigger than any matinee idol you can think of, and he had the press clippings to prove it. "There wasn't a movie star that could touch him," George Goodale, who was the Angels' publicist, once told me. "I know. I kept count myself."

The adulation didn't stop with that, however. Neil Simon was in the throes of creating a TV show called *You'll Never Get Rich* and he needed a name for the conniving Army sergeant Phil Silvers was going to play in it. Simon went through a multitude of possibilities, but there was one name he couldn't get out of his mind, the name he read every day on the sports page, the name that almost chose itself for him: Bilko. Nothing like that ever happened to Mickey Mantle.

Still, it took me a while to fess up to the hold that Bilko had on me. The problem was my parents' loyalty to the Hollywood Stars. Owned by the founder of the Brown Derby, haunted by the memory of the time they played in short pants, the Stars weren't much to look at in 1956 once you got past two fallen bonus babies, Paul Pettit and Jim Baumer, and a cadaverous second baseman named Spook Jacobs. The Angels, on the other hand, were a work of art featuring Gene Mauch, Bob Speake, and George Freese as well as Stout Steve. But my mother and father cared not; Gilmore Field, the home of the Stars, was in a better neighborhood than Wrigley, so that was that.

Ever the obedient only child, I did my best to root for the Stars along with them, but I could feel myself backsliding, being lured astray by the thunder in Bilko's bat. I thought I might be saved the next season when the Stars imported Dick Stuart, who was fresh from a 66-homer campaign in Lincoln, Nebraska, that prompted him to dot the *i* in his first name with a star. Then Stuart bashed five home runs in the Stars' first four games and I was sure he could turn me around. At last the Stars had someone getting the royal treatment that had theretofore been reserved solely for Bilko.

One of Stuart's first stops was Twentieth Century-Fox, where he found himself posing for a picture with the bounteously endowed Jayne Mansfield and having his fancy tickled by a question he must have been waiting for all his life.

Steve Bilko was not as big a star on the Los Angeles Angels in the American League as he'd been with the Los Angeles Angels in the Pacific Coast League.

Courtesy California Angels

"How come you're getting the headlines and I'm not?" La Mansfield asked.

"Because I'm hitting the long ball," Stuart replied.

Bilko was speechless. Talking wasn't his game, hitting was. So he stuck to his strength while the new kid in town flapped his jaw, neglected his swing, and wound up suffering exactly the fate you might imagine. The last time I saw Stuart in a Stars uniform, he was standing forlornly in right field at the end of a Sunday doubleheader replete with his strikeouts and errors; hot dog wrappers were swirling around his feet, and boos were cascading down on him. Soon afterward, he was dispatched to Atlanta, and from there back to Lincoln. Bilko, meanwhile, was piling up 56 more homers for the Angels. That made 111 in two seasons, establishing him as a legend of sorts and teaching me about the insight that baseball can provide into the men who play it.

To my way of thinking, there is no other sport that reveals so much about its performers as human beings. Baseball players aren't hidden by helmets and shoulder pads, nor are they separated from the rest of society by their runaway pituitary glands. Give or take the stray Dave Parker or Eddie Gaedel, they resemble everyday people and they function in an arena where you can follow their every move, talk to them, yell at them, maybe even reach out and touch them. Watch ten games in person in a season—really study them from batting practice until the final out—and you should be able to identify the loafers, the brooders, the pranksters, the head cases, and the just plain good guys.

Steve Bilko was just a plain good guy. I imagined as much when I was eleven years old, and twenty-two years later, when I was a sports columnist for the *Chicago Sun-Times*, I learned it for a fact. Death had taken Bilko by surprise at forty-nine and I wanted to write a farewell, but I had never gotten any closer to him than the stands were to the diamond. So I started calling his old friends, and slowly there began to emerge a picture of a gentle galoot who always got a breaking pitch instead of the break he needed. One erstwhile Angel remembered how deeply touched Bilko was that a team executive went to the airport to greet him when he blew into town. Another recalled Stout Steve trying to repent for a night of beer drinking by locking himself in the bathroom, padding the cracks around the door with towels, and turning the place into a steam bath. And everybody agreed it was too bad he didn't hit his prime a little later, when the majors were expanding and the pitching was thinning out. "If Steve had come along in the sixties, he would have been a hell of a big-league player," said Bob Scheffing, his manager during the glory years on the West Coast. Instead, Bilko came to symbolize a breed that is now extinct.

All those home runs he hit for the Angels signaled the beginning of the end of an era when a big lug could drag his Louisville Slugger from one minor league outpost to another and make a living. As the majors were growing, the minors were shrinking, changing, chasing kids back to the real world before they had a chance to grow old swinging from the heels. Never again could there be a Joe Hauser in Minneapolis, a Howitzer Howie Moss in Baltimore, a Joe Bauman in Roswell, New Mexico. It was the twilight of the long-ball gods, and only two of their spiritual descendants, Randy Bass and Moe Hill, would survive into the seventies and eighties. But neither of them ever matched what Bilko accomplished in the two best seasons of his career. Hardly anybody did. And I'll tell you something else that set him apart from the pack: when he went back to the big show in 1958, he took a pay cut.

Things didn't go any better on the field. Bilko started the season in Cincinnati, then got a return ticket to L.A., which had stepped up in class with the Dodgers. In both uniforms, he looked lost, and he had the statistics to prove it. No wonder he was back in the bushes the next year. I got to see him play there because my family had moved to Salt Lake City and he passed through town with the Spokane Indians. But somehow his presence didn't mean as much anymore. I was getting older and my horizons were expanding, my requirements for my heroes were getting stricter. Maybe I even thought of Bilko as a mirage. He wasn't, of course. He was the real thing. I would learn just how real after he died.

The news shook loose memories of how Bilko hung on to do honorable work for the L.A. Angels of the expanded American League, and how he hit 20 homers in the first of his two seasons with them. I seemed to recall also that he got to play in Wrigley Field West again. Yes, but only in 1961, an old teammate told me. I started to say that was too bad, because Wrigley was where I would always picture him, and then I was silenced by a bit of history that made everything right. On the last day of the '61 season, in the last game ever played in his old launching pad, Stout Steve Bilko said thanks for the memories the only way he could; he hit the last home run in the park's history. It was one of those rare moments when justice is poetic.

John Schulian has written television scripts for *Miami Vice, Hooperman, The "Slap" Maxwell Story, L.A. Law, Wiseguy,* and *Midnight Caller,* for which he is co-producer. He spent ten years as a sportswriter in Chicago and Philadelphia, and was voted number one sports columnist in the country at the Associated Press Sports Editors 1980 Convention. He is the author of *Writers' Fighters & Other Sweet Scientists.*

GEORGE VECSEY on

MARV THRONEBERRY

He materialized years later in the beer advertisements, rubbery-shaped and sad-eyed as a basset hound, musing, "I still don't know why I'm in this commercial." His line was a stroke of genius by the copywriters because probably three-quarters of the new generation had no idea why this man was cavorting with the stars.

Who was this Marv Throneberry, anyway?

It wasn't much of a clue to know that his nickname had been Marvelous Marv back in the lunatic summer of 1962. The new style is rap-music braggadocio, a boxing champion being totally unashamed of legally changing his name to Marvelous Marvin Hagler. The era of irony is gone. When Marvin Eugene Throneberry—note the initials, please—was in his prime, such as it was, it was a tweak of affection to label him Marvelous Marv.

The fact is, he didn't appreciate reporters circling his locker, didn't appreciate fans dancing on the dugout roof in his honor, didn't appreciate his teammate Richie Ashburn feeding him lines, at least not at first. He was the personification of a dreadful but captivating expansion team, the New York Mets, and people flocked out of the subway to chant his name, and he hated it.

This was no way to treat a ballplayer who was going to be another Mickey Mantle. This was no way to treat a Yankee. What was he doing in a Met uniform? Even then, he didn't know why he was in this commercial.

Back in the summers of 1956 and 1957, this man had hit 42 and 40 home runs in the rarified air of the Yankees' minor league farm in Denver. He joined the Yankees and dreamed of playing alongside the great Mantle, but most of their association came during batting practice or in the clubhouse. The ball didn't travel so far at sea level.

Throneberry was shipped to Kansas City and then to Baltimore, but in 1962 he received his big break. The New York Mets were founded in the expansion draft, and after one month of the season it was very clear they needed another first baseman.

In early May, the Mets traded for Throneberry, aged twenty-eight, from the cotton fields of west Tennessee. He was being given a chance to play regularly in the Polo Grounds, right across the Harlem River from Yankee Stadium—but never had that river seemed so wide.

In Yankee Stadium, the business was winning a third straight pennant, the middle of five pennants, as it turned out. In the Polo Grounds, the manager was Throneberry's old boss, Casey Stengel, who had won ten pennants in twelve years with the Yankees. The Old Man still desperately hated to lose, but he knew what he had to do—mug and clown and create the image of lovable little Metsies, stumbling around in their playpen.

Casey installed his former Yankee farmhand at first base. At 6'1", 190 pounds, Throneberry was a solid-looking left-handed hitter.

"Not a great hitter," Throneberry would call himself. "But a sweet hitter."

At first, the fans were indifferent to the Sweet Hitter. Like it or not, he was destined for a different kind of glory.

His legend began on a lovely Sunday afternoon on June 17. In the top of the first inning, he planted himself in the baseline during a rundown and was charged with interfering with the Cubs' runner. In the bottom of the first, he slugged what seemed to be a two-run triple, but he was called out for missing first base.

The seventy-one-year-old manager scrambled onto the field to argue with the umpire, but Stengel was intercepted by his first-base coach, Cookie Lavagetto.

"It won't do any good, Casey," Lavagetto said. "He missed second base, too."

Marv's fielding lapse eventually led to four Chicago runs. His base-running eventually cost the Mets at least one run. The Mets lost the game, 8–7, but a star was born.

There were three factors in Throneberry's becoming a folk hero. The first was that the Mets had inherited imaginative New York fans who had been bereft since the Dodgers and the Giants moved to California in 1958. Another factor was that the New York papers had assigned the best and the brightest reporters to this fledgling team, and they caught the fun of this team of vagabonds.

A third factor was that by the luck of uniform numbers, the name-plate "No. 2 Marvelous" was placed alongside "No. 1 Ashburn" in the Mets' clubhouse. Richie Ashburn was a two-time batting champion playing out his last season, fiery enough to keep going after running into the center-field fence, but also perceptive enough to know that something marvelous was happening in the next locker.

"Tell them how you're going to throw a party for your fans," Ashburn told Marv, "in a phone booth."

Ashburn realized there was something different about his lock-ermate after spotting a photograph of a beautiful woman, with very little on, hanging in Marv's locker. A few days later, Ashburn saw the woman in the stands, more substantially clothed. When Ashburn asked who it was, Throneberry replied, "That's my wife." Not every ballplayer displayed revealing pictures of his own wife.

Ashburn's teasing brought out the country-boy comedian in Throneberry, made him realize he might as well enjoy his celebrity.

Marv began making self-deprecating jokes, like telling reporters before a doubleheader, "Hey, I've got good news for you. I'm only playing in one of the games today."

Soon the fans were chanting, "Cranberry, strawberry, we love Throneberry." One night five fans printed the characters M-A-R-V-! on their T-shirts and danced on the dugout roof. They were ejected, but turned their shirts inside out and paid their way back into the ballpark.

Marv's greatest moment came the night he wound up coaching first base after a series of ejections and pinch-hitting maneuvers. With two men on base and two outs in the ninth and the Mets trailing by two runs, Marvelous Marv was called in to pinch-hit. He strode in from the coaching box and drilled a three-run homer to end the game, and had to make a curtain call from the steps of the rickety old clubhouse dressed only in his underwear—which was torn, of course.

Marvelous Marv was not the only opera-buffa hero. There were pitchers like Roger Craig and Alvin Jackson, just good enough to lose heartbreakingly. There were two pitchers named Bob Miller. There was a catcher named Choo Choo Coleman who called everybody Bub. There were a few dozen third basemen. There was a strapping left fielder named Frank Thomas who hit 34 home runs and served thousands of meals on the Mets' chartered flights.

And there was Rod Kanehl, a former Yankee farmhand who was remembered by Stengel for hopping a fence to chase a ball during a long-ago intrasquad scrimmage. Kanehl had never played in the major leagues until Stengel claimed him in 1962—and Kanehl made the most of it, playing seven positions, letting himself get hit by a pitch with the bases loaded, and exploring the subways so regularly that people called him The Mole. Stengel called him "My Little Scavenger."

Because of raffish heroes like these, the Mets almost immediately became as popular as the crusty Yankees across the river. Some young reporters who had to shuttle back and forth between the two teams would spend part of their Yankee hitch on the phone inquiring what awful fate had befallen the Metsies today.

The charm of the Mets was lost on certain American League types who were so accustomed to being bludgeoned by the Yankees that they became like hostages who identify with their captors. A certain Midwest sports columnist—let's call him Sid Hartman to disguise his identity—used to rage at the instant fame of the Mets.

"Throneberry couldn't even play for the Yankees," harrumphed our mythical Mr. Hartman. "Kanehl couldn't even play AAA ball. What's so great about bad ballplayers?"

Met fans saw it differently. They paraded to the rusting, pigeon-befouled Polo Grounds carrying bedsheets and tablecloths with slogans and imprecations. They put the humor and the energy of New York into a ball club that lost 120 games. They insured the success of the new National League franchise in New York. They celebrated Marvelous Marv until Tom Seaver could be invented.

By the end of the season, the balding man with the reddish sideburns was a mythic figure in New York, not quite DiMaggio, not quite Robinson, not quite Mays, but the most celebrated Met of all. In years to come, he would acquire the reputation of a dreadful ballplayer, but let the record speak for itself: In 1962, Marvelous Marv Throneberry batted .244 with 16 homers and 49 runs batted in for 116 games. Not marvelous, but not terrible.

He had served a purpose on the field and in the public eye, but the Met management ticketed Marv for oblivion in 1963. He went 2 for 14 in early pinch-hitting roles and was shuffled off to their minor league franchise in Buffalo. The last words we heard him say were, "I ain't done yet." The next time anybody saw him was in the beer commercials. The new generation had no idea who he was, but Met fans of a certain age felt the irresistible urge to dance on a dugout or wave a bedsheet.

George Vecsey is a sports columnist for the *New York Times*. He is the author of *A Year in the Sun*, *The Harlem Globetrotters*, and *Frazier-Ali*, and coauthor of Loretta Lynn's autobiography, *Coal Miner's Daughter*, Martina Navratilova's autobiography, *Martina*, Bob Welch's autobiography, *Five O'Clock Comes Early: A Young Man's Battle with Alcoholism*, and Barbara Mandrell's forthcoming autobiography.

TERRY PLUTO
on

SUPER JOE
CHARBONEAU

Joe Charboneau and I had a couple of things in common, but drinking beer wasn't one of them. He poured his Bud through his nose. (Okay, he did use a straw.) I used my mouth. But that's another story. With Joe Charboneau, there's always another story. Charboneau was perhaps the most storied ballplayer in history, and notice that the word is "storied," not "best" or "talented" or "fastest." He was far more story than ballplayer, and for better or worse I was the guy who wrote most of them.

He had a dog named Diarrhea for obvious reasons and a daughter named Dannon, once again for obvious reasons—he liked the yogurt. He said he was a descendant of Tossiant Charbonneau, who along with Indian princess Sacagawea, had helped Lewis and Clark through the Northwest Territory.

With Charboneau, the temptation is just to tell the stories, but none of them tell his story.

The year was 1980, the month was early March, and Charboneau was in the batting cage at Hi Corbett Field in Tucson, Arizona. This was his first spring training with the Cleveland Indians as a player, my first as a sportswriter. He was born on June 17, 1955, and I was born five days earlier. Such things are important when dealing with the Indians, whose last pennant was in 1954.

So Charboneau and I were twenty-four during that spring of 1980. That means we were being conceived when the 1954 Indians, a team that had won 111 regular-season games, more than anyone in baseball

history, were about to blow four games to the New York Giants in the World Series.

The Indians haven't been in the World Series since, and if anyone symbolized what a cruel tease baseball could be in Cleveland, it was the storied Joe Charboneau. He had come to a team that hadn't even been in contention since 1959, a team with the worst overall record in baseball since 1960. It was a team with Herb Score in the radio booth, the same Herb Score many were convinced would be the next Sandy Koufax before the world even knew Sandy Koufax. That's because Herb Score was a lefty who could throw the hell out of the ball and throw it over until he was struck in the eye with a line drive off the bat of Gil McDougald in 1957. It wasn't long after that Score became another Jerry Coleman in the broadcast booth, telling fans such as myself: "Leon Wagner hits a fly ball deep to right. . . . Will it be fair? Will it be foul? . . . It is."

Or he'd tell us: "There's a two-hopper to Eddie Leon, who catches it on the first bounce."

Or he'd tell us: "Swing and a miss, called strike three on poor Joe Azcue."

Believe me, Herb Score was a perfect symbol for the Indians.

Back to the spring of 1980, back to Charboneau hitting line drive after line drive. The guy swung like a right-handed George Brett and in the minors he hit like one—.350 at Class A Visalia in 1978, .352 at Class AA Chattanooga in 1979. I already knew about Joe Charboneau before I ever saw him, but I soon found that hardly anyone knew *all* about him.

When that first workout was over, I sat down in the dressing room with Charboneau and started the old routine of interviewing a new face from spring training. Those folks in the snows of Cleveland had no idea what they would read the next day, and I certainly had no idea what I was about to write.

That's because Joe Charboneau started telling stories. The amazing thing was that most of them were true.

If you had any doubts, he'd show you the scars.

"See my nose?" he asked.

Yes.

"I can drink beer through it . . . with a straw," he said.

A couple of his minor league teammates would indeed swear that Charboneau could do just that. They also said he could open a beer bottle with his forearm. No big deal, I'd seen guys do that, I said.

But how about with his eye socket? they asked.

I wasn't sure I wanted to see anyone do that.

Charboneau had also broken that same nose about eight million times when he fought bare fisted and bare chested in boxcars near a migrant camp where he grew up in Santa Clara, California.

"The winner got thirty bucks, the losers got twenty," he said. "They weren't fights, they were brawls. Like human cock fights. They would last a couple of minutes at the most, and when you'd lose, you'd find yourself on your hands and knees, shaking and throwing up because usually someone had kneed you in the balls. A bunch of Mexicans would bet on us, and when you got beat, the Mexicans would swear and spit on you."

Which brings us back to the nose.

"I got it busted again and I was tired of going to the hospital," he said. "So I took a pair of vise grips and a re-set myself."

I suddenly didn't like the way my stomach felt.

On and on he went, about how he couldn't throw because his right shoulder had been slammed up against the walls of the boxcars during fights, or even out of the boxcars and landing on the tracks.

There was more.

When he was a kid, he was watching television and saw a snake swallow an egg . . . whole.

"I can do that," Charboneau told his friends, and they immediately went to the kitchen, where he swallowed the egg, but it became stuck in his throat.

"One of my buddies whacked me on the back and it broke the shell," he said. "Then it went down, but I never did that again."

But he did eat six cigarettes in order to make five bucks. And he did try to eat a shot glass—another trick he saw on the tube—and ended up with a bloody mouth.

"I promised myself that I'd never eat glass again," he said sincerely.

Of course there was more.

He had been bit by a spider on his cheek, by a turtle on the toe, and shot by an arrow in the side, and he'll show you the scars to prove it.

One day he wanted to climb a fence to steal some cherries from a nearby farmer's field and cut his arm on the barbwire. He didn't want his mother to know about it, so he went home and with the help of a friend, put three stitches into the wound with fishing line.

He'd roll up his sleeve and show you the scar.

Charboneau also got a tattoo on his other arm when he was in high school. He sister screamed at him and Joe got the message that there would be hell to pay when his mother got home from work. Rather than face the wrath of his mother, Charboneau grabbed a razor blade and cut the tattoo off his arm.

Believe me, you don't want to see the scars.

In the minors, he had an infected tooth and went to the dentist. He was told that the dentist wanted to do a $250 root canal and cap job. Charboneau didn't have the money, but when he went home, he did have a razor, a pair of pliers, and a bottle of whiskey.

Believe me, you don't have a stomach strong enough to hear the rest of that story.

"It cost me five bucks and I just yanked it out," said Charboneau.

After a while, you heard so many stories that you just started to laugh. And Charboneau would smile as he told his newest tale of self-surgery.

Naturally, there was more.

Before reporting to spring training with the Indians in 1980, Charboneau said he had done 500 sit-ups a day, was bench-pressing 400 pounds, and God knows what else. Anyway, he lost 47 pounds during the winter. That's because he went from weighing 190 to 240 late in the 1979 season. "First, I got the mumps, then I pulled a groin muscle and sat around for the last six weeks of the season," he said.

Charboneau also was on a strict liquid diet—Budweiser.

After listening to all this and more, I did it. I named him Super Joe, after Super Joe from Kokomo, although it dawned on me years later there was no Super Joe from Kokomo but Shoeless Joe from Hannibal, Mo. The guy seemed to be right out of *Damn Yankees* or Ring Lardner.

As the man himself said, "Things just happen to me."

I can attest to that. In the spring of 1980, the Indians played an exhibition game in Mexico City and I was standing with Charboneau and some other players (all in their uniforms) in front of Maria Isabel Hotel awaiting the bus that would take us to the stadium. A grisly little man ("A Charles Manson type," Charboneau would later say) approached Joe with a pen and paper as if he wanted Charboneau's autograph.

"Where are you from?" I heard the guy ask Charboneau.

"California," said Joe.

Then the guy took a red Bic pen and stuck it right into Charboneau's side. Charboneau screamed, about six players leaped, and this Charles Manson and the pen lay on the sidewalk, covered with blood. Charboneau went to the hospital. The would-be assassin went to the police station where he was fined fifty pesos, which was worth $2.27 in 1980.

Why $2.27?

"Because the judge said a pen wasn't a deadly weapon," said Charboneau.

Also in spring training, Charboneau and a few of his friends ended up in a brawl outside a Tucson dive with some bikers. Charboneau proved to be very adept at dribbling people's heads off the roof of a car. There are more fight stories involving people swinging pool cues and people smacked in the face with glass beer mugs, but you don't need to hear them.

The nice part of this story was that Charboneau could indeed hit, and he hit enough (.289, 23 homers, and 87 RBI) to become the 1980 American League Rookie of the Year. On opening day before 61,573 at Cleveland Stadium, Charboneau had a homer, double, and single. The nickname began to stick, and by mid–season he had 500 registered members in his fan club, the largest ever according to the

Indians front office. He had an agent, a fellow named Dan Donnelly whose previous claim to fame was running the best damn heating and cooling company on Madison Avenue in Lakewood, Ohio.

"I liked Dan," said Charboneau. "He was nice to me when I first came to town and he owned his own business, so I figured he could handle mine."

He also had his own song, "Go, Go, Joe Charboneau."

"I liked it," Super Joe said. "It's a punk-rock song and I'm a punk-rock ballplayer."

Joe Charboneau liked everything and everyone, and for a year, everyone liked him. But this story ended up like everything else that has ever happened to the Indians since the year Charboneau was born. He pulled a groin muscle and limped through the last month. At the end of the 1980 season, Donnelly decided he could also be a literary agent and arranged a deal with Stein & Day Publishers for a Super Joe book, to be written by Burt Graeff of the old *Cleveland Press* and myself. After weeks of wheeling and dealing, Donnelly said the advance was five grand—to be split between Graeff, Charboneau, and myself.

Well, we wrote the book and it came out in late April of 1981. By the middle of May, Charboneau was back in the minors. By late May, baseball was on strike and Charboneau was bothered by a disk problem in his back and a confidence problem at the bat. He had taken to sleeping on an army cot in the Charleston (West Virginia) Charlies clubhouse, right next to the washer, dryer, and dirty socks and jocks on the floor.

"I figured I needed to get back into baseball, really into it," said Charboneau. "I want to eat and sleep it."

He also got to smell it.

By August of 1981, the American League Rookie of the Year was all the way back in Class AA Chattanooga, where he was sleeping in an apartment, but still not hitting. His back pain had become so severe that he was spending most of his time coaching first base. This meant he had another story—that of the first player to be a big-league rookie of the year in one season and a Class AA first-base coach less than a year later.

Charboneau made a couple of brief appearances with the Indians in 1982. He later gave baseball another shot with Hawaii in the Pirates chain, but by June of 1984 I found him checking IDs in a Buffalo bar and playing softball. As of late 1988, he was Joe the Bartender in a pub near Phoenix.

CULT BASEBALL PLAYERS

Obviously, there were more stories, but that no longer was the point.

What happened?

Charboneau will tell you it was the disk trouble in his back that led to a couple of operations. The Indians will admit the guy did get hurt, but they will also mention that he was the classic case of too much, too soon.

The intriguing thing about the rise and the fall of Super Joe was that neither event seemed to surprise him. He had told friends before the 1980 season that he would be the rookie of the year, saying it in the same way you'd mention that the sun will rise tomorrow. But when he went on the skids, he was still the same Joe, still gracious, still with more stories. This was a guy who grew up living in sixteen apartments and houses, each progressively worse, "until our furniture was nothing but a picnic table and some wooden benches." This was a guy who put his body in a boxcar jammed with drunken migrants hoping to make thirty bucks, a guy who stitched his own cuts and pulled his own teeth hoping to save a few pennies. This was a guy who slept with his first baseball bat and caught toads and sold them for a quarter each in order to earn enough money to buy his first glove.

Finally, this was a guy who had seen a lot of things go wrong and seemed to know that they would go wrong for him again. He had one Indian summer and a lot of painful years before and since. It brings to mind something former Cleveland manager Frank Robinson said when asked about Charboneau and his old team: "Never forget that Indian fever is nothing more than a twenty-four-hour virus, so don't let anything that happens to that team excite you."

Terry Pluto has covered baseball for the *Baltimore Evening Sun* and the *Cleveland Plain-Dealer,* writes a column for *Baseball America,* and covers basketball for the *Akron Beacon-Journal.* He is the coauthor of *Weaver on Strategy* (with Earl Weaver), *A Baseball Winter* (with Jeff Neuman), *Super Joe* (with Burt Graeff), and *Sixty-one* (with Tony Kubek).

ART SPANDER on

BO BELINSKY

There's a quote from Bo Belinsky that bounces around like a bunt on Astroturf. It's a commentary on life more than sport, distilling our hopes and frustrations and wariness into a few poignant comments.

"I had my moments," Bo said after he wandered far enough into history to gain perspective.

"I have my memories. If I had the attitude about life then that I have now, I'd have done a lot of things differently. But you make your rules, and you play by them. I knew the bills would come due eventually."

So many warnings. So many questions. So many doubts about present and future. It's a theme as old as mankind, a story of checks and balances, of forethought and intuition. And of hindsight.

Looking back on the young Belinsky, I think of the heroine of *Evita*. He, too, had his moments and had his style. He, too, thought he'd be young forever and didn't worry what life would hold ten, twenty, or thirty years in the future. He, too, did things his way, without fear of the consequences.

Robert Belinsky—nicknamed Bo, for boxer Bobo Olson—was on his way from the moment in 1962 he came up to the Los Angeles Angels, now the California Angels. He was on his way to infamy. And irony. And antipathy. And sympathy.

Did any major leaguer ever receive more publicity for accomplishing less than Belinsky? On the baseball field, that is. Indeed, he had unions with movie starlets, endorsements by Walter Win-

chell. But he won a total of only 28 games during a big-league career that covered six seasons, and he never earned more than $18,000.

Five of those wins came in succession at the start of the 1962 season and included the first major league no-hitter in Southern California history.

Belinsky knew how to hold a baseball, a blonde, a cocktail glass, a steering wheel of a Cadillac convertible, and for all too brief a time, our attention.

And then like some meteor that flashes across the sky, he burned out and disappeared, surfacing in the mid-1980s in Hawaii, where, having achieved the once unforeseeable goal of a fiftieth birthday, Bo was residing in relative seclusion.

"I finally decided that I was put here to live," he told us. "Nothing complicated or sophisticated. Just to live life."

Do we recall style more than substance? Is the sizzle invariably more tantalizing than the steak? How did Bo Belinsky, who seemed to embody all the qualities attributed to left-handers, mythical and actual, gain his place in sporting lore?

They say everything depends on timing. Belinsky's timing was perfect. Southern California in the early sixties wasn't yet what it would become, a melting pot of the rich and weird where everybody thinks he's a star. Anybody a little different got noticed, especially by us sportswriters new to the major league beat.

Bo was already in the headlines and the starting rotation before the Angels, in only their second year of existence, escaped from training that spring of 1962.

Arriving in the big time after six years in the minors, Belinsky was hardly a paragon of humility. On the contrary. He thought so much of the talent that had been utilized to compile a 9-10 record at Little Rock the previous season, Bo staged a contract holdout that ended with a poolside press conference at the Desert Inn in Palm Springs.

The Dodgers had moved to L.A. from Brooklyn before the 1958 season. In 1959, they won the World Series. In 1962, after four seasons in the Los Angeles Coliseum, with its forty-foot screen in left field, they were installed in their own, new park, Dodger Stadium. The Angels would be, too, only they would call the place Chavez Ravine.

The Dodgers were the establishment. The Angels were the family from the wrong side of the tracks who were going to live in the rich uncle's home. Anything to make them more respectable. Why not try a few stories about a thin, dark-haired, good-looking guy who used to hustle pool in Trenton, New Jersey, and was agreeable to self-promotion?

Hurrah for Hollywood. The Angels' caps in those days were embellished by a halo on the crown. We learned it wasn't quite typecasting.

Bo supposedly was half Jewish, which was good enough to balance the Dodgers' Sandy Koufax, who was all Jewish. Both were lefties. Both were easterners. On May 5, 1962, a Saturday night, Belinsky pitched the no-hitter, beating the Orioles, 2–0, at Dodger Stadium . . . uh, Chavez Ravine. On June 30, 1962, Koufax pitched the first of his four no-hitters, beating the Mets, 5–0, at Chavez Ravine . . . uh, Dodger Stadium.

Bo beat Sandy to the punch. And to the glitz. Koufax would merely pitch his way into the Hall of Fame. Belinsky would become a legend in our minds, the flawed hero, unable to control his fastball and at times himself. But hey, this was the stuff of the silver screen, if not the sandlot. This was flash and glitz and alas, a tumble into oblivion. It was the American version of Icarus flying too close to the sun.

Bo, and Dean Chance, his comrade in arms—usually the arms of some lovely female—were either striking out some opposing batter or going out to some posh nightclub. Bo dated Ann-Margret, Tina Louise, Paulette Goddard, a DuPont heiress, and even, for god's sake, Queen Soroya.

He would become engaged and disengaged to actress Mamie Van Doren, who was blond and busty. "I need her like Custer needed Indians," Bo said after the breakup. There was a party every night and seemingly a newspaper story every morning.

Belinsky threw a screwball two decades before we'd ever heard of Fernando Valenzuela. Belinsky was a screwball. Bill Rigney, the Angels manager in their formative years, thought Bo should have been a 15-game winner every season. "It takes a certain dedication and energy that I didn't always give it," Belinsky said some time ago, speaking to Ross Newhan of the *Los Angeles Times*, one of those who knew Bo when.

"I'd like to have been Steve Carlton or Nolan Ryan or Sandy Koufax, but it must be boring going out there expecting to win all the time. I had that first year with the Angels, and it was total excitement. A new team. My rookie year. The no-hitter. Tinseltown. Meeting all the famous people. Playing for Gene Autry, who had been one of my idols. I was a guy who never had anything handed to him, but every dog has his day. I wouldn't trade five and oh and the no-hitter for anything."

It's refreshing, I suppose, to discover someone without regrets, somebody who doesn't moan about opportunities wasted—and they were—or chances squandered. And yet, it is to wonder what Bo could have done on the diamond if he didn't do so many things off. I was working for United Press International back then, covering Angels games, watching Bo at close range and like many others hoping to the end that he might someday reform. It was not to be.

Bo didn't last very long with the Angels. The team tried nearly everything and nearly everyone in an attempt to reform him. There were fines. There were lectures. There was even a brief association with Albie Pearson, a preacher-to-be, as a roommate. "I was just Bo's answering service," said Albie. "I never saw him at night. I just roomed with his suitcase."

Finally, after an incident in which he allegedly used a can of shaving cream to clout old-time sportswriter Braven Dyer, nearly three times Bo's age, Belinsky, in 1964, with an overall record of 20–28 with the Angels, was traded to the Philadelphia Phillies.

Bo would pitch for the Phils, Houston, Pittsburgh, St. Louis, and Cincinnati before the career came to a close in 1970 with the Reds' farm team at Indianapolis.

There would be eight more major league victories, then alcohol and drug problems and failed marriages with onetime *Playboy* centerfold Jo Collins and paper-goods heiress Jane Weyerhauser, whom he met while rescuing her in the Hawaii surf. In 1986, Belinsky would marry for a third time.

"I'm semiretired," Belinsky said from Hawaii sometime ago. "It's a humble existence. Nice people, clean air. I'm like Dean Chance, who's in the carnival business. Money is not our God.

"If someone told me twenty years ago I'd be sitting out in the Pacific watching palm leaves rustle, I'd have said, 'No way.' It's just that there comes a time when you have to slow down."

We hear so much about life in the fast lane. Is there something to life in the parking lot? Would Bo have been better off out of the spotlight?

"I was an egotistical bastard," said Bo. "I came to the Angels as a kid who thought he had been pushed around by life, by minor league baseball. I was selfish and immature. I went the only way I knew how. I didn't play the game according to Hoyle, and I couldn't understand when people started stepping on my toes in retaliation. I thought I was a gracious, understanding person, and I went on thinking it until I found myself face down in the gutter."

Belinsky was either ahead of his time or behind the eight ball. He tried amphetamines, booze, prescribed drugs. "I look at a ballplayer throwing six hundred thousand dollars away today and think he's insane. But that's what I was."

Desperation drove him to rehabilitation. For maybe the first time, Bo listened to advice instead of his heart. He's been sober for years.

"I feel very fortunate," said Bo. "I took a run at baseball and was surprised that I was able to do what I did. But I probably got more out of twenty-eight victories than any major leaguer in history. Anybody can be a known star if he wins three hundred games. Let him try being a known star winning only twenty-eight games. I did."

That may not have been the right way, but it damn sure was his way.

Art Spander is a sports columnist for the *San Francisco Examiner* and the *Sporting News.* He is the author of *The Art Spander Collection* and coauthor of *Golf: The Passion and the Challenge* (with Mark Movely). He was California Sportswriter of the Year in 1980.

DAN SHAUGHNESSY
on
TONY CONIGLIARO

If you liked baseball and grew up in New England in the sixties, Tony Conigliaro was your guy.

Ted Williams was a god who'd taken his place alongside Ruth, Zeus, and the other mythological figures. Carl Yastrzemski, Williams's successor, was stoic, almost aloof.

Tony C. was our guy. He was young, handsome, built for Fenway, and best of all, he was local. He was no Southern Californian invading Fenway on a six-month work visa. He shared our accent and he knew how to drive the rotaries. The emergence of Conigliaro gave hope to Little Leaguers in Groton, Massachusetts, and Groton, Connecticut. Tony C. made it. So could we.

The Red Sox were not very good in those days, and New England youths who missed the Williams era had little to cheer about. The Sox were eighth or ninth every year, and good old boys like Pinky Higgens and Billy Herman had no clue about how to turn it around.

Fenway Park was not the Cheers Bar/tourist trap that it is today, and there was no rivalry with the hated Yanks. The Sox didn't expect to draw a million (in the eighties it's a letdown if they don't get two million), and .500 ball would have been cause for a postseason parade. The sagging Sox were down there with the Senators and the A's, battling to stay out of the cellar.

But we had Curt Gowdy at the mike and Dick Radatz in the pen, and in 1964 we had a nineteen-year-old kid who could hit the long ones. A local kid.

I was ten years old when Conigliaro started hitting homers in

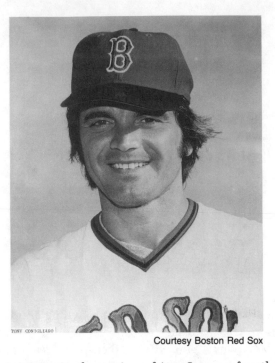

TONY CONIGLIARO

Courtesy Boston Red Sox

Scottsdale, Arizona, in the spring of '64. I was a fourth-grade, first-year Little Leaguer. He was a teenager, two years out of Swampscott High School, and he was making an impression on the big boys. Each day, the morning paper raved about the tall phenom from Swampscott, Massachusetts.

Conigliaro had played only one year in the minors, but his cactus-league clouts made it impossible for the subterranean Sox to cut him.

The Red Sox opened their 1964 season in Yankee Stadium. I do not need reference books to verify any of this. When you are ten, you know more about your team than you will ever know again, even if you grow up to be a professional baseball writer. And you remember.

Tony Conigliaro almost grounded into a triple play in his first major league at-bat. With two on and nobody out, he hit a hard grounder to third: 5–4–3. He had pretty good speed and was able to beat the relay to first.

On April 19, 1964, the Sox came home and dedicated their Fenway opener to the memory of John F. Kennedy. The assassination was still on everybody's minds. My older sister found shelter in the Beatles. I had Tony C.

He was untarnished. We had memorized all of the limitations of his teammates, but Conigliaro still had none when he came to Fen-

CULT BASEBALL PLAYERS

way for the first time in a Red Sox uniform. He was nineteen. He was infinite.

Conigliaro homered on his first at-bat. This was the kind of drama we would learn to expect from Tony C. He clocked a Joel Horlen fastball and hit a parabolic shot over the left-field wall. Bobby Kennedy, Ted Kennedy, Carol Channing, Gene Tunney, and Stan Musial were among the 20,211 fans on hand. I watched from home, glued to a black-and-white Zenith that had a clothespin channel-changer.

He hit 24 homers that year, batting .290 and missing six weeks with an assortment of injuries. He crowded the plate, much like Frank Robinson. Pitchers hit him a lot. But he hit them back. At the age of nineteen, Conigliaro smacked 24 homers in the big leagues. At the age of twenty, he led the American League with 32 homers. He remains the youngest player ever to lead a league in homers. He was also the youngest to ever hit 100.

"He might have been the guy to break Ruth's and Aaron's records," Oriole ace Jim Palmer told me years later. "With his swing, in that ballpark, there's no telling how many he would have hit."

Beyond the substance, there was style. Tony C. made the gossip columns, dated Mamie Van Doren, and appeared on *The Merv Griffin Show*. He cut his own 45 records. We heard "Little Red Scooter" (Penn Tone Records) on the radio. Best record I ever heard. He did a duet with Dionne Warwick.

He made headlines. Tony C. was late. Tony C. was fined. Tony C. was news.

There were a few other good Red Sox players during the lean years. Felix Mantilla made an All-Star team, Frank Malzone was wrapping up a nice career, and young Yastrzemski had already won a batting title before Tony C. arrived. But how could you warm up to Yaz? Yastrzemski was from Long Island. He was mechanical, married, and boring. Tony C. was a loose cannon. He lived on the edge. And he was local. He was hope that you, too, could make it to the big show.

On the night of August 18, 1967, Tony C. stepped to the plate to face California Angel righty Jack Hamilton. There were two outs and nobody aboard and the score was 0–0. The surprising Red Sox were only three and a half games out of first place. This was Boston's impossible-dream season. The young Sox were delivered from mediocrity by new manager Dick Williams and Tony C. already had 20 homers by mid-August.

It was a hot summer. Newark and Detroit were on fire. Muhammad Ali had just been stripped of his title for refusing induction. It was the Summer of Love on the streets of San Francisco, and everybody everywhere was listening to *Sergeant Pepper's Lonely Hearts Club Band*.

My father and I were driving to Cape Cod to pick up my twenty-year-old brother, who was working in a restaurant for the summer. My brother had to be an usher in my sister's wedding the next day, and we made the 200-mile round-trip to get him to the church on time. We had chocolate-covered caramel cookies in the front seat, and the Red Sox on the radio. We were somewhere on Route 3 South when Hamilton's pitch (was it a spitball?) splattered against the side of Tony C.'s face.

California catcher Bob Rodgers watched as Jim Lonborg, Mike Ryan, Buddy LeRoux, and Fred Federico carried the stretcher that carried Tony C. José Tartabull pinch-ran for Conigliaro and scored the first run in what would be a 3–2 Red Sox victory.

That run won the game and you could say that the game won the 1967 pennant for the Red Sox. I do. Boston took the flag on the final day of the season, beating the Twins and Tigers by one game. I'll always think of Tony C.'s hit-by-pitch as the winning run for the '67 season.

That fall the Red Sox played in their first World Series in nineteen years and reestablished a winning tradition that carried into the late eighties. But Tony C. didn't play again in 1967 or '68. When vision in his left eye improved, he came back, homering on opening day in 1969. He hit 56 homers in the 1969 and '70 seasons, then was dealt to California. I stopped paying attention to Red Sox baseball. I was a teenager. I was a basketball player. There were movie dates and cars and jobs. It seemed like the Orioles were in the World Series every year, but who cared? Tony C. didn't play for the Red Sox anymore.

He retired after hitting .222 in 74 games with the Angels in 1971. He came back again in '75 and was Boston's designated hitter early in the season. He hit two homers for the '75 Red Sox, went to Pawtucket, retired for good, and watched the '75 Series on television like the rest of us. No more comebacks for the Comeback Kid. It was finally over for Tony C.

He was a sportscaster in San Francisco, trying out for the Red Sox color commentator's job in 1982, when he got hit with something harder than Hamilton's fastball. A massive heart attack felled Conigliaro, and today he remains incapacitated and lives with his brother Billy, requiring round-the-clock nursing care.

Ken Tatum, Stan Williams, Orlando Cepeda, Steve Renko, Mark Clear, Don Baylor, and Larry Parrish have worn No. 25 since Tony C. was dealt to the Angels. The number didn't look right on any of those players. Boston Red Sox No. 25 will forever belong to Tony C.

Dan Shaughnessy is a sports columnist for the *Boston Globe.* He is the author of *One Strike Away: The Story of the 1986 Red Sox,* and coauthor of *Courtside: The Fan's Guide to Pro Basketball* (with Gary Hoenig).

I first heard of Dick Allen in 1964, when I was in spring training with the Twins in Clearwater, Florida. He was known as Richie Allen then and was being called a "can't miss" prospect with the Phillies. In fact, he had been handed the third-base job after having played with the team the previous September. Philadelphia had never had a lot of black players and no black superstar, so he was getting more attention than the average rookie. I read the stories about him hailing from Wampum, Pennsylvania, where he had excelled in baseball and led his high school basketball team to 82 straight wins and two state titles. His older brother, Hank, and younger brother, Ronny, also were star athletes. Hank would make it to the majors in 1966 and hang on for seven years with Washington and the Chicago White Sox. At one time Ronny was considered as good a prospect as Dick, but he only got to the big leagues for a cup of coffee in 1972. Richie was here to stay and make an impact.

As it turned out, I didn't face Dick until after he'd had a couple of outstanding seasons and his fame had grown accordingly. It was in an exhibition game in Clearwater, and just looking at the guy, I was impressed. He had the build of an NFL running back and was very agile, fast, and powerful. And man, could he hit. Fortunately, we were in different leagues and I wouldn't have to pitch to him when it counted. At least not until 1972, when he was traded to the White Sox and proceeded to tear up the American League.

Here's a guy who didn't even report to Chicago until April 1, because of salary negotiations, yet after hitting only off the pitching

Courtesy Chicago White Sox

machine for a few days, clubbed two homers on opening day. Later
that year, he tied a record by hitting two inside-the-park homers in
Metropolitan Stadium. I didn't pitch that game, but I still distinctly
remember those two screaming line drives that wobbled like knucklers in center. Bobby Darwin charged in but didn't lay a glove on
either ball. They both ended up at the wall, while Allen easily circled
the bases. The more I saw Allen the more I realized what an amazing
player he was. I didn't know then that I'd soon have the privilege
of playing with him. This came about when I was traded to the White
Sox in August 1973.

The trade that brought me to Chicago was my first, so I was
stunned, upset, and disoriented. I sort of felt out my new teammates
and immediately became aware of the great respect everyone on the
club had for Dick, as he now called himself. If there ever was a team
in which there were twenty-four guys at a particular level and one
guy who was head and shoulders above the rest, it was the White
Sox of the early seventies. Other than Wilbur Wood, there weren't
a lot of big names or players in their prime. Dick had instantly become
Chicago's star and leader. He was particularly supportive of younger
players like Terry Forster, Goose Gossage, Jorge Orta, Bucky Dent,
and Bart Johnson and had told them, "Get on my back and I'll give
you a ride." And they did. And he did. Dick had almost carried an

average team to a championship in 1972, when he led the American League with 37 homers and 113 RBIs and was elected MVP.

In those days any black player who didn't act like the establishment wanted them to, on and off the field, was automatically labeled a militant. Dick had gotten that tag. Over the years I had heard stories about him. In Philadelphia there had been his much-publicized fight with teammate Frank Thomas. There had also been a mysterious run-in with police who found him pushing his car along the road one night after it had run out of gas. News reports claimed Dick cut his hand smashing his taillight. Dick had a terrible relationship with the Philadelphia press, which portrayed him as a bad guy and helped turn fans against him after his Rookie of the Year season. He began wearing his batting helmet in the field because Phillie fans kept throwing things at him. Allen supposedly countered by writing nasty messages in the dirt. After several extremely productive but difficult years in Philadelphia, Allen was sent to the Cardinals in 1969 in the historic Curt Flood deal. He had a big year, but something happened and he was traded to the Dodgers. There was another bad incident with, I believe, Willie Davis, and after only a year there, too, he was sent packing. I'd heard those stories, but I really didn't know the details. I learned early in the game that you can't judge anyone by their reputation. You can't believe the press or what you hear coming down the baseball grapevine. You really have to get to know that individual personally before drawing any conclusions. And that's how I felt about Dick Allen.

As we got to know one another, we'd talk shop and share our love of horses. Occasionally we'd go out to the track with Wilbur Wood and Chuck Tanner. I remember Dick saying, "What great athletes these horses are, but they're like human athletes. They might look like great physical specimens, but you don't know anything until you find out what's inside them. You might be better off getting a horse that doesn't look so great but has heart." Allen appreciated heart in human athletes, too, which is why we got along so well.

Dick called me Old-timer, and like the other players, I called him Mose, which was short for Moses, because he had taken the Sox out of the wilderness. I remember those times he'd come into the clubhouse and ask, "Old-timer, are you pitching tonight?" When I'd say I was, he'd get a gleam in his eye and say, "Oh, boy." He loved that I pitched quickly and kept things alive in the field. I'd turn around and wink or talk to him. This kept him in the game and, I like to think, gave him a little extra motivation. He certainly did well in games that I pitched.

I remember the night I went after my 200th career victory against Cleveland. It was tied early in the game, but they got the bases loaded with nobody out. I gave up a double-play grounder and they turned it, short to second to first, where Dick was playing. Dick had a habit of flipping the ball to the umpire at the end of the inning, and after the double play he automatically flipped the ball. Of course, the umpire jumped out of the way because there were only two outs. As the ball trickled into short right field, the runner on second circled third and came home to give the Indians a two-run lead. I got the next out, and as we were trotting off the field, Dick said confidently, "Don't worry, Old-timer, I'll get those back for you." Well, Dick proceeded to hit two home runs and drive in five runs. I got my 200th win, 7–3.

One of my all-time favorite wins came when I hooked up with Nolan Ryan in Chicago. Ryan had a no-hitter going for eight innings and about a dozen strikeouts. The Angels had scored one run early in the game when Frank Robinson homered. I quietly retired the Angels in the top of the ninth, and as we trotted to the dugout, a familiar voice said, "We're going to win this one, Old-timer. I'll get something started." Dick led off the inning by hitting a routine two-hop grounder to Dave Chalk at third base. All Chalk did was take one extra little step and keep the ball in his glove a shade too long, and Dick beat it out for our first hit of the game. Dick then upset Ryan on the bases and moved to second on a bunt. The Angels made an error, Ken Henderson got a single, and Bill Sharp hit a sacrifice fly, and we won 2–1. It was clear that without the leadoff spark that Dick provided we wouldn't have won and Ryan would have pitched a no-hitter. But that was the type of player he was. Dick wasn't just a power hitter. He would do whatever was needed to help win a ball game. He had great instincts and good training, which, he admitted, went back to playing for Gene Mauch in Philadelphia.

He was one of those athletes we read about but don't think exist who can always defy the odds, who enjoy defying the odds. I remember cold days at Comiskey, when the wind would be blowing in, and we'd say, "Nobody's going to hit one out of here today." Bill Singer was going for the Angels one day that statement was made. Dick looked over at me on the bench with a gleam in his eye. He didn't have to say anything because I could tell he was thinking, "Yeah? Watch me." And he got up there with that 42-ounce bat that he swung. He cocked it over his shoulder so far that the end of the bat and the barrel pointed almost directly at Singer. Then he uncorked and hit a pitch well up into the stands in left center field, where the bullpen meets the grandstand. It must have gone about 425 feet into the teeth of the wind. That day everyone else was hitting their best shots and the outfielders were catching them on the warning track. Dick just wasn't like everyone else.

I can attest to Allen's strength. In Kansas City in 1973, our pitcher, Stan Bahnsen, hit big John Mayberry with a pitch. Mayberry charged the mound and I ran out there to try to break up the fight. While trying to separate Bahnsen and Mayberry, I was struck by a left hook thrown by Mayberry. I was knocked down and rolled around on the mound. When all the dust cleared, I looked over toward first base and there was Dick, who stood about 5'11" and weighed 185, holding John Mayberry, who was about 6'5" and 235 pounds, in a bear hug, with John's spikes about six inches off the ground. I only wish Allen would have caught him before he clocked me.

I didn't see Dick have many confrontations, but I do remember his approaching teammate Ron Santo after he'd fired his batting helmet around the dugout in a rage a couple of times. Santo had just come over to the South Side and wasn't having the success he'd had all those years with the Cubs. He was a highly emotional player and couldn't calmly cope with his slump. Finally Dick walked up to him and quietly said, "Why don't you use your energy to figure out how to hit the pitcher instead of throwing helmets around?" The dugout got as silent as a tomb because nobody in their right mind (Santo, luckily, was in his right mind) was going to stand up to Dick. Without question Dick was one of the strongest men in the league and certainly the strongest player on our team.

During his years in Chicago, Dick received much negative press for arriving late to the ballpark and refusing to take batting practice. While I don't want to defend or condone Dick's actions, let me say that as his teammate they didn't really affect me. If Dick could do his job, it didn't make any difference what he did or didn't do in preparation for the game. Chuck Tanner was the first manager I had who had a different set of rules for everyone. For instance, in spring training after I won twenty games for him, he had no problem with my getting my daily workout over in the morning so I could play golf in the afternoon. He felt Allen had earned special consideration for having taken the team from nowhere into pennant contention and upped the attendance to 1.3 million from about 400,000 in 1970, when Tanner became manager. A few of the more insecure players resented Dick's special treatment, but no one could really knock him because he produced on the field. We used to kid about Dick's tardiness. It would be about twenty-five minutes before game time and someone would venture, "I wonder if Mose will be here." Then all of a sudden he'd come sashaying in with his hat pulled down over his eyes. It was kind of like Superman going into a phone booth. He'd put on his uniform and go sit in the dugout, then go out in the field and do his thing. And nobody did it much better than he did those few years in Chicago.

I think "misunderstood" is the word that best applies to Dick Allen. He loved the game of baseball between the foul lines, but it was very difficult for him to deal with all the attention that was drawn to him by the press. We'd sit in the dugout and he'd look up at the fans and the writers and sigh, "If I could just play the game." I really didn't feel the Chicago writers were unfair to him, but he must have had some deep bitterness toward all members of the press that dated back to his troublesome days in Philadelphia. He also had bad memories of what it was like to be a young black player on the Phillies' farm team in Little Rock, Arkansas, and in Florida during those early years of spring training. That stayed with him a long, long time. It would have been ideal if we could have put him in a vacuum and just brought him out to the stadium and let him play ball, then let him go home and do what he wanted to do. Because dealing with the other stuff shortened his career.

Dick wasn't one to get down on himself if he didn't do well. He was even-keeled about the game. However, the selfish play and emotional outbursts of other players affected him deeply. I'd tell him, "Everybody's different—play how you play and don't let it affect you. That's the manager's problem." I remember seeing the frustration in Dick in the September of 1974. At the time he was leading the league in homers and RBIs and you might think he'd be enjoying such a season. But Dick called a team meeting and announced he was retiring. He'd had enough. We lived in the same apartment complex and that night I visited him. Dick was a loner and I was really flattered that he considered me enough of a friend to confide in me. He told me that he had done everything he could for the ball club, but we were going from being on the verge of beating Oakland for the division title to playing less than .500 ball. I just said, "Man, there's too much baseball in you—there's no way you can walk away from the game." He shook his head and said, "I can't tolerate playing with guys who don't do the necessary things it takes to win and only care about their stats and themselves." He was sincere about that. He was "a baseball player" and whatever it took to win was his motivation. He didn't like guys going onto the field without the same approach to the game.

Dick did have more baseball in him and the next year returned to the Phillies. After the 1975 season, I knew the White Sox were going to shop me around for some young players because the team wasn't going anywhere. The next thing I knew, I got a call saying I was traded to Philadelphia for a couple of prospects. Dick had suggested me to Phillies owner Ruly Carpenter, who was on the hunt for a left-handed pitcher. So Dick and I were reunited in 1976. Though we didn't go all the way that year, Dick got a chance to play on a divisional winner. We got knocked off by the Big Red Machine in the championship series, but I know it was a real thrill for him, and for all of us, to be on a winning team—something they hadn't had in Philadelphia since 1950. That helped erase a bit of the frustration Dick experienced when the Phils collapsed at the end of 1964.

After the season, Dick, as had mysteriously happened to him in previous years, wasn't on the roster anymore. I drove to his farm outside Philadelphia. I said, "I heard about your horses." He took me to his barn and showed me around. I was in my jeans so we grabbed a couple of pitchforks and mucked out the stalls and talked horses and baseball. When it was over, we were hot and thirsty. It was Election Day, so most lounges were closed, but there was an open restaurant down from his farm and we went there and talked them into serving us wine in coffee cups. Then we drank together and reminisced about how much fun we'd had playing major league baseball and the good year we'd had in Philadelphia. Once again, Dick lamented, "I just wish I could play the game and enjoy myself and enjoy my teammates, and not have to worry about the off-the-field stuff."

It's unfortunate that Dick Allen's off-the-field incidents and his bad relationship with the press have diminished his career in many people's eyes. Because if you look at the raw numbers—he hit 30 homers six times and over .300 seven times—the man built a pretty good case for himself to be a Hall of Fame candidate. Yes, there are those who question his character and his heart. Maybe people don't think of Dick Allen in terms of courage or heart, but that's how I remember him. Once he got between the lines, which are my fondest memories of Dick, he truly was a courageous athlete, who played with a lot of heart and put a lot into all phases of the game.

I occasionally get the chance to see Dick at old-timers' games. When you look at him, you'd swear he could play in the majors today. What makes me believe that—besides that he's in great shape—is that if you watch him take the field and stand on first base, you'll suddenly see the broadest smile you can imagine. I'm reminded of that line by Kevin Costner, the star of *Bull Durham*: "I'm never happier than when I'm making movies." In Dick Allen's case, he was never happier than when he was playing baseball.

Jim Kaat is a baseball broadcaster for the Minnesota Twins and CBS. He pitched in the major leagues for twenty-five years, winning 283 games.

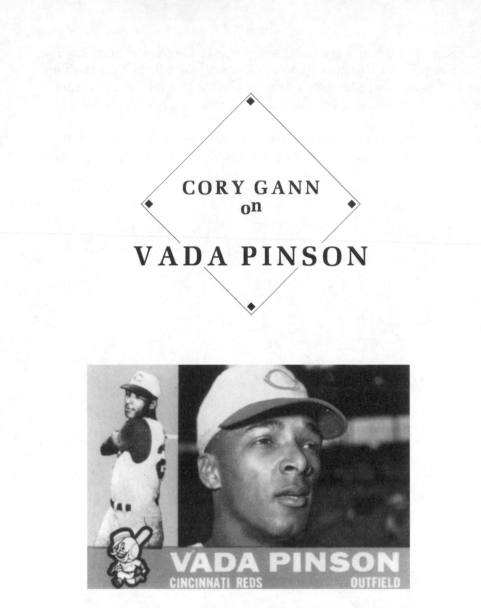

CORY GANN
on
VADA PINSON

1960 Topps: Copyright © The Topps Company, Inc.

Obscured by the Dodgers' *Boys of Summer* glory years and the rising star of the Milwaukee Braves, the Cincinnati Redlegs of 1956 were one of the great power-hitting teams of all time. In fact, they smashed 221 home runs, tying a still-standing National League record reached only once before, by the '47 Giants. Five players had big-homer seasons: Rookie of the Year Frank Robinson (a rookie record, 38), muscular first baseman Ted Kluszewski (35), slugging outfielders Wally Post (36) and Gus Bell (29), and even catcher Ed

Bailey (a career high, 28). But these slugging Reds finished third, two games behind the Dodgers. They scored more runs than anybody, but with 221 dingers they should have scored even more. Only Robinson crossed the plate more than 100 times, and only Kluszewski had more than 85 RBIs. Except for the exciting young Robinson, the Reds were slow, plodding, and powerful, more likely to score on a solo homer than by stringing hits together. You might say they were like a machine—a big, but rusty, red machine.

The next year their home-run production dropped a bit and the team dipped to fourth place. It was obvious that for the Reds to improve they would have to change their style and rely more on pitching, speed, and defense and less on homers. In December, Post, a vital part of the Reds' dependable and seemingly intransigent outfield, and the great Kluszewski, were traded. The following spring, line scores from training camp revealed that funny things were going on with the Reds. Game after exhibition game a strange configuration of letters kept showing up in the second spot in the batting order. What was a Vada Pinson? This was before I'd heard the accolades. Vada Pinson, it turned out, was one of those kids who was getting "a look" in spring training, and it was turning out to be an unusually long look at that. As the team barnstormed it's way north for those last few games before Cincinnati's traditional opening day, this swift left-handed hitter was still getting looked at. No doubt he had a good chance to make the team, but I wondered when they were going to give the real outfielders some starting time, all playing together, before the real gates opened.

In fact, Pinson tore up the Grapefruit League and was the rookie media sensation of Florida. Birdie Tebbets, the Reds' manager, played a reverse psychology game by letting him play every day. "I wanted him to do something wrong for a few games so I could send him down. I just couldn't believe he was ready for the big jump." Pinson never did what Tebbets was counting on. On Opening Day, he was the starting right fielder, batting second.

And I was sold. His meteoric jump from Class C to the majors overshadowed what he'd done in the California League. So the number that really made my eyes light up was his birth date. I've always believed that a player's birth date is a vital stat that is unappreciated by most fans. I know it helped me learn subtraction. In those days, players born after 1930 were still considered young with lots of prime time left in their careers. Mantle and Mays were the bellwethers, of course, by which everyone was compared, and they were both born in '31. Occasionally a '34 or '35 creeped onto the backs of newer players' baseball cards. But Pinson's card stood out because it had these telling birth-date numbers: 8–8–38. '38! A nineteen-year-old phenom starting in right field meant peace of mind until I was well out of college! Now all I had to worry about for the next fifteen years were injuries.

As it turned out, 1958 was not to be Pinson's first big year. In the second game of the season, against the Pirates, he clubbed one of the better-remembered Cincinnati grand slams. A great start, but from then on he began to press. That would be his only homer of the season in 96 at-bats and account for half his RBIs. It was a prophetic blast that started a controversial, career-long relationship Pinson had with home runs. Baseball writers lined up behind the theory that he tried to hit too many of them and that his power efforts detracted from other aspects of his offense. I don't ever remember being disappointed with his homer output or upset that he occasionally went for the fences. For instance, in 1959, his first full season, he stroked 20 homers and still put together great stats in other departments. He led the National League in runs with 131 and doubles with 47, had the first of his four 200-hit seasons, stole 21 pre–Maury Wills bases, and hit .316. It was a Rookie of the Year season if there ever was one, but Pinson missed out on the basis of six too many at-bats the year before. Instead, the rookie award went to Willie McCovey, who got to bat only 192 times. It was an example of the quirky way in which Pinson seemed to miss out on the limelight.

Following his impressive '59 season, writers started to trip over each other trying to describe his potential. It was a crescendo of accolades building to a consensus conclusion that he was going to be "the best." *Look* ran a three-page picture spread peppered with descriptive words like "graceful," "lithe," and "stylish." "Is He the Nearest-Perfect Player?" headlined the *Saturday Evening Post*. My favorite quote was from Fred Haney, fresh from managing the Braves. "For now—Hank Aaron," said Haney. "For the future, there's no doubt about it—Vada Pinson." Coverage of Pinson became a comparison orgy. Mays and Mantle were the main targets. Pinson's vault from the deep minors to the majors got a statistical workover next to Mantle's. He expropriated the "fastest man" title without a whimper. Way before Sparky Anderson built a career on platitudes, Reds general manager Gabe Paul implored us to "imagine a Mantle who doesn't strike out and a Mays who steals sixty bases. That's how good Pinson can be."

Reds fans know the comparison game can be a nightmare. Take for instance when two network commentators insisted on comparing

Frank Pastore's pitching form with Tom Seaver's. "It's the spitting image," they would say, just as the guy at bat invariably homered off Pastore's Seaver-like form. Pastore wasn't another Seaver. And Pinson never did become the equal of Mays or Mantle. But he was a tremendous talent who had several outstanding seasons. And he was just what the Reds needed at the time.

Pinson's average dipped to .287 in 1960—it was one of the game's curiosities that he'd take turns batting below and above .300 for his first nine seasons. His critics unfavorably compared that year to his exceptional 1959 campaign. But Pinson still scored 107 runs, clubbed a league-leading 37 doubles, and matched his homer output. Ever since I associated Pinson with the number 20. It was the number I could pencil in each spring when I predicted his homer totals. It was pretty much automatic during his years with the Reds (he hit between 20 and 23 homers six times), like his guaranteed 600 at-bats (nine times), 90 runs (eight times), 30 doubles (seven times), 10 triples (five times) and 20 stolen bases (seven times). It was more than a satisfactory number considering everything else he could do at the plate, on the base paths, and in center field, where he shifted to in 1960.

The 1961 edition of the Reds was commonly described as Pinson and Robinson and a bunch of ragamuffins and was picked to finish in sixth or seventh place. But with Pinson and Robinson leading the way, and "ragamuffins" Gordy Coleman, Gene Freese, pinch hitter Jerry Lynch, reacquired Wally Post, and old standby Gus Bell helping out a solid pitching staff, the Reds zoomed to the top of the standings. Pinson nestled into the third spot in front of Robinson to form an incredible cleanup combination. Robinson won the MVP, Pinson hit .342 while collecting a league-leading 208 hits, and the Reds took one of the most improbable pennants since the Giants' 1951 miracle. But would it be immodest of this Reds fan to say that I honestly wasn't surprised? After all, the lumbering Red Machine of five years back had been rebuilt with a Pinson piston sparking the attack.

Although they didn't win another pennant in the ensuing years, Cincinnati remained a strong contender, and their third-place hitter continued to have fine seasons, even topping 100 RBIs in both 1962 and 1963. But Pinson's stats were never the primary concern of his confident devotees. They were excited by his speed, the conviction that anything in play, on or near the ground, was potentially a hit. In fact, Pinson's speed was to become the focus of another major controversy that was to dog his career—sportswriter Earl Lawson's contention that more drag bunts would catapult him past Dick Groat to the batting title in 1963. Pinson didn't win that title (neither did Groat), but Lawson's column brought to a head a feud between the two that had been festering for the better part of two seasons. The clubhouse scuffle that followed resulted in Pinson's arrest on assault and battery charges—charges that Lawson dropped only after a hung jury failed to find Pinson guilty. In any event, it wasn't the bunts I was concerned about when Pinson was setting up in the batter's box, or when I was "being" Pinson in a backyard Dodgers-Reds simulation.

One of the joys of my youthful devotion to baseball was a methodical effort to copy the style of each and every major leaguer I ever heard of. I remember practicing Musial's crouch, and as Mantle, being better from the right side than the left. Most of these stances and postures required some contortions and were major impediments to successful batting and throwing. Ott's leg had to come up before each stroke; Wagner's and Cobb's hands had to be split at the bat handle; and having Mordecai Brown on my team meant gripping the ball with only three fingers. But mostly I was the Reds against the Dodgers, and that required eight distinct poses on my part, from Don Blasingame down to Johnny Edwards. I remember wielding a heavy bat for Gordy Coleman while swinging from the heels. And Frank Robinson was the hardest. You had to crowd the plate closer than you wanted to be and cock your wrists so the bat was parallel to the ground. Robinson tended to get into slumps in our game. . . .

And there was Vada Pinson. Pinson was my introduction to the virtues of grace and style. As far as I was concerned, his swing defined hitting in the game of baseball. With that distinctive two-inch choking up on the bat, he swept his arms letter-high across his body in a totally relaxed position, and the bat loomed motionless as merely an extension of his hands, like they used to talk about Hogan's driver or Heifetz's bow. It has always surprised me that many great players didn't have beautiful swings, but Pinson's was a perfect compact stroke. The story Fred Hutchinson, the Reds' vociferous manager in the sixties, used to tell was that visiting players liked to stand on the dugout steps to watch Pinson take his cuts in batting practice. "I've only seen them do that for a handful of guys," Hutch remarked, and the names that came closest to mind were Musial and Mays.

Pinson and Robinson were such an entrenched combo (they were also inseparable friends) that it is easy to forget how effectually Pinson was tied up with Pete Rose's start in the big leagues. Although not quite as explosive, the rookie's surprise claim of the second-base job in 1963 paralleled Pinson's unexpected arrival on the scene in

1958, especially in that their respective managers gave them "the job is yours until you lose it" treatment. But whereas Pinson took over a vacated outfield spot, Rose's ascension was at the expense of Blasingame, who was popular among a cliquish group of Reds at the time. Rose's all-out hustle also didn't sit too well with his new teammates, who showed their displeasure by avoiding him off the field. Except for Pinson, who befriended the newcomer and began to hang out with him on road trips. Robinson joined the two, and it was the image of this trio palling around that started to perturb the Reds' front office. In one of baseball's unseemly sidebar incidents, Rose was called in by the Reds' top brass and was admonished for his friendship with two black players.

On the field, Pinson, Robinson, and Rose were a veritable juggernaut of hits. During Pinson's eleven years with the Reds, from 1958 through 1968, this Reds threesome had eight 200-hit seasons: Pinson had four, Robinson had one, and Rose had three of his eventual ten 200-hit campaigns. In 1965, Rose and Pinson finished one-two in the National League hit race, with 209 and 204 respectively, and with Robinson's 172 thrown in, you have to wonder how they finished no higher than third. Desperately in need of pitching, Cincinnati sent Robinson to Baltimore for Milt Pappas that winter, in one of the most awful trades in baseball history.

Pinson and Rose remained together for three more years until Pinson suffered his most serious and slowing hamstring injury. This occured, according to some reports, during a Rose-sponsored winter basketball game for charity. The injury I feared all along had finally come to pass. After a disappointing '68 season, Pinson's Cincinnati career came to an end. He was traded to St. Louis for pitcher Wayne Granger and Bobby Tolan, a young lefty-swinging outfielder with some power and great speed who the Reds hoped would become another Pinson. Vada would play another seven years for four clubs, but his last real hurrah came in 1970 when he slugged a career-high 24 homers for Cleveland, the Reds' intrastate rival. It was the year that the Reds made it back to the top, and no doubt Pinson would have loved to have been part of the party.

Was he too highly touted at the beginning of his career? Was he plagued by a ballyhoo of expectation beyond what anybody could realistically have achieved? And once he was finished, was he given adequate consideration as one of the top players of the sixties for putting up splendid, though not Hall-of-Fame-caliber, numbers? In retrospect, his story stands apart from his impressive statistics and the Reds' finishes from year to year. Although serviceable, that information does not do justice to this fan's mind-set each time Pinson would stride to the plate. At crucial points in the game, when the Reds were one hit away from victory, his swing and speed made Vada Pinson as good a bet as anyone in baseball to do some significant damage.

Cory Gann is an early-childhood educator in Seattle. In the early seventies, he was the sports columnist Benny Bozo of the *The King Street Trolley,* an underground paper in Madison, Wisconsin.

SAMUEL FULLER on

BABE RUTH

As a copyboy breast-fed on ballplayers by Ford Frick, Damon Runyon, Jim Jennings, Sid Mercer, Burris Jenkins, Jr., and Ring Lardner, it was no sweat to get a free ducat to Yankee Stadium or the Polo grounds from Bill Farnsworth, sports editor of the *New York Journal*.

Old Henry Hudson, who got inning-by-inning figures on his telegraph, his ear cocked to the attached empty can of Velvet pipe tobacco amplifying the *click-clack* of hits, strikes, walks, and errors, would often fill me in with tales of Stuffy McInnis, Jack Barry, Eddie Collins, Walsh's spitball, Christy Mathewson's fadeaway, Carl Mays's submarine, Big Train Johnson, Grover Cleveland Alexander, Tris Speaker, and Home Run Baker.

I never saw them in action nor away from the diamond.

But I saw Babe Ruth hit a home run many times and saw him once in the City Room of the *Journal* near Park Row.

The year 1927 was one of champs . . . in many fields . . . Ty Cobb, Rogers Hornsby, Lindbergh's flight, Al Jolson's *The Jazz Singer*, Helen Wills won at Wimbledon, Ziegfeld's *Showboat*, Dempsey lost to Tunney, and my idol smashed his legendary 60th home run.

What a year. And what a moment when Babe Ruth charged in with a grin as wide as his arm, sweeping toward six five-gallon watercoolers on stands in the City Room.

"Gentlemen," Babe Ruth announced, "that bathtub gin is poison."

Courtesy New York Yankees

He was right. Not water. Just Prohibition gin.

He waved. Six uniformed cops carried in six cases of illegal whiskey. Congratulations and toasts replaced working against time for the next edition. The cops joined the drinkers.

When they ran out of paper cups, I made cups for them by folding copy paper—a trick Bill Farnsworth showed me. He'd learned it from Henry Hudson.

Watching Babe Ruth up close my awe had a different sensation. He exchanged humorous banter with Farnsworth, Burris Jenkins, Jr., the sports cartoonist, and Hype Igoe, who wrote a witty sports column, "Pardon My Glove."

They were all there. Big newspaper names and those that would become big. They loved him and he loved them. But it was far from a star-press gibble-gabble get-together. I sensed right there that, like me, they were tasting the same goddamn awe. He was King of Swat who could point at a spot in the bleachers and slam a homer to that exact spot. It wasn't ego. It was the highest form of his art: professionalism. He enjoyed the humor of it as much as the fans and the sportswriters. You could tell how much he loved the game. But more important, how much the game loved him. He must have been in awe of baseball as much as I, all of us, were in awe of him.

Why? What makes a man a hero? What made fanatics need to claw at him, touch him, or just stand like statues staring at him? And why this baseball player in particular, when so many of them since the first cry of "Play Ball!" was heard had attracted fans, wild fans, speechless fans, roaring fans?

It could be magic. It could be the way he jogged from base to base and you got deaf when he reached home plate. It could be the right moment was there, the right man and the right fans.

He was a symbol.

Not just a symbol of baseball. That goes without saying. But a symbol of excitement the world needed, at least Uncle Sam's world. He was not only the most famous baseball player in the country.

He was far more than that.

He was the balls of America. Romantic balls. Proud balls. Competitive balls. Had he lived in the days of knights, they would have thrown a coronation for him. We know that there were other players through the years, great, great players. And today there are great players.

Why was this man a giant above them? To me, he was.

Maybe he was just throwing a spell over me. A spell that never left me. That spell bothers me. The word bothers me. He was a true knight. His horse his legs. His sword his bat. His helmet his cap. His armor his Yankee uniform. He didn't kill a giant. He killed the New York Giants.

He was the aura every kid wanted to be like.

When he left the *Journal*, I followed him down the street. Kids mobbed him. It was the reincarnation of Charles Dana Gibson's drawing of kids following their idol, John L. Sullivan . . . but one thing was different. That was a drawing and I had to imagine that scene and what the great John L. meant to those kids following their Pied Piper.

But Babe Ruth was flesh. No fairy tale. All flesh that made me explode with a joy still within me. A joy of contagious love and pride and awe. He was a two-legged miracle joking with the kids. His picture was on page one of every newspaper.

The kids wanted his autograph. He plucked out a big bill for the newspapers.

Zookie shook his head, grinning. "It's on me, Babe."

He asked each kid his name and wrote it on the front page and autographed it and gave each kid the whole newspaper. When he ran out of newspapers to sign, I saw the kids looking at him and I realized I never knew a kid who didn't play baseball with Babe Ruth on his mind.

I got to be a crime reporter on the New York Graphic and assistant sports editor. Ed Sullivan, who would be a Broadway Columnist and eventually launch the classic TV variety show, took me to Beefsteak Charlie's for dinner. He had invited two other guests. One was Tex Rickard, who promoted fights at Madison Square Garden.

The other guest was Babe Ruth.

That aura intensified. Babe Ruth grinned. All he said was, "You're the kid who was on the Journal."

Then he told Ed Sullivan about the gin in the water bottles. I felt proud to be part of his memories.

You can call Babe Ruth an alchemist at work with his bat. You can say his world was baseball and he owned the world because of a bat. And I agree. But to me, when Babe Ruth died, he took baseball with him. My interest in baseball has passed on, but he never took that aura from me. He always comes back, even today, when I hear "Play ball!"

Samuel Fuller started as a copyboy with the *New York Journal* and worked as a crime reporter on the *San Diego Sun* before becoming a novelist, screenwriter, and the director of such films as *The Big Red One, Steel Helmet, Fixed Bayonets, White Dog, Pickup on South Street, Shock Corridor, The Naked Kiss, The Crimson Kimono, Run of the Arrow, Underworld, U.S.A., Forty Guns, I Shot Jesse James,* and *Street of No Return.*

STEPHEN LONGSTREET on

BABE RUTH

In the late 1920s, when the Sultan of Swat was King of New York, I was a young art student doing drawings (title heads) for the *New Yorker* and Sunday items for the *Brooklyn Eagle*, the *Herald-Tribune*, and other publications. I was also trying to put together a play for Broadway to be called *High Button Shoes*. When I had the time and the money, I'd take the train out to Yankee Stadium to watch what may have been the greatest team in baseball history. The Yankees had several genuine stars and two immortals: the young iron man Lou Gehrig and the one and only Babe Ruth. The remarkable Ruth, who began as a great southpaw pitcher for the Red Sox, was then in the prime of a peerless career that would produce 714 homers, a .342 lifetime average, and indelible memories for all of us who saw him. Since I was a young boy, I kept a scrapbook on major league players, and the most space was devoted to the Babe, the heroic slugger whose unprecedented homer feats—including his record-setting 60 homers in 1927—excited the entire nation, and whose charismatic personality and overwhelming popularity were enough to rescue the sport whose image had been tarnished by the Black Sox scandal.

The first time I had seen Babe Ruth outside of Yankee Stadium was back in 1925, when they were shooting a baseball picture called *The Pinch Hitter* at the Rutgers University baseball field in New Brunswick, New Jersey. The film starred Constance Bennett and Glenn Hunter. One day a big Packard motorcar drove up and everyone got excited when word got around that Babe Ruth was inside.

They kept us kids back when he stepped out, but there he was under a checkered cap and looking just like in his pictures. The product of a Baltimore orphanage, Ruth loved kids, but I don't remember if he waved at us—perhaps he didn't see us. I just stared and stared. He left soon and I never did find out why he'd come in the first place. Someone suggested that maybe he was supposed to show Glenn Hunter how to hit a baseball. But he never did.

Later on I'd often see Ruth in Lindy's taking care of a big meal. Unfortunately, in Lindy's, where the show people hung out, a shy young man didn't just rush up to a celebrity and ask for an autograph. Of course my scrapbook grew fatter with the stories and pictures of Ruth that appeared every day in every New York paper. Everything he did, on and off the field, was newsworthy in his town. At one time I decided to write a play about the era's greatest sports attraction. In those days I was always writing novels and plays that no one wanted, and the Ruth play never got past a few pages of notes. What was there to *The Babe Ruth Story* but how a chubby boy with chicken-bone legs had a habit of hitting home runs? I decided there wasn't enough for a plot and gave it up. But I kept watching him in Lindy's while he held court and thrilling to his remarkable exploits on the ballfield. There has never been a greater, more exciting player. Nothing compared to watching Ruth hitting long homers way over the short right-field fence and then proudly circling the bases and tipping his cap, but even his mighty whiffs were worth the price of admission.

So imagine my excitement when one day an Englishman who called himself Ralph Sims asked me to do a promotion drawing of Ruth for a project he was developing. He claimed to have acquired from Ruth the rights to sell in England "The Babe Ruth Hot Dog." I asked for $25 to do the drawing—and stated I'd like to do it from life, with Ruth posing for the picture. He said that Ruth was out of town, couldn't I do it from a photo? I said I'd much rather do it from life and have Ruth sign it. After all I was a Ruth fan, and since Ruth was one of the most famous people in America, I figured a Ruth drawing or two signed by him would look impressive in my collection. Sims said of course, he'd have me meet Ruth as soon as he got back to town. I was a simple youth in those innocent days and was so excited that I'd soon be meeting and drawing my idol.

As I gathered from Sims's spiel, he would form or had formed an English company to produce the exclusive "Babe Ruth Hot Dog" in England, where they ate something called a banger. I asked if a Ruth Hot Dog wouldn't sell better in America, especially in New

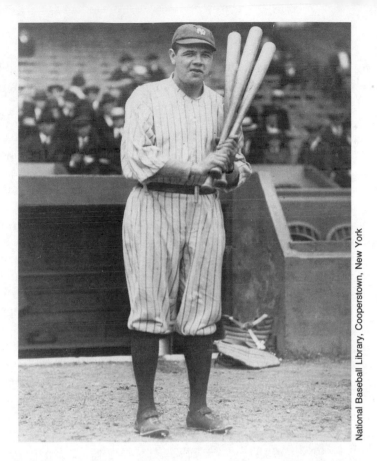

York, especially at Yankee Stadium, the "House That Ruth Built."
Sims smiled, patted my shoulder, and explained that Ruth's contract
forbade him to endorse a ballpark product in America, and he told
me confidentially, Ruth had plans to bring out his own hot dog when
he retired. Frankly, in those days I didn't care about or understand
big business deals. I was just an ex-sandlot kid who was nuts for
Babe Ruth to sign one of my drawings. And I could have used the
$25. In fact, I asked for an advance and Sims said sure, he'd get a
corporation check to me right away.

While Ruth and the Yankees were on the road, I did some sketches
of Ruth to limber up, and when they came back to town, I phoned
Sims at his hotel and said I was ready. Sims said fine; Ruth was
going to pose for some newsreel shots and he'd take me over to meet
the great man. At last.

But it rained and Sims told me that the newsreel shooting was
off—bad lighting, he explained. Although disappointed about the
postponement, I remembered the $25 advance I'd been promised.
Sims said he had "the chit" but it was in British pounds—he'd have
it converted into U.S. currency. It seemed that rain or shine, some-

thing always kept me from sketching Ruth in person. And the bank sure was taking its time converting pounds into dollars. Now I may have seemed a real dope for still not being overly suspicious, but Sims was such a marvelous talker, and such a great salesman. I went along for two weeks of delays. But even a dope comes out of his haze in time, and I began to wonder about Sims. I was also short of cash. The freelance newspaper market for drawings was in the midst of a slow season, and I had rent to pay, and eating in the automat may have been nourishing but it wasn't filling. . . .

I had friends on several papers, like Milt Gross on the *Mirror* and Ralph Barton, whose drawings were everyplace and who knew everybody. I began to talk to them about Mr. Sims, the English businessman—and then I told them about his Babe Ruth Hot Dog Company. Milt said it was a con game for sure. He knew one when he heard one, but I still felt Sims had sounded *so* sure, so real, so encouraging. I decided I'd wait a day or so before confronting Sims. Then I called him at his hotel and told him all the delays seemed peculiar. He assured me, as only he could, that things were ready and set, that the company had all the cash, and that all the factories in England were already producing hot dogs. I was too eager a young man—he understood me, he said, *youth* and all that. For sure, in two days I'd meet Ruth, do my drawing of him, and as a bonus, I'd get an *extra* $25. It seemed like my lucky day.

However, Barton had told my story to a private detective, as a joke—what a dumb kid I was. The detective called on me and asked me to join him and visit Sims. Just to check, kid, nothing else. As a favor to Barton.

At the hotel I asked for Mr. Sims and the clerk asked if I were a friend. The detective explained we were just checking a business deal. The clerk said Mr. Sims had left—with several weeks of bills unpaid. They were holding his trunk. My heart sank. We checked the bank Sims claimed he was using—they had never heard of him. We went to the British consul—no Ralph Sims was listed; no known British citizen of that name was listed.

Several Broadway characters told the detective that a cockney con artist had been pushing something about a Babe Ruth company to tourists from the tall timber who showed an interest in sports. Some seemed to have laid money on the line when Sims used the name of the most marketable figure in the country—for what they didn't know.

Neither I nor anyone else in New York City ever saw Mr. Ralph Sims again. And no one in England ever ate a "Babe Ruth Hot Dog."

However, Milt Gross kindly took me to Yankee Stadium and I finally got to meet Babe Ruth. There was no time to do a sketch of Ruth at our brief meeting, but he did graciously sign my program. It was an exciting experience, but being nothing like what I'd been anticipating, so much like a dream, that I don't remember it as well as I should. However, I do know that I didn't say a word to him about the "Babe Ruth Hot Dog" scam.

Over the years, I kept my Babe Ruth–autographed program with a prized Lou Gehrig baseball card and my baseball scrapbook. I managed to hold on to the rare Gehrig card when my *High Button Shoes'* lyricist Sammy Cahn hinted that he'd like to add it to his collection. But I am sorry to say that I didn't cherish the Ruth–autographed program enough because I gave it to Al Jolson when I was writing *The Jolson Story.* That was in 1947, when Ruth was long gone from the game and only a year away from his death. Jolson was a baseball nut who said he collected signed programs of great ballplayers but had no Babe. I didn't want to give him my signed program, but Sol Skolsky, the film's producer, said Al wouldn't be happy with my script until I presented him with the Ruth autograph "on his birthday"—a very vague date. Skolsky must have gotten lessons from Mr. Sims. In the end I gave Jolson his "birthday" present (I still wonder what happened to that program). I gave in when Harry Cohn, the head of Columbia Studios, began giving me odd looks and talking of hiring a *new* writer. I think Babe Ruth would have understood— some days you have to do what you have to do. Sorry, Babe.

Stephen Longstreet wrote the award-winning play *High Button Shoes,* such films as *The Jolson Story, Silver River, Uncle Harry,* and *Stallion Road,* and such books as *Storyville to Harlem: Fifty Years in the Jazz Scene, Our Father's House,* and *God and Sarah Pedlock.*

ROBERT WUHL
on
ROGER MARIS

I ran into my house, went downstairs to the recreation room (or "reck" room as we referred to it), and turned on the Emerson to Channel 11. . . .

It was A MOMENT. One of those "Where were you when . . . (fill in the blank with 'Kennedy was shot,' 'Neil Armstrong walked on the moon,' etc.)?" To a nine-year-old New York Yankee fan in 1961 this was equally important. Roger Maris hit his 61st home run of the year.

In 1961, in the New York Metropolitan area, the Yankees were the only game in town. Although my father would relate to me in stirring detail the exploits of the Brooklyn Dodgers and the New York Giants, I was too young to have any firsthand knowledge that New York had actually had two more teams. All I knew about the Dodgers and Giants were that they were on the other side of the country and were part of the foreign league, the National. With the insurrection of the Mets still a season away, for me there was only the Yankees, and being a left-handed-hitting right fielder, Roger Maris became my hero.

Maris had joined the Yankees the previous year, arriving in a trade from the Yankees' unofficial major league farm team, the Kansas City Athletics. The trade paid immediate dividends. In 1960, Maris hit .283, led the league in RBIs (with 112), slugging average, home-run percentage, and was runner-up to teammate Mickey Mantle in home runs (with 39), runs scored, and total bases. He was named

the American League's Most Valuable Player. In addition, he homered in his first World Series at-bat.

The 1961 baseball season was unlike any other. The American League had expanded its membership with the addition of two new teams. Seeing the impact the Dodgers had had on the West Coast, the AL, wanting a piece of the California pie, established the Los Angeles Angels. The new Minnesota Twins were in actuality the old Washington Senators now transferred to the Twin Cities, making the new Washington Senators franchise the other expansion team. Are you still with me? The more things stayed the same, the more they changed.

The AL also expanded its schedule from 154 to 162 games. This, of course, was done in the best interests of baseball. (Read: more playdates, more money.)

What they hadn't counted on was that by adding eight additional games, there would be more at-bats, and more opportunities for records to fall (something the NFL would experience years later when they expanded their season from fourteen to sixteen games).

Expansion also had another side effect. By adding two more rosters, it watered down even further that most valuable of all baseball commodities—pitching.

This was immediately evident. Although plenty of great pitchers were still flourishing—people like "Yankee Killer" Frank Lary, Jim Bunning, Whitey Ford, Juan Pizzaro, Bill Monbouquette (a candidate for the most-vowel team), Jim "Mudcat" Grant, and Camilo Pascual—pitching was at an all-time premium, and lesser arms tried to no avail to sneak lesser fastballs past salivating veterans.

That summer, baseballs went out of the park in record-breaking numbers. The league totals went from 1,056 home runs hit in 1960 to 1,534 hit in 1961, more than a 45 percent increase.

If you were a Yankee fan, it was Valhalla.

The Yankees crushed 240 home runs. Two hundred and forty! Maris and Mantle hit 115 home runs between them. *Just between them.* (To put this into perspective, consider that in 1989 the AL's *three* homer leaders, Fred McGriff (36), Joe Carter (35), and Mark McGwire (33), had 104 combined. That's still 11 short.)

The M&M boys, as they were referred to, just went wild. I remember witnessing a July doubleheader in which Mantle took over the league home run lead by hitting two dingers, only to watch it disappear when Maris hit four! Most of my colleagues (it's tough to refer to third-graders as peers) were for Mantle. He had the tradition, he had the name, and he had their hearts. I opted for Maris.

I think it was the swing.

Roger Maris had *the* perfect Yankee Stadium swing. Short. Quick. Powerful. Left-handed. The sight of number 9 in pinstripes, Maris, whacking ball after ball over the right-field porch of the Stadium remains as indelible as any baseball memory I have. (It is ironic that the man whose swing most resembled Maris's, Graig Nettles, would also wear number 9. Perhaps 9 should be the first uniform number to be retired not because of a certain player but a certain swing.)

To give you an idea of how strong the 1961 Yankees were, the Detroit Tigers won 101 games—and finished 8 games back! By September, it was generally assumed that the pennant race was over. But another, more interesting race was still being waged—the competitive assault by Maris and Mantle on Babe Ruth's single-season home-run record.

To my age group, this was great. Go get 'em. Sure, we had heard of the Babe. Loved and respected the man. But this was now! This was a day-to-day event. And I could see it live. Sixty home runs in a single season. Besides, this was in New York, where it's *supposed* to happen.

But to another generation, a generation who had grown up with Babe Ruth and had not so long before fought and won a great war, this was wrong.

Television journalism wasn't yet "up close and personal"; this was still the heyday of the powerful newspaper sports reporters like Jimmy Cannon and Dick Young, people who had fond memories of the Babe and had canonized him. "Oh, sure, Babe was a womanizing, egomaniacal, alchoholic prima donna, but he was *our* womanizing, egomaniacal, alchoholic prima donna."

Through August, both players were ahead of Ruth's 1927 pace. But in September, Mantle went down with an ailment, missed a number of games, and dropped out of contention, eventually finishing with 54 homers. Now there was only Maris. Mantle, the foremost target of the Yankee boo-birds until Maris's arrival in New York, had been the scribes' preference. True, he was a country bumpkin to the New York sophisticos, but at least he wasn't nearly as intense as Maris. An introvert, Maris wasn't the type of copy they wanted. Unaccustomed to the avalanche of media attention and unprecedented pressure, he probably didn't handle it as well as possible, but who could? Nowadays he would be buffered by a team spokesperson, an agent, and a battery of attorneys.

The sportswriters portrayed him as a moody, sullen, nasty, selfish player who didn't deserve to break Ruth's record. "Roger Maris top the Babe? He couldn't." Or more possibly, "He shouldn't."

So they changed the rule. Or rather put an asterisk next to it.

Ford Frick (rhymes with "dick"), the commissioner of baseball, determined that should Maris break the record he would have to do it in 154 games; otherwise the record would read, Ruth, 60 in 154 games, Maris, 61 in 162 games, thereby keeping the record (and presumably the world) pure. It was particularly galling that Frick didn't bother to change the rule at the time the 162-game schedule was conceived, but did it during the season! Make no mistake, this was the "Roger Maris isn't going to blemish our sacred world of baseball" rule.

Going into the 154th game, Maris had 58 home runs. In the third inning of that game he hit number 59, but that was all. The Babe's record was safe. The world, according to Frick, could sleep peacefully.

Maris hit number 60 four games later (game 158), but stayed tied with Ruth going into the final day of the season. Then, in the fifth inning, with Boston's Tracy Stallard on the mound, came THE MOMENT.

I ran upstairs from the recreation room and out of my house, jumping and screaming, "He did it! He did it! He did it!"

"Okay, but what's he gonna do for an encore?"

The fans didn't turn against Maris, the media did.

The following season, Maris's numbers included a more-than-respectable 33 home runs and 100 RBIs (down from 142), giving him three straight 30+ home-run, 100+ RBI seasons, if not three straight MVPs. Good, but not the Babe. ("See? We did the right thing.")

Plagued by nagging injuries the following years, his production sagged, and in 1967, he was traded to the St. Louis Cardinals for Charlie Smith. (And how come no one's campaigning for *his* election to Cooperstown, huh?) I was hurt that the Yankees had dealt Maris—it was like losing a family member. But at the same time I felt relieved for him. I believed that he would flourish in a less-judgmental environment.

The Cardinals fans, as knowledgeable as they come, expected a moody, sullen, sour malcontent. Instead they got Roger Maris. A hustling, hard-nosed, tough winner.

In his first at-bat in a Cardinals uniform, he stretched what appeared to be a routine single into a hustling double. The fans applauded, and with one at-bat Maris was more appreciated in St. Louis than in the past five seasons in New York. He became an important cog in St. Louis's pennant-winning teams in 1967 and 1968.

Maris retired after the 1968 season, but he had impressed Gussie Busch so much in just those two seasons that the Cards' owner awarded him a much-coveted Budweiser distributorship in Florida. (Can you imagine George Steinbrenner awarding Carlos May a shipyard?)

Unfortunately, bad luck continued to plague Maris. In the years that followed, Maris's physical maladies got worse. They included Bell's palsy and finally, cancer, which silenced him on December 14, 1985.

Every January when the balloting approaches, the question is always brought up: "Does Roger Maris belong in the Hall of Fame?" His detractors point to 1961, saying that the 61 home runs was fluke. That he never again even hit 40 homers in a single season. That with Mantle hitting behind him, Maris had a big advantage. "Yeah, he broke it, but he had another eight games. Nah, nah, nah-nah-nah."

This still doesn't diminish the feat.

Nor does it do Maris justice. Ask anyone who ever played with him. To a man, they extol his virtues. A fine and daring baserunner, Maris was also a rifle-armed outfielder who cut down many a base-runner foolish enough to attempt to take an extra base, and who would routinely dive into the right field stands to take home runs away from opposing batsmen. In an era that featured marvelous right-fielders, Kaline and Clemente (both, need I add, Hall of Famers), only Maris's name was brought up for comparison.

The question of Maris's belonging in Cooperstown is moot. The fact is that Roger Maris is already in the Hall of Fame.

Most Home Runs in a Single Season, Roger Maris, 61 (1961).

Robert Wuhl appeared in the films *Bull Durham, Batman, The Holly-wood Knights, Blaze,* and *Good Morning, Vietnam.* He has performed stand-up comedy across the United States.

DAVE
ANDERSON
on

HENRY AARON

In the quiet of a hallway high in the New York Sheraton, Henry Aaron realized he had left his room key in his room. Rather than go down to the front desk, he asked a chambermaid to let him in with her passkey.

"I can't do that," the chambermaid said.

"I'm one of the baseball players," he said.

One of the baseball players. That's how Henry Aaron described himself to that chambermaid. And his gentle sincerity eventually persuaded her to use her passkey. But she never recognized the man who had described himself as one of the baseball players.

The only one with 755 home runs.

Of all the times I've been around Henry Aaron, of all the home runs I've seen him hit, that small moment defined him better than any other. And there were many small moments over more than two decades after we, in a way, broke in together. He was a twenty-year-old rookie with the Milwaukee Braves in 1954 when I went to spring training with the Brooklyn Dodgers for the first time. I was covering the Dodgers for the *Brooklyn Eagle,* and upon my return from Florida, a cityside rewrite man and a delightful cynic, Clarence Greenbaum, sneered and said, "Well, kid, what did you see in spring training that you never saw before?"

"Henry Aaron," I said.

"Who?" asked Clarence.

"Henry Aaron," I said.

He was Henry Aaron then, not Hank, and that's why he's always

Henry Aaron connects for his record 715th home run.

been Henry to me. Not that I was a talent scout. I had simply been listening to the Dodgers talk about him. That year the Dodgers had traveled north with the Braves by train, stopping for exhibition games in Mobile, Birmingham, Nashville, and Chattanooga, and the more the Dodgers saw of Henry Aaron, the more they talked about him.

"This kid," I remember Jackie Robinson saying, "is a hitter."

Not a home-run hitter. None of the Dodgers, or anybody else for that matter, believed then that he would hit 755 home runs. But if they had been told that his batting average for twenty-three major league seasons would be .305, none would have been surprised. And then, season by season, his home runs began to add up—400, 500, 600—and when his total reached 700, the countdown to Babe Ruth's record 714 began. When he had 712 entering the last week of the 1973 season, I went to Atlanta along with about a dozen other out-of-town sportswriters. Before the night games, he would sit at his locker with us for about an hour in what were more casual conversations than interviews.

"Are you enjoying all this?" he was asked one night.

"I refuse," he said with a big grin, "to answer that."

It wasn't easy for him to enjoy it. Not after having answered many of the same questions for months. But he tolerated it patiently. And throughout his career he performed the same way: stoically, without flair, without emotion. He seldom created headlines with anything except his home runs.

"But things do bother me," he was saying at his locker. "I just react differently than other people. Some guys go oh for four and throw their helmets or kick things, but I think, Why did I pop up? Why did I strike out? This is how to teach my kids—to sit down and figure it out."

His attribute was consistency. Thickly muscled through the chest and shoulders, his body supported that consistency. So did his mental outlook.

"The reason I'm not showing much emotion in all this," he said, "is that I've been doing it through the years. I don't recall having a bad year. I think my best year was 1959 for hitting the ball. I hit .355, but for a long time I was well over .400, then I sprained my ankle running after a fly ball in the old Philadelphia ballpark. I stepped on a bottle. I didn't begin to think of myself as a home-run hitter until I was around a few years. When I got older and stronger, I also got more selective with the pitches I hit, and that turned me into a home-run hitter. Then it was my responsibility."

Rubbing the big yellow callus at the base of his left palm, he smiled.

"I realized," he said, "that home-run hitters drive Mercedes or Cadillacs."

"What kind of a car do you drive yourself?" one of the sportswriters asked.

"I have a Caprice," he said, referring to a Chevrolet. "It gets me around."

In the laughter, he noticed that it was almost six o'clock, the time when the Braves regulars took batting practice. He stood up, put on his white Braves' shirt with the big 44 on the back, then he adjusted his red, white, and blue cap.

"Let me go hit," he said.

Suddenly, on Saturday night, he hit his 713th homer. Now he needed only one more to tie the Babe's record, two to break it. With his first swing in the first inning off Jack Billingham in the Braves' 1974 opener in Cincinnati, he hit a line drive over Pete Rose's head and over the left-field wall in Riverfront Stadium. And the next day, an off day in the schedule, he stood in the lobby of the Netherlands Hilton and reflected on the 714th home run.

"It was just a fastball," he said. "To me, the homer I hit off Billy

Muffett of the Cardinals to win the 1957 pennant is still my favorite. But the 715th probably will mean more. Then you're standing out there alone, you're not sharing it with anybody."

The following Monday night, April 8, 1974, the Braves returned to Atlanta for their home opener. Al Downing, a sturdy left-hander, started for the Los Angeles Dodgers, but when Aaron led off the second inning, he walked without taking the bat off his shoulder. Four balls, one called strike. With each pitch, the crowd was hushed in silence. Not a murmur, not a stir. Each of the 53,775 customers had been transfixed by the anticipation of history. And when Aaron walked up to the plate in the fourth inning, they were transfixed again.

"It was a fastball," Downing would say later of his first pitch. "Right down the middle of the upper part of the plate. I was trying to get it down to him, but I didn't, and he hit it good. As he would."

In that instant when the bat struck the ball, the sound is what I'll always remember. The sound that's baseball's version of a thunderclap, the sound that momentarily was the only sound in the ballpark, the sound of Henry Aaron's 715th home run. And as that sound faded, another sound erupted, the roar of the crowd as the ball soared high and deep toward the left center-field fence. And over it.

On the dirt base paths Henry Aaron was trotting past Babe Ruth into history. And at home plate, surrounded by an ovation that splashed over him as if it were a waterfall of appreciation, he was met by his teammates, who attempted to lift him onto their shoulders. But he slipped off into the arms of his father, Herbert, Sr., and his mother, Estelle, who had hurried out of their special box near the Braves' dugout.

"I never knew," he would say later with a laugh, "that my mother could hug so tight."

With that 715th home run, he was, as he predicted, "standing out there alone, not sharing it with anybody." And as he sat in an interview room near the Braves' clubhouse, he sounded relieved, but drained.

"You don't know," he said, "what a weight it was off my shoulders, a tremendous weight."

With that 715th home run, he had transferred that weight to the shoulders of every slugger who even dreams about surpassing Henry Aaron's eventual total of 755 homers. Think of it this way: If somebody averages 35 homers for twenty seasons, he will still need 55 more to equal that total.

His 755 homers constructed his monument, but it's not his only monument. More than a decade later, he still held the major-league career records for runs batted in (2,297), total bases (6,856), and extrabase hits (1,477, including 624 doubles and 98 triples).

He would retire from baseball after the 1976 season, but in spring training in Arizona with the Milwaukee Brewers that year, another small moment occurred.

"Some of that adrenaline has left me," he said somewhat wearily. "It hasn't been the same since the Babe Ruth thing. It's not that you don't see the ball. It's that your mind and your hands don't react like they used to. And the ball you used to hit out of the ballpark lands at the base of the fence."

He was waiting to go into the batting cage and he talked about the toughest pitchers he had faced.

About how Curt Simmons had been the most difficult pitcher for him to read because "he hid the ball so long behind his hip." About how, of all the good pitchers he had faced, he hit Don Gullett the best because "he didn't change speeds on me, everything was fast." About how the fastest pitchers he had faced were Sandy Koufax, Jim Maloney, Nolan Ryan, and Bob Gibson. About how Robin Roberts had the best control. Then he turned and moved toward the batting cage.

"Excuse me," he said. "I hit now."

In the batting cage he hit a few sharp grounders, then he hit a high drive to left field that had the look of a Henry Aaron home run. But the ball landed at the base of the fence.

But over his twenty-three seasons, 755 of the balls Henry Aaron hit didn't land at the base of the fence. Not bad for just one of the baseball players.

Dave Anderson is the Pulitzer Prize–winning sports columnist for the *New York Times*. His books include *Frank: The First Year* (with Frank Robinson); *Hey, Wait a Minute, I Wrote a Book* and *One Knee Equals Two Feet (and Everything Else You Need to Know About Football)* (both with John Madden); and *Shooting for the Gold: A Portrait of America's Olympic Athletes.*

LAWRENCE S. RITTER on

CHIEF MEYERS

An honor roll of the game's greatest catchers always includes the Big Six—Bench, Berra, Campanella, Cochrane, Dickey, and Hartnett—and usually Ernie Lombardi as well. Long before any of them wrapped themselves in armor, however, a powerfully built 195-pound six-footer, wearing the uniform of the New York Giants, was for a while every bit their equal. His name was John Tortes (Chief) Meyers and he came to the Polo Grounds in 1908 from a remote Cahuilla Indian village high up in southern California's San Jacinto Mountains (via an unlikely detour through the ivy-covered campus of Dartmouth College).

Today, such recognition as the name "Chief Meyers" might evoke derives largely from the fact that in 1910 he succeeded Roger Bresnahan as the Giants' first-string catcher and from then through 1915 was the immortal Christy Mathewson's regular batterymate. Back in his heyday, though, the Chief needed no reflected glory—his fame rested solely on his own broad shoulders because he was widely recognized, by teammates and opponents alike, as the best all-around catcher in the major leagues.

He earned that status in part with an enviable reputation as an astute handler of pitchers. "The Chief understands my style so well," Matty once said, "that we hardly need signs to communicate." He was also far and away the hardest-hitting catcher in the game, batting .332 in 1911, .358 in 1912, and .312 in 1913. The Giants won the National League pennant in each of those years. He was traded to Brooklyn in 1916 and promptly wound up behind the plate in a

Courtesy Lawrence S. Ritter

fourth World Series, catching for the Dodgers. By that time he was thirty-six, however, and his playing days were just about over.

I first met Chief Meyers in 1964 at his home in Rialto, California, a suburb of Riverside, when I was traveling around the country searching out old ballplayers, interviewing them for a book that was later published as *The Glory of Their Times*. The Chief was eighty-four years old then (he was born on July 29, 1880), and it had been almost half a century since he'd donned a mask and chest protector. But his energy and enthusiasm were contagious. I soon discovered that he knew as much about baseball's present as its past, since he often attended games in Los Angeles as a guest of the Dodgers and Angels. Indeed, he even made occasional road trips with the Dodgers at the invitation of owner Walter O'Malley.

We talked all day and long into the evening. We talked about Giants' manager John McGraw, about Christy Mathewson and Jim Thorpe, the great Indian athlete, about Babe Ruth and Casey Stengel

CULT BASEBALL PLAYERS

and W. C. Fields (yes, W. C. Fields!), all of whom the Chief knew well, and about the changes that had taken place in baseball—and in America—since the turn of the century.

The Chief also reminisced about his student days at Dartmouth College. "The biggest regret of my life," he said, "is that I never graduated with my class, the Class of 1909. I was born in a small Cahuilla village and I went to school there. Then my family moved to Riverside when I was about eleven or twelve, and I went to the public schools here. I didn't even think of going to college right away after high school. Instead, I caught for various semipro teams around here, in southern California and Arizona and New Mexico. However, after a few years of that I applied for admission to Dartmouth and was accepted, which was a great thrill for me.

"In the 1700s, you know, Dartmouth College established a fund for the purpose of providing scholarships for any qualified American Indians. That fund still exists today, although few Indians know anything about it. I didn't know about it myself until I came in contact with Ralph Glaze while I was playing semipro ball in Albuquerque in the summer of 1905. At the time, Ralph was a student at Dartmouth, where he was on the baseball and football teams; later, he pitched a few years for the Boston Red Sox.

"Ralph told me about Dartmouth, and through his efforts and the information he obtained for me, I eventually got admitted. I was the first Cahuilla to ever get such a wonderful chance, so in September of 1905 I left home and went east to Hanover, New Hampshire, to avail myself of the opportunity.

"However, as I said, I never got to finish. After my freshman year my mother got ill so I came back to California. Mother eventually recovered, but by then it was too late to return to Dartmouth. You know, Dartmouth is just like the Giants: once a Giant always a Giant. Mr. McGraw instilled a spirit there that never left you. And this is quoted from Chaucer: once a Dartmouth, always a Dartmouth. You never lose that affection for the old school. Regardless if you just get in there and get a cup of coffee, they instill that spirit into you that lasts. Dartmouth men are very, very close, all over the world."

The next time I saw the Chief was a year later, in 1965, when he flew to New York on a road trip with the Dodgers as guest of owner Walter O'Malley. Together, we went to and from Shea Stadium with the ballplayers on the team bus and hung out in the Dodgers' locker room before and after each game. On the last of the Dodgers' three days in New York, when we boarded the bus for the ballpark, I couldn't help but notice that the Chief was lugging along a shopping bag. Seeing my curiosity, he only winked and said cryptically, "All shall be revealed, young man, to those who bide their time."

At the Stadium, the Chief suddenly disappeared from the locker room about twenty minutes before the game was scheduled to start. As I made my way alone to our seats behind the Dodgers' dugout, I was surprised to see my friend as one of a small group standing at home plate. The loudspeaker blared forth that a ceremony was taking place wherein Chief Meyers, who had caught for the Dodgers in the 1916 World Series, was presenting his old uniform to Yogi Berra, former Yankee catcher, now a Mets' coach. It was meant as a symbolic gesture, the announcer explained, a bridging of the generations between one of the best catchers of the old days and one of the best of more recent times. There was applause, and then Berra and the Chief headed back to the Mets' dugout, with Yogi carrying the Chief's old uniform.

I am indebted to writer Donald Honig, who was standing in the dugout, for knowledge about what happened next. According to Honig, Berra placed the old uniform on the bench. Meyers approached him and smiled. "You don't really want this, do you?" he asked. Yogi shrugged. The Chief nodded in agreement, gathered up his uniform, stuffed it back in his shopping bag, gave Berra a handshake and a pat on the back, and was on his way.

With an intrigued Honig trailing behind him, the Chief found me in the stands. "Come on, let's have some fun," he said. "We're going to pay a visit to my old friend George Weiss."

Crusty old George Weiss had become president of the Mets following a lengthy career in a similar role with the Yankees. It was news to me that they were old friends, but I was beginning to realize that there was more to Chief Meyers than met the eye. "I don't know if you fellows realize it," the Chief said as the three of us made our way upstairs to the Mets' administrative offices, "but Mr. Weiss was once my employer. The year was 1917 and he hired me as playing manager of his minor league New Haven team. Well, you *do* know that there was a war on then, World War I, and on Opening Day, when the band played and they raised the flag out in center field, I was stricken with an acute attack of patriotism that refused to go away. After the game, without a word to anyone, I went downtown and joined the Marines. Never did return to the ballpark. At the very least, I certainly owe Mr. Weiss an apology."

George Weiss was sitting behind his desk when we arrived, waiting for Meyers, who took from his shopping bag a small but bulky cloth, drawstring bag. He held it in his hand as he spoke.

"Mr. Weiss," he said, "many years ago, when I was barnstorming in Vancouver, I received a gift. The stones in this bag were given to me by some Kwakiutl Indians. They said the stones would bring me good fortune and long life. I have enjoyed both. And now, with the same sentiments, I would like to present them to you. I hope that you will accept them as a belated but heartfelt apology for my sudden and inexcusable departure in 1917."

So saying, Meyers undid the drawstring and poured onto Weiss's desk a number of small, scruffy-looking stones. Weiss stared down at them and then looked up at the expressionless face of his benefactor. For a moment, each man seemed to be daring the other to smile, but both faces remained impassive.

"Thank you, Chief," Weiss said, "no apology has ever been necessary, considering the cause for which you departed." Then he stood up and the two men shook hands.

Outside in the corridor a few minutes later, Honig asked the Chief, "Was that true about those stones, that those what's-their-name Indians gave them to you?"

"Kwakiutl," the Chief said. "They live in the Vancouver area. A noble people."

"But what about the stones?"

Meyers smiled. "God knows where they came from," he said. "They've been at the bottom of an empty flowerpot in my basement ever since I can remember. But it was a fine little ceremony, wasn't it?"

The following year the Chief was back in town, this time for a party celebrating the publication of *The Glory of Their Times*. He stayed almost a week, appearing on a number of radio and television programs, including *The Ed Sullivan Show,* and during that time arranged to visit the Dartmouth Club in New York where he proudly presented an autographed copy of "our book," as he always called it, for placement in the Alumni Alcove.

That evening after dinner, the Chief said he wanted to tell me something. "Hardly anyone still alive knows about this," the Chief said, relaxing in a big easy chair, a twinkle in his eye, "but I think you should be one of the few. It's about my matriculation at Dartmouth. The fact of the matter is that not everything happened precisely as recounted in our book.

"I did indeed meet Ralph Glaze when we were both playing ball at Albuquerque in the summer of 1905, and Ralph did indeed tell me about Dartmouth's scholarship fund for Indians and help me get admitted. Of course, Ralph had an ulterior motive: in his mind's eye he could already see me up at bat or crouching behind the plate with the name 'Dartmouth' stitched across my uniform shirt! For my part, the idea of actually going to college was beyond my wildest dreams.

"But admission to Dartmouth wasn't as simple as it sounds, because actually I'd never even graduated from grade school, much less from high school. Indians have never been encouraged to get a lot of education, you know. However, somehow Ralph came up with someone else's high school diploma. The name on it was 'Ellis Williams,' and whoever this Ellis Williams was, according to his diploma, he was only five feet six inches tall and had red hair. I was six feet tall and my hair was coal black. But apparently Ralph had friends in the Admissions Office because despite these obvious discrepancies, I was duly enrolled for the fall semester of 1905 under the name Ellis Williams Tortes Meyers.

"That term I took courses in history, Spanish, biology, and Chaucer, and with the help of tutors I did reasonably well in all of them. In the spring term, though, word got out that something wasn't exactly kosher, and President Tucker called me into his office. I had never met him face-to-face before and I was frightened. I still remember thinking that he looked like a treeful of owls, with eyes like an eagle's. On his desk, among other papers, I could see 'my' high school diploma, the one that said height, five feet six, and hair, red. However, President Tucker was very nice about it. He wound up saying he'd like me to stay at Dartmouth but that I needed better preparation to be able to pass all the courses that were necessary for graduation. He even said he'd help me get into a good college preparatory school and not to worry about tuition expenses.

"On reflection, though, I decided to give pro baseball a whirl instead. It so happened that Billy Hamilton was the baseball coach at Dartmouth, and he also managed the Harrisburg team in the old Tri-State League. I asked him if he'd give me a tryout with Harrisburg and he said yes. That's how I got started, and then, as you know, two years later I was on the New York Giants, understudying Roger Bresnahan. That was also a dream come true, but even so it will always be the biggest regret of my life that I didn't graduate with the Class of '09."

.   .   .

The last time I was in touch with Chief Meyers was a Christmas letter he sent in December of 1970. "I am not any too well," he wrote. "My eyesight is failing, getting quite dim. Just read the headlines now. No fine print. It is quite some chore for me to write, as you can see by my handwriting. It looks like the sun is getting down pretty low on the old Chief. Maybe Bresnahan got a bad finger and soon Mr. McGraw will be calling for a catcher. Who knows what is going on up there. Don't let this disturb you, my good friend. I am not a quitter."

Seven months later, the call for a catcher did indeed come. John Tortes Meyers—known as Jack to his family and as Chief to everyone else—died of natural causes on July 25, 1971, four days before his ninety-first birthday.

Upon hearing the news, my mind drifted back to the words he had spoken when he was in a reflective mood during our first meeting, seven years earlier. "I guess," he had said, recalling an old Indian quotation, "I am like an old hemlock. My head is still high, but the winds of close to a hundred winters have whistled through my branches, and I have been witness to many wondrous and many tragic things. My eyes perceive the present, but my roots are imbedded deeply in the grandeur of the past."

Good-bye, my friend. I will miss your wry wit, your rare wisdom, and above all your gentle nature. Those who knew you will love you forever.

Lawrence S. Ritter is the author of *The Glory of Their Times, The Babe: A Life in Pictures* (with Mark Rucker), and several other baseball books, including *The Story of Baseball,* for young readers; and coauthor of *Principles of Money, Banking, and Financial Markets* (with William Silber). He teaches finance at New York University.

JOAN MELLEN on

JIM BOUTON

A cult figure in baseball has to be more than just one of the game's colorful or memorable characters. He's a player of whom true appreciation demands special taste. Meet Jim Bouton, who while pitching in 1970 wrote the controversial baseball exposé *Ball Four* and simultaneously changed the face of sportswriting and our conception of what it means to be a professional athlete.

He sits behind his desk in a small, modern office building in Teaneck, New Jersey. At fifty, he's very slender and lithe, so that he seems smaller than the six feet at which he's listed. His hair is no longer the color of spun gold. It's pale, somewhere between gray and blond, and his face is lined, especially when he laughs. He seems a man at peace, not driven, not yearning for days of athletic prowess that will never come again, and he speaks with relish of all that has happened to him.

In high school, he had read Jim Brosnan's seminal *The Long Season*, a diary of the scholarly pitcher's 1959 season with the Cardinals and Reds. Brosnan took notes and produced a less than glamorous view of baseball. Nicknamed "the Professor," Brosnan anticipated Bouton by achieving consideration for another vision of manhood: the athlete who reads, who speaks up for his rights—he opens with his maddening attempt to negotiate for a living wage—and who is not beneath writing about it.

What impressed Bouton about *The Long Season* were "the quote marks on the page. I got excited. It wasn't a writer talking about these guys. They were talking among themselves." When he came to write

Ball Four, he decided, "I'm going to do the same thing." Bouton added a sense of the absurd, a deep-seated iconoclasm, and an unrelenting commitment not to let the parsimonious and cruelly indifferent owners off the hook. He proposed that the tough, tobacco-spewing brute, all brawn and no brains, is in actuality a sad victim of management. Despite the media attention and high salaries for the elite, no athlete is one of the chosen, but more often than not only half a man, one who founders once his body succumbs to time.

Go back in time. It's 1951. We are in the fourth grade and have been given the afternoon off from school, and so we find ourselves five blocks from home at Yankee Stadium in the upper deck in deep right field. There is only one baseball player within our vision. He's young, he doesn't seem much older than us. He's blond, muscular, and unconflicted. He's chewing bubble gum and he's crouched in his stance, concentrating hard while forming perfect round bubbles.

"He looks like he's sitting on the toilet," observes my friend Byrna matter-of-factly.

Mickey Mantle is nineteen and we're nine. He's the man we, if we dare hope, two little dark-haired Jewish girls from the Bronx in plaid skirts and white blouses with shiny-red viscose ties, want to grow up and marry. The ironies of Jim Bouton would not have appealed to us at all. Not then. Not until we grew up.

I was twenty when twenty-three-year-old Jim Bouton brought his flattop to the Bronx in 1962. While on his high school team, "Warmup" Bouton had wanted only to get called from the bullpen and into a game. Maybe he could play college baseball. And now he was a Yankee!

He had always loved the game, from childhood days as a New York Giants fan. The family moved to the Midwest, but Bouton remained loyal to his team. Once in Chicago, he hung over the visiting Giants' dugout, his legs held by his brother Bob while he begged Alvin Dark for an autograph. "Take a hike, son, take a hike," Dark told young Bouton. That line was at once adopted as the Bouton family put-down.

But far from having had his feelings hurt, Jim Bouton was ecstatic: "We had an actual quote from a major league baseball player," he remembers. "Sure, he was telling us to bug off, but he told us to bug off."

One day during that same season I fell for Mickey Mantle, the Bouton boys, clutching their scorecard outside the ballpark, got the signatures of Giants Willie Mays and Alvin Dark and Eddie Stanky and Larry Jansen. And Bob said, "Boy, wouldn't it be great to be a famous baseball player? People would want your autograph. What would you sign your name like?"

Jim looked down at the scorecard, at the poor penmanship of the Giants, and concluded, "Well, if you were a major leaguer, you'd have to scribble your name because you'd be in a hurry all the time."

And so Jim Bouton scrawled his name on the scorecard, the twelve-year-old scribble side by side with all the old Giant greats. On that day, he wasn't an iconoclast, but a fan, like any kid.

Eleven years later, a New York ballplayer himself, he was tickled to be a teammate of Mickey Mantle and Whitey Ford. He walked around with a silly grin on his face. Back home, he delighted his folks with quotes—what "Ellie" said in the clubhouse, what "Mickey" said. He related that after his first big-league win, an 8–0 victory over the Washington Senators, "Mickey" had laid down a path of towels leading to Bouton's locker. He thought, "I don't know how long I'll stay in the big leagues, but how ever long I'm here it's great, it's a bonus, more than I expected. This is fun and I'll try to make the most out of it." From the beginning, he knew there was a world outside baseball that sooner rather than later would claim him. It was his acceptance of this truth that gave him the perspective to see baseball for what it was.

It wasn't long before irony overtook him, and Jim Bouton, promising Yankee pitcher, set his foot on the path to becoming Jim Bouton, outcast. It began innocently. One day he had been joking around when Roger Maris turned and glared and said, "You got a ball game today!" Bouton started to see the Yankee heroes as men of flesh and blood. Joe Pepitone refuses to take the field if his uniform isn't skin-tight. Whitey Ford finds unique ways to doctor the ball while Yogi Berra likes to call fastballs because they're easier to catch. Hung over, Mantle hits a home run only to squint up at the stands and say, "Those people don't know how tough that really was." Like players around the league, his teammates are expert Peeping Toms, always in quest of "beaver" and finding unique ways of looking up the skirts of the women sitting in the stands. Mickey Mantle no less than lesser men.

The kid whom Alvin Dark told to "take a hike" now watched as Mantle pushed aside the kids asking for his autograph, even almost closing a bus window on some of them. On the other hand, Bouton took pleasure in signing autographs. He even admits to hanging around the hotel lobby, hoping people would come over and ask for his signature.

To his teammates, writers were "a necessary evil," and they would talk only to those who would write good things about them. "Watch out for those writers, especially that fucking Leonard Shecter," Bouton was warned about his future collaborator on *Ball Four*. Meanwhile a bunker mentality reigned with Ralph Houk getting the team together and inspiring them to play well "because the writers don't want us to win." Bouton tells this story with incredulity because "this was the early sixties when the Yankees were winning every year!" Bouton enjoyed talking to writers. Before one World Series game, he did his imitation of Frank Fontaine's "Crazy Guggenheim," (a weird-voiced bar character on *The Jackie Gleason Show*), infuriating Moose Skowron and John Blanchard, who belonged to the old school. Already he knew he was not to make a career out of baseball; he would never be a coach. He saw no reason not to combine hard work and fun.

The men with whom he played, he tells me, were people who had been told they were special since the third grade. Their lives had been defined by their learning to perform one specific task well, and in this effort they had been isolated by their community and family. They grew up with a simplistic view of the world. They gravitated to the quick slogan, becoming victims of the right wing, which mindlessly equates sports with chauvinism. The more they relied on one narrow skill, the more terrified they became of what would happen if they lost it. Toward the end of their careers they really got scared because they hadn't prepared to do anything else. The sight of Bouton reading a book caused them to doubt themselves, these people who spent their whole lives sharpening skills that had no marketability once they turned thirty-five. We are light-years from the athlete as hero.

Meanwhile something fateful was happening. Jim Bouton was becoming a clubhouse lawyer. He was amazed one day when Clete Boyer took a poll among the players to determine what they thought was a fair minimum salary and the answers ranged from $7,000 to $12,000.

"Twenty-five thousand!" piped up Jim Bouton.

"For crying out loud, what are you talking about?" he was scolded.

"Hey, everybody in this room has a Ph.D. in hitting or pitching," said Bouton. "What's that worth? We're the top six hundred in the world at what we do. In an industry that makes millions of dollars. And we have to sign whatever contract they give us? That's insane. We should be making twenty-five thousand dollars minimum and go up from there!"

At that instant, Bouton became a "flake" and, worse, a trouble-maker. Shunned by his Yankee teammates, he was left standing alone in hotel lobbies while the other players drifted off to dinner. As he says in his second book, *I'm Glad You Didn't Take It Personally*, he became a "deviant."

But while his relationship with his teammates became strained, he remained on their side. Ownership was the player's enemy. Even Mantle is a victim. He is given a vitamin shot by a Yankee doctor with an unsterile needle and winds up with a bleeding abscess on his hip. Johnny Keane, Yankee manager, pressures Mantle into playing when he's hurt. The players know the rule: Keep your mouth shut.

Bouton had two splendid seasons with the Yankees. In 1963, he won 21 games while losing only 7, with an ERA of 2.53. He earned $10,000 that year and had to hold out two weeks to get a tiny raise. He proved he was underpaid when he went 18-13 in 1964, with an ERA of 3.02. He thinks he did his best postseason pitching in the

1963 World Series against the Dodgers, when he lost his only start, 1–0 to Don Drysdale, yielding only a first-inning run and 4 hits in seven strong innings. But in 1964, more experienced, he won both of his starts against the Cardinals and posted a brilliant 1.56 ERA. A fierce competitor, he was known as "Bulldog."

Then in 1965 came a sore arm, and the fastball was gone, and unless you win, which he did only nine times in the next four seasons, the intense windup where his cap falls off with every pitch—the Jim Bouton trademark—is no longer so charming. He was sold after the 1968 season, not because he was a clubhouse lawyer, he acknowledges, but because he wasn't pitching well enough.

Jim Bouton sat in the bullpen in 1969, warming up for the-once-and-not-to-be-future-expansion-team the Seattle Pilots, Vancouver in the minor leagues, and finally with the Houston Astros, a pennant contender. He foundered on the Pilots, briefly being demoted to Vancouver. He could not gain a hearing either from Joe Schultz, whose managing amounted to telling his players to "Get that old Budweiser," or pitching coach Sal Maglie. Bouton wanted to learn to survive on only one pitch, a newly developed knuckleball, as quixotic as that seems. "But," he writes, "I was asking to do something unorthodox, and unorthodoxy does in baseball what heresy does in the priesthood."

To his new teammates, he was a mystery. He signed petitions and spoke out against the Vietnam War. He was a strong union supporter in the locker room. He was also a guy who sat in the back of the bus reading, a threat to those who never read, and for whom books represented a world to which they had no access. As on the Yankees, his politics frightened his teammates. After he called Billy Graham a "dangerous character," no one in the bullpen would speak to him for three days.

By day he took notes, diligently reading them into a tape recorder each night. When he couldn't take notes, as at a clubhouse meeting, afterward he'd race to the bathroom, close the stall, and sit on the seat writing down what had been said. Later people would accuse him of making some of it up. "Who could have created Joe Schultz?" Bouton laughs. "You couldn't dream up those guys."

Bouton believes the veracity of *Ball Four* would have suffered had he been a star rather than a reliever who won only two games and saved two others all season. "If I were a publisher," Bouton insists, "and you asked, 'Would you like a book by a major star or a third-string catcher?' I'd say give me the book by the third-string catcher. He's the guy who's going to tell me what I need to know.

That's where the irony's going to come; that's where a book with real meat is likely to be." During that season in which Bouton wrote *Ball Four*, his insignificant role in the pen permitted him to be a writer first and a player second.

And so Bouton wrote his ground-breaking book, which detailed his 1969 season and looked back on his years with the Yankees. Unself-consciously, armed by indignation at how the Yankee management had treated him and the other players, he began by not viewing the status quo as sacrosanct. From inside, he observes. First he laughs. He shows who these guys really are—not "heroes" but men who are more flawed than us because they are unaware of their flaws. He writes of their faults, their quirks, their sins. He discusses their sexual antics. He reveals that to be up for a game, some players become addicted to "greenies" and nobody minds. At times, he turns dead serious.

By today's standards of exposé, his revelations have been supplanted by far more lurid accounts of the night lives of athletes. Bouton contends that he told only about 25 percent of the sexual exploits to which he was witness. Asked about the scene in *Bull Durham* in which a player makes love in the locker room before a minor league game, Bouton swears that not only was that realistic, but that he had seen sexual intercourse in the locker room *during a game*, in the major leagues.

So Bouton didn't alienate the powers that be by "telling all" or by depicting the adolescent escapades of his teammates, and so robbing us of our heroes, but by exposing what he knew firsthand about the business of baseball. With a light but firm hand, he revealed, indubitably, how the owners care about nothing but their profits. Callously they trade loyal players; ruthlessly they keep salaries of the majority indecently low; and neither the mental nor physical well-being of the players is of much concern to them. Bouton told how hard it was for a player to make a living. He described contract negotiations, showing how little leverage players have. He recalled how the Yankees' Dan Topping haggled with him over an extra $500 a year. He broke the rule by which players were forbidden to tell each other their salaries, lest they band together and suggest parity.

His book would alienate the sportswriting establishment, led by Dick Young, who called him a "social leper" and then told Bouton he was glad he "didn't take it personally." He broke the sportswriter's unwritten rule not to write about what they really saw, a rule honored since the day Babe Ruth revealed himself naked in a hotel while in pursuit of a woman and the sportswriters "did not see it," to the nights Mantle, Martin, and Ford painted the town red. Of course, the sportswriters were angry that Bouton had done what they knew they should have been doing. And so the best reviews came from serious authors such as Roger Angell, Wilfred Sheed, and David Halberstam, who equated Bouton's revelations with Sy Hersh's breaking the story of the My Lai massacre.

Bouton had known that the owners and writers would find *Ball Four* anathema, but he was surprised that the players did not respond more positively. He thought they would say, "Hey, this is our story, Jim's telling what it's really like, how the owners take advantage of us, how they push us around, how they abuse us. It's about time somebody did that." But they didn't. Instead they accused him of violating their privacy and tarnishing their image. "Jim who?" Mantle responded when he was questioned about the book. To this day he has not spoken to Bouton. What also annoyed them was that it wasn't a star who had written *Ball Four*, someone, by their logic, whose athletic prowess permitted his telling this story. Instead the author who took us behind the scenes was a peripheral relief pitcher whose days in the game were numbered. "Fuck you, Shakespeare!" Pete Rose yelled out to the mound one day.

No matter, Bouton remained the advocate of the ordinary ballplayer. As Marlon Brando says in *On the Waterfront* after speaking out against the bosses on behalf of unappreciative dockworkers, "I'm glad for what I did." Bouton says, "I wanted to nail those guys because they really stole money from the players and they owe that money to the players and the players are entitled to it as old-timers and they should get it from the owners." He reveals his fantasy: "Mickey Mantle and Warren Spahn and Carl Yastrzemski and Ted Williams form a picket line around a baseball stadium on opening day, telling fans they shouldn't cross the line until the owners today pay those old-timers what they were worth." Is it any wonder that Bouton alone among retired Yankees is not invited back for Oldtimer's Day?

Bouton's major league career seemed over after the 1970 season, in which he was 4-6 with a 5.42 ERA for the Astros. He wrote his second book, served as a McGovern delegate at the Democratic National Convention, and even acted in a 1973 Robert Altman movie, *The Long Goodbye*, playing the playboy killer, and in an ill-fated semifictional CBS sitcom, *Ball Four*, which he cowrote. He tried his hand as a TV sportscaster and was as much an irritant to television management as he'd been to baseball management. Here was a guy who refused to read all the scores. He produced sports stories about ordinary people, while he chastized the TV stations that would not cover the real sports news because they were in partnership with professional sports. When he said just what he thought of Evel Knievel's jump over the Snake River, for which ABC, the station for which he was working, had bought the rights, he was fired. He was the kind of sportscaster who encouraged the viewers to play sports themselves rather than watch it. Pass on the "junk" that starts at noon and come back at six for the actual game, he advised on Super Bowl Sunday, prompting CBS to ax him.

Bouton's heart wasn't in reporting sports, but in participating in them. So he launched a comeback with the renegade Portland Mavericks, and in 1978, after having won 13 games in half a season with Savannah, he returned to the majors with the Atlanta Braves. The sportswriters called it a publicity stunt. They were wrong. He had come back to play the game he loved. "I didn't want the comfort of going to bed at night and saying I didn't pitch well today, but it'll make a good book. I wanted to lay myself on the line and make it or not make it. I didn't want to have anything in the wings. I wanted to fully experience the joy or the sorrow of whatever was going to happen there."

He could have returned to the majors for the 1979 season because he pitched creditably during that comeback year at age thirty-nine, but he didn't. There was a divorce and what he calls, quaintly, his "midlife crisis." He had proven his point. But he wished the media had given him credit for working hard and accomplishing something no one had done before. He had hoped to be given credit for the process, the effort, his having climbed a veritable Jacob's ladder. There seemed little point in continuing after that, and he retired. "Once you've climbed the mountain and you get to the top," Bouton speculates today, "why would you want to stay there? You get down and you move on."

At fifteen, Jim Bouton used to hand out cards for his lawn-mowing business. Today, he runs a successful business that offers personalized baseball cards. He is also copartner in Big League Chew, shredded bubble gum that looks like tobacco and is sold in a pouch. He paints, does stain-glass work, gives motivational speeches. He also pitches for the semiprofessional Teaneck Merchants, brandishing— what else?—the knuckleball. "I hold my own," he says, smiling. "Sometimes they kick my ass and sometimes I win. Just like before."

If Jim Bouton remains only a cult figure, his long-overdue perceptions the province of a happy few, it is because sports remains in our culture one of the last bastions of provinciality, of narrow-mindedness and of exploitation. If you agree with Bouton, you must begrudgingly concede that there may be no such thing as a hero, that ballplayers, however glorious they seem on the field and however worthy they are of our applause, may not be such terrific people. I think Jim Bouton appeals to our increasing need to speak out for ourselves, not to conform, and to defy complacency by rebelling. He suggests that we raise our voices in protest against unfairness, injustice, and iniquity. He encourages us to take risks. He teaches us to trust ourselves. He's an original, this clubhouse lawyer, a thorn in the side of the money-men, a Maverick, a misfit reading a book in the back of the bus.

Joan Mellen is the author of *Bob Knight: His Own Man* and nine other books. "Workin' on the Chaney Gang" was voted one of the best sports stories of 1987 by the *Sporting News.*

GEORGE
KIMBALL
on

BILL LEE

Bill Lee once supposed that a highly disciplined Buddhist monk could probably make a baseball disappear, only to materialize again in the catcher's mitt.

"That," he said, grinning, "is my idea of a relief pitcher."

He wasn't the first product of a sixties education to grow a beard and get caught up in politics, but he was surely the first major league baseball player to visit mainland China.

When he returned from that trip (he was part of a delegation of radical American athletes), he thoughtfully brought me a pack of "Phoenix" cigarettes.

"These are the cigarettes that killed Chou En-Lai," he said as he handed them over.

He wasn't the first ballplayer to be influenced by rock and roll, but after Warren Zevon wrote "The Ballad of Bill Lee" he was the first to have a rock song recorded about him since Mickey Mantle and Willie Mays in the early fifties.

Indeed he was probably the first big-leaguer to come clean about smoking marijuana, though after a careful review of the interviewer's tape he realized he'd only said he "used" the stuff. So he backtracked and claimed that what he really meant to say was that he sprinkled pot on his buckwheat cakes each morning. When then-commissioner Bowie Kuhn insisted on pursuing the matter, Lee, armed with a battery of lawyers, went right to the mat with him—and in a compromise settlement finally agreed to a $250 fine provided he could

CULT BASEBALL PLAYERS

Courtesy Boston Red Sox   Courtesy Montreal Expos

specify the donee. He wrote the check out to an obscure Indian mission in Alaska.

It was a teammate named John Kennedy who dubbed him "Spaceman," though he was very much of this earth. Never before or since has a baseball player so captured the essence of his fandom as did Lee, who fitted in with the burgeoning mobs of Cambridge students, Back Bay hippies, and the radical subculture that adopted Fenway Park in the early 1970s. The Red Sox management tried for the longest time to muzzle his antics, fearful that he might somehow offend the team's clientele, but Lee had long since perceived what it would take the others a full decade to figure out: The very people to whom he was playing *were* the Red Sox's new clientele.

The fans loved him because he was different, and sportswriters loved him because he was quotable. His teammates tolerated him because he won (though when the day came that he no longer did, he predicted long ago, "I'll wind up facedown in the Charles River.")

Baseball people, who are always looking for easy answers, decided that it was probably because he was left-handed and therefore weird. Lee himself thought about that more than once: "If the right side of the brain controls the left side of the body," he proposed, "and the left side of the brain controls the right side of the body, then that means left-handers are the only ones in their right minds."

I can offer personal testimony on the matter of Bill Lee and the

Work Ethic. The countercultural *Boston Phoenix* for which I was writing hired Spaceman to cover the 1977 World Series. The idea was supposed to be that I would record his thoughts and impressions, but after several days of carousing in New York and a night at the Eliot Lounge, neither of us was in much shape by the time we got to the newspaper offices. I woke up the next morning in a panic, with less than an hour and a half remaining before both pieces were to be filed, only to discover two stories neatly stacked on my desk. Lee had written not only his own column but mine as well.

It has been twelve years since Lee staged his one-day strike, a measure taken in protest of the Red Sox's trade of his friend Bernie Carbo to Cleveland. (When he returned, they fined him a day's pay, or $533 in 1978 dollars; Lee asked if they wouldn't triple the fine and give him the rest of the weekend off.) Lee's explanation of the walkout: "They keep saying we're all supposed to be a family here. If you're a family, you don't send your children to Cleveland."

By the end of the year they'd had enough, the manager Lee had dubbed "The Gerbil" and the rest of them. They traded him to Montreal for an obscure utility infielder and figured they'd heard the last of him. On an opening day ten years later Bill Lee walked into Fenway Park in civilian clothes, and from the moment the first person recognized him the ovation built up as it swept the stands, and soon he was doing curtain calls from his seat in right field. He was like the Pied Piper: he could still have walked out of the park had he a mind to, and taken 30,000 people with him.

He won 17 games three years in a row, and later, when his arm was truly gone, won 16 for Montreal on guile alone. His lifetime record against the despised Yankees was bettered by only two men in history: Babe Ruth and the Chicago Black Sox's Dickie Kerr, and Kerr, pointed out Lee, may have been the greatest pitcher of all time: "Had to be. He won two World Series games when eight guys on his team were trying to lose."

He even made one All-Star team, in 1973, an occasion that brought him face-to-face with his first big-league manager, Dick Williams. Williams convened his pitching staff and prefaced his remarks by supposing that a few of them might have been used in the previous day or two and be a bit arm-weary. "Any of you think you can't get these guys out?" He asked. Lee slowly raised his hand.

"You pitch Sunday? Or Monday?" asked Williams.

"Neither," replied Lee. "You asked if we were sure we could get these guys out. I'm not sure I can get any of them out."

The All-Star game and the '75 Series against the Reds were,

claimed Lee, not nearly as emotional as pitching in the College World Series: "There we weren't playing for money. We got Mickey Mouse watches that ran backwards."

When the Red Sox abandoned their traditional blue cap in favor of a two-toned red model with a blue bill, Lee registered his disgust by adding a beanie propellor before he wore the new cap onto the field for the first time.

Lee was also, briefly if unsurprisingly, baseball's first known convert to Pyramid Power. It didn't exactly require a quantum leap for the rebellious Yossarian who complained about designated hitters and artificial turf to turn it up a notch and start making public statements about "planet-polluting owners" or, in the case of the hated Yankees, "Billy Martin's brownshirts."

The latter came after one of those classic New York–Boston free-for-alls in which Graig Nettles separated Lee's left shoulder and nearly ended his career. The brawl had its genesis in a home-plate collision between Lou Piniella and Sox catcher Carlton Fisk and quickly spread throughout Yankee Stadium.

Much later that night, once Lee had returned from the hospital, the Spaceman, pitching coach Stan Williams, and I were looking for a cure in a mid-Manhattan saloon when Piniella chanced in alone. He apologized profusely, bought a round or two, and disappeared into the evening. I remarked that the Yankee outfielder had seemed genuinely contrite about the whole affair.

"What else was he going to do?" Lee said, laughing. "This time there's three of us and one of him."

Actually, Lee had good reason for avoiding baseball fights. Prior to his conversion to pacifism he had staged a one-punch KO of Elisio Rodriguez when the catcher had charged the mound during a Puerto Rican winter league game in 1970.

Only in the next day's papers did he learn that he had knocked out a legendary Puerto Rican golden-gloves champion. On his team's next road trip, he was jumped by a whole army of Rodriguez cousins and brothers who saved face by bashing Lee's in. "The set of teeth I got was better looking than my old ones anyway," he said later, shrugging off the incident.

Lee was well on his way to winning the seventh game of the 1975 World Series when he threw his infamous "Leephus" pitch—a tantalizing, slow curve—to Tony Perez, who slammed it over the left-field wall to pave the way for Cincinnati's comeback victory. Lee refused to be daunted about his choice of weaponry ("I lived by that pitch, and now I died by it"), but noting that Reds manager Sparky

Anderson had somewhat prematurely nominated *his* hurler Don Gullett for the Hall of Fame as well as to pitch the seventh game, he remarked cheerfully that "Gullett's going to the Hall of Fame, but I'm going to the Eliot Lounge," a hip watering hole a few blocks from Fenway Park.

He hadn't done much to endear himself to hidebound South Boston conservatives with his remark that "Judge Garrity's the only man in this town with any guts," a reference to the federal judge who had ordered and implemented busing as a solution to the de facto segregation of Boston's public schools.

In the wake of that outcry, in fact, Lee received a long, vituperative, and rambling letter from arch-conservative Boston city councillor Albert (Dapper) O'Neil, which concluded with the politician's observation that "on my worst day I could still outpitch you."

Lee replied with a letter of his own: "Dear Councillor O'Neil," it began. "I think you should be made aware that some idiot has gotten hold of your stationery. . . ."

No Nukes. The Equal Rights Amendment. He was for them—or against them—all. Long before it became fashionable, he made it a practice to report for work by jogging the eight miles to Fenway Park from his home in suburban Belmont. Later, in his Montreal incarnation, he wound up on the disabled list when a startled cat interrupted one of his training runs. When the cat leapt in front of Lee, Spaceman leapt in front of a taxi.

When manager Darrell Johnson, using a rainout as a pretext, juggled the Sox's World Series pitching rotation and pushed Lee back to Game Seven, Spaceman explained, "That's what Zeus did when he raped Europa. He asked the sun god Apollo to stay away for a few days."

He wasn't—not even close—the first cerebral ballplayer, but he must certainly have been the first to expound at length on the Coriolis effect as it pertains to the thrown baseball—in a *Playboy* interview:

"I have a mediolateral synapse of the humerus, a culmination of wrist flexation and pronation which causes the ball to use Newton's Law instead of trying to be Nolan Ryan and oppose Newton's Law. He tried to make the ball go up in a world that is basically going down. I just let gravity help my ball and make it sink; that's because of the pronation. You've got all these muscles in your back and in the shoulder. The summation of those forces with the pronation causes the ball to spin away from right-handed batters and gives them the illusion that it's a good pitch to hit, but at the last minute it's not. It's a kind of entrapment. . . ."

CULT BASEBALL PLAYERS

That was the theory, anyway. On another occasion Spaceman put it into even better perspective.

"If Nolan is the 'Ryan Express,' " he said, laughing, "I guess I'm the Marrakesh Express."

His departure from the major leagues came in 1982. In an episode reminiscent of the Carbo incident, he became enraged when the Expos released his friend Rodney Scott. Lee tore off his uniform and spent the afternoon shooting pool in a Montreal saloon. When he returned to the ballpark the next day, his own release papers were waiting for him. He signed the forms "Bill Lee, Earth '82."

He had always proposed to disappear into the sunset and never be heard from again, but in 1988 he reappeared, this time as the presidential candidate of something called The Rhinoceros Party. His campaign slogan was "No Guns, No Butter." Outside the cheap seats at Fenway Park, he didn't get many votes at all. But those he still won, hands down.

Thirteen years ago, right after *Star Wars* had been issued, Lee and I agreed to serve as volunteers at a Halloween "Haunted House" to benefit the Boston Children's Museum. They dressed him up as Chewbacca and me as Darth Vader, and hundreds of kids passed through the place. Upon encountering us, it seemed as if every one of them would invariably go up and shake Chewy's paw and then try to kick Darth in the balls, or worse. I even got bruises on my forearms from where kids had whacked me with their laser sticks.

We were allowed to take a beer break after forty-five sweaty minutes or so, and Spaceman agreed to switch costumes for our second set. I still don't know how he did it, but not one of the little bastards laid a hand on Darth Vader the whole time Lee was wearing the black suit and Nazi helmet. I'd been hanging out with the guy for the better part of a decade, and I had always suspected there was some ephemeral magic to him. Now I knew it.

George Kimball is a sports columnist for the *Boston Herald*. He is the coauthor of *Sunday's Fools: Stomped, Tramped, Kicked and Chewed In the NFL* (with Tom Beer).

MARTY
SUTPHIN
on

TUG MCGRAW

Then the makers of that wonderful baseball film *Bull Durham* were dreaming up cult-hero names for their characters, they had to settle for Crash Davis, Nuke Laloosh, and such.

Not bad. But the greatest baseball name of all time had already been taken—immortalized on the real diamonds of The Show by a wondrously weird left-handed relief pitcher.

Tug McGraw. The Tugger.

If you could look up that name in the dictionary, the definition might read: left-handed reliever; animated; emotional; a flake.

But McGraw was not just a left-hander, he was a southpaw screwball specialist.

And not just any reliever, but a "closer," the game-saver of the bullpen.

Animated: Try bubbly bundle of energy. A windup toy that never ran down.

Emotional? He coined a battle cry that motivated a last-place team (and a city) to the World Series.

Flaky? Was his book, *Screwball*, named for his best pitch or himself?

It must have been ordained that McGraw would pick up the nickname "Tug" somewhere along the way. Frank Edwin, Jr., just wouldn't do. Actually, his aunt gave him the label within hours of his birth, as his mother nursed him. "What a little tugger," she observed. It stuck, and generations of baseball fans to come would be forever grateful to her.

Courtesy New York Mets

My love affair with McGraw began in 1969, the year that New York Mets manager Gil Hodges persuaded his struggling young pitcher to switch from starter to stopper.

I had grown up in New Jersey idolizing the Brooklyn Dodgers of the Reese-Reiser-Robinson era, but the Bums and I left that area for greener pastures about the same time. Fortunately I came back to New York in 1962, just in time for the birth of the Mets.

My old Dodger loyalties were rekindled in the Mets, and the fervor peaked in 1969 when that lovable band of irreverent young men moved from major league doormat to world champion.

In a 1977 *Harper's* article, "Tom Seaver's Farewell," a baseball fan named A. Bartlett Giamatti referred to that future Hall of Famer as "a man of such qualities of heart and mind and body that he transcends even the great and glorious game."

Seaver may well have been the heart, mind, and body of that amazing Mets team, but I believe Tug McGraw was its soul.

My children were eight, six, and four years old in 1969. What better way to introduce them to baseball than to take them to Shea Stadium to watch McGraw, truly an animated ambassador of the game.

Baseball was always exciting—and fun—when Tug was playing, from the time he dashed from dugout to pen to warm up, to the glorious moment when he would stride from the mound in triumph, thumping his glove against his thigh.

In between, he might dust his armpits with the rosin bag or stick out his tongue at a batter who had reached base. That may not seem like the stuff of legends, but it was enough to touch a young fan's heart.

By 1973, when McGraw convinced his struggling team and New York City that "You Gotta Believe," my kids were hooked—on Tug, the Mets, and baseball.

I remember one evening with my son Mike, high up in Shea's upper deck, with McGraw on the mound. Jerry Grote got hurt, and the Mets brought in their only other catcher, Duffy Dyer. I turned to Mike, who was a catcher at pre–Little League level, and told him as seriously as I could that he might have to play if Duffy got hurt, too.

Mike thought about that a while, studying the enormous stadium complex that enveloped us. Finally, he said, "How do I get to the field from here?"

Somehow, I'm sure Mike felt that, if Tug was pitching, he could catch. After all, wasn't the Tugger just a big kid himself?

But it was not only youngsters who identified with Tug. The rarity of McGraw gave him a unique relationship with fans of all ages.

"I did most of my growing up in front of the fans," Tug told me years later. "As a young player, much of what I was experiencing— all the things that were happening in the sixties—was played out in the arena. I carried all my experiences onto the field. All my reactions were on my sleeve. I shared all my feelings with the fans—joy, exuberance, and pain. It was part of growing up and learning how to cope."

It always seemed to me that McGraw was a natural crowd pleaser. He did what he did by nature, not by design. He didn't set out to put on a show, as some others have done. There was nothing phony about his enthusiasm, his emotion.

McGraw confirms that nearly all his mound antics were spontaneous: "I had to do things to release my nervous energy. I could become paralyzed by nervousness, so I would do something crazy to put things in perspective, to say, 'Hey, remember, this is supposed to be fun.' "

Once, needing one out to finish a tight game and feeling that tense feeling coming on, he remembered some friends in the stands, friends he had argued with the night before about whether a balk could be called with no one on base. In the middle of the next windup, McGraw "balked" wildly, falling to the ground in the process. No violation was called, and Tug assured the anxious trainer who rushed to the mound that he was okay. He then retired the batter, winning both the game and the argument with his pals.

"Fans did not have any trouble reading me," McGraw says. "My attitude was: This is a great life. I'm more than willing to share it with you."

Even on the road, Tug seldom got a bad time from the crowd. Once, he recalls, he expected the worst but was able to defuse the situation.

In a game in Los Angeles against the Dodgers, Tug had lost his cool and his concentration after a strategy move he disagreed with went sour, and in frustration he drilled the next batter, Bill Russell, precipitating a brawl.

McGraw knew he would be the villain on his next visit to Dodger Stadium, so he showed up for batting practice that day in full military fatigues, including helmet and flak jacket. Not to be outdone, Russell found a giant boxing glove somewhere and came out to challenge Tug. Then they both attacked a TV type who tried to interview them. The fans loved it, and there was no danger of Tug's being booed after that.

If the crowds loved McGraw, the feeling was mutual.

"When you need that extra," he once said, "you look up there [at the fans], and there it is. I just keep saying to them, 'Give it to me, give it to me.' "

McGraw was much more than showman or cheerleader, of course. He was a tremendous competitor who relished coming in with the game on the line. "Somedays you tame the tiger," he said, "and some days the tiger has you for lunch." On most days the tiger went hungry.

Dividing his colorful career almost evenly between the Mets (1965–74) and the Philadelphia Phillies (75–84), his record over twenty major league seasons was 96-92, with 179 saves—sixth all-time at his retirement—and 825 games pitched—ninth all-time. He held the National League record for career-innings pitched by a reliever (1,302), and the career-saves records for both ballclubs, 95 in Philadelphia and 84 in New York.

Oddly, McGraw wasn't used in the '69 World Series, as the Mets starters breezed to a five-game triumph over Baltimore. In the '73 Series against Oakland, he appeared in five games, winning one and striking out 14 in 13 innings as New York lost in seven games.

In 1980, McGraw was boss of the Phillies bullpen and pitched in four of the five games Philadelphia won to beat Houston in what, at that time, was viewed as baseball's best pennant playoff.

But records aside, it was McGraw's inspirational leadership that figured most prominently in spurring the '73 Mets and '80 Phillies to their World Series appearances.

Tug was not a practical joker or initiator of clubhouse pranks, like Seaver was. He says he wasn't a clubhouse leader either, in the formal sense of the word. But the others certainly got inspiration from his positive attitude.

McGraw on McGraw in the clubhouse: "In difficult times—and we had many in the early days on the Mets—they'd wonder, 'Doesn't anything bother him?' No matter how bad things got, my attitude was, 'It's great to be in the Bigs, and don't ever forget it.' "

It was the summer of '73 that marked the high point of my love affair with McGraw. The Mets seemed hopelessly sunk at the bottom of the NL East that August when Tug, who had been struggling, stirred the team and its fans with the rallying cry, "You Gotta Believe."

McGraw recalls the day the "YGB" fervor started, over lunch at his home with his wife and a friend. They suggested Tug's first step to get back on track was to believe in himself, and they sent him off to the park saying, "Remember, you've gotta believe."

"I kept repeating that to myself as I drove to Shea," McGraw says. "I started chanting it, like a mantra. By the time I got to the park I was really pumped up, a maniac. When I got out of the car, I screamed, 'You gotta believe,' to the fans in the parking lot. I screamed it at the security guard, and into the clubhouse."

As fate would have it, then Mets chairman M. Donald Grant chose that day to give a rare pep talk in the clubhouse. At one point Grant said, "You men have got to believe in yourselves." As if on cue, McGraw jumped up, yelling, "That's right, you gotta believe, right on, Mr. Grant."

Tug's exuberance almost did him in. Grant thought McGraw was mocking him, and it took some fast talking from the pitcher afterward to convince him otherwise.

The rest is history. The slogan was soon in daily headlines, on every fan's lips. It became almost a holy thing. Nuns held up "You Gotta Believe" signs at Shea. My kids designed YGB posters and composed "Amazing Mets" parodies to the tune of "Amazing Grace." And the Amazin's rallied to take the pennant with an 82-79 record, as McGraw caught fire down the stretch.

The most compelling image of those days was McGraw's hustling from mound to dugout after a victory or save, rhythmically pumping his glove against his right thigh—a big kid barely able to contain his emotion.

That glove-pounding McGraw signature developed in Triple A ball, in 1968, the day after Tug got married. He was a starter then, and he pitched a 2-hit shutout that day. After each inning, as he returned to the dugout, he would tip his cap to his bride in the stands. But all he got in return was a negative shaking of her head. Afterward she told him why: "You tipped your cap to a lot of women when you were single. I want a special sign." And so the glove routine was born.

What Mets fan could have known after the YGB season that just one year later, in one of many trades that would send the team's fortunes plummeting, The Tugger would be sent to the Phillies?

Soon after arriving in Philadelphia in 1975, McGraw underwent surgery to remove a benign tumor on his back. Then, in typical Tug fashion, the fiery lefty bounced back, won the hearts of a new team and city, and wound up pitching in five more playoffs and one more World Series.

The 1980 season was inspiration time again for Tug. He came off the disabled list July 17 and allowed only 3 earned runs in more than 50 innings the rest of the way. He appeared in 12 of the Phils' final 15 games that year, including all 5 in the NLCS against Houston and 4 of 6 in the Series win over Kansas City. He had 4 postseason saves and was on the mound for the final outs of both the League Championship and World Series.

A Philadelphia tugboat company immediately renamed one of its crafts the "Tug McGraw," because "no one works harder."

A major league pitcher needs more than a hard-work ethic, however, and McGraw had quite an assortment of pitches. In addition to his specialty, the biting scroogie, he had a curve, a slider, and several fastballs. There was his "Peggy Lee fastball." He says that when he threw that one, "I took something off it and the hitter said, 'Is that all there is?' " Then there was his Cutty Sark fastball, which sailed, and his John Jameson fastball, which was straight, "like Irish whiskey should be."

Tug was asked after the 1980 World Series if relief pitching wasn't mostly mental. Not so, answered McGraw. "If that was the case, I'd be in the trainer's room soaking my head in ice. I've never been paid a dime for my brains."

Such clubhouse quips and quotes always made McGraw a favorite of sportswriters and fans. Question: "What's the difference between grass and artificial turf, Tug?" McGraw: "I don't know; I never smoked artificial turf." Question: "What will you do with your new raise, Tug?" McGraw: "Ninety percent I'll spend on good times, women, and Irish whiskey. The other ten percent I'll probably waste." Question: "How did you meet your wife, Tug?" McGraw: "I met my wife in a New York bar. We had a lot in common. We were both from California and we were both drunk."

But for me, his most endearing quality was his attitude between the lines—his contagious enthusiasm for the game.

Where did that come from? I asked him.

"In the beginning, every time they put the ball in my hand, it was fun and exciting. I never knew what was going to happen. Later, as I developed pitches and strategies, it was just as much fun anticipating what would happen and seeing how it turned out. They say that hindsight is always best, but nothing can replace the moment.

"In the sixties, I was in the Marine Corps Reserve, training for riot duty. My brothers were in peace and freedom movements. There were lots of tensions off the field. The ballpark was the one place where everything made sense. You could share the electricity and feelings that developed. Everyone in the park, players and fans, sharing the same feeling. To be one of the athletes who was able to do that—share those feelings with the fans—was the greatest."

McGraw's enjoyment and passion for the game was as evident in his last-place days as it was when he struck out Willie Wilson with the bases loaded in the ninth inning to save the final game of the 1980 World Series.

After that high moment, Phillies president Bill Giles said, "There are only two players about whom I could say, 'Gee, I love that guy.' One was Pete Rose. The other was Tug."

When he hung up his spikes on February 14, 1985, McGraw said, "Maybe it's appropriate that I announce my retirement from the playing field on Valentine's Day. I've had a love affair with baseball. . . . The game stole my heart and I was never a jilted suitor."

Legions of baseball fans feel the same way about Tug McGraw.

Marty Sutphin is a supervising editor with the Associated Press.

JOE
MANTEGNA
on

ERNIE BANKS

"Let's play two today!" *That* seemed to be Ernie Banks's answer to everything.

Among young boys growing up in Chicago during the fifties, Ernie Banks idolization was a common malady. At that point, the Cubs' last pennant, in 1945, didn't seem so long ago, and the flame of hope burned strongly that with the slim, young, homer-hitting shortstop leading the way, our beloved team would soon be world champions again. Needless to say, we kept waiting. Yet, despite all those traumatic ninth-inning defeats, the endless losing streaks that saw the Cubs tumble down the standings and out of pennant races, and the years of frustration, we continued to come out to Wrigley in droves. Ernie was mostly responsible for that. While we watched this graceful player with the strong wrists and confident smile put up record-breaking numbers, we also noticed that he never complained about his team's bad luck or bad talent, never stopped playing the game with joy, never stopped giving his all, never lost his proud demeanor, and never acted like anything but a winner. He was the symbol of the Cub fan's undiminishing resilience. If he could be happy to come to the park each afternoon, then so could we.

But what was the magic of number 14? Of Mr. Nice Guy, Mr. Cub, Mr. "How bad can life be as long as there is beautiful Wrigley Field"? What was it that caused things like the Chicago City council to take a vote as to whether a statue of Ernie Banks would be more appropriate for Daley Plaza than the Picasso "bird" that would eventually nest there?

In retrospect, I clearly know what it was. Ernie Banks truly was a hero. In every sense of the word. And the particular statistics that made him one won't necessarily appear in a record book; nor did they have much to do with getting him elected to the Hall of Fame.

What stats? I submit: Not once did Ernie Banks get thrown out of a game. Not once did Ernie Banks demand a trade in order to make more money or play on a pennant contender. Not once did Ernie Banks criticize his manager, his owner, or his teammates in the press. These may not seem like very interesting stats, except when you weigh them against today's supposed heroes. In our era of bad boys and brat packs, of drug tests and fisticuffs (even among players on the same team!), it's reassuring to find that rare figure who stands out because he *didn't* throw tantrums, *didn't* get into fights or question calls, and *didn't* surround himself with the hoopla and controversy so common among today's high-paid and high-profile baseball celebrities.

I recall one game in the sixties, when Ernie, by then an All-Star first baseman, had hit a couple of homers against the Giants. In his third time at bat, he caught a fastball in the ribs. The crowd went nuts, the team went nuts, *everyone* went nuts but Ernie. He got to his feet and trotted down to first. He subsequently was out for a week due to the injury. A month or so later in San Francisco, facing the same pitcher, Ernie again had a big day and once again got dusted with a fastball. I'll never forget that painful look he directed toward the mound, not expressing anger but rather disappointment at why someone would try to hurt him for just doing that thing he loved to do so much: play great baseball. Ron Santo expressed all our feelings when *he* charged out of the dugout for the mound, not willing to turn the other cheek, as Ernie so often and gracefully did. As a boy, Ernie was a role model I was fortunate to have. As a father, I can only hope for such role models in my child's life.

Suddenly Ernie Banks had been playing sixteen years and it was 1969, an exciting year for both me and the Cubs. I was in Chicago doing my first professional play, *Hair*, the love-rock musical, and the Cubs were on top of the National League, rolling unheeded toward their first pennant in almost twenty-five years. As our costuming in the show was very free-form, I often wore a tie-dyed Ernie Banks T-shirt in the second act. One evening the stage manager informed me that Ernie Banks was in the audience. I was more nervous that performance than on opening night. At the curtain call I boldly walked to the front of the stage and asked Ernie to stand and take a bow. The roar of love and appreciation that crowd gave him warmed me as no applause I've ever gotten for myself, then and since. As a return gesture, he invited me to be his guest at the ballpark the next day, so I had the additional thrill of spending an afternoon in the clubhouse and dugout of Wrigley Field with my childhood hero. I'm sure I still hold the record for Cub dugout visitor with the longest hair.

The pain of the ultimate collapse of the '69 Cubs passed, but no Cub fan was ever really the same after that. I think it was partly because we all realized that it was probably Ernie's last chance for a World Series ring. We were already looking back at his tremendous career, as if it were over. One could only appreciate how good Ernie was by realizing how mediocre most of the Cub teams he played on were. How good would Mantle or Aaron or Clemente have been if opposing pitchers were able to pitch around them for most of their careers? Yet Banks won two MVPs with awful Cub teams and hit over 500 homers playing, at least until the arrival of Billy Williams and Ron Santo, on teams on which he was the only threat in the lineup.

The seventies started, my career was beginning, and Ernie's was ending. In 1971, after nineteen years in the big leagues—all with the Cubs—Ernie hung up his glove. In 1977, I had the pleasure to co-author a play called *Bleacher Bums*, which takes place at Wrigley during a Cubs-Cardinals game. At the play's conclusion, one of the characters recounts his version of the ideal ending to a mythical World Series. It also happens to be mine:

> If you're smart, tomorrow, you'll bet on the Cubs. 'Cause to-morrow they're gonna win. 'Cause they're mad now. And they're not only gonna win tomorrow, they're gonna win the rest of this series, and then they're gonna pull three games out in Montreal, and then Frisco. And Reuschel's gonna be a 20-game winner. And so is his brother. And Sutter won't lose a game in relief. Do you believe it? His earned run average is gonna be .00000001. And they're gonna take the pennant! And then at the end of the season, guess what? The Sox win, too! Can you see it, Marv? They're gonna call it "The 50¢ Series" because that's what the El costs to go back and forth between here and Comiskey. And they're gonna go down to seven games, Marv. And in the seventh game they're all tied up and it turns into a pitchers' duel. And they go into the twenty-third inning and you know what happens? They bring *Ernie Banks* out of retirement and he hits a home run right into my lap and they win!"

Ah, if only all dreams come true. In 1984, the Cubs once again knocked on destiny's door. Coincidentally, I was again in a Broadway play, doing a role that would win me a Tony award, so I began to think important years for me and the Cubs were unavoidably linked. They won their division. Chicago went berserk, and the highlight was when the Cubs honorally activated Ernie so they could bring him along for the inevitable Series against the Detroit Tigers. All that remained in their way was the San Diego Padres. The Padres? Forget it, it was going to happen, Ernie would finally get his ring, and the world would be right again. Well, you know the rest. The Cubs blew it. On the night they lost it, I wore a Cubs hat during the curtain call of the play I was in—a weak gesture, but a proud one.

Until the unexpected emergence of the 1989 Cubs, the odds of Ernie's getting that World Series ring seemed mighty slim. But as far as I'm concerned, a ring on every one of his fingers could not raise his esteem in my eyes and those of countless others. And not just because of his marvelous exploits as a player, as those are well recorded for all to admire. Ernie's a winner because of the man he is. An eternal optimist in an increasingly pessimistic world may seem corny, but I'll take it. Thanks for being my hero, Ernie. Not just to the boy I was, but to the boy-in-the-man I am. In my mind and heart, you've already hit that Series-ending homer.

Joe Mantegna is an actor whose stage credits include *Glengarry Glen Ross*, for which he received a Tony, and *Speed-the-Plow*, and film credits include *House of Games* and *Things Change*. He is the coauthor of the play *Bleacher Bums*.

JEAN SHEPHERD on
ZEKE BONURA

These days, I must admit, I'm getting bored with the endless baseball "Memories" that are popping up continually in the sleeker magazines. Crammed in with reviews of obscure French movies and countless four-color ads featuring angry, hawk-faced, blond women wearing six-hundred-dollar cashmere sweaters, these Proustian memoirs are mostly of a piece. They are usually written about the old Brooklyn Dodgers, occasionally the New York Giants, and more rarely the Yankees of the Roger Maris Age. Thus, these teams have become the official literary-memory teams of America. I've even spent some cocktail-party time with these writers and have found that if you try to entertain them with your memories of, let us say, the Cleveland Indians or the Cincinnati Reds, their eyes glaze over and they begin muttering about Carl Furillo or Gil Hodges. The only thing to do is head for the bar and forget about talking baseball, real baseball.

For myself, and no doubt millions of others, I feel vaguely culturally deprived, because even though a lifelong baseball fan, I have hardly a trace of Dodger-Memory. In fact, during my most crazed fan days, I didn't give a damn about the literary Big Three: the Dodgers, the Giants, or the Yankees. Since my youth was spent worshiping an American League team, the Dodgers and the Giants were as foreign to me as the smaller Balkan nations. The Yanks popped up occasionally as a hated enemy, so my memories of them are mostly painful. My team was, and is, the Chicago White Sox, an organization that truly represented the civic soul of Chicago; a history replete with

cosmic scandal, endless second-rate-ism, not to mention decades of mediocrity. Yet, somehow, White Sox fans can never free themselves of their White Sox virus. Even in Chicago, the local press barely reports their daily doings, while the Cubs, up on the North Side, are lavishly applauded for every victory, and even their defeats are honored. Ted Koppel, on *Nightline*, does a whole show on The Cubbies, as they are called, not once but several times. I doubt whether he even heard of the Pale Hose. He has that innocent, prosperous look of the true yuppie Cub fan. White Sox fans tend to have dark shadows around the eyes and the somewhat furtive look of guys who spend a lot of their time going to union meetings, bowling, and washing down Polish sausage with whatever beer is on sale this week at the 7-Eleven.

My Old Man, since he was born a few blocks south of Comiskey Park, in the heart of the tough Irish neighborhood that spawned the likes of James T. Farrell and the *Studs Lonigan* trilogy, was, like his whole gang, dedicated to the Sox. So it was natural that I, in my turn, would be part of the small but dedicated downtrodden Chicago minority who followed the Sox religiously, at home and on the road. When they were home, the cool voice of Bob Elson, the most laid-back baseball announcer who ever lived, calmly described the endless battles that the Sox fought with the St. Louis Browns, who seemed to play hundreds of games a year against the Sox. He was in direct contrast to the hysterical hyper-rantings of the Cub announcers, who performed more like shills hawking snake oil than baseball men. Elson was soothing to listen to, and he had the habit of occasionally turning the mike over to injured Sox players to do the play-by-play for a couple of innings. I looked forward to the days when Elson would say, "Well, look who's here. It's Zeke Bonura in the booth with us today. How's your back?"

"It hurts a little, Bob, but it ain't real bad."

"Fine, Zeke. We miss you in the lineup. How'd you like to do a couple of innings . . .?"

Then would begin the funniest half-hour ever heard on radio. Zeke made Jack Benny come off like an undertaker. He was naturally funny and didn't know it. A typical Zeke-ism would be: "Would you look at that swing? Wow . . . " . . . (Zeke is watching the ball and has also forgotten he is on the radio.) . . . "Holy smokes, would you look at that?" . . . (At this point, thousands of fans listening to the game are going crazy over what the hell Zeke is watching.) . . . Zeke continues chaotically: "Boy . . . " . . . (Another pause.) . . . Finally, he lets us in on the secret: "That was the highest pop-up I ever seen! Whoo!"

Zeke could even make pop-ups exciting, and some of the things he said about various ballplayers who came to bat were hardly fit for a family audience. He was candid to a fault. In fact, after one of his radio stints, Zeke got into at least five fights because of the things he had let out during the broadcast.

Zeke Bonura was a lumbering first baseman who hit the long ball better than most, was a legendary nonfielder, but was truly beloved by White Sox fans of the time. Every day The Old Man would come home from the office, and the first thing out of his mouth would be, "What did Zeke do today?" He didn't necessarily mean did Zeke get a hit today. Zeke did a lot of things. I will give you an example of pure Zeke-iana. The Sox manager, a tough, round, cigar-smoking ex–third baseman of outstanding skills named Jimmy Dykes, fought a continual battle in a hopeless dream to keep Zeke on the straight and narrow. Zeke's trouble was that he truly loved fun. The Sox had taken off on a road trip in the middle of the summer, during the sultry heat of the Midwest. Before their departure, it was announced that Zeke was now disabled due to a bad back and would stay home during the trip to "rest and get treatment." He had allegedly twisted his back in a futile attempt to field a ground ball that eluded Zeke's concrete glove and rolled out to the bullpen, thus turning a sure out into a triple. Zeke laughed, tossed his glove in the air, and waved to the crowd, which cheered back. The next day, the Sox left for Cleveland, with Zeke among the missing due to his "bad back." They dropped three straight games.

They next moved on to St. Louis, where the Browns were fielding a team even worse than the White Sox. The Sox dropped four straight, highlighted by the embarrassment of a Brownie relief pitcher with a .043 batting average smashing a grand-slam home run to conclude the final game. Dykes was quoted about the event: "Bullfrog threw him a grapefruit my mother coulda put away." He was referring to "Bullfrog" Bill Dietrich, a Sox pitching ace of the period who had more than a passing resemblance to Kermit the Frog. He didn't pitch much better either.

Next it was Detroit. Detroit was even more hated than the Yankees, if possible. They savagely dismembered what was called the Sox Pitching Corps, while taking four out of five. Hank Greenberg clubbed the Sox pitchers sadistically. He was quoted in the *Chicago Tribune* as saying, "I love to see them Sox come to town."

Dykes countered with: "They're lucky we didn't have Zeke with us. He's hittin' a blue streak these days."

The White Sox finally won the final game because it was rained out in the sixth while the Sox happened to be ahead by a slim run.

Suddenly the city was electrified. A headline in the *Herald-Examiner* read: "ZEKE BONURA SUSPENDED." The subhead read: Dykes says "I caught Bonura dancing the damn cha-cha at the Chez Paree. What kind of bad back is that?"

Well, I tell you, the Sox fans were agog. On the one hand, they couldn't blame Zeke for wanting to dance the cha-cha at the Chez Paree, since most of them could not afford the price of admission, but on the other hand, Zeke sure as hell hadn't helped the White Sox during the past three weeks while he was getting his "rest." Zeke was suspended for two weeks. The day after he was benched, he was quoted thusly: "I was dancin' the cha-cha because my doctor says it's good for my back. Also, Xavier Cugat was at the Chez, and I couldn't miss him."

Candid to a fault. Dykes replied, "That's pure baloney, but you sure can't help lovin' the guy."

Truly spoken. Zeke is no longer with us, but there are countless White Sox fans of ages past who will never forget that Zeke Bonura made a bad team fun to watch, and his nickname, "Banana Nose," when chanted by a Sunday-afternoon doubleheader crowd—"BA-NANA NOSE, BANANA NOSE, BANANA NOSE"—was a pure hymn of love. I, for one, love him still.

Jean Shepherd created (wrote and narrated) the feature film *A Christmas Story*. His other films include *Ollie Hop Noddle's Haven of Bliss, Phantom of the Open Hearth, The Great American Fourth of July and Other Disasters,* and *The Star-Crossed Romance of Josephine Cosnowfki*. He is a renowned radio raconteur and the author of *In God We Trust: All Others Pay Cash, A Fistful of Fig Newtons, Ferrari in the Bedroom,* and *Wanda Hickey's Night of Golden Memories & Other Disasters*.

IRA BERKOW
on
EDDIE WAITKUS

I don't remember what I did or even what I thought when I heard about the shooting, but I know I have never forgotten it.

The bullet that tore through the chest of Eddie Waitkus, the first baseman for the Philadelphia Phillies, ripped a hole through my idea—a nine-year-old boy's fantasy notion—that sports was not a part of the real world, and that athletes were greater than mere mortals.

The rifle shot that exploded in that hotel room that night in Chicago exploded the following day on the front pages of newspapers all across the country.

The shooting remains with us even though it happened so many years ago, on that warm, quiet night of June 14, 1949. The incident is now a part not only of our national history, but it provided a scene in our literature, and our print and celluloid mythology. In one of the most dramatic moments in the The Natural, a novel by Bernard Malamud, published in 1952, and which years later was made into a Hollywood motion picture starring Robert Redford, an unsuspecting major league baseball player is shot in a hotel room by a woman wearing a dark veil.

I believe I felt closer to it than many, and closer, oddly, to Waitkus, though, of course, I didn't know him personally.

I was a boy growing up in Chicago, living several miles away from Wrigley Field, and from the Edgewater Beach Hotel, that sprawling, pink, castlelike building on Lake Shore Drive, where Waitkus was shot.

I went to the Cub games regularly with my friends, having only about a year before discovered baseball, and like so many American boys, having the game and its players and the legends swiftly sinking deep into my consciousness, and my heart.

I also played first base in sandlot games. In my neighborhood, it seemed that first base was less than a glamorous position. It wasn't pitcher, say, or shortstop or center field. And being younger than most of the guys I played with—but tall for my age—I gravitated, or possibly was shunted, to first.

In 1948, the Cubs had an excellent first baseman named Eddie Waitkus, who would be traded that winter to the Phillies. The Cubs were always trading some of their best players, which is how they managed to remain such a miserable team for so long, and why, after all these years, they continue to cause their passionate fans so much grief.

Waitkus, meanwhile, had a cool and buttery style around the bag. He was left-handed and I was a righty, but I still tried to imitate his wonderful and yet almost comical little midair jitterbug of stretching, catching the ball, and toeing the base all in one smooth motion. He was six feet tall, lean, with sharp Slavic features, and as I recall from waiting with my friends after games at Wrigley Field for the players to emerge from the clubhouse, with warm, rather slanted eyes.

The players came out all slicked-back hair and deific. They signed autographs, or didn't, hurrying and pushing through the crowd. I remember Waitkus being fairly patient. I admired him, but I was hardly alone. I found out later that a Chicago teenager, someone I

CULT BASEBALL PLAYERS

assume stood in some of those crowds with me waiting for the players after games, was also very fond of him but in a totally different way. Her name was Ruth Ann Steinhagen.

She talked about Waitkus constantly, dreamed about him, even built a little shrine in her bedroom with newspaper photos of him. In a report later prepared by the chief of the Cook County behaviorial clinic in response to an order from the felony court, which found her deranged, she admitted:

"As time went on I just became nuttier and nuttier about the guy, and I knew I would never get to know him in a normal way . . . and if I can't have him, nobody else can. And I then decided I would kill him."

Steinhagen, age nineteen, purchased a secondhand rifle, checked into a room at the Edgewater Beach, where Waitkus was staying with the Phillies during a series against the Cubs, and sent a message to the front desk for Waitkus.

The message said that a woman named Ruth Ann Burns wished to see him in her room—Room 1297-A. Steinhagen had decided to use a pseudonym, but typically strange, only for her last name. The message added that it was about "something important." The time was close to midnight. Waitkus, a bachelor, decided to go up to her room to see what this mystery was all about.

Decades later, when writing about the incident, I received a letter from Edward (Ted) Waitkus, Jr., a lawyer in Boulder, Colorado, and we subsequently spoke on the phone.

"My dad was an easy-going, trusting guy at the time, and kind of flippant with women," recalled Ted Waitkus. "He walked into her room and said something like, "Well, babe, what's happening?' He didn't know anything about her, that she was so crazy about him she even learned Lithuanian, which was Dad's heritage. I guess she was a fanatic in the way the guy who shot John Lennon was. Then she went into a closet, took out the .22, and shot him. The first thing he said was, 'Why'd you do that?' "

His father told him that it was hard to believe that "a little bullet could make you feel as though six men had slammed you against the wall."

Waitkus, Jr., added that his father's recovery from the shooting was "miraculous." Eddie Waitkus returned the next season, played the entire 154-game schedule for the Phillies, the team nicknamed "The Whiz Kids" that year, won Comeback-of-the-Year honors, and played in the World Series. In the Series, Waitkus batted a respectable .267, slightly down from the .284 average during the regular season, and the .306 he was hitting—and incidentally, leading in the all-star-game balloting at the time—when he was shot, some sixteen months earlier. The Phillies lost to the Yankees in four straight games, but Waitkus told his son that "the World Series was the high point of my career."

"The shooting changed my father a great deal, as you might imagine," said Ted Waitkus. "Before, he was a very outgoing person. Then he became paranoid about meeting new people, and pretty much even stopped going out drinking with his teammates, which is what I guess they did in those days.

"When she was about to be released from the mental hospital after only a few years—they said she had fully recovered—my father and my family fought to keep her in. My father feared for his life."

Despite the pleas, Ruth Ann Steinhagen was released; Waitkus never heard from her again.

Waitkus was sold by the Phillies to the Orioles in 1954, then sent back to the Phillies midway through the 1955 season. He retired as an active player after that season, having compiled a .285 batting average during his eleven-year major league career.

He had got married and had two children, a daughter and a son. Born and raised in the Boston area himself, Waitkus now remained there, working summers as an instructor at Ted Williams's baseball camp. Waitkus made banquet talks, collected his baseball pension, and, his sister, Stella Kasperwicz, would recall, "pretty much took it easy."

"After baseball," said Ted Waitkus, "Dad had some trouble finding himself."

On the morning of September 16, 1972—a little more than twenty-three years after the shooting—I opened the *New York Times* and happened to run across a modest-sized obituary notice on Edward Stephen Waitkus, former major league baseball player. He was dead at age fifty-three.

"Different doctors through the years have expressed the theory that the stress of the shooting, combined with the four operations, allowed the cancer to take hold," said Ted Waitkus. "Cancer of the lung or esophagus can take up to twenty years or more to be fatal. My dad was never diagnosed as having cancer. It wasn't until after the autopsy that this came out. So I think Ruth Steinhagen was more successful than she thought."

I remember reading the Waitkus obituary and thinking how the shooting was the beginning of a heightened awareness for me of senseless violence and tragedy. Many more times would I experience that terrible feeling in the pit of my stomach of helplessness and rage. It was there after the murders of John Kennedy and Robert Kennedy and Martin Luther King, and when I learned of the sniper Whitman, the malevolent Manson, and the terrible slaughter in Vietnam. And again, only weeks before the death of Waitkus. I had recently returned from Munich, from covering the 1972 Olympics, where the eleven Israelis had only recently been killed in the most grotesque fashion.

In the *Times* obituary on Waitkus it noted that he died in the Veterans Administration Hospital in Boston (Waitkus had served four years in the military during World War II). Through the hospital I was able to reach Waitkus's sister.

Mrs. Kasperwicz told me that Eddie had retained an interest in sports and had watched the Olympics and talked about the Arab terrorists who had shot the Israelis.

"Eddie thought it was awful," she recalled. "He said that none of us will ever be the same because of it."

I understood, I told her. I said I also had felt that way about a similar incident that had occurred many years before, when I was a boy growing up in Chicago.

Ira Berkow is a sports columnist for the *New York Times.* He is the author of *Pitchers Do Get Lonely and Other Sports Stories, The DuSable Panthers: The Greatest, Blackest, Saddest Team from the Meanest Street in Chicago, The Man Who Robbed the Pierre: The Bobby Comfort Story, Oscar Robertson: The Golden Year 1964,* and *Red: A Biography of Red Smith;* coauthor of Rod Carew's *Carew* and Walt Frazier's *Rockin' Steady: A Guide to Basketball & Cool;* and editor of *Hank Greenberg: The Story of My Life.*

MIKE
DOWNEY
on

WALT (NO NECK)
WILLIAMS

WALT
WILLIAMS

OUTFIELD
WHITE
SOX

After the California Angels drafted and signed a left-handed pitcher with no right hand, I got to thinking about the outfielder with head and shoulders but no neck. Oh, I suppose that Walt (No Neck) Williams did have *something* to connect his chest and chin, some sort of windpipe, but it was barely visible to the naked eye, let me tell you. I mean, the man had absolutely no Adam's apple. He had more of an Adam's grape. Had he been the one who blabbed to Woodward and Bernstein, they would have immortalized him as "Shallow Throat." The poor guy could not even wear a necklace, because, you see, he was neckless.

Bad baseball gag of my own creation:

Question: Which big-league ballplayers have had physical deformities?
   Answer: No Neck Williams, Three Finger Brown, and Sixto Lezcano.

Okay, different jokes for different folks. Naturally, I would not wish it to be perceived that the Man With No Neck belonged in the circus, flanked by the tents of the Bearded Lady and the Man With the Two-Foot Tongue. Walt Williams had no neck the way some guys have flat feet, the way some kids have buck teeth, the way some women have tits that don't quit. It was just a physical peculiarity of his, one that made him stand out above the crowd—or rather, not. That lack of neck made Walt Williams different, unique, adorable. He was the Cabbage Patch outfielder, cute as a teddy bear. So what if no doctor could take his temperature during a fever, since the thermometer would enter one end of Walt Williams and protrude from another? So what if the man saved a fortune on scarves? So what if the man never had ring around the collar, because he had no collar?

Some details: Walter Allen Williams is five feet, six inches high, from head to toe minus neck, and one of the smallest things ever to grow in Texas. As a baby in Brownwood, Texas, there was a typhoid scare going around, and everybody needed shots. Baby Williams, evidently, took his in the neck. This story could very well be apocryphal, but that's the way the family legend went.

When Williams broke into the majors with the Houston Colt .45s in 1964, Paul Richards and Eddie Robinson, who had sent for him, were waiting at the hotel when Walter walked in. Richards poked Robinson and said, "Hey, Eddie, look at this guy. He aint' got no neck." Williams did not take it personally, because he figured they were thrown at the sight of him—not because of his neck, but because of his size. "I was leading the California League in hitting," he remembered, "and I guess everybody thought I was a big guy, because I had big statistics."

Later on, though, when "No Neck" became fastened to his first name the way "Yogi" was to Lawrence, "Duke" was to Edwin and "The Man" was to Stan, Williams came to resent it.

"Nicknames stay with you longer than regular names," he reasoned.

And who wanted to be known throughout eternity as No Neck? Williams felt the way Charles Hickman must have felt, around the turn of the century, when he was playing the outfield for Boston and New York and Cleveland, and was known to all as Piano Legs. There are nicknames that are flattering, such as Splendid Splinter and Hammerin' Hank, and then there are nicknames that are merely descriptive, in a less than generous way, such as Pee Wee or Dizzy. Nobody yearns to be called Dizzy. Nobody sets out to become No Neck.

Were Walt Williams a wonderful ballplayer, perhaps he would be remembered mostly for that. What he was, though, was an adequate major-leaguer, a dogged little hitter with an ax-chopper swing who looked as though he came to the plate with a miniature bat, and a struggling little fielder whose trouble with depth perception occasionally turned routine fly balls into suspenseful adventures. After only ten games with Houston, it took Williams three years to get back to the majors, but when he did, he gave the Chicago White Sox six decent seasons, including a .304 average in a career-high 471 at-bats in 1969.

It was during this period that No Neck not only became a particular favorite of the fans, but an unmistakable presence in the clubhouse, helped by the turquoise satin Nehru jacket he went out and bought himself after coming into some money. What the crowds liked in what they saw of Walt Williams was his hustle, including a Pete Rose-esque sprint to first base even after a walk. Grover Resigner, a White Sox coach at the time, advised him to run to first and gain attention for his hustle, telling Williams, "You're never going to be a superstar. So, try harder than everybody else."

No Neck did. When Cleveland acquired him in a trade in 1973, players were asked to participate in the Indians' annual goodwill trip around the state during the off-season. Only Williams volunteered. The next year, however, even after batting .289 in 104 games, he was off to New York, for two seasons with the Yankees that would end his big-league life.

Not so his baseball life. The No Neck show went international, first to Japan, later to Mexico. From 1976–78, he became No Neck the Nippon Ham Fighter. And a funny thing happened to him in

CULT BASEBALL PLAYERS

Japan. Instead of becoming popular, he became unpopular. For some reason, Japanese pitchers started throwing at No Neck. His batting average was among the league's best prior to the All-Star Game, but he had already been hit by pitches eight times, and he was getting sick of it. So sick, that when one more pitcher popped him, Williams charged the mound, intending for once to change Hit By Pitcher in the box score to Hit On Pitcher.

Turned out, though, that even No Neck's Nippon teammates did not side with him. When they ran out onto the diamond, it was to rescue the pitcher, not to reinforce the hitter. Not only did they pull Williams away from his victim, they joined in with the opponents and threw punches at him. Williams was eventually suspended for two weeks and fined $3,000, but he was told he could play in the All-Star Game if he apologized to the pitcher.

So sorry, he said.

After three years in Japan and three in Mexico, Williams went back to his hometown of Brownwood, where he became sports director of the community center there, and where he worked with juvenile delinquents as well. Although it was 1980 when he retired, No Neck today is still younger than Tommy John, and still full of youthful enthusiasm. When he played his last major league game, he was only thirty-one years old.

One December day after the 1987 season, the White Sox were eager to add a black coach to their staff, to comply with equal-opportunity guidelines, so Larry Himes, their general manager, made an appointment to interview Walter Williams, who had not held a baseball-related post in eight years. No Neck pulled up to the hotel in his block-long Caddy, then walked into the lobby in a brown leather jacket, T-shirt, and gym shoes. Larry Himes, remember, was the guy who fined several of his players the previous season for violating dress restrictions, including the wearing of socks. He was a stickler for proper attire, the sort of guy who probably detested the fact that the White Sox were obliged to wear, well, white socks.

Whatever was said at their meeting, Walt Williams did, regardless of wardrobe, make a good first impression on Himes. He got the job—first-base coach of the Sox—and we can only assume that when he stepped into the room, Larry Himes did not exclaim, "Hey, look, this guy ain't got no neck!" We also can only assume that if Himes ordered him to put on a tie, Williams's reply must have been, "On what?"

How nice to see him again. Personally, I would not have cared if Walt Williams had undergone a neck-transplant operation and was

made to resemble Audrey Hepburn. Resent your nickname? No, no,
No Neck. We like you just the way you are, so keep your chin up.
Such as it is.

Mike Downey is a syndicated sports columnist for the *Los Angeles
Times* and the *Sporting News.*

PETER BAIDA
on
HOYT WILHELM

In 1958, when I was eight years old, something special happened in Baltimore. It was the arrival of a baseball player unlike any we had ever seen. He had a funny name, Hoyt, and a funny pitch, a knuckleball that fluttered goofily toward the plate at a speed of about nine miles per hour. He was thirty-five years old, and everyone knew he was near the end of an undistinguished career. In fact, he was fourteen years from the end of a career that lasted until 1972. By that time Hoyt, the old man who hobbled into Baltimore in August of 1958, had pitched in more games than any man in baseball history. No one has topped him yet.

I had discovered baseball in 1957. By 1958, I had all but memorized the baseball record book. So I knew what the Orioles were getting when they picked up Hoyt from Cleveland for the waiver price in the dog days of their sixth consecutive mediocre season.

What the Orioles were getting, I knew, was a relief pitcher who had kicked around in the minor leagues (and served in the military) for about a decade before finally making it to the majors with the New York Giants in 1952, who had had some good seasons and some not-so-good ones, and whom Cleveland was willing to let go for next to nothing despite his 2.49 earned run average. Perhaps his 2-7 record did not impress them, perhaps they figured that a thirty-five-year-old with a funny name and a funny pitch did not have much of a future.

What happened after the Orioles picked up Hoyt on August 23 may be as unlikely as anything that has ever happened in baseball

Courtesy Baltimore Orioles

history. The Orioles' manager, Paul Richards, was a baseball genius whom no one yet recognized as a baseball genius. A lanky Texan who had been a journeyman catcher in the 1940s (321 career hits; career batting average of .227), Richards decided to put Hoyt in his starting rotation. Why not? What else would a manager do with a pitcher whose total number of starts in his first 361 major league appearances had been exactly zero?

As an eight-year-old who already knew more about baseball than he would ever know about any other subject, I have to admit that I was skeptical. My skepticism lasted until September 20. That was

CULT BASEBALL PLAYERS

the day when Hoyt started in Baltimore's Memorial Stadium against a Yankee team whose lineup included Mickey Mantle, Moose Skowron, Hank Bauer, and Elston Howard.

Hoyt no-hit them. I remember listening on the radio in my bedroom while the mighty Yankees marched up to the plate and back to the dugout, up to the plate and back to the dugout, batter after batter, inning after inning, hour after hour. Nothing like this had ever happened in any Baltimore baseball game in the brief time since I had discovered baseball the year before. In fact, I learned later, nothing like this had happened in a major league Baltimore baseball game since Jim Hughes no-hit Boston on April 22, 1898, in the days when there were Orioles with names like John McGraw, Hughey Jennings, and Uncle Wilbert Robinson. As for the Yankees, nothing like this had happened since Virgil Trucks of the Tigers stopped them cold on August 25, 1952.

Thirty years later, looking at the box score of Hoyt's masterpiece and reading the account of the game in the *New York Times*, I discover details that time had pushed out of my mind. The starting pitcher for the Yankees was Don Larsen, who never would have tossed the most famous game in baseball history if Baltimore had not traded him to the Yankees after he pitched his way to 3 wins and 21 losses for the impossibly incompetent Orioles of 1954. The losing pitcher was not Larsen but the left-hander whom Baltimore's radio announcers always called "little Bobby Shantz." (Remember him? He was 5'6" tall; 139 pounds; 24 wins and 7 losses for the Philadelphia Athletics in 1952; sixteen years in the big leagues!)

Hoyt's performance, wrote *New York Times* sportswriter John Drebinger, "was all the more amazing because more than half of it was staged in a drizzling rain." Hoyt himself, Drebinger noted, was "regarded as virtually a washout at the beginning of the season." The game was played "before a cheering crowd of 10,941" and was won, 1 to 0, on a seventh-inning home run by Orioles catcher Gus Triandos. (Remember him? "Big Gus"; thirteen years in the majors; came to the Orioles in the same trade that sent Larsen to the Yankees.) Gus's homer in Hoyt's no-hitter was his 30th of the year, tying the American League single-season record for home runs by a catcher— a record set by Yogi Berra in 1952, duplicated by Berra in 1956, and broken by Lance Parrish in 1982, whose record was topped in turn by Carlton Fisk in 1985. Ah, baseball!

Thanks to Hoyt, Gus still has a place in the record books, though probably not one that he wants. Gus caught most of Hoyt's starts in 1959, when Baltimore catchers set the all-time record for most passed balls in a 154-game season. Thirty-eight of the 49 passed balls came with Hoyt on the mound.

By the end of the '59 season, Hoyt had become a cult figure in Baltimore. That year, working mostly as a starter, Hoyt won 15, lost 11, and led the league with a 2.19 earned run average. In one stretch he won nine straight games, including three shutouts. Two of the three were back-to-back beauties, a one-hitter and a four-hitter, against the Yankess. Hoyt must have been a little off, people in Baltimore said, to let the Yankees get four hits.

Other fans who cherish Hoyt's memory will never forgive me if I fail to mention that '59 was not the only year he led the league in earned run average. In his rookie season with the Giants, Hoyt led the National League in games pitched with 71, earned run average with 2.43, and winning percentage with .833. He won fifteen games and lost three—a remarkable start to a career that got more and more remarkable.

But it was not just his level of performance that made Hoyt special. Baseball is the most unpredictable of sports, and the knuckleball is the most unpredictable of pitches. I can remember sitting with my father at Orioles games in the late fifties and sixties—Hoyt was again a full-time reliever by 1961—and I can remember the buzz that would ripple through the crowd as "Old Sarge" ambled in from the bullpen, with his head tilted oddly to one side as if he had a permanent crick in his neck.

Everyone knew, once Hoyt came in, that the most unpredictable of sports had just become doubly unpredictable. Hoyt threw the knuckler on perhaps forty-eight out of every fifty pitches. It was a beautiful knuckler: it might dive, soar, flutter, float, skid, speed up, slow down—sometimes it even seemed to stop and head back toward Hoyt, then resume its sixty-foot journey toward home plate. No one, *no one*, knew what the ball would do once Hoyt let it go. The batter did not know. The catcher did not know. Hoyt himself, as he freely admitted, didn't have the slightest idea.

His fans were ecstatic about Hoyt, but Baltimore's catchers—Triandos, Clint Courtney, and Joe Ginsberg—desperately needed help. Paul Richards came up with the solution. On May 27, 1960, he introduced "the big mitt"—a catcher's glove 50 percent larger than the one used for other pitchers. The mitt, no longer legal, became part of Hoyt's legend.

In 1962, at the age of thirty-nine, Hoyt posted an ERA of 1.94—the first time he had gone under 2.00 for a full season. He was rewarded by being made part of a big off-season trade with the White

Sox—a trade that brought the great shortstop Luis Aparicio to the Orioles.

Though we rarely got to see him pitch, my father and I continued to follow Hoyt's career with avid enthusiasm. We were typical of others whom I have met over the years—the people who were not merely fans of Hoyt but informal members of a kind of secret society. When we talked about Hoyt, our eyes lit with a special delight. For me, the delight was intensified by the discovery that Hoyt had been born on July 26, 1923—twenty-seven years to the day before I was born. Even now, when I am asked my birthday, I reply, "July twenty-sixth, the same day as Hoyt Wilhelm and George Bernard Shaw."

Like wine, Hoyt got better as he aged. For the White Sox, pitching strictly in relief, he turned in an earned run average under 2.00 for five consecutive years: 1.99 in 1964, at age forty-one; 1.81 in 1965, at age forty-two; 1.66 in 1966, at age forty-three; 1.31 in 1967, at age forty-four; and 1.73 in 1968, making 72 appearances at age forty-five. Maybe some reliever will top that performance one of these days, but I'm not holding my breath.

All good things must end, and Hoyt's career came to an end after the 1972 season with the Los Angeles Dodgers. In his next-to-last season, at age forty-eight, his ERA had been a respectable 2.70, though he had pitched only twenty innings. In any case, Hoyt would have been fifty in '73, and no one wanted a fifty-year-old reliever.

Hoyt set several career records: most appearances by a pitcher (1,070), most appearances in relief (1,018); most innings in relief (1,870); and most relief victories (124). His career ERA was 2.52. In 1985, he became the first relief pitcher to be elected to the Hall of Fame.

Some people—people such as me, for instance—think that Hoyt's career was one of the most extraordinary in baseball history. Once we start talking about Hoyt, it's hard to get us to stop. At this very moment, for instance, I can't resist mentioning that in addition to his feats as a pitcher, Hoyt was renowned for his ineptitude as a batter. His career average of .088 speaks for itself. In twenty-one years in the big leagues, Hoyt hit exactly one home run, and he hit it the first time he stepped to the plate, in 1952. You can look it up, as Casey Stengel used to say.

Hoyt's fans wanted him to pitch forever, and some of us still think that he could have. These days, I'm told, he lives in Sarasota, Florida, but I doubt that it would take him long to get in shape if some team needed him to save a few games in the stretch run of a tight race. The knuckleball, as Phil Niekro demonstrated after Hoyt, takes next to nothing out of a pitcher's arm. I can imagine Hoyt at seventy, strolling out of the bullpen with his head tilted oddly to the side, while the catcher grimaced and a buzz of excitement swept through the crowd, and no one had any idea what would happen next.

Peter Baida has written on topics ranging from business to baseball in such publications as *American Heritage, The Atlantic, American Scholar, Forbes, Manhattan, inc.,* and the *Harvard Business Review.* He is a fundraiser for the Memorial Sloan-Kettering Cancer Center in New York City.

DIANE COLE
on
BROOKS ROBINSON

In my home office, directly above my word processor, hang the portraits of three famous men whose lives and faces never cease to inspire me. They are Charles Dickens, Samuel Johnson—and Brooks Robinson.

If you wonder at the last name, clearly you have never lived in Baltimore, a town that still talks of running Brooks for mayor, and from which, on July 31, 1983, some two thousand citizens in thirty chartered buses and twelve private planes traveled north to Cooperstown to pay tribute to the greatest-fielding third baseman of all time on his induction into the Baseball Hall of Fame.

Brooks Robinson: Every Baltimore Oriole fan worthy of the name knows that in the course of twenty-three years of exquisite leaping, diving, lunging, and belly flopping at third base, Brooks came to own virtually every fielding and endurance record at that position. These include sixteen—count 'em!—consecutive Gold Glove awards for the years 1960–1975, and lifetime marks among third basemen for most games (2,870), most putouts (2,697), most assists (6,205), most double plays (618), and perhaps most significant of all as a statistical measure of a player's fielding greatness, both most chances accepted (8,902) *and* highest fielding percentage (.971).

This Oriole fan finds these facts enchanting because, growing up in Baltimore, she was smart enough to say yes whenever her big brothers happened to find themselves with an extra ticket for their Sunday-afternoon excursions to Memorial Stadium. Sitting perched above the third-base line, the three of us had what I still consider

Courtesy Baltimore Orioles

the best seats in the house because they gave us what I have come
to think of as a "Brooks's eye" view of the game. Inning after inning,
week after week, season after season, this is what we saw:

Glaring into the afternoon sun, Brooks, a gangly six-footer, would
edge slightly forward and squint toward the plate, anticipating the
ball's path before the ball was struck. Suddenly he would lunge to
his side, spear a white blur, fall full-length with his face in the dirt,
crawl onto his elbows, and finally, all in one swift motion, hurl the
ball across the infield to nail the runner at first with plenty of time
to spare.

"Routine play!" my brothers would exclaim knowingly, before
adding, even more knowingly, "Routine by Brooks's standard, that
is."

And what other standard was there? For all twenty-three years
of his career, 1955 through 1977, Brooks played for just one team,
Baltimore—more years than even Ty Cobb played for Detroit. Though
his cleats could leave no more than a ghostly imprint on the infield
at Memorial Stadium, Brooks's acrobatic leaps and vaults form a
central part of the city's collective memory. As a result, my brothers
and I, along with every other Baltimorean who grew into sports
consciousness during the years of Brooks's reign, will be forever
doomed to sigh with yearning, anger, and despair whenever some
lesser player at third base (that is to say, anybody else who dares to

play the position) can't even get near the kind of brutally slashed line drive that Brooks would magically spear, snare, or scoop up and transform into an easy double play.

Ask any Baltimorean about Brooks at third and you'll hear all this and more. You'll hear about poetry and dance, about how Brooks's sheer energy and athleticism gave his movements a peculiar grace and balance, regardless of how awkwardly he lurched as he hurled the ball toward first.

These glittering memories glow at the very core of any bona fide Oriole fan, and rightly so. But they should not entirely overshadow Brooks's achievements at the plate. His lifetime average over twenty-three years was a respectable .267, with a slugging average of .401. In those years, he amassed a total of 2,848 hits, including the 268 career home runs that made him the leader among American League third basemen, until Graig Nettles surpassed him.

And let's not forget 1964, his MVP year. That season, Brooks led the league with 118 RBIs and batted .317, second only to Tony Oliva, and ahead of both Elston Howard and Mickey Mantle. In a show of power, he hit 35 doubles and 28 home runs, racked up a total of 319 bases, and achieved a slugging average of .521. Naturally—it seems so obvious that one almost doesn't have to say it—Brooks also led league third basemen in putouts (153), assists (327), double plays (40), and fielding average (.972).

For many seasons, Brooks seemed to be Baltimore's best-kept secret. In spite of his fabulous 1964 MVP season; in spite of his dramatic home run in his very first World Series appearance in the first inning of the first game of Baltimore's 1966 romp over Los Angeles; in spite of Baltimore's enthusiasm for Brooks Robinson, Frank Robinson, and baseball in general, the rest of the baseball world seemed not to appreciate Brooks as we did.

Alas, the 1969 World Series did not help any Oriole's cause. After sweeping Minnesota in the league playoffs, the Orioles were heavily favored to vanquish the Mets. And so, when my brothers invited me to accompany them to the second game of that ill-fated series, we self-assuredly took our usual seats above the third-base line and settled in for a gloriously balmy October afternoon of fun.

It was not fun. In the bottom of the ninth, with the Orioles behind 2–1, with two men on and two men out, Brooks, who had driven in the Orioles' only run in the seventh, came up again. This is it, I thought! And it was—the saddest baseball memory of my life. Brooks bounced a chopper to third. He ran valiantly, he ran hard. But Brooks, the man with the fastest set of reflexes on the infield, was one of the slowest runners on the base paths. Brooks was out. The Orioles lost this game, lost the next three games, lost the world championship. And it turned out, I had witnessed Brooks's only hit in the entire five-game series.

And then came the glorious World Series of 1970—Brooks's series.

Perhaps the Orioles entered this series, against Cincinnati's Big Red Machine, with the same trepidation as their fans, still hurting from 1969. But Brooks Robinson assured us almost immediately that the cruelties inflicted this year would all be against Cincinnati—and almost all inflicted by him.

It did not take long. In the sixth inning of the first game, Brooks backhanded a fierce drive by Lee May down the left-field line, and with one of his patented off-balance throws, converted a guaranteed double into an out at first. Not yet convinced, the next day May lined another bullet toward Brooks; this time, Brooks came up with a double play.

After that, Brooks's glove is all that Cincinnati or the whole world saw: Brooks scooping up a ground ball; Brooks spearing a line drive. Inning after inning, whether he was springing to his right, lunging to his left, or throwing from his knees, the fielder with the ball was always Brooks. Then, most spectacular of all, the third game brought the belly flop seen round the world: Brooks's headfirst dive to snare a Johnny Bench line drive, end the Reds' sixth-inning rally, and virtually shut down the opposition for the duration of the Series.

Away at college, I watched this brilliant display in the dormitory TV room, a central gathering place where fans of all rooting persuasions came to be awed by Brooks's virtuosity. By the Series' end, a sense of astonishment and wonder filled the air, especially when the ninth inning of the Series' fifth and final game provided Brooks with a last shining moment—a diving leap to his right to grab Johnny Bench's final attempt to get anything, even a foul ball, past Brooks's glove. When Brooks fell to earth again, the ball safely caught, all around me heads were shaking in disbelief. Now the rest of the world knew what we Oriole fans had always known.

Afterward, Brooks's glove was immediately claimed by the Hall of Fame. His bat could have been, too. Brooks's two home runs, two doubles, and five singles set a five-game Series record for most total bases (17), and also tied the five-game Series record for most hits (9). In addition, he hit safely in every game, batted .429, drove in six runs, and scored five.

That is why Brooks won the MVP award for the 1970 World

Series, but that is not the only reason why he has earned a place in my personal Hall of Fame.

Few superstars would have bothered to respond when a proud father sent his daughter's articles on baseball to them. Brooks wrote back twice—and both times he wrote separate notes to Dad and me.

He also sent the glossy black-and-white photograph that hangs directly above my word processor. Although by this time Brooks had retired to the broadcast booth, the picture captures him with his Orioles cap tilted slightly upward, and he is smiling gently as he squints into the camera as if he were squinting toward home plate— just the look I remember from my seat above third base.

"Diane, My Best to you, Brooks Robinson," his backward-slanting autograph reads.

My best to you, too, Brooks. And thanks.

Diane Cole is a contributing editor to *Psychology Today* and has written for many national publications, including the *New York Times, The Wall Street Journal,* and *Ms.* She is the author of *Hunting the Headhunters: A Woman's Guide.*

HILMA WOLITZER on

JACKIE ROBINSON

The first subversive act of my young adult life occurred in the mid-1940s, in a school playground in Brooklyn, where I was just hanging around with a few friends. Someone a little older, a skinny boy with glasses and a clipboard, approached and asked us to sign a petition to allow Negroes to play in organized baseball. Although I had grown up in what I'd always thought of as a "liberal" family, the kid with the clipboard had to explain what all the fuss was about segregated baseball. The subject had never come up at our dinner table.

My friends refused to sign the petition, and one of them even muttered something about "Communists." I was, in those days, sheeplike in my conformity to the crowd—a pretty common adolescent affliction. "If your friends all jumped off a cliff, you'd jump, too," my mother would frequently complain. This time I decided to jump first, but no one else followed. While I scrawled my name and address on the petition, another girl hummed "Red Sails in the Sunset." I remember how rapidly my heart was beating, what a big deal it suddenly all seemed.

I was *almost* a baseball fan in those days, largely because my father and my favorite uncle were, and I enjoyed their animated, male company when they sat near the radio and listened to a game. So I often listened with them, especially to the Dodgers' games, and gradually I learned the ground rules and the various players' names and positions. If I wasn't quite sure what a balk was, and didn't really understand the logic of the infield-fly rule, I liked the background excitement of the crowd, Red Barber's soft drawl, and even the af-

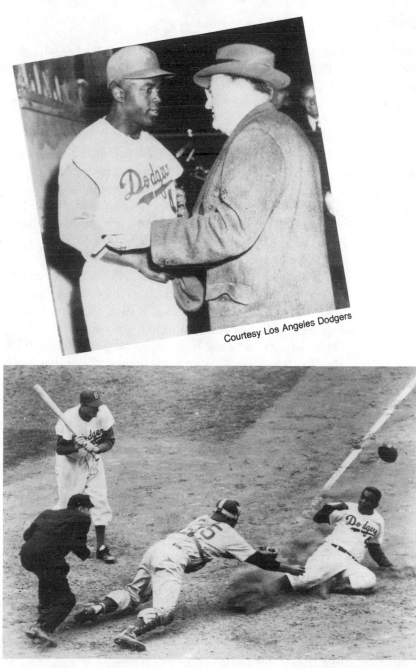

Courtesy Los Angeles Dodgers

Courtesy Los Angeles Dodgers

Top photo: Robinson with Walter O'Malley, who became the majority owner of the Dodgers after Branch Rickey's departure.

Bottom photo: A classic photo of Robinson stealing home against the Cubs in 1952.

fectionate, amusing nicknames of some of the players—Cookie, Pee Wee, Frenchy, Pistol Pete. I cheered when the Dodgers were winning and booed when Walker or Reiser was "robbed" of a hit. But it was only after Jackie Robinson came down from the farm team in Montreal to join Brooklyn that my interest in baseball became instantly, sharply focused, that I became a dedicated fan.

One of the beauties of listening to baseball, rather than seeing it played, is the work of the imagination. A similar analogy might be made between reading and watching television. Radiocast baseball depends a lot on the style of the sportscasters and the ability of the listeners to visualize the players and the action. I remember thinking of Pee Wee Reese as an agile midget, of Frenchy Bordagaray as romantically, languidly handsome—something like Charles Boyer. In 1947, when Jackie Robinson became the pioneer black major-leaguer, I imagined that he looked exotically different out there, and I thought I heard a difference in the crowd's response to him, a jeering among all the cheering. I experienced something like anxious pride whenever he came up to bat. Hadn't I put him there practically by myself?

I didn't actually *attend* a ball game until the middle of that 1947 season. It was a night game at Ebbets Field, and the Dodgers were playing the Giants. The look of the diamond itself surprised me. It was like a stage setting under the lights; even the infield grass seemed unnaturally green. And the actors! Like all celebrities, they were both wonderfully glamorous and disappointingly ordinary in person. Pee Wee Reese wasn't nearly as short as I'd imagined, and Duke Snider was impressive, but not particularly regal, as his name suggested. Jackie Robinson *was* conspicuously dark among all the white players, but what you soon fixed on was his quickness and grace, in the field and at bat. Baseball, I saw, was a kind of ballet, with continually improvised movements, and Robinson was its premier danseur. His stance at the plate was deep, the bat held high. He'd rub one hand on his hip, then grip the bat again, and I wondered if this was a nervous habit, if he was only wiping off his sweaty palm. After he reached base, with a hard line drive to left, he dodged and danced and bluffed going, to the crowd's delight and the pitcher's distraction. And he eventually did steal second, running swiftly in his distinctive, pigeon-toed gait, then sliding in to just beat the throw. So *this* was baseball! By the time the game was over (with the Dodgers winning, naturally), I decided that Robinson's hip rubbing wasn't a nervous gesture at all; no one who played that well could possibly be nervous.

It was only much later that I read the details of Jackie Robinson's historical passage into the majors. I learned about owner Branch Rickey's decision to integrate the Dodgers, his choice and summoning of Robinson, and the proposition that included one crucial edict: *Robinson must not overtly react to racist attacks.* It was understood by both men that such attacks were inevitable—during their legendary meeting, Rickey even acted out a series of probable abuses, in a kind of minipsychodrama. Robinson is reported to have said, "I get it. What you want me to say is that I've got another cheek." He finally agreed to Rickey's terms, but the concession must have been agonizing for him; he was an aggressive, hot-tempered man, one hardly inclined to be passive in the face of bigotry.

I learned that there had been other petitions besides the one I'd signed with such youthful fervor in the playground. One of them, circulated by a Dodger player, demanded that Robinson *not* be brought down to join the team. Volumes of vicious, threatening letters were sent to both Robinson and Rickey. And Red Barber, the southern-born announcer, almost decided to quit broadcasting for Brooklyn when he heard of Rickey's decision to break the color barrier. By his own admission, Robinson's palms *were* often sweaty, at least during that initial season. As expected, there were taunting insults from the stands, and savage physical assaults by opposing players during the course of the game. The segregation of travel and recreational facilities incurred further indignities. Despite the growing support of his teammates, and the extraordinary bond between Robinson and his wife, Rachel, he must have suffered moments of profound loneliness and rage. But he endured it all, somehow, with astonishing self-control; his only revenge was the superb playing that led to his being named Rookie of the Year.

Five years later, I voted in my first presidential election. Pulling the switch in the voting booth, I was reminded of the thrill I had felt—a sense of participating in history—when I signed that baseball petition in the playground. I'd realized a while back that the signature of a minor in such a major controversy probably hadn't mattered at all, except to me. And my official vote, for Adlai Stevenson (in 1952, and again four years later) didn't carry the day, either. Yet I continue to vote and to sign petitions, often with a feeling of deep frustration, if not complete futility. And I know that Stevenson wasn't a lesser candidate for losing those elections—it takes a kind of valor just to run, especially against the odds.

Jackie Robinson ran against the odds, too, and against the grain of intense and disgraceful public opinion. Of course, he was a winner in every sense of the word—a brilliant athlete, a man of remarkable willpower and integrity, the groundbreaker for all the gifted black players who followed him. He kept his word to Branch Rickey, under brutal circumstances, and the integration of organized baseball was accomplished. But ultimately he *stopped* turning the other cheek—on and off the ballfield. He became an ardent and outspoken activist for civil rights, instead of relaxing in the comfortable climate of his own success, and that was his truest heroism.

Hilma Wolitzer is a Mets fan and the author of such novels as *Ending, In the Palomar Arms, Silver,* and *Hearts.*

ROBERT
SILVERBERG
on

KARL SPOONER

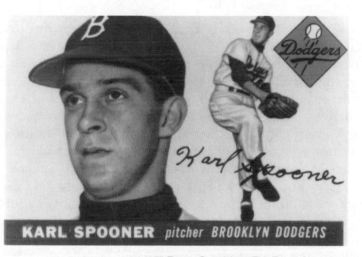

KARL SPOONER *pitcher BROOKLYN DODGERS*

1955 Topps: Copyright © The Topps Company, Inc.

He certainly got everybody's attention, for a little while. Coming up from the Texas League at the tail end of the Dodgers' miserably disappointing 1954 season, he was given his first big-league start late in September against the Giants and struck out 15 in the course of fashioning a 2-hit shutout. Three or four days later he started again, against the Pirates, and struck out a dozen more, en route to another shutout. In his first two games, 27 strikeouts and no runs—an unparalleled accomplishment.

That was it for the Dodgers, and Karl Spooner, in 1954. The regular season came to its end the week he arrived to stage his astounding and unexpected little flourish. But he and I and anybody else who cared at all about National League doings spent the winter feverishly wondering what this guy was destined to accomplish in the year to come, after that sort of start. Thirty wins? Forty? Five hundred strikeouts? Twenty shutouts? An entire unscored-upon season? It was your basic baseball fantasy. Anything seemed possible. Nobody had ever seen a rookie turn in two back-to-back pitching jobs like that.

And then in spring training in 1955, Spooner hurt his arm, and he never did much worth noticing again. He had his moment of glory, and it was so dazzling that no one who was following baseball at the time of Karl Spooner's debut has ever been able to forget it. But the moment was heartbreakingly brief. It was almost as if he had sold his soul to the devil for eighteen innings of baseball brilliance, and the devil had turned up very promptly indeed to present his promissory note.

I was nineteen that year, a Brooklyn boy who had grown up within walking distance of Ebbets Field, and I was still more or less in the grip of my boyhood fascination with the Dodgers. But I was also a very scholarly college kid, up there at Columbia studying Faust and Oedipus and the other great tragic figures of literature. And at the same time I was beginning my own career as a professional writer, and as I struggled to construct my first publishable stories, I was inordinately sensitive to such things as irony, the prankishness of fate, and the poignancy of the human condition. So Spooner's astounding rise and fall was a big deal for me. Not only did I see in it all sorts of significant literary resonances, but I had hoped with truly passionate intensity that this guy would be the invincible blow-'em-away pitcher that the Dodgers had never quite been able to find, and my disappointment was extreme when he failed to move into the slot that in my hyped-up imagination I had reserved for him.

The postwar Dodgers, of course, were the dominant team of the National League—the team of Snider, Hodges, Robinson, Reese, Furillo, Campanella. In 1946—they had Reese and Furillo then, not yet any of the others—they finished in a first-place tie with the Cardinals, then lost two agonizing playoff games. (I was in the sixth grade that year. It was the beginning of my education in baseball frustration.)

The year 1947 brought a pennant, a crazy seven-game World Series with the Yankees, and another defeat. And 1948 was Boston's year, a bleak, depressing season for the Dodgers, but now the famed Boys of Summer were assembling and maturing—I saw Campanella's first game and could tell you right away that he was Hall of Fame stuff and the big years were coming. For most of the next decade the Dodgers either would be league champs or would manage to lose out at the last minute in some uniquely harrowing way. In 1949, another pennant, another Series loss to the Yankees. In 1950, a close race with the Phillies, and the championship lost on the final day of the season. In 1951, the horrendous frittering of a 13½-game lead, another playoff, the crushing Bobby Thomson home run to give the Giants the pennant. Then two easy championships in 1952 and 1953, and two more losses in the Series—they seemed inevitable—to the Yankees. The dreary 1954 season, when the Dodgers were hardly ever in contention, seemed a strange anomaly.

Of course I knew what was missing. The Brooklyns had home run hitters galore, some elegant basestealers, splendid relief pitchers, and a few extraordinary defensive players. But where was the big starting pitcher? Ralph Branca, who did the job in 1947, never quite got it together again. Don Newcombe, the huge rookie of 1949, per- formed heroic deeds on the mound and even at the plate, but he was often mysteriously inconsistent when it counted. Carl Erskine, Preacher Roe, and Russ Meyer won a lot of games, but they did it by cleverness and stealth, not by overpowering the hitters. A guy named Rex Barney, who had a big year in 1948, might have been one of the real power throwers, but his extraordinary skills did not include the basic one of getting the ball over the plate.

So we were all ready for Spooner. He was twenty-three years old in 1954, a left-hander, big and strong and superconfident. When he was a kid, he said, he terrified everyone with the accuracy and force with which he could throw snowballs. Pitching for Fort Worth, he averaged better than one strikeout an inning all season, routinely striking out a dozen or more batters per game. The word on him was that his fastball was not only hard but moved around in a way that wasn't easy to believe.

With the 1954 season already in the tank, manager Walter Alston had nothing much to risk by giving the rookie Spooner a start against the Giants that final week. I remember listening to the game—college kids didn't have television sets in 1954—in mounting astonishment. The Giants had the pennant clinched and weren't disposed to knock themselves out that day, but even so, they seemed utterly helpless. Spooner got into trouble in the first inning and struck out Bobby Hofman with the bases loaded to end it. He struck out just about everyone else, too. The record for most strikeouts in a single game back then was 18. Spooner got 15 his first time out.

A fluke? Who could say? We all waited for the second start, which I think came on the very last day of the season. And it was pretty much a repeat, 1–0 Brooklyn, 12 Spooner strikeouts, 5 hits, no runs. Plainly this guy was a superman. But then the curtain came down on the Dodger season, and we were left with a long winter of frenzied speculation. The new Walter Johnson? The new Christy Mathewson? Time alone would tell.

Time told a lousy story. Spooner, perhaps overeager, threw too hard in spring training and pulled something in his shoulder. The great fastball was gone after that. In the regular season he proved to be quite vincible, winning 8, losing 6, striking out a commendable but unspectacular 78 batters in the 98 innings he pitched. But he seemed to be regaining some of his rookie form as the season went along: he did manage one shutout, and in the World Series, pitching relief, he struck out five Yankees in three innings. That gained him a start in the sixth game, when the Dodgers, leading the series 3–2, needed only one win for their first World Series victory in history. What a chance for Spooner to replay 1954's late-season miracle! The fantastic promise redeemed, the strikeout phenom bringing Brooklyn the long-craved triumph at last!

Alas. He was bombed for five runs in a third of an inning. The Dodgers lost, and it remained for Johnny Podres to produce the historic Series-clincher the next day. Spooner never pitched for the Dodgers again. During the winter his arm troubles worsened. He spent 1956 in the minor leagues, did nothing there, took a chance on arm surgery in 1957, tried to make the Cardinals' roster in 1958, and was released in spring training. He found a job refinishing floors, worked as a bartender, did a turn as a carpenter. I suppose he lived more or less happily ever after, now and then looking back in wonder at those sunlit autumn days of 1954. He pitched two blazing games one September week that gave him an eternal place in baseball mythology, and that was that for Karl Spooner, the king of might-have-beens.

Perhaps the worst irony of all is that the gods of baseball had actually decreed that it was Brooklyn's turn to get an absolutely invincible pitcher about that time; but Spooner showed up six months early to claim the job. The opening wasn't quite available yet. A kid named Sandy Koufax, who joined the team the following year, got it instead. But that's another story.

Robert Silverberg is a Nebula and Hugo Award–winning science fiction writer and editor. His books/novellas include *Nightwings, The Masks of Time, Up the Line, To Jorslem, Tower of Glass, The World Outside, A Time of Changes, Dying Inside, Born with the Dead, Lord Valentine's Castle, Majipur Chronicles, Master of Life and Death, The Book of Skulls,* and *Sundance.*

GERALD
GREEN
on

PETE REISER

It really ended for Pete Reiser in 1947 when he slammed into the center-field wall at Ebbets Field, caught Cully Rickard's line drive—the bases were loaded—and collapsed.

In the clubhouse a priest administered the last rites of the Roman Catholic Church to the Brooklyn Dodger star. Reiser had fractured his skull, dislocated both shoulders, and fallen into a coma.

He was never the same after that last battle with the hated wall. But he kept on playing, racing after the deep ones, sliding headfirst, throwing strikes from the outfield, crippled, battered, and scarred at age twenty-eight.

Talk about doomed heroes! Pistol Pete (his name was Harold; the nickname derived from his affection for westerns) made the ancient Greeks look like sissies. He was a youth who had it all—talent, desire, courage, an exuberant competitive spirit. And he came to grief—because of these admirable traits.

I saw Reiser play perhaps twenty times at creaky Ebbets Field. In the bleachers (pavilion, 55¢) or the more elegant grandstand seat ($1.10), I watched the kid from St. Louis race after fly balls and line drives, duck beanballs, steal bases, throw perfect pegs to the infield, and above all, *hit*. A switch-hitter in the minors, he batted exclusively left-handed for the Dodgers, digging in at the plate and defying pitchers to hit him. Though never a home run belter, he hit with power and was a brilliant contact hitter. In the clutch, he was a terror to opposing pitchers. Injured, nursing battered ribs or a throbbing skull, he would limp to the plate and connect for a game-winning hit, often

CULT BASEBALL PLAYERS

a riposte to some pitcher who'd dusted him off. And all this, mind you, with a smile, an affable manner. Reiser was never a showboat, a holler guy, one to bad-mouth teammates or opponents or jaw with umpires. He didn't have to. He had almost too much talent for one man. He knew not fear. And he played with the abandoned joy of a child.

And yet . . . and yet . . . some fatal flaw persisted and doomed him.

In Greek tragedy, in Shakespeare, heroes fall because of some lesion in their character. Othello's jealousy, Macbeth's greed, Lear's ego. But Pistol Pete was too good to be true. He played with dedication, boundless energy, heedless of his own safety, and invited disaster. We loved him for it, suffered with him, prayed for him, and those of us who rooted for the Dodgers in the forties remember him with an affection that is never maudlin, an admiration that he earned a thousand times over.

Consider some facts before confronting the decline of this magnificent man. In 1939, as a nineteen-year-old rookie shortstop/second baseman in Florida, he batted twelve times from both sides of the plate against the best big-league pitchers and hit *three homers and five singles and walked four times!* In 1941, his first full year in the majors, he led the National League in batting with .343, in slugging with .558, in doubles with 39, in triples with 17, and runs with 117. He was a spectacular centerfielder, a daring baserunner, an inspiration to a team of stars. And he was twenty-two years old.

But there was always the wall.

Center field in Ebbets Field was a cement-hard sloping monster. No padding, no warning track. For Reiser, it did not exist, or if it did, it was an enemy that had to be defied. Like Ahab's white whale, or Mallory's Everest, it had to be challenged, because it *existed*. As did all ballpark walls. Or a bean-balling pitcher. Or a catcher blocking the plate. They used to say of Bobby Layne, the potbellied quarterback, he never lost a game—he just ran out of *time*. In Reiser's case, one could argue that he never muffed a ball—he just ran out of *space*.

Bill Heinz kept track of Pete's injuries. Eleven times carried off the field. Nine times he came to in a hospital or the clubhouse. Once he broke a bone in his right elbow and taught himself to throw lefty. Seven of the nine times he crashed into walls, he either fractured something or dislocated a shoulder. Twice he was beaned. Once he was operated on for a blood clot on the brain.

In later years, coaching for the Cubs, Reiser recalled, "I ran into the wall only twice that I hurt myself—in 1942 and 1947. Hell, any ballplayer worth his salt has run into a wall. I'm the guy who got hurt doing it, that's all."

He underestimated the damage wreaked on his beautifully coordinated body. By 1942, he was having dizzy spells and headaches, experiencing severe weight loss. Yet he played on Army teams, showing the same reckless courage, once tumbling into a gully and further maiming his right shoulder. They wired the shoulder and Pete came back to Brooklyn after the war. But the magic was gone.

It shocked me, reading the record book, to discover that Reiser, after leaving Brooklyn, played for the Braves, the Pirates, and the Indians. It was the early fifties and a new dynasty had come to Ebbets Field. His career dwindled into wisps of the old Reiser talent. In 1952, his last year, he hit .136 in 34 games for Cleveland.

He died of a respiratory ailment, aged sixty-two, in California.

Yet how can a Pete Reiser die?

He's in our memory, cherished, clear and bold on a steamy July day in Brooklyn. The grass gleams, the sun is high. For all the wrong bettors, the disappointed, those who nurture the memory of loss, dead friends, vanished loves, ambitions unfulfilled, Pistol Pete is always there, daring the pitcher to pick him off, slapping the high, hard one to the opposite field, and forever battling his enemy, the wall. He meant so much to so many of us. We cried when we learned of his death. . . .

Good God, the measure of the man!

Hospital beds and doctors' orders could not restrain him. Once he was beaned by Ike Pearson of the Phillies on the fifth day of the season. Doctors made him promise not to play for a week. But he suited up and sat impatiently on the bench. In the eighth, with the score at 7–7 and the bases loaded, Pearson relieved. Durocher told Reiser to pinch-hit. Wobbly on his feet, Reiser hit the first pitch over the fence for a home run. (As always, he made it tough for writers of fiction.)

The following year he chased an Enos Slaughter fly in St. Louis, struck the wall, and for the first time in his career, dropped the ball. Unconscious, he was hospitalized. The team doctor pleaded with him to sit out the season. (The reader is surely ahead of me.) Two days later Reiser joined the Dodgers in Pittsburgh. In the fourteenth inning, Durocher had no pinch hitters left. He called on Reiser. So Pete smashed a certain "triple" that knocked in the winning runs. Limping and dazed, he only made it to first base and collapsed. He came to in the hospital where Durocher told him, "You're better with one leg and one eye than anyone else I got."

And so we remain in awe of this gifted youth—forever star-crossed and doomed. But never a loser, never one to dog it, never a whiner or complainer. To me, an aging fellow who has had a remarkably unsuccessful career as an intramural softball player and a tennis hacker, a defeatist who battles migraine and nervous stomachs, he remains forever golden, a rare and precious human being.

Damn that wall.

Gerald Green is the author of *Holocaust, Wallenberg,* and *The Last Angry Man.*

STEPHEN JAY GOULD on

DUSTY RHODES

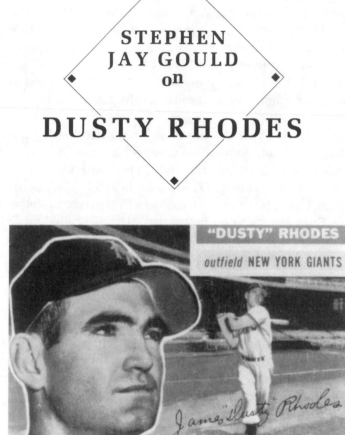

"DUSTY" RHODES
outfield NEW YORK GIANTS

James "Dusty" Rhodes

1956 Topps: Copyright © The Topps Company, Inc.

Circumstance is the great leveler. In a world of too much predictability, where records by season and career belong only to the greatest players, any competent person in uniform may produce an unforgettable feat of the moment. A journeyman pitcher, Don Larsen, hurled a perfect game in the World Series of 1956. Does Bill Wambsganss, with his unusual name and strictly average play as an infielder, ever evoke any memory beyond the unassisted triple play that fortuitously fell his way in the fifth inning of the fifth game of the 1920 World Series?

CULT BASEBALL PLAYERS

All ship's carpenters are named "Chips," all radio engineers "Sparks." By a similar custom, anyone named Rhodes will end up with the nickname "Dusty." James Lamar (Dusty) Rhodes, an alcoholic utility outfielder from Mathews, Alabama, made me the happiest boy in New York when he won the 1954 World Series for the New York Giants, all by himself. (I will admit that a few other events of note occurred during these four short days—Mays's legendary catch off Vic Wertz among others—but no man, and certainly not a perpetually inebriated pinch hitter, has ever so dominated our favorite days of October.)

The 1954 Cleveland Indians were probably the greatest team of my lifetime. They compiled the best record of the modern era, 111-43 for an incredible winning percentage of .721. (I just turned forty-eight, and no other team on my watch has come close to breaking .700. The 1939 Yankees, another of our century's greatest clubs, squeaked by the barrier at .702 when I was minus two. People forget the ironic fact that the Yankees, who won the American League pennant in every other year between 1949–1958, actually compiled their best record of the decade by coming in second to the Indians at 103-51 in 1954). With a pitching staff of Bob Lemon, Early Wynn, and Mike Garcia (not to mention an aging, but still able, Bob Feller), Cleveland was an overwhelming favorite to slaughter my beloved Giants with dispatch.

The Giants won that World Series in the greatest surprise of modern history (matched only, perhaps, by the 1969 Mets, whose victory, or so George Burns tells us, was the only verifiable miracle since the parting of the Red Sea). Those two Series, 1954 and 1969, have two other interesting elements in common, but in each case the 1954 Giants provide the cleaner and more memorable case. One, both the Giants and the Mets were overwhelming underdogs, yet both won commandingly with four straight victories. But the 1969 Series lasted five games, because Baltimore beat Tom Seaver in the first contest; the Giants put the Indians away in four—clean, simple, and minimal. Two, both victories were sparked by the most unlikely utility ballplayer. Al Weis (remember Big Al?) won the Mets' first game with a two-out single in the ninth, then tied the last game with an improbable homer. Dusty Rhodes fared even better. He won, tied, or assured victory in each of the first three games. By then, the Indians were so discouraged that they pretty much lay down and died for the finale.

If Leo Durocher, the Giants' manager had been able to call the shots, Rhodes wouldn't have been on the team at all. In fact, Durocher told Giants' boss Horace Stoneham that he would quit as manager unless Rhodes were traded. Durocher had two objections to Rhodes: he couldn't field, and he couldn't stay sober. Stoneham agreed and put Rhodes on the block, but no other team even nibbled. As Durocher said, "Everybody else had heard about Mr. Rhodes, too. Any club could have claimed him for a dollar bill. Thank the Lord none did." Durocher was appeased by Stoneham's honest effort, and even more by Rhodes's stellar performance as a pinch hitter in 1954, when he batted .333, in that role at 15 for 45.

Rhodes won the first game of the 1954 Series with a three-run homer in the tenth (after Willie Mays had saved the game with his legendary catch off Vic Wertz). It wasn't the most commanding home run in the history of baseball, but they all have the same effect whether Carlton Fisk grazes the left-field foul pole in Fenway Park or Mantle hits one nearly into orbit. I loved the old Polo Grounds, but it had a bizarre shape, with a cavernous center field and short fences down the lines to compensate. The right-field corner sat at a major league minimal distance of 258 feet from home plate. Dusty just managed to nudge one over the right fielder's outstretched glove—an out anywhere else.

In game two, Durocher called upon Rhodes earlier. Wynn held a 1–0 lead in the fifth, but the Giants had two on and nobody out. Rhodes, pinch-hitting for Monte Irvin, dumped a single to center, tying the score. In the seventh, he added an insurance run and silenced the grousing about his "cheapie" of the day before by blasting a massive homer that was still rising when it hit the upper facade, 350 feet from home.

Durocher, on a roll, inserted Rhodes as an even-earlier pinch hitter in game three. He came in with the bases loaded in the third inning and knocked in two more runs, including the ultimate game-winner, with a single.

All this happened long ago, but my memories of joy and vindication could not be more clear or immediate. I had taken all manner of abuse, mostly from Dodger fans, for my optimism about the Giants. I had also bet every cent I owned (about four bucks) at very favorable odds. I ended up with about fifteen dollars and felt like the richest kid in New York. I'd have bought Dusty a double bourbon, but we never met, and I was underage.

Dusty Rhodes was a great and colorful character, but a strictly average ballplayer who had a moment of glory. You will find him in record books for a few other items—he once hit three homers in a single game, two pinch-hit homers in a single inning, and has the most extrabase hits in a doubleheader. But he was no star during his seven-year career, all with the Giants. People tend to focus on great moments and forget averages. They then falsely extrapolate the moment to the totality. Thus, many fans think that Dusty was a great pinch hitter throughout his career. Not so. As Bill James points out, Dusty's career pinch-hitting average is .186. He could do no wrong in 1954, but his pinch-hitting averages in his other six years were .111, .172, .250, .179, .152, and .188.

Who cares? Our joys and our heroes come in many modes and on many time scales. We treasure the consistency of a Ted Williams, the resiliency of a Pete Rose. But we hold special affection for the journeyman fortunate enough to taste greatness in an indelible moment of legitimate glory. We love DiMaggio because he was a paragon. We love Dusty Rhodes because he was a man like us. And his few days of majesty nurture a special hope that no ordinary man can deny. Any of us might get one chance for an act of transcendence— an opportunity to bake the greatest cake ever, to offer just the right advice or support, even to save a life. And when that opportunity comes, we do not want to succeed because we bought the lucky ticket in a lottery. Whatever the humdrum quality of our daily life, we yearn to know that, at some crucial moment, our special skills may be exactly right and specially suited for the task required. Dusty Rhodes is a symbol of that hope, that ever-present possibility.

Last I heard, Dusty Rhodes, still fighting the demon rum, was working on a tugboat in New York harbor. The past can set a cruel standard but can also provide solace. I only hope that Dusty Rhodes, the agent, continues to feel even half the pleasure that I, a mere observer, experience whenever my thoughts turn to the Polo Grounds and the early autumn of 1954.

Stephen Jay Gould is a professor of geology and the Alexander Agassiz Professor of Zoology at Harvard University. He is the author of *Wonderful Life: The Burgess Shale and the Nature of History, The Flamingo's Smile, Ever Since Darwin: Reflections in Natural History, The Panda's Thumb: More Reflections in Natural History, Time's Arrow, Time's Cycle: Myth and Metaphor in the Discovery of Geological Time, The Mismeasure of Man, Ontogeny and Phylogeny,* and *Hen's Teeth and Horse's Toes.*

JOHN KRICH
on
MANNY MOTA

Is this how private deities are born? Nobody else seemed to take notice of his annual wizardry. After all, he was too dark, with a face lost in the shadow of his cap brim, a determination that couldn't be gauged at a distance. He was too foreign, another one of those products of U.S. Marine invasions who come north to stage an annual, symbolic reconquest through sheer force of will, who played this ultimate Yankee game with such flair and bravado that it seemed made for them. When he was young, he was traded too often, playing for four different teams in his first eight years, shunted from one bench to the next—have bat, will travel. His name rarely appeared on the starting lineup card, and it was a funny, diminutive, alliterative name to boot. He did his good work too quickly and too late in the game. He was gone from the game and the country before he'd been noticed, striking and slashing at the first opportunity, daring failure or success to come as quickly as possible. He hit .304 in a twenty-year career with the Giants (1962), Pirates (1963–1968), as part of an amazing center-field platoon with lefty-hitter Matty Alou, Expos (31 games in 1969), and Dodgers (1969–1982), and always seemed to have one of the highest averages in either league—was I the only one who took note?—but he never could get enough at-bats in a season to qualify for a batting title or get listed among the leaders. He was never voted the most valuable player, either of his league or his team, though he won as many games as any of his contemporaries ever did. He won't ever be considered for the Hall of Fame, though he performed his specialty better than any man ever asked to do it.

He was the greatest pinch hitter of all time, with a record 150 hits, but he won my undying adulation for being the ultimate marginal man, box-score afterthought, legal alien, minority. Manny Mota was the quintessential Latin player: unknown and underrated, unseen (he played in the field only sixteen times in his last eight years) and uncredited (except for the vicious rumor that he holds the major league record for killing fans—two—with line drives into the stands), oppressed and vengeful, speechless and ageless and faceless. Like any good God.

All praise be to the All-Seeing One of the seeing-eye grounder, Swami Motoji of the pinch hit, the Zen master of the swiftly slashed single to right! All credit to this sinewy sage in sanitaries, this Dominican magician with a wand of Tennessee ash, this calculating Espanish everyman who regularly and miraculously triumphed over all aches and hesitancies! In the religion of baseball, I belonged to the congregation of the denomination of Mota—and genuflected before his baseball card mounted on an index card that formed a fabled talisman that my pals dubbed "the Mota chip." I reveled in that ultimate Zen moment of the Latin game when Manny rescued the 1977 pennant for the Dodgers along with his *numero uno* nervous disciple, Vic Davalillo—who wasn't just some punk scrub late-inning substitute, but the all-time Venezuelan hit-leader, idolized as "Victico" in Caracas, along with being the brother of Pompeyo Davalillo. Down to their last out in the playoffs with the Phillies, Davalillo calmly bunted for a hit with two strikes. Doubling the karma, Mota loaded up and followed with a pinch double over Luzinski's confused head—shocking Philadelphia into submission. I was amazed when my high priest proved himself a veritable immortal, reactivated at forty-four, brought back year after year for a few key September hits. This was the man who inspired the old baseball saw, "He could fall out of bed on Christmas morning and get a hit."

Probably because he did just that for many years of winter ball in Santo Domingo—where I couldn't resist traveling to pay my respects. For years, Mota has managed the Licey Tigers, affiliated with the Los Angeles Dodgers for whom he coaches in the summertime. Down here, he's Manuel, a respected *veterano* and *gloria nacional*, grooming himself for the call to lead a big-league club that will probably never come for someone this Negroid or exotic. After a game at Estadio Quisqueya, I sneak into the plushest locker room that L.A.'s pocket change will buy. Carpeted, soft-lit, with a steam room, just like in the *mayores*. I have to talk my way into the divine Mota's lair past an equipment manager. Mota's just showered, though all he's done today is fill out a lineup card. How can he refuse an audience when I can peek through to see he's armored in nothing but a towel?

In the buff, a mere mortal. Mota looks like he's ready for another comeback. While I'd thought of him as having made the most of the least through self-knowledge, one look at Mota without his clothes shows me this is no otherworldly type. This monk knows only discipline, discipline, discipline. He's all rippling sinew: if he were a dish, he'd be tough and chewy. He's one grisly, tough-meated critter of an *africano*. Even his face has muscles. His cheeks a perfect Nautilus bony. His skin is so black that his eyes are hardly distinguishable. Is it surprising that the greatest pinch hitter of all time should exist in a state of permanent squint? His mouth doesn't smile, and his brilliant teeth only gnash. This man is at once dried-out and dangerous. He is utterly humorless from squeezing out every drop of potential. My reception is icy, but I can't help blurting out the brilliant speech I've been preparing since I landed: "You're my favorite player. I have all your baseball cards."

He offers none of the Hispanic hospitality that usually puts me at ease with Latin players. Some occult Motaesque signal to his assistant lets me pass into the inner chamber. I can shoot a few questions toward him while he dresses. Mota's soon wreathed himself in several layers of gold chain. He looks calculating even in boxer shorts. And what knowledge am I seeking from my Godhead in the flesh? How it feels to shoot a grounder through the right side? Instead I assess his current state of enlightenment by the rows of photos that he has framed and hung in an ascending pyramid on the fake-wood paneling behind his desk. At the bottom of this hierarchy are stock publicity shots of Mota's favored contemporaries: the McCoveys, Stargells, Gibsons. All signed with some variation of "To my good buddy, Manny, the toughest out this side of the Pecos." No Dominicans, I notice. None of his many sons and daughters, who, I seem to remember reading, all have variations of the same name.

On the next rung of angels, documentation of Mota's presence in heavenly antechambers: Mota shaking hands with Lyndon Johnson, Mota shaking hands with Dodger owner Peter O'Malley. I'd settle for shaking hands with Mota! Everyone is holy to somebody else. On the top rungs are the genuine pantheon—those whom even the great Mota serves. First Tommy Lasorda, his current boss, the prophet of Pollyanna, whose stigmata bleed Dodger blue. On the same level, Ronald Reagan, current overseer and pharaoh of the empire of the baseball, el líder maximo. Above this temporal power reigns a spiritual one. And who is at the apex but an unctuous, greased-back Al Campanis, longtime Dodger director of player personnel, the same "good baseball man" who said blacks lacked "the necessities" to manage?

Leaning back in his swivel chair with a devil-may-care attitude, Mota looks ready to guide even the most lamentable of men. He does his best imitation of John J. McGraw of Miller Huggins, an imitation of how every manager imitates every other. Now Mota repeats the lessons he learned from his former Pirate skipper Danny Murtaugh, Lasorda, and all those he's played under, discounts baseball's obvious discriminations by saying, "If you act like a man, you're going to get treated like a man." The game's golden rule—but did it really apply in the South in the fifties? Mota, the man, like Mota the hitter, is unswerving. This Mota is the only Mota I'm going to get. I'm neither surprised nor disappointed. I will always have the ninth-inning rallies he initiated seemingly just for me. And I will always have my faith, the wisdom to guide me through life, the Ten Commandments of Motaism:

"1. Humility is the better part of a batting average.
2. A hit is better than a walk, a bunt even better.
3. It is wiser to stumble and to set forth than to swing tall and never arrive.
4. Don't wait for your pitch. Don't have a pitch. Get that bat off your shoulders, keed.
5. Know your role and don't overreach it. Expand within your limitations.
6. There is a lot of green grass out there and only eight fielders.
7. Get your head in the game. You never know when someone might need you.
8. Choke up on reality.
9. Keep your third eye on the ball.
10. Whatever you do in life, always make contact."

John Krich is the author of *El Béisbol*, about baseball in Latin America. His articles on baseball and travel have appeared in publications throughout the United Sates. He also contributed the essay on Vida Blue to this volume.

GERALD
PEARY
on

CONRADO MARRERO

Miraculously, he had been listed in the Havana telephone directory and when called, agreed to come meet us. A taxi pulled up in front of the Hotel Nacional, where we were guests of the First Latin American Film Festival in 1979, and out stepped a squat, white-haired man with a bull neck and a patterned acetate shirt, a jacket slung over his shoulder, and a Cuban stogy stuck in the corner of his mouth. Conrado Marrero, sixty-eight-year-old Havana resident and one-time ace pitcher for the Washington Senators (1950–1954), swaggered into the hotel lobby.

He would never recall the first time we met. It was in the spring of 1954, after the big-league teams broke Florida camp and bused slowly north. Each year, they would stop and suit up along the way for games, including a single exhibition contest in Columbia, South Carolina. At this particular game, an immensely excited nine-year-old stood by the first-base fence accumulating autographs.

I had gone through the hard-hitting Cincinnati Reds already, securing signatures from Ted Kluszewski and Johnny Temple and others, and now I sought out the Reds' rival: the lowly Washington Senators, "First in war, first in peace, and last in the American League." Sighting a pitcher warming up fifty feet away, I began yelling, "Connie! Hey, Connie! Over here!" Over walked Conrado Marrero, whom I knew well from his baseball card. And an amazing thing happened. He gave me the obligatory autograph and touched by my enthusiasm, handed me a present: a major league Spaulding baseball. I had never forgotten his shy smile, or that kindness.

And now, in the Hotel Nacional lobby, we worked hard to break the ice, for Marrero reasonably was puzzled, and a bit suspicous, about the telephone call to his house. The translator for the occasion, Roger L. Simon (screenwriter-author of *The Big Fix* and other acclaimed detective stories), pointed to me and explained, in Spanish, that I had seen Marrero play.

"Where?" Marrero demanded. "Columbia, South Carolina," I answered. Marrero nodded in recognition, and we had passed a crucial test. For the first of many times, Marrero's eyes twinkled, and in rasping, colloquial Spanish, he began the story of his long baseball career. He rattled off the events of his life in staccato sentences, jumping backward and forward in a chronology every bit as convoluted as in a Gabriel Garcia Marquez novel.

"I was born in 1911, on April twenty-fifth," Marrero announced, proud that he has lived to be an old man, and still a strong one. He had been a sugar cane cutter as a youth, working six long days a week in the provinces in order to play Havana pickup games on Sundays with his *compañeros*. Marrero managed a reputation based on his once-a-week amateur pitching schedule. In Havana, nobody was better. He had a fancy curve, an effective slider, and perfect control. Had a coach taught him? Marrero wagged his finger. "No," he said, and pointed to his brain. "I taught myself."

By 1938, he was a twenty-seven-year-old pitcher at the peak of his talent. But where were the major league scouts? Had everyone so quickly forgotten Dolf Luque, "the Pride of Havana," who between 1914 and 1935 had won 193 games in the big leagues? Marrero would spend ten more years as a nonprofessional before a Mexican team sent someone to offer a contract. In 1947, at age thirty-six, he finally turned professional and journeyed to Mexico to pitch.

Most major league teams were beginning to sign black players. The Washington Senators instead imported Cubans, resuming a tradition it began prior to World War I. Washington rosters in the late forties and early fifties contained such Cuban players as Roberto Ortiz, Sandy Consuegra, Julio Moreno, and Fermin Romero "Mike" Guerra. In Havana for winter ball, Marrero was signed by Senators scout Joe Cambria. In 1950, he became a thirty-nine-year-old rookie pitcher in the American League.

Marrero was laconic about his five major league seasons, but this is what we gathered: that "Mr. Griffith, owner of the Senators, was a friend of mine" and that "the manager, Bucky Harris, talked to me a lot," and that, though he was one of only a few Spanish speakers, "I felt fine. I spent time with my buddies." His only discomfort was over the shortening of his first name to "Conrad" and then "Connie" as a convenience for American fans.

But Marrero was a big-league pitcher at last, helping the Senators stay competitive with the St. Louis Browns and Philadelphia Athletics—at the bottom of the American League. His best season was 1952, when he was 11-8 as a forty-one-year-old starter, with a 2.88 ERA. His belated success was celebrated throughout baseball-crazy Cuba.

The big-league records show that Marrero won 39 games and lost 40, totals not unlike those of Satchel Paige (28-31), who passed decades of stardom in Negro League ball. Marrero matched arms against Paige on more than a few occasions, both in and out of the majors. "Sometimes he won, sometimes I did," Marrero tersely said.

In all, Conrado Marrero accumulated more than 400 victories in a career mostly uncatalogued and virtually unknown in the U.S. What if Marrero had been summoned to the major leagues at a normal age, eighteen or twenty strong pitching years earlier?

Marrero's approval of the Washington organization encouraged a young pitcher from Cuba, Camilo Pascual, to sign on with the Senators. They roomed together when the future-great Pascual was a raw rookie. Marrero, old enough to be his father, was demoted to the bullpen. He was released in 1955, at age forty-four. While he returned home to live with his family in Havana, other Cuban ballplayers were just leaving home for U.S.: Pedro Ramos, Julio Becquer, Tony Taylor, Chico Cardenas, José Valdivielso, and many more.

But Marrero still had some pitches left in his throwing arm, especially since he had added the knuckleball to his repertoire. He played winter ball in Nicaragua until he was forty-seven, and then, in 1958, he got a front-office job with the Triple-A Havana Kings and also worked as a scout for the Boston Red Sox.

"I was a scout for two more years after the Revolution," Marrero continued, now without prodding. "I signed three Cubans, but they only made it to the minor leagues. Relations with the United States broke down, and it was over. After the U.S. embargo, I worked teaching baseball to children."

Marrero remained on call for the Castro government (as is still the case according to an official I spoke to in Canada's Cuban consulate). He showed young players how to pitch. A national hero, he became a celebrity goodwill ambassador (the hotel maître d' pumped Conrado's hand as if this were Fidel himself), but also a serious worker in the Cuban Ministry of Sports. "In Cuba, players are better now than before the Revolution, because there are so many participants in amateur ball," he said, approving of the government's ban on professional sports.

Had Marrero ever regretted his decision to leave the U.S.? "Yo soy Cubano [I am Cuban]," he answered, shrugging his shoulders.

At last it was time to explain my sentimental reason for tracking Marrero down. I told him what had happened at that long-ago exhibition game against Cincinnati. Sitting there in Havana, I shook Marrero's hand and thanked him for spring 1954.

Soon after, he pushed toward me the photograph of a handsome young Conrado early in his Cuban baseball career. He asked that I write my name on it, and then the ex-sugar cane cutter penned his signature. "Muchas gracias," I said. "Every twenty-five years, you give me a present!"

Gerald Peary is a contributing editor to American Film; writes frequently on pop culture topics for the Toronto Globe and Mail, the Los Angeles Times, and Boston publications; and has written or edited six film books. He teaches journalism and film at Suffolk College in Boston.

CULT BASEBALL PLAYERS

TOM
MORTENSON
on

MINNIE MINOSO

Born Saturnino Arrieta Orestes Minoso Armas in Perfico, Cuba, in what is rumored to be 1922, he's known affectionately as "Minnie" Minoso. As a player, he was one of the most exciting performers I ever saw; of former stars, he is one of the most affable, modest men I have ever interviewed (his only stipulation is that I not quote him in broken English); as a personality, he is still adored by his fans. In Chicago, where he had his most productive seasons and still resides, he is a cult figure on the level of Ernie Banks. He's the White Sox fans' favorite, a unique and marvelous individual, a baseball institution that transcends the sporting world.

Most of us can't think of baseball without Minnie Minoso crossing our minds. The "Cuban Comet" is truly the "Constant Comet": he's the only man to ever play major league baseball in five decades—the forties, fifties, sixties, seventies, and eighties. And it's almost a certainty that he'll be making an appearance in the 1990s, too. When he steps up to the plate, the fans and the entire baseball world—probably even the opposing pitcher—will be pulling for him to get a base hit.

This would give him 1,964 hits in an impressive career that included eight All-Star games, three Gold Glove awards for his play in left field, three American League stolen-base titles, three triples titles, four 20-homer seasons, four seasons with 100 runs, four seasons with 100 RBIs, eight years above .300, and a .298 lifetime average. Minnie also held the record for many years for most consecutive seasons of leading the league in being hit by pitches. He also

held the record for most times being hit during a career—192 (since broken by Ron Hunt and current record-holder, Don Baylor). I still remember his fearlessly crowding the plate in his familiar crouched batting stance. He was susceptible to being hit by any inside pitch, but there was little doubt that he was also the target of brushback pitchers, like other gifted early black players such as Jackie Robinson, Sam Jethroe, Luke Easter, and Larry Doby. He was willing to accept a few bruises to live his dream of being a major-leaguer.

It hadn't been an easy dream to realize. Minoso grew up in Cuba in the twenties, about 120 miles southeast of Havana. Like many poor youngsters on the island, he worked long hours in the fields cutting sugar cane. Undoubtedly, that's how he developed strength and endurance. He tells me that he can't remember when he didn't play baseball. He does remember that at the age of eleven, when there was difficulty organizing a baseball team on a sugar plantation, he would recruit players and manage the team himself. Minnie went to high school in Perfico, but since he wasn't allowed to go to school and play baseball, too, he quit school and went to Havana. There he took a job with the Ambrosia Candy Company and joined a semipro baseball team, playing third and pitching occasionally.

In 1946, Minnie progressed to the Marianao team in the Cuban Winter League and established himself as one of the stars on the island. He was voted Rookie of the Year and in 1947 signed a contract with the New York Cubans of the Negro National League. After watching Minnie play for the Cubans, Cleveland Indians scout Abe Saperstein (who founded the Harlem Globetrotters) sensed he was destined for the major leagues. On Saperstein's recommendation, the Indians' maverick president, Bill Veeck, who gave Larry Doby the opportunity to be the American League's first black player in 1947, and also signed Satchel Paige and Luke Easter, purchased Minoso's contract.

Minoso was nearly 28 years old when he broke in with the Indians in 1949. The 1949 Cleveland yearbook compared his talents to those of Doby, the team's star: "The parallel between the Cuban-born Minoso and Doby is amazingly exact. Not only are they exceptionally fleet of foot and possessed of exceptional throwing arms, but each has a tremendous amount of apparently effortless power."

Unfortunately, Minnie didn't get to showcase his talents in 1949, playing in the field only seven times and making only sixteen plate appearances. He spent most of that season and all of 1950 tearing up the Pacific Coast League for the Indians' San Diego farm team. It took until 1951 for Minoso to get his first real shot at the major leagues and he made the most of it. However, it was with the White Sox, not the Indians. At the time, Frank "Trader" Lane was general manager of Chicago. He had been trying to pry Minoso from the Indians for some time and finally did so in a complicated seven-player three-team deal, in which the Athletics were the third party. The trade would make Lane look like a genius. In his first at bat in Comiskey Park as a member of the Sox, Minnie crushed a 430-foot home run into the far left-center-field grandstand—and wiped out the grudging reluctance of the Sox fans to accept a black player. Minnie ended the 1951 season with a .326 average (second only to Ferris Fain's .344), leading the league with 14 triples and 31 stolen bases, and being selected by the *Sporting News* as the American League Rookie of the Year. His hustle and all-out play seemed to ignite the White Sox and excite their fans, as attendance soared to over one million for the first time in years. Minnie was described as the heart and soul of the club and the inspiration for the slogan "The Go-Go Sox." Minnie recalls that it was longtime Chicago broadcaster Bob Elson who nicknamed him the "Cuban Comet."

Through the next few years, Minnie continued to fire up the White Sox. They climbed from fourth in 1951 to third in 1952 (for five years!) and finally to second in 1957. But while Minoso produced on the field, it couldn't have been too easy for him. Minnie not only suffered the prejudice and indignities other black ballplayers endured, especially during the early part of his career, but also had to adjust to a foreign country and a population that didn't speak Spanish. If these hardships bothered Minnie, he never let it show; he simply won over us fans, teammates, and team management with his sense of humor, infectious smile, charm, exuberance on the field, and of course, immense talent. If being thrown at by opposing pitchers bothered Minnie, he never let it show. I remember that he'd just get up, dust himself off, and trot down to first base. However, I also remember that he'd often steal second base on the very next pitch.

In December 1957, the Sox, desperate for pitching, made a brash move: They traded Minoso back to Cleveland for Early Wynn and outfielder Al Smith. Chicago fans were heartbroken and outraged. They heaped abuse and insults on Smith, not because he was black but simply because he was not Minnie Minoso. Unfortunately for Minnie, he missed appearing in a World Series with the White Sox in 1959. He was, however, a big part of an exciting second-place Indians team that is remembered fondly by fans for its cast of unique characters. Minnie's colorful compadres included Billy Martin, Jimmy Piersall, Vic Power, Mudcat Grant, Gary Bell, and Rocky Colavito.

The White Sox reacquired Minoso for the 1960 season. Happy to be home, he debuted with a pair of homers and 6 RBIs. Although he was closing in on forty (by his account), he could still hit and run. He batted .311 (his eighth .300 season in ten full seasons), led the league with 184 hits, including 32 doubles and 20 homers, drove in 105 runs (his most since 1954), and stole 17 bases. Obviously, his return to Chicago didn't dampen his spirits at all. He signed a new contract for 1961, for $50,000. Three of Chicago's four newspapers reported different ages for him.

Minoso had a solid season in 1961, although it was subpar for him. He slipped to a career-low .280 and dropped in every offensive category but runs and walks. For the first time, he had trouble with pitchers other than his old nemesis Hoyt Wilhelm ("I couldn't hit the knuckleball. He knows it, too. I told him"). This would be his last year as a full-time player. In 1962 he was traded to the St. Louis Cardinals, his only National League team, and suffered a fractured skull and broken wrist when he slammed into the Busch Stadium wall trying to catch a drive off the bat of Duke Snider. It was typical of Minnie's all-out hustle. He played just 39 games that year and was traded to the Washington Senators in 1963, batting just .229 in

315 at bats. In 1964, he returned to the White Sox again, playing in just 30 games in what was long assumed to be his final major league season. (However, he would still be playing in the Mexican League in 1973, at age fifty.)

But the White Sox reactivated him in 1976, and he came to the plate eight times as a designated hitter. On September 12, he became the oldest player in major league history to get a hit. He was fifty-three years old when he was the starting designated hitter in a double-header against the California Angels and singled in his first at-bat against Sid Monge. Previously, Nick Altrock of the 1929 Washington Senators held the record for the oldest player to get a hit. Minoso was nine months older than Altrock.

In 1980, the White Sox brought Minoso back for two pinch-hitting appearances, making his playing career span five decades.

Minoso has not returned to Cuba since 1960. He makes his home in Chicago and is a member of the White Sox public relations staff. As a goodwill ambassador, "the symbol of the old tradition of the White Sox," according to Sox community relations manager Paul Reis, Minoso enthusiastically makes special appearances on the team's behalf. Reis told me one story to illustrate Minoso's character:

"Minnie was scheduled to make an appearance in a western sub-urb of Chicago. We got a call from the people where the event was to take place that Minnie was late. I thought that it was really unlike Minnie to be late or miss an appearance. Well, a couple of days went by and the incident sort of slipped my mind. Then I received a nice thank-you note in the mail telling me what a great guest Minnie had been. I later found out that the reason Minnie was late was that he had stopped along the freeway to help a lady with a flat tire. He took the tire off, drove it to a service station in his own car, had it fixed, returned, and put it on her car himself—all while dressed in a busi-ness suit. And he still made it to the appearance."

Reis recalled another incident that involved Minnie and a sales representative with whom he was supposed to appear in the Chicago metropolitan area. "They were taking separate cars, and since the salesman knew where they were headed, he asked Minnie to follow him in his car. They take off down the freeway and all of a sudden, Minnie passes the guy like a shot. He's chasing another car ahead of him at about seventy-five miles per hour. All the time, the sales rep is wondering what's going on. Well, the car Minnie's chasing pulls over and Minnie leaps out of his car and opens his trunk. He takes out a couple of White Sox caps and gives them to the people in the car. It seems that all this happened because those people waved to him. He probably didn't give it a thought that the reason they recognized him was because his license plate reads MIN-OSO."

Having seen Minoso at appearances for the White Sox, I can easily understand why he's so popular with fans of all ages. It would be difficult, if not impossible, to find a more responsive autograph signer. He's been known to wear a button on his lapel that reads "Just ask, I'll sign." He greets everyone who lines up for his autograph with a friendly smile and a handshake. He takes additional time with kids, often asking them about how they are doing in school. They adore his outgoing personality. They shower him with affection and he returns it tenfold with genuine sincerity. He simply loves the attention. During his playing days, Minnie was famous for staying long after the other players went home to sign autographs for fans. Then after about an hour or so, he'd excuse himself to take a shower and get out of his uniform. He'd tell anyone who hadn't gotten an autograph or who wanted to ask questions to meet him outside the park. He'd tell them where his car was and stay there until everyone who wanted a Minnie Monoso autograph got one.

One honor that has eluded Minnie has been election to baseball's Hall of Fame. I suggest that had he played in the majors throughout the prime of his career that he would have an honored place in Cooperstown. It's likely he would have accumulated the 3,000 lifetime hits that guarantees induction. In his typically diplomatic style, Minoso says it doesn't bother him to be excluded. He says his legion of fans are the Hall of Fame to him. He tells me he has no regrets. "I'm proud of everything," he says, "I'm proud to have been a baseball player."

Tom Mortenson is the editor of *Sports Collectors Digest.*

JOHN LITHGOW on
TED KLUSZEWSKI

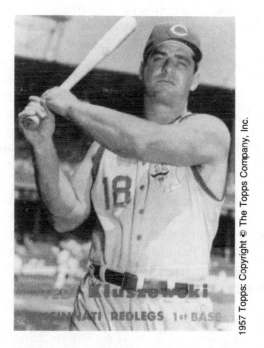

1957 Topps: Copyright © The Topps Company, Inc.

The movie business is a funny thing. I recently played a broken-down vet in a film called *Distant Thunder*, a man who's never met his own son. In an early scene, the son opens a cigar box from among his dad's old, abandoned effects. Atop a pile of mementos is a baseball card from the old man's boyhood, back in the fifties. Whose face is on the card? Unbeknownst to me, and by the wildest coincidence, the prop man had picked my childhood hero, Ted Kluszewski, "Big Klu," from that not-very-big Red machine, the mid-fifties Cincinnati Redlegs. Imagine my astonishment watching the film for the first time and seeing Klu's handsome, steely-eyed face grinning up at me from inside that box! The coincidence had a special kick since I'd already agreed to reminisce about Kluszewski in print. I figured our names were somehow destined to be linked.

Something was surely at work in my ten-year-old head and heart that made me focus on this ungainly giant on that marginally competitive team all those years ago. The memory of Kluszewski had enlarged him in my personal pantheon as I've grown older. Perhaps it's because in many ways I've grown up to resemble him. Comparing Klu in his prime to myself in mine, the similarities resonate: both Buckeyes, both big men, genial if shy, who have taken star-supporting roles in several less-then-stellar seasons of our respective games, and both with thorny surnames that set us metaphorically apart from our more accessible, pronounceable teammates. It was always you and I, Klu, from the beginning.

The beginning was in 1955 when baseball dawned on me like the first look at the green grass of Crosley Field while emerging through one of its creaky grandstand gates. I was ten. Suddenly the Redlegs took on gigantic importance to me. I donned a yellow belt with its quaint bandoliered flamboyance and guarded younger children as they crossed the street by my school, every morning and afternoon. Why? Because after an entire school year of this, we safety patrols were all promised Redlegs tickets in the spring. I insisted that my parents fill up our black Studebaker with Sohio gas and nothing but. Why? Because at each visit to the Sohio station I could claim a free glossy photo of yet another Redleg. A budding Leroy Neiman, I spent hours drawing meticulous pencil pictures of Redlegs in action, for my own one-of-a-kind yearbook. (God, I wish I still had it!)

The *real* yearbook, of course, was scripture to me: I memorized every word. The numbers, however, I ignored. Statistics never held for me the compelling fascination of those thumbnail bios, complete with birthplace and date, marital information, hobbies, and "ancestry" (the first time I'd ever seen the word) of Gus Bell, Wally Post, Johnny Temple, Joe Nuxhall, Roy McMillan, Ed Bailey, the great rookie Frankie Robinson, and of course, Big Klu. It was by this means that I learned that Kluszewski was a Polish name (!) and that Ted's hobby—so attractive!—was woodworking. I also remember a photo of Klu lounging backyard-style with his pretty wife. I had to admit he was heavy for a baseball player (I didn't know he'd been a football star at Indiana), and his face was almost too kindly. But in my eyes these were aspects of his unlikely heroism.

And then, of course, there were the Kluszewski biceps. I'm quite sure that I first encountered the entire concept of "biceps" in connection with Big Klu. The Redlegs uniform of the day featured a sleeveless white shirt with tight red sleeves extending down to the elbow—a look the Pirates made more famous a few years later when Mazeroski single-handedly did in the Yankees. There were no red sleeves for Ted Kluszewski. His naked pneumatic arm muscles rippled in the sunshine, visible from the farthest reaches of Crosley Field. With typical modesty, Ted let it be known that he found the tight sleeves of his trendy uniform to be too confining, constricting his bearlike home run swing. But he wasn't fooling me. I knew that, deep down, he was showing off. There was a hidden strain of arrogant barbarity under that fey demeanor.

Too hidden, perhaps. Big Klu was probably not as feared a hitter as he should have been, considering his home run stats and hefty batting average. Sadly, he was a laughable first baseman. And his nature was the precise opposite of that far-more-celebrated Reds leader of the next decade, the fire-breathing Pete Rose. It is certainly no accident that Kluszewski's Redlegs were congenital losers while Rose's Red Machine was one of the most successful recent baseball dynasties. But to a small-town Ohio boy, hoping that the world he grew up in would give equal honor to qualities of strength and kindliness, Big Klu, "the gentle giant," was my natural mentor.

A while ago a fellow named Danny Peary asked me to write about my boyhood baseball hero, be he ever so famous or obscure. He even provided a list of unsung heroes to jog my memory. I phoned him right away and laid claim to Kluszewski without even consulting the list. I guess I assumed Klu's name wouldn't even be there (it was). Peary was delighted I'd picked Big Klu, an old favorite of his, too. "I guess you heard he died last month," he said, over the phone. It was the first time I'd thought about or talked about Ted Kluszewski in at least ten years, the first time I'd said his name aloud. To hear of his death that moment (and so recent! *another* coincidence!) was exquisitely sad. Kluszewski was part of my discovery of baseball— its excitement, fun, and heart-stopping significance—and of the sometime goodness of the people who play it. His death felt like the loss of something precious I'd forgotten I owned. To my surprise, I miss him.

John Lithgow won Tony Awards for his performances in *M. Butterfly* and *The Changing Room*. He received Oscar nominations for *The World According to Garp* and *Terms of Endearment*. His other films include *The Adventures of Buckaroo Banzai, Harry and the Hendersons, Twilight Zone—The Movie, Blow Out, The Manhattan Project,* and *Distant Thunder*.

LEONARD KOPPETT
on
YOGI BERRA

When Lawrence Peter Berra first appeared at Yankee Stadium in the closing days of the 1946 baseball season, he had long since been called Yogi by his friends, but not yet by strangers. One of the famed Yankee sluggers at that time was Charlie Keller, whose muscular arms and bulky shoulders emphasized his fearsome impression of extraordinary power and earned him the nickname "King Kong" Keller. Yogi's torso, at least in outline from a distance, seemed to be a smaller version of Keller's, and he also represented (by reputation) a home run threat from the left side of the plate and was also supposed to be an outfielder. So to the Yankee fans of the day, the newcomer Berra was known as "Little King Kong" before "Yogi" became not only familiar but inseparable from his identity.

His roommate was Bobby Brown, who also had played with him at Newark in the top rung of the Yankee farm system. They were very different. Keller's powerful frame was topped by a face that could be called ruggedly handsome; Yogi's was better described as lumpy-friendly; but Bobby had classic good looks and was called Golden Boy, not because he had yellow hair and hailed from California (the Golden State), but because he had received the then-unheard-of sum of $50,000 as a signing bonus. He was one of the first avowedly "scientific" hitters, had been to three colleges, was preparing himself for medical school, and was clearly an intellectual. Yogi, whose schooling in the St. Louis district called The Hill could best be described as sporadic, was clearly not an intellectual.

Now skip fast-forward about forty years.

Dr. Brown is now president of the American League. He was part of the Yankee team that won five straight World Series (1949–54), with certain interruptions for military service; he had become a highly successful heart specialist, settling in Texas; he had reentered the baseball scene by becoming a part owner of the Texas Rangers and took on the league presidency after retiring from medicine.

Yogi is now a coach with the Houston Astros, in the National League. He was a much bigger part of those Yankee teams, and a dozen others. He has compiled the most massive World Series statistics of any player. He has been Most Valuable Player three times. He has been voted into the Hall of Fame. He has managed the New York Yankees and the New York Mets into the World Series (losing both times in a seventh game). He has prospered in outside business as well as in baseball and has for decades been one of the most recognizable public figures in America.

That Bobby Brown should reach his mid-sixties as an all-around success surprises no one; all the ingredients were always visible.

But how come this Italian kid from an immigrant-dominated neighborhood in St. Louis, locally overshadowed by his garrulous buddy named Joe Garagiola, winds up even more successful? His assets weren't visible at all.

Until you got to know him.

Then you found that intelligence—the ability to grasp, understand, remember, and utilize the information about you—is not diminished by lack of "book learning" and smooth speech; that sincerity—the honest wish that all associates do well—cannot be faked and carries its own reward; that the ability to rise to occasions and perform best under pressure is a gift, to be appreciated wherever it is found; and that being an always-willing worker with an absolute minimum of egotistical considerations is a bigger part of winning than a picture-perfect appearance or glib demeanor.

People have made fun of Yogi all his life—but with affection and respect, a truly potent combination for popularity. But it was Yogi's ability to accept and absorb the teasing, cheerfully and amicably, while never letting go of a firm grip on his own values, convictions, and determination, that made the popularity permanent. In the brightest of publicity spotlights, for more than four decades, Yogi remained completely himself—a rarer and more difficult accomplishment than making the Hall of Fame.

And the keynote has always been incongruity. Unimposing body, great athletic ability; mangled words and phrases, surprising sense and insight; humble beginnings, then wealth and honors; at times ridiculed, blamed, fired, defeated, and treated unfairly—but never losing his dignity, in his own eyes or the world's. And of course, the name itself, acquired when he did headstands as a training device among the kids on The Hill.

It started with the very first anecdote circulated about him back in 1946. Yogi read sports pages for information (which he had the knack of memorizing in an apparently bottomless data bank) and comic books for literary experience. Brown, the med student, was lugging around his thick copy of *Gray's Anatomy*. Eventually, Yogi asked him, "How'd that book come out?"

A sign of ignorance? Sure. A dumb question? Not if it's based on ignorance. What could be more reasonable than to expect so long a book to resolve its plot?

Soon afterward, he produced one of his earliest celebrated malaprops. Being converted to a full-time catcher, Yogi had trouble mastering the defensive side of the job. The Yankees brought in Bill Dickey, his illustrious predecessor, as a coach, making Berra his special project.

"He's going to learn me all his experiences," Yogi explained.

Poor grammar? Sure. Correct sense? Absolutely.

About a popular restaurant: "Nobody goes there anymore, it's too crowded."

About his qualifications when suddenly promoted to Yankee manager at the end of his playing career: "Sometimes you can observe a lot just by watching."

About a performance of the opera *Tosca* during a visit to Milan: "We liked it. Even the music was good."

About close ball games and pennant races: "It's never over until it's over."

As with all other much-quoted sages, many remarks attributed to him were made by someone else—but the fact of attribution, the desire to have Yogi's imprimatur on the ludicrous-but-valid-and-insightful observation, is the true measure of his impact. The prelude "As Yogi Berra said" lends prestige, authenticity, and humor to the one who uses it—and in the process, establishes Yogi's status in a way outright praise could not.

Outright praise is inescapable when one discusses him as a player. His ability as a hitter was the basis of his excellence; his defensive play didn't match his offense, but it was of high quality in its own right; and his intuitive grasp of the mental aspects of winning baseball games was exceptional, the part of him most often underrated.

At bat, he could pull anything, even a pitch not in the strike zone, against any kind of pitcher. That's what made him particularly dangerous in late-game situations, along with his gift of concentration/relaxation in the right proportion. His 358 homers, 1,430 runs batted in, 75 World Series games played, are merely statistics. Key hits—game-winners, rally-prolongers, momentum-changers against the toughest pitchers—were his hallmark.

As a catcher, quickness was his forte: quick hands, quick feet, blocking low pitches, pouncing on bunts. And he was durable. In a six-year stretch, he caught more than 140 games a season five times.

And his baseball brain was first-rate. He could analyze what he couldn't verbalize. About the right pitch, the right play, the right estimate of a player's ability, he would simply be correct a larger portion of the time than most people. Casey Stengel, his manager who teased him about being "my assistant manager," noted that characteristic early in Yogi's career. It's the reason that, as a manager himself, he won pennants in both leagues, and as a coach contributed to so many others.

Why did fans love him? Well, he produced, of course; he came through for their team when rooting interest was at its height in clutch situations, so why wouldn't they love him? But beyond his own team's fans, he had appeal because he never said or did anything mean; his persona was entirely nonthreatening; and his face, voice, and name were instantly recognizable and unforgettable.

Most of the greatest baseball stars—Ty Cobb, Ted Williams, Rogers Hornsby, Joe DiMaggio, even Sandy Koufax—projected an air of aloofness, partly out of shyness, partly out of the inherent aggressiveness that helped make them great. The ordinary person feels awed but uncomfortable, dazzled if not intimidated, in their presence. But Yogi, by reputation as well as in his undistinguished size and appearance in civilian clothes, was obviously accessible and not to be feared.

There's a special category for baseball stars of this type: Dizzy Dean, Goofy Gomez, Pee Wee Reese, Stan the Man Musial—an amalgam of the right nickname, a gregarious personality, and a projection of wit or softness in manner. At the mention of their names, let alone in their presence, people's faces light up.

At his career peak in the middle 1950s, Yogi held out for more money. (He wanted $55,000 that year, when that was near the top of the scale.) At the annual New York Baseball Writers dinner that winter, we did the following sketch:

Two bleacher fans are playing cards and complaining. Ticket prices went up, the hot dogs are lousy, they're unemployed and beset with domestic problems, broke, bitter, and completely cynical. Then Berra's name comes up. "Poor Yogi," says one, "can you imagine them not giving him his $55,000?"

"Yeah," says the other, "what lousy cheapskates. Poor Yogi."

Whatever the quality of the sketch (it did get a few laughs), it was an accurate reflection of the universal response to "Yohg," as his friends came to call him. People empathized with him. His existence brightened the scene.

Among other things, Yogi was a tireless moviegoer and instinctive critic. He became a competent actor (playing himself) in commercials (including his classic Yoo-Hoo ads), and wound up with his own one-minute television spot reviewing movies. Like Joe DiMaggio as "Mr. Coffee," he became better known to the next generation as a character in TV commercials than as a baseball player. One of them encapsulated his special viewpoint. He is asked to rate movie-actor dogs and says his favorite is Rin Tin Tin.

Courtesy New York Yankees

"But Rin Tin Tin is dead," says the voice-over.

"Yeah," says Yogi. *"Now."*

Bobby Brown, trained by his father from the age of five to swing a bat with purpose, rises to the highest levels of medicine and baseball administration. Yogi Berra, St. Louis street kid, becomes identified as a philosopher of his time. Truly, only in America.

Leonard Koppett is editor emeritus of the *Times-Tribune* in Palo Alto, California. He covered baseball from 1948 to 1978 for the New York *Herald-Tribune, New York Post,* and *New York Times.* He is the author of *A Thinking Man's Guide to Baseball.*

ROY
CAMPANELLA II
on
ROY CAMPANELLA

A Sunday doubleheader in St. Paul, Minnesota, a memorable Father's Day, June 20, 1948. My father was catching for the local Dodger farm team. He hit two home runs, and just after six P.M. my birth was announced to the crowd at the ballpark. Later that week my father received the other good news he had been waiting for: Branch Rickey wanted him to join the Dodgers in Brooklyn. It has always seemed appropriate that my birth coincided with the advancement of my father into the major leagues.

The youngest of four children, Roy Campanella was born in Philadelphia in 1921. His father, John Campanella, the popular owner of a fruit and vegetable market, was white, a first-generation Italian American. His parents came from Palermo in Sicily, where the rhythm of peasant life is affected by the sounds emanating from church bell towers. *Campanella* means "little bell" in Italian; *campanilismo* symbolizes the spirit of the rural peasantry in Italy. John married Ida Mercer, a lovely, intelligent black woman. They met considerable resistance because of their integrated marriage, but the question of color never posed a conflict in their household. Although it never was important to my father or our family, in retrospect it is another unfortunate example of bigotry in America that my father's origins have been much less acknowledged by Italian Americans than African Americans.

By the time he was fifteen, Dad was playing in a tough sandlot league, more than holding his own against men in their twenties. That same year, 1936, he was recruited by the Baltimore Elite Giants of the Negro National League. This meant being on the road for as

much as two months at a time and occasionally catching as many as four games a day. While he had power and natural ability, he greatly benefited from the instruction of a mentor, "Biz" Mackey, the seasoned manager and catcher of the Giants. Mackey provided the insights Dad would need to develop defensively. He also taught him "the art of enlightened conversation," or how to break a batter's concentration by initiating light chatter.

During the winters Dad played in such places as Cuba, Puerto Rico, Mexico, Panama, and Venezuela, where he also was a manager. He was as popular in the winter-baseball circuit as in the Negro Leagues. But here, too, he had difficulties with a color caste system. When I was eight, he told me of having once stood in line at the post office in Panama, where there were separate queues for white, brown, and black people. He told me many other stories of degrading scenes of white racism, taking place in America and Latin America, before and after he joined the Dodgers, to prepare me for manhood and give me a context for understanding his approach to life. Most of my father's fans may not understand that his ability to see beyond the bitterness and disillusionment, which can result from facing years of prejudice, is based on deep religious convictions and the intelligent, pragmatic conclusion that "living well is the best revenge."

After nine years with the Giants, my father spent time in the Dodgers' farm system with Nashua, Montreal, and St. Paul. He was already twenty-six when he joined Brooklyn. Though he detested the racism that had prevented African Americans from playing in big leagues until 1947, he was not angry knowing that a player of his caliber should have started in the majors five years earlier. Instead he embraced this opportunity. He wanted to carry the torch for Josh Gibson, whom he idolized, and other Negro League stars who would never get his chance. Also, he just loved the game too much to be bitter—his life was and is baseball.

He was the first black catcher in the majors. Branch Rickey knew that the bigotry Jackie Robinson faced as a black infielder from fans and opponents could be worse for my father, because a catcher was responsible for "calling the shots." A former catcher himself, Rickey simply advised that he use his natural leadership skills, immense knowledge, and intuitive sense of the game to develop highly individualized relationships with the Dodger hurlers. He pointed out that if race came between him and a pitcher, their relationship could rapidly deteriorate. My father agreed. This did not mean he would become a "yes" man who would accept their racial slurs. A passive approach would have undermined his authority and eliminated the essential element of mutual respect. As it turned out, my father's sanguine personality was perfectly suited to Rickey's proposed strategy. White pitchers like Carl Erskine, Johnny Podres, Clem Labine and Ed Roebuck developed close, trusting relationships with him. Of course, the same could be said about black pitchers such as Don Newcombe and Joe Black.

Rickey came to call him "the perfect receiver." He had a quick, analytical mind that contributed to the team's defensive strategy, an encyclopedic knowledge of hitters' strengths and weaknesses, excellent fielding ability, and was a master at handling pitchers. "He took charge of his pitchers," attested Rickey. "He assumed authority."

As a hitter, my father always had power but worked hard to bat over .300 in his three MVP seasons. He learned by studying other hitters. He particularly admired Joe DiMaggio because of his consistency, Ted Williams because of his concentration, and Henry Aaron because he proved a ball could be driven if you use your wrists. As in everything he did on the field, my father took great pleasure in hitting. He was proud of his many homers with the Dodgers, including 41 in 1953, then a record for major league catchers. But he spoke with more excitement about his homers in exhibition games in the South in 1946–47. He felt a sense of triumph in having homered off white pitchers in segregated ballparks where black fans were forced to sit in the unshaded bleachers.

Dad always had a sense for the dramatic. On October 2, 1953, he was scheduled to be the featured guest on the premiere of Edward R. Murrow's *Person to Person*. That afternoon, the Dodgers played the Yankees in the second game of the World Series. The Dodgers' PR man joked it would be great if he had a good game before appearing on national TV in prime time. So he homered in the bottom of the eighth to win the game, 3–2.

He made everything look easy. He was just in that circle of greatness where talent coincides with opportunity and dreams come true. While proud of his achievements, he *never* boasted or infringed on others. He had a distinct sense of dignity and humility. He was at peace with himself. Which isn't to say he didn't get depressed if he got injured or disappointed if he had a bad game. He always wanted to do better. He'd advise me, "There is no need to compete with other people. The important thing is to try to be better each time you have a chance at something. Compete against yourself."

As a youngster I spent a lot of time at wonderful Ebbets Field. I'd sit in a box seat near the Dodger dugout. Even during important games, my father was never too busy to acknowledge me and ask if I was hungry or thirsty, and being very protective, to remind me not to eat too many hot dogs or go running around the stadium, which I did anyway. Until I was about five or six I'd cheer wildly any time he hit the ball, even if he made an out. I distinctly remember one time when he grounded out to second and I jumped up and applauded. He turned to go back to the dugout and I said, "Good try, Dad!" He smiled and said, "Not good enough." The fans around me laughed, and that was the first time I realized there were other people in the park watching my father, that it wasn't just a private thing the two of us shared.

Even as a young boy I could tell he was one of the best players. I remember when Willie Mays, a close family friend, took a big lead off first and my dad noticed him leaning and picked him off from a squatting position. I was as startled as Mays. "It's all in the wrist," Dad explained to me, like a magician revealing his secrets. I remember his hitting home runs. I also remember his getting triples because

CULT BASEBALL PLAYERS

Young Roy with his famous father. Courtesy Roy Campanella II

fielders underestimated his speed. He was much faster than you'd think when you saw his hefty, squat physique. In the stands, I shared my father's enthusiasm on the field and I also felt excitement and a sense of danger. Once a baserunner rounded third, and I could tell by the way he was charging home plate that he intended to spike my father. Dad moved gracefully to the right, planted one leg, and while tagging him out, kicked him in the ass (so hard that the strap on his shin guard broke) and sent him flying. He did it all in one motion and it was so beautiful.

Sitting so close, I could also hear the racist remarks coming from the opposing dugout that were directed at my father, Jackie Robinson, and the other black Dodgers. Eddie Stanky, when he managed the Cardinals, was particularly abusive and encouraged his players to emulate him. Casey Stengel is so beloved that it may surprise some people that he was particularly insulting to blacks; he was a racist who used the word "nigger" as if he thought it were appropriate.

Many strangers commonly assume it was wonderful growing up Roy Campanella's son. They are right but for the wrong reasons.

While I am very proud of my father's accomplishments and cherish our father-son relationship, living on borrowed importance has never brought me any pleasure. As a youngster I would occasionally ask my friends to introduce me as just "Roy" when meeting other children. I learned to accept the extra attention and curiosity because it was usually given out of respect for my dad, but it was difficult to adjust to the persistent name-association game I was forced to play with the general public. "Are you related to . . . ? Is your father really . . . ? I felt so bad when he had his accident. Is your father still alive? I'm from Brooklyn and I loved watching your father play. Let me shake your hand, it's an honor. . . . Didn't you want to follow in your father's footsteps?" In retrospect, had I not been an "all-star" Little Leaguer, playing baseball as a youngster could have been a miserable peer-pressure experience. Also, it's fortunate that I knew at an early age that I wanted to be a filmmaker and my parents encouraged me to pursue my dreams. "Do what you love most," Dad advised, "and make sure you can earn a living at it."

My father and at times our entire family have been under a microscope of media and public attention. In the mid-fifties, when we'd go to restaurants or out shopping, my father would constantly be approached by sports fans and well-wishers seeking autographs. On weekends a steady stream of onlookers would cruise by our home in Glen Cove, Long Island, pointing at our house. Inside was a close-knit family. I was the first child of my father's marriage to my mother, and his first son; both my parents had children from prior marriages. My father had two daughters, Joyce and Beverly, who lived with their mother in Philadelphia but visited often, and my mother had a son, David, who was five years older than me and lived with us. My brother Tony was born two years after me, and in 1953, my parents had a daughter, Ruthe, whom we affectionately nicknamed Princess. My father owned a liquor store and every year a photo of a different child would be on the calendar he gave to his customers— I used to think it strange that people all over Harlem had my picture hanging on their walls. In the mid-sixties, my father would adopt Joni and John, the children of his third wife, Roxie.

My parents were loving but also strict. They placed a high value on discipline. My father never read Tolstoy but his philosophy certainly reflects the saying "The only true happiness comes from honest hard work and sacrifice." Although we had a housekeeper, the kids were expected to participate in all of the domestic chores. But it wasn't always work. The boys often played catch with my father. And we enjoyed his hobbies, like his extensive collection of electric trains and his passion for fishing. Some of our happiest weekends were spent on our yacht, fishing in the Long Island Sound.

My parents were adamant that their kids get a good education and continually encouraged us to go further than what was being taught in school. As a youngster with a voracious appetite for the written word, I developed a passion for Ernest Hemingway. Before reaching my midteens I had read all his work. (I was struck that Hemingway's definition of courage as "grace under pressure" seemed an accurate description of how my father handled tough situations on and off the field.) Years later, my father revealed that when the Dodgers were in Cuba in the late forties, he and Jackie Robinson were the only Dodgers not invited by Hemingway to the author's home. An oversight? Papa Hemingway specifically requested that the Dodgers not bring any black ballplayers. As my father explained, he had not spoken of this encounter when I was a teenager because he didn't want to discourage me from reading, Hemingway or any other authors.

"Celebrity is a mask that eats into the face," observed John Updike. My father would reply, "Only if you let it." My father's "public mask" is an honest but selective representation of his private self. Nothing about him in public is artificial, especially the kindness he displayed in the 1950s to children at Ebbets Field and at such places as the Harlem YMCA. In public and during press conferences, Dad always expressed himself in terms that could easily be grasped by the public. He is a complex man but knows it doesn't make sense approaching an interview as if it were a therapy session. Even so, the press has on many occasions taken his comments out of context and even worse, invented thoughts he never expressed. Jules Tygiel, in his much praised *The Great Baseball Experiment*, states that "when young black Dodgers would complain about discrimination, Campanella would call them aside and explain, 'You're in the big leagues now. It's nice up here. You're getting an opportunity to show what you can do; don't louse it up for everybody else.' " In fact, my father never tried to stop other blacks from complaining about discrimination. His good-natured, optimistic approach to life never meant that in public or private he was an apologist for discrimination. There were numerous examples of his standing up to racists on and off the field. In a minor league game a white player, Sal Yvars, deliberately threw dirt in my father's face as he squatted behind the plate. My dad's response was immediate and forceful: "Try that again and I'll beat you to a pulp." Tygiel even mentions an ugly incident in 1953 when Lew Burdette, who was notorious for throwing beanballs at black players, twice knocked down my father and then yelled, "Nigger, get up and hit." My father got up and charged the mound.

My father was unfairly characterized by some sportswriters as being less committed to civil rights than Jackie Robinson. But the fundamental difference between them was style and not substance. In the early fifties, we lived in the same neighborhood, St. Alban's, Queens, and they would drive to work together. There were no great debates. They both detested racism and wanted to see the full benefits of democracy extended to all Americans of African descent. Both resented being treated as second-class citizens, but they expressed their resentment in different ways. For instance, after an exhibition game in Miami, they approached a cab to take them to the Lord Calvert, the impressive black hotel where we stayed. They were rejected by a white driver. "Jackie wanted to stay there arguing with the fool," my father recalls, "and I told him it didn't make sense because he wasn't listening to us." Besides, my father didn't want to do business with the driver. The driver never changed his mind and Jackie finally agreed with my father that they should call a private car. Both Robinson and my dad hated such racial terrorism, and that is what segregation and apartheid really are, but neither could change things that moment outside a ballpark in Miami. Whether hot or cool, no African American was going to ride in that racist's cab.

Both men were inspiring role models to American youth and authentic heroes to African Americans. So it is a disservice for sportswriters such as Tygiel and Lowell Reidenbaugh to stereotype Robinson a "militant" and my father a "conservative." Such labels are easily revealed as false when the actions of both men are examined in relation to the political persecution of Paul Robeson by the House Un-American Activities Committee. Branch Rickey urged both Robinson and my father to testify against Robeson at a committee hearing. Robinson agreed—a decision he would always regret—and my dad declined. Years later, Paul Robeson, Jr., would tell me with touching sincerity how deeply his father appreciated my dad's refusal to denounce him. My father told me, "White people will use you to attack other blacks, be careful of that. For instance, the sportswriters use me to attack Jackie—that's why you can't believe anything you read. I respect Mr. Rickey, but why should I denounce Paul Robeson? I told Mr. Rickey I'm a baseball player and I don't need to get into politics." In fact, Rickey, as would Walter O'Malley, counseled players not to get involved in political issues, inadvertently providing my father with an acceptable justification for not speaking out against Robeson.

My father always saw himself as a baseball player and not a social crusader. But he was deeply committed to the civil rights movement led by Martin Luther King. He and Robinson knew Dr. King because they stayed at his home in Atlanta when the KKK threatened to kill them if they played in an integrated Dodger exhibition game. Dad never considered Dr. King too "militant." He firmly believed, as did my mother, in his nonviolent philosophy for social change and supported sit-ins and other civil rights demonstrations. He recognized that Malcolm X was militant and didn't agree with all his conclusions, yet he didn't object when I regularly played his recorded speeches when I was older.

In 1959, about a year after my father's tragic auto accident that left him a quadriplegic, our family traveled to the West Coast to attend "Roy Campanella Night" at the Los Angeles Coliseum. Dodger owner Walter O'Malley had organized a spectacular tribute exhibition game that was attended by 94,000 adoring fans. We all cried when everyone lit matches to honor my father and the entire coliseum was like a huge birthday cake. The applause was thunderous. It was a beautiful, touching evening. But our trip was marred by the Jim Crow treatment we received at the Sheraton Hotel in Los Angeles. The management informed my parents that no blacks were permitted to use the pool facilities. My parents were livid. After unsuccessfully protesting to the hotel manager, my dad complained to O'Malley. The Dodgers subsequently withdrew all business from the hotel. My father's style may not have been combative, but it was not passive. He initiated change. I was ten years old at the time and was filled with such anger and resentment—I wanted to inform on the hotel to the 94,000 fans who had been so nice to my father and, I was sure, would have been appalled by what had happened. My father told me, "Regardless of what you've accomplished, regardless of how much education you have, there are some people who will still treat you as a second-class citizen just because of race. But I hope you never let anyone convince you that things should be like that." And I never have.

Many of the roads I have taken return to the lessons of my father. His life has certainly been an example of turning adversity into a valuable lesson for self-development. Dad is a firm believer in willpower. He is a wellspring of courage and conviction. He is a true competitor and spirited team player. He is the quintessential athlete.

In the late sixties, I read Zen and the Art of Archery. It told how Zen archers are able to repeatedly achieve bull's-eyes while blindfolded and in total darkness. They use bows that are unusually difficult to pull and require not just strength but a powerful skill that eludes most archers. I discovered a surprising similarity between my father, as a ballplayer, and these Zen archers. My father had the same distinctive power. He was in perfect harmony with the game of baseball.

Roy Campanella II is a filmmaker with a background in anthropology, which was his major at Harvard University. He has directed the feature *Not Without Laughter;* the PBS documentary *Passion and Memory,* about blacks in films; episodes of such television series as *Lou Grant, Hooperman, Frank's Place, Dream Street,* and *Wiseguy;* and the television movies *Quiet Victory: The Charlie Wedemeyer Story* and *Body of Evidence,* which he also produced.

EDWARD HERRMANN on

LOU GEHRIG

"He used to pick up bobby pins."

"Bobby pins?"

"Yeah, bobby pins! You wanted to know his habits, didn't you?"

"Yes, yes, Mrs. Gehrig."

"Well, we'd be walking and talking about the day's game or the guys on the team or how much he loved *Tristan and Isolde*, and suddenly he'd stoop down and pick up a hairpin, you know, and he'd fiddle with it as he walked along. He'd never pick up anything else."

"Did he work out at home?"

"No. Didn't have to. He went through all that when he was a kid at some German gym on Second Ave. in the eighties. He had all the muscles he needed. He liked to stay as loose as he could. I guess he did some Swedish stretching exercises at the piano. When I took him to the ballet, he loved it. He thought dancers were the best-conditioned athletes of all."

"Did he feel awkward going to the ballet and opera?"

"When I took him to *Tristan and Isolde*, he insisted we slip in a side entrance. He said life would be impossible in the dugout if any of the bench jockeys discovered he went to the opera. It was his first opera so he didn't know what to expect. His jaw dropped open. A whole new world opened up to him. We went to every performance. But around the other players, he was ashamed of his feelings."

"Did he get tense?"

"Well, he took the game very seriously. When the Yankees were in town, after the game I'd drive down to the stadium and pick him up. If they'd lost, he never said a word. For two or three hours, until I put dinner on the table, he'd sit in a chair in the living room and not say anything. I knew he was going over every single pitch, every single chance he had, or anybody else had, and trying to figure out how they lost the game, how they could have won, how he could have done better. Little by little, I mean a word at a time, I'd bring him back and he'd start to go over things. He took losses real hard."

"Did he resent Babe Ruth's getting more attention than him?"

"Never. When Ruth left, the team tried to make Lou the glamour boy. He hated it. They stuck him in a movie, and he had this big, forced, silly grin. He just wanted to get out of there. He was acutely embarrassed. Lou hated extracurriculars. He just wanted to play baseball."

"About his illness . . ."

"It was terrible. . . . He never complained."

"Did Gary Cooper get him right?"

"Not really. He was all right, but he was always a little nervous. He looked uncomfortable in the uniform—didn't move like a ballplayer. Not quick and graceful like Lou."

"Is there anything you want me to get over about him—any quality he had that I could try and express?"

"He was a square guy. Just a wonderful . . . square, honest guy. Try to get that."

Try indeed. I didn't do a very good job of portraying Lou Gehrig in the 1978 television movie *A Love Affair: The Eleanor and Lou Gehrig Story*. What made it so tough was that I could find no "key" to his character. There was no strangeness, there was nothing spectacular about him. As Eleanor Gehrig told me, he was just a square, honest guy.

In terms of their illnesses, I couldn't really draw on my portrayal of Franklin Roosevelt in two earlier television movies. Roosevelt had an illness he could live with; once he overcame the initial shock, he got back into politics. But Gehrig had a degenerative disease that made him weaker and weaker. Just before he was diagnosed, the Yankees came through Detroit on the way to Chicago. Hank Greenberg told me that Gehrig was still working hard, doing wind sprints. In Chicago he went to the Mayo Clinic and found out what was wrong. The next time Greenberg saw him he was tired and listless, not able to run around. Breathing became progressively more difficult. For an athlete so strong, who loved physical activity so much,

CULT BASEBALL PLAYERS

it must have been devastating that he could no longer concentrate on the simple game, no longer pour everything into it.

Being a baseball fan, I well knew of Gehrig's great stats and importance to the game and cared how I portrayed him as a ballplayer. I worked like hell to learn to bat and throw left-handed. And I did it. At least I could make it look plausible. For *Pride of the Yankees*, they had to dress Cooper in a uniform with the letters backward, film him throwing right-handed toward third, then reverse the negative. True! I even got contact lenses so I could hit the ball and not have to fake it. But I'm a miserable athlete and Lou was magical. I didn't look like I could hit .340 lifetime or play in 2,130 consecutive games.

Luckily for me there wasn't much baseball in the script. It was mostly about a man and a woman who find exactly the right partner and rejoice for the rest of their lives—despite Lou's tough, unscrupulous mother and his fatal illness. As he said in his incredible farewell speech, he absolutely believed he was "the luckiest man on the face of the earth," not only because he had had a remarkable career with the Yankees, but because he had Eleanor. Until he met her, Lou experienced emotional starvation. There was nothing effete about him—he was just a quiet, sensitive man in need of emotional release. She came to represent that to him, and I think that's why he became so devoted to her. Eleanor appreciated that Lou was a patient, deep man, and though she was, like my own mother, an Irish–American with a fast, intuitive mind and an impatience for intellect, she was glad that Lou was the more intelligent and better educated of the two. She was a strong woman who provided the protection he needed. She didn't mind spending her life looking after him, taking care of finances and other business, and giving him freedom to shine on the diamond. I don't know why they never had kids, but being alone, they just became closer and closer.

So in the movie, I had lots of intimate scenes with the wonderful Blythe Danner, who played Eleanor. And it went pretty well. Eleanor Gehrig sent me a letter after the film was broadcast. I cherish it more than I can say. But I don't agree with her that I was better than Gary Cooper. On the other hand, I may have gotten as close to that straight, generous heart of Lou's as he did. Which isn't to say that we weren't both far, far away from him—in the bushes somewhere.

Lou Gehrig. The Iron Horse. What a gentle, powerful, decent man he was. No show, no razzmatazz. Hank Greenberg told me he never jumped away from a dust-off pitch. He just moved his chin back and stood his ground. How could anyone really portray that kind of hero? If offered the choice of being able to ride across the screen like two-time Oscar-winner Gary Cooper or hit like Lou Gehrig, there'd be no question which this actor would take. Thanks and kiss that baby good-bye!

Edward Herrmann starred in the television movies *A Love Affair: The Eleanor and Lou Gehrig Story, Eleanor and Franklin,* and *Eleanor and Franklin: The White House Years,* for which he won the TV Critics' Circle Award. On Broadway, he won a Tony Award for *Mrs. Warren's Profession* and the Theatre Guild Medal for *Plenty.* His films include *The Paper Chase, Annie, The Great Gatsby, The Purple Rose of Cairo, The Lost Boys, Reds, Compromising Positions, Overboard,* and *Big Business.*

HEYWOOD HALE BROUN on

JOE DIMAGGIO

When I was a boy—when the milkman still had a horse, when a sign in your window told how big a block of ice you wanted—the out-of-school reading of my peers included books about Baseball Joe and the Merriwell brothers, Frank and Dick.

These young men, in addition to being remarkable players, were paragons of virtue, men of honor, believers that victory was not victory if it was tainted with questionable tactics. As I grew older, I learned that the world was a much more complicated place than the fictional diamonds of sunny-ended boys' books, and by the time I had become a professional baseball writer I was on my way to that cynicism which we call "realism" or "maturity."

Then I met Joe DiMaggio and discovered that "maturity" was less exciting than purity, the dedication governed by a code that Joe brought to the game. Joe did not seem to me as happy-go-lucky as the players of my favored fiction, but that was because, as we all discover, the maintenance of honor in a pragmatic world is a difficult task, rather like going up hill while carrying a tombstone at a horizontal angle. It never gets easier.

"You never know what a gentleman is," wrote Scott Fitzgerald, "until you cease to be one," and constantly measuring one's actions against a set of ideals is wearing and gloomy business.

When I joined the Baseball Writers' Association in 1941 as a green reporter for the New York newspaper PM, DiMaggio had already put in five years of distinguished major league play. Older colleagues told me that he was polite but remote and not one for swapping yarns in the dining car on road trips. From my junior position at the end of the press box I didn't essay to talk to him at all, but we were thrown together by chance when he hurt his foot sliding into a base in Philadelphia's old Shibe Park, and returning to New York by train, shared a seat with me.

I asked if he was going to consult a doctor about his injury and saw his taciturnity give way to a torrent of angry words. It seemed that doctors who had done nothing for the knee injury he brought with him to the Yankees had further contributed to his pain by burning him with a diathermy machine and were constantly urging him to try various deadening shots, apparently unaware that to a person who goes all out, the mutings of danger signs are an invitation to permanent injury.

To a man striving for perfection, as DiMaggio constantly was, the tinkerings and patchworks of doctors were maddening and occasionally inept intimations of mortality.

"I'll last a lot longer in baseball," he said to me, "if I stay away from doctors altogether."

I was honored to be his confidant in this conversation, but I had little occasion to improve on it as I was shortly summoned to military service. I saw Joe next in 1946 when, not much more experienced as a writer and still working for my small-circulation newspaper, I was standing in the lobby of the Ben Franklin Hotel in Philadelphia and wondering how to kill the time until it was a suitable hour to

Courtesy New York Yankees

go to the ballpark. To my happy surprise the supposedly reserved DiMaggio hailed me and issued an invitation to coffee. Pleased but puzzled, I realized that he certainly had no interest in planting a story in my paper, the equivalent of putting it in a bottle and throwing it in the ocean, and came to understand as we chatted pleasantly and inconsequentlally about our Army years that he was obeying a Merriwell rule. As the leader of the team he had an obligation to make new boys feel at home, and little as he may have wanted to spend time with an unimportant stranger, he did the job with easy grace and none of the condescension that people doing The Right Thing sometimes show.

Our next encounter tested his principles heavily if accidentally. I had been assigned to write a piece about him for a now-forgotten magazine and had made a date to meet him at the Edison Hotel where he maintained a suite. On the chosen day I called from downstairs on the house phone and found myself talking to a man in distress.

"That's right," he said slowly, "I promised you. The thing is, it's my day with the boy," a reference to Joe, Jr., who lived with his mother, Dorothy Arnold, the ex–Mrs. DiMaggio. "Well, I told you today, so come on up." I was aware that these visits were precious to the lonely father and pointed out that another day would do as well and that he should devote the day to the pleasures of his son. There was a pause after this, and Joe said in a voice between doubt and hope, "But I gave you my word." I told him to forget that, but he persisted once more. "You release me from the promise?" he said, and as solemnly as one knight talking to another about a question of tournament protocol, I told him that I released him from the promise. He thanked me with great warmth and for some time thereafter showed me gratitude with a share of his normally sparing dugout conversation.

I am indebted to the late Jimmy Cannon, perhaps Joe's closest friend among the writers, for a story that I think best illustrates Joe's complex but unswerving devotion to honor.

In the first game of the 1947 World Series between the Yankees and Dodgers, Jackie Robinson, always a zealous player, strayed a little beyond zealotry and threw a rolling football block on Phil Rizzuto when the little Yankee shortstop had gotten out of the baseline after completing a double play. There was a little booing, and then the incident, like the inning, was over.

Later in the game DiMaggio hit a routine grounder to Pee Wee Reese, who threw over to Robinson, an inexperienced first baseman who put his foot right across the bag, an invitation to a legal and painful spiking, which DiMaggio managed to avoid with a sideways leap.

After the game Cannon asked him why he hadn't stepped on Jack's foot after what the Dodger had done to Rizzuto, and DiMaggio, after a moment of consideration, said, "I thought about it running down to first base, and then it occurred to me that Phil's an Italian, I'm an Italian, and Robinson is black, and I didn't want them to think it was the guineas against the niggers. If Phil was black or Robinson Italian, I guess I would have done the spiking."

As Cannon remarked, that was a lot of sociological thinking for three and a half seconds of running, but the wheels of the inner DiMaggio had so long been trained to turn in the direction of decency that the decision was made instantaneously with the appearance of the foot across the bag.

In addition to the restraints Joe imposed on himself, there was his generosity, strange in a basic puritan, about the problems of others. It was during that same World Series that Joe sent word to the press that he wanted to see them, and in an extraordinary statement spoke in defense of the Dodger outfielder Pete Reiser, who, normally brilliant defensively, had had a terrible time in the Stadium center field. Joe explained to us the nature of the autumn haze, which made it difficult to judge fly balls, lectured us on deceptive trajectories, and in general tried to make us see that Reiser was up against a special phenomenon that erased much of the blame. We all made notes, and as we were leaving, someone asked if Joe didn't have all the same problems. He grinned suddenly, murmured, "Oh, don't worry about the old man," and turned back into his locker to show that the conference was over.

Forgiving his faults, Joe was unforgiving about conduct and deplored much of the so-called "feistiness" that had been introduced by combative managers such as Leo Durocher. When Charlie Dressen, a Durocher disciple, joined the Yankees as a coach, he once demonstrated his disagreement with an umpire's decision by flinging towels and batting helmets out of the dugout. He was in the midst of this mess-making when a sharp command from DiMaggio stopped him and brought him to Joe's side.

"Go out and pick that stuff up—now" was the order. Dressen started to justify his action, looked at the stone face before him, and gathered up the detritus. Later DiMaggio told him, "Charlie, on this ball club when we don't like decisions, we don't throw things. We hit home runs."

So also I remember a night game in 1948 when, a little of the snap having departed from his wrists, he hit what appeared to be a home run until, at the last moment, it drifted foul by a foot or so. He was well on his way to second base at the moment of failure but walked back with no display of dismay to pick up the bat and wait for the next pitch. In the dressing room I asked why he didn't release some frustration by jumping on his cap or throwing up his arms.

He gave me the kind of look he must have given Dressen and said, "Heywood, I can't do that." The meaning was clear—and had a wonderful and justifiable arrogance about it. Second-raters who substituted scrappiness for greatness were entitled to such demonstrations. The greats must pay for their greatness with dignity.

As full of Freud as one can only be after a year of college Psychology I, I warned him that such conduct led to ulcers, unaware that it already, in his case, had.

I didn't see him again for seventeen years, during which I pursued a career in the theater without ever quite catching it, but when, as a TV newsman, I ran into him again at a spring-training base, his first words to me were, "Heywood, that ulcer? I got it."

In his personal life as in his professional, DiMaggio was always deeply concerned with questions of honor and interpretations of his code of behavior, interpretations that were sometimes as complicated as an argument on a constitutional point, but since his personal life is just that, no comments on it will appear here except one. Like many perfectionist people, he liked to have a hanger-on to whom abstractions and ideals were well down the list of priorities. The first of them was Jimmy Ceres, the kind of man who was always asking you to estimate the price of an overcoat, so he could triumphantly top your figure and add the constant comment, "Class, huh?" His chatter did not disturb Joe's ruminations, but the simple sound of his voice kept loneliness and the impersonal but urgent demands of celebrity seekers at bay. An assortment of Damon Runyon types succeeded Jimmy, but the picture that stays in my mind is of Joe staring at something beyond the wall while the current jester made the simple sounds of companionship.

For proof of Joe DiMaggio's greatness as a player, there are magnificent statistics, the lifetime .325 batting average, the 56-game hitting streak, and the 361 home runs, and the plaque in the Hall of Fame. Engraved in the minds of those who saw him are the perfect hip-pivoting swing and the long strides that seemed always to bring him directly under anything that didn't go over the fence. Yes, he was a great ballplayer, but also he was a fictional character who came out of the pages of juvenilia into real life. Nowadays athletes use press agents to create images for them, images that will lead to success in postgame commerce or politics.

Joe DiMaggio achieved success, but without scheming. He did not craft an image. He simply was and is one.

Heywood Hale Broun is a renowned sportswriter, broadcaster, lecturer, and actor.

ANDREW SARRIS on

TED WILLIAMS

Ted Williams was simply the best and purest hitter I have ever seen. Purity, however, is an acquired taste, perhaps even a perverse one. It has little or nothing to do with character, virtue, intellect, morality, geniality, and good old American team spirit, honored throughout our history more in the breach than the observance. Even so, Williams lifted individualism to a new plateau in supposedly collectivist sports when, on the occasion of his being walked with the bases loaded in the last of the ninth to force in the winning run for his Boston Red Sox, he threw his bat up in the air in disgust at not having been given a good pitch to hit. This was the mark of a Romantic virtuoso standing alone on a mountaintop with a unique gift separating him from the rest of humdrum humanity. An Enos Slaughter, a Pete Rose, an Eddie Stanky, would have exuded triumph at such an outcome. Indeed, the tireless Slaughter would have run at full speed to first base. A Minnie Minoso would happily have offered his body as a target to squeeze in the winning run. Williams stood proudly aloof from such pragmatic considerations. His role in the dramatic spectacle of baseball was that of the majestic flailer of a wooden club at the swiftest and most treacherous projectiles that could be launched by a strong-armed hurler.

I just happened to admire Williams's sublime single-mindedness more than did most Boston fans and sportswriters. For them, the stubborn slugger committed the unpardonable sin of disdaining to doff his cap to the public after concluding his home run trot around the bases. Williams had other PR problems as well. Even in his self-imposed solitude, he did not perform in a competitive vacuum. There were Joe DiMaggio and Stan Musial, justifiable legends in their own right, and ostensibly more-dedicated team players to boot. There were such group nemeses as the accursed (to Boston backers) New York Yankees during both the Joe McCarthy (1936–1943) and Casey Stengel (1949–1960) championship dynasties; and to a lesser extent, the 1946 St. Louis Cardinals and their always bothersome left-handed pitching; and the 1948 Cleveland Indians, managed by Lou Boudreau, who invented the infernal "Ted Williams shift" that overloaded the infield on the right side to reduce the left-handed slugger's pull-hitting productivity.

It was almost held against Williams that he performed better in All-Star games—the winning home run in 1941 that erased two previous National League home runs by Arky Vaughan; two homers of his own in 1946, the second a spectacular blast off Rip Sewell's maddening blooper pitch—than in the 1946 World Series and in crucial pennant-deciding games for his own team. This proved, his detractors claimed, that he was not a "clutch" hitter despite a lifetime .344 average and six batting crowns. Williams did not help matters by often exchanging batting tips with opposing players, and by never questioning an umpire's decision. Once, as legend has it, an umpire who remembered that Williams's eyesight was better than his own asked the batter if a pitch he had called a strike had actually been over the plate. "No," answered Williams softly.

A native New Yorker who lived part of my childhood a few blocks from Ebbets Field, I grew up in a largely Italian neighborhood in the years just before the Dodgers became fashionable even in Brooklyn, where the local team received about the same respect accorded the Boston Bees. I remember the year everything changed. In 1939, the Dodgers slipped past the fading Giants into third place, only the second time since 1920 they had finished higher than their crosstown rivals. Suddenly, the kids were excited about the Dodgers. Previously, they had rooted for the Yankees in the '36 and '37 Series, whereas the fathers stayed with Carl Hubbell and the Giants. I was so alienated from the other kids that I started rooting for the Detroit Tigers because I had seen pictures of Charlie Gehringer and Mickey Cochrane on a Kellogg's Corn Flakes box. Joe DiMaggio was an instant sensation in my neighborhood, but not for me. I would come to admire Ted Williams, who broke in with the Red Sox in '39 and immediately began to put up incredible statistics.

Though I couldn't play baseball worth a damn, I loved baseball statistics. I spent hours poring over the league batting averages in

Courtesy Boston Red Sox

the Sunday papers. Baseball was something I could worship book-
ishly in private along with all the other trivia one found in newspapers and almanacs. To this day, I can name all the presidents and
most of the state capitals. But in my childhood I did not know that
the cumulative score of every baseball game ever played averaged
out to five runs for the winning team and three runs for the losing
team. Hence, the significance of the 3.00 earned run average as a
dividing line between good and bad pitching, and by somewhat more
arcane calculations, of .300 as the dividing line between good and
bad hitting. When Ted Williams hit .406 in 1941, his third season,
without the benefit of the sacrifice-fly rule, he set a mark that will
probably never be equalled again, although no one suspected that at
the time.

Stephen Jay Gould, in *The New York Review of Books* of August
18, 1988, states flatly that Ted Williams's .406 average takes second
place in 1941 to Joe DiMaggio's 56-game hitting streak, "both the
greatest factual achievement in the history of baseball and a principal
icon of American mythology." One does not have to demean Di-
Maggio's feat to suggest that the Williams-DiMaggio debate is remarkably complex. At one time, there were rumors of a straight trade
of the two players so that the two superstars could avail themselves

of closer fences in their power fields. Of the two, DiMaggio was the more victimized by the vast "out" spaces of Yankee Stadium's left-center field.

Bob Feller, the Cleveland fireballer, once observed that he had an "out" pitch for DiMaggio, but none for Williams. This comparison was unfair to Joe D. because Feller was thinking of (and exploiting) the deep alley in Yankee Stadium's left-center field, whereas there was no comparably expansive playing area in Fenway's right-center field. On the other hand, Williams never had a chance to come close to DiMaggio's hitting streak simply because pitchers walked Williams too often. In fact, both the 1954 and 1955 batting crowns were denied him because his official at-bats fell short of the 400 required. There was a brief period when the Red Sox lineup boasted eight .300 hitters, but opposing moundsmen still pitched around Williams as if he were the only genuine threat on the team. By contrast, Yankee left-handed sluggers such as Gehrig and Keller in one era, and Berra in another, took much of the pressure off DiMag.

The fear that Williams inspired as a hitter was not based either on the raw power of a Mickey Mantle or the beer-barrel-chested physique of a Babe Ruth or Hack Wilson, the 5'6" slugger who was endowed with all sorts of upper-body strength. The Splendid Splinter was Williams's sobriquet, attesting to his tall, lean build. Williams's power derived from his extraordinary eye-wrist coordination and the ruthless logic of his swing. His rising-line-drive home runs were positively Euclidean in their trajectories. I saw Mantle, completely fooled by a Preacher Roe spitball, lunge out and pound the moist pellet into the center-field bleachers in Ebbets Field. By comparison, the mentally confident authority of Williams's pounding a misguided pitch made the victimized pitcher feel as if he had not done his homework. I saw pitchers arduously nick all the corners to get Williams out, then serve up a grapefruit to overrated shortstop Vern Stephens, and watched him slap it to left field as if he were the intelligent hitter and Williams were the dunce.

Nonetheless, there was an aura around Williams for a worshiper of pure form such as myself. One of my abiding perversities in the contemplation of athletic activities is my tendency to root for the favorite over the underdog. I detest upsets. When I decide that A is superior to B, I expect A never to lose to B. (When that happens too often, I begin looking in B for the hitherto hidden formal beauties I had somehow overlooked.) I expected and counted on Williams to perform well, and my confidence was almost always rewarded.

There was something else about Williams that attracted me. He was so quintessentially "American" for an urban ethnic such as me that I felt the same kind of soft-focus squishiness I experienced in the most romantic movies, coupled with the magic spectacle of a sport linking the heroic with the aesthetic. The numbers speak for themselves even with the four lost prime seasons in two military tours of duty for a man once accused of being a draft dodger by the rabble-rousers of the press. Anyone who has seen Ted Williams swing a bat—and I would cite particularly John Updike for his eloquent tribute to the Fenway Thumper—has had the privilege of witnessing amazing grace under pressure.

Andrew Sarris is a professor of film at Columbia University. A film critic for the *Village Voice* for almost thirty years, his books include *The American Cinema, Confessions of a Cultist,* and *Politics and the Cinema.*

TIM HORGAN
on
JIMMY PIERSALL

A crusty Boston baseball writer took scalpel in hand one day in the summer of 1952 and quickly cut to the heart of the matter. "Jimmy Piersall," he ventured, "threatens to become the greatest attraction the Red Sox have ever had, if he doesn't get hit by a pitched ball first."

The wild-eyed rookie out of Waterbury, Connecticut, came perilously close to doing both that incredible season. In fact, for a few zany months he was even more popular than his renowned teammate, Ted Williams.

Piersall, who much to his dismay had opened the season at shortstop, became a one-man, three-ring circus. He took deep bows after his every catch, flapped his arms like a seal, shook his fist at the crowd, and loudly berated the umpires every chance he got.

After moving to right field, his natural habitat, he shadowed centerfielder Dom DiMaggio all the way to the dugout between innings, mimicking his Groucho Marx lope as the fans hooted and howled.

One notorious June afternoon, the twenty-two-year-old rookie even harassed the revered Satchel Paige, then pitching for the St. Louis Browns. In the ninth inning, with the Red Sox trailing badly, he told Paige he was going to bunt, then made good on his promise, beating it out for a hit. On the base paths, he mimicked Paige's delivery and oinked like a pig. Paige had pitched thousands of games without getting perturbed, but somehow this youngster got to him.

On that one day, Satchel Paige lost his composure. Piersall sparked what turned out to be a six-run, game-winning rally.

Off the field, Piersall fought with Battling Billy Martin, then the New York Yankees second baseman, in a runway at Fenway Park. And after being rescued by three samaritans passing by, he fought with Red Sox pitcher Maury McDermott in the clubhouse.

Piersall's antics captivated every prim and proper Bostonian, if not his teammates, rival players, umpires, manager Lou Boudreau, or the Red Sox hierarchy.

Finally, inevitably, Jimmy Piersall went over the line and around the bend. He allegedly spanked the four-year-old son of Red Sox shortstop Vern Stephens in the locker room. Although Jimmy denied it and there were no eyewitnesses, he was banished to Boston's Southern Association farm club in Birmingham, Alabama.

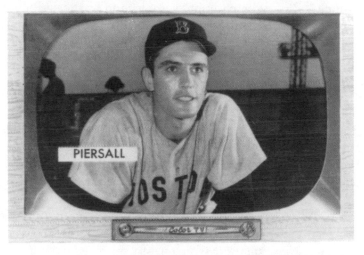

1955 Bowman: Copyright © The Topps Company, Inc.

His behavior was even worse there, but the talented rookie was soon recalled, went berserk shortly after his return, and was rushed to the Westborough State Hospital, where he underwent shock treatments. End of season.

Piersall later revealed that his bombastic debut was a total blank. He didn't remember a thing from the time he walked into the lobby of the Sarasota Terrace Hotel in January 1952 until he awoke in the violent ward of the mental institution seven months later. Even so, he'd been permanently inscribed in baseball lore.

Jimmy Piersall's breakdown and recovery were detailed by the late Al Hirshberg in the best-selling book *Fear Strikes Out*, which later was made into a popular movie starring Anthony Perkins. As a result, Piersall became an international celebrity as well as a cult hero, but not surprisingly, he panned the film.

"I don't know why they ever picked Anthony Perkins to play me," he mused in a subsequent book, *The Truth Hurts*. "He threw a baseball like a girl. I hated the movie."

A few years previous, and more to the point, Piersall had pointed out, "The film focused too much on my difficult relations with my father. It never mentioned the fact that my mother had spent a lot of time hospitalized for a mental problem."

He never denied his own mental problems. In fact, he wrote in *The Truth Hurts*: "Probably the best thing that ever happened to me was going nuts. Whoever heard of Jimmy Piersall, until that happened?"

Well, I'd heard of him, and so had the rest of us kids in the Naugatuck Valley, where Jimmy was a legend by the age of fourteen, playing, and starring, in a league featuring men twice his age. He was such a gifted athlete that he also put Leavenworth High on the map by leading it to the New England basketball championships, scoring 29 points against Durfee High of Fall River in the final at Boston Garden. He was even on the Boston Celtics' negotiation list, but he had long been destined for a baseball career. "I learned to catch and throw a ball before I learned the alphabet," recalled Jimmy, who never complained about that.

He had been an only child growing up in the run-down East End section of Waterbury, a mill town, during the Great Depression. His father, John, a moody housepainter, was a baseball fanatic and in some minds, pushed his son too far, too fast, too hard. Jimmy would always play the role of the brilliant eccentric prodigy. He is, when it suits him, funny, smart, outspoken, and outrageous. And he writes, "I'm crazy as a fox." I think that statement best describes Jimmy Piersall.

I began covering baseball for the *Boston Herald* in 1955, by which time Piersall had settled in as Boston's centerfielder. Although I had also grown up in Waterbury, I went to Crosby High and was a couple of years older, so in those days I had known him only by athletic reputation. As a Red Sox fan, I had cheered the exciting Boston outfielder, worried about his mental health, and marveled at his fielding, like everyone else, but I still hadn't met him. In my new position, I introduced myself to Piersall, mentioning the Waterbury connection. Maybe it was because we had the same hometown, but I always found him to be extremely friendly and cooperative, more so than most of his teammates. I'd bring friends, the uncle who raised me, and even my uncle's priest, over to meet him, and he'd willingly pose for pictures with them by the dugout. He even gave me instructions on how to box Ted Williams ("Just get inside!"), although there was no reason to believe I would require such information.

I loved to watch Jimmy play baseball. I've always felt that his zaniness obscured the fact that he was an extraordinary player. He was a smart doubles hitter who batted a respectable .272 in seventeen-year major league career for the Red Sox (1950, 1952–57), Indians (1959–61), expansion Senators (1962–63), New York Mets (briefly in 1963), and Angels (1963–67). His best average for Boston was .293 in 1956, and he hit a career-high .322 for Cleveland in 1961, finishing third in the league. But it is his fielding that I remember most. Fans not only came to the park to see Piersall's antics but also to see him play the outfield. Much of his popularity was due to his being a colorful performer. Whether in right or center, he played extremely shallow. He wasn't that fast, but he had the best anticipation of anyone I've ever seen and seemed to have run ten strides by the time the ball left the bat—somehow he reached everything. Jimmy contended that Dom DiMaggio was the best centerfielder, but I think Jimmy was as good. Ted Williams, in left, was even willing to put up with his antics because he trusted Piersall next to him—with other centerfielders, he always feared a collision.

By every informed opinion, Piersall was a Hall of Fame fielder, even after he had hurt his arm irreparably in a throwing contest against Willie Mays in 1954—a typically foolish Piersall endeavor.

"I thought Joe DiMaggio was the greatest defensive outfielder I ever saw, but I have to rate Piersall better," Casey Stengel said after watching Piersall rob Mickey Mantle of a homer.

Raved Red Sox general manager Joe Cronin after watching Piersall rob the Senators' Mickey Vernon of a home run at Fenway Park, "That was the best catch I've ever seen." The next day, after Piersall robbed Vernon again, Cronin said, "I take back what I said yesterday. *That's* the best catch I've ever seen."

Proclaimed the venerable Bill McKechnie, when he was the Red Sox third-base coach at the end of a long career, "That kid Piersall gets balls Tris Speaker wouldn't have reached."

The kid appreciated the compliments; but that didn't stop the irrepressible Piersall from lambasting Stengel, Cronin, and many another baseball demigod after he'd retired as a player in May 1967 to "sell" baseball as the Angels' PR man.

. . .

I spoke to Piersall about his long, eventful playing career during a brief reunion of Waterburians at the Buena Vista Country Club, just outside Disney World, of all places, in 1977. At the time, he was tuning up for his latest role as the Chicago White Sox No. 2 broadcaster behind Harry Caray, a match that might have been made by Don King. Sportswriter Dave Nightingale and I arrived on the course early in the morning to discover Piersall in a particularly vivacious mood, talking a mile a minute, and howling like Tarzan of the Apes after swinging wildly and hitting balls a thousand miles into the jungle: "Aweeyaweeyaweeyaw!"

"I'm happy to be alive!" he explained to some curious onlookers.

We were there to play golf, but I took notes as he cheerfully talked baseball. He began reviewing his eight years with his first love, the Red Sox, but frowned when the name of Tom Yawkey, the club's late owner, was mentioned.

"Somebody said I made an obscene gesture at Mr. Yawkey after I hit a home run for the Cleveland Indians," Jimmy told me. "But I never did that and I wrote a letter and told him so. He was too good a guy for me to do that, one of the two guys in baseball who never told me a lie."

Piersall's angular face brightened as he recalled playing for Casey Stengel and the early, futile Mets.

"Casey was an old man by then," he related. "He'd fall asleep during the game. So one day he's sleeping on the bench and the grounds crew is smoothing the infield and I went into the runway and yelled as loud as I could. Casey woke up and right away started flashing all kinds of signs to the grounds crew. I thought I'd die laughing.

"Then I hit my one hundredth career home run and ran the bases backward and Casey was so mad that he cut me. But I got six thousand dollars severance pay for one month, which made it my best payday in baseball, although I'd hit only .194 for the Mets. He did me a favor."

Piersall rejoined the Angels as a free agent as well as a free spirit. "My last four years were my best in baseball," he said, "because Fred Haney ran the club and he's the only other guy in baseball who never lied to me. The other people in baseball try to con you, which is why I'm thrilled to see the players today get all that money. Now the shoe is on the other foot."

Piersall, who had nine children by his first wife, Mary, and has eighteen grandchildren at last count, just missed the big money but has no regrets. I think he prefers to live by his wits. He once told me, "My name will get me through the office door—but once in, I have to do the job." He had seen smart, "sane" players get through the door and then discover that their names could no longer carry them. Piersall was always willing to work hard, whether he was playing ball or selling potato chips.

As Piersall describes it, his postplaying career has been an odyssey in itself. He spent his first two years out of baseball in Virginia, as general manager of the Roanoke Buckskins, a pro football team. "I knew nothing about football," he confessed, "but I knew how to sell tickets. I just hired a good coach and told him, 'I'm an easy guy to work for. All you've got to do is win.' "

The coach didn't follow instructions and both of them got fired. Piersall then became a manager, not of a baseball team, but of a Roanoke hotel. He soon checked out of the hotel business and returned to baseball as Oakland A's owner Charles O. Finley's right-hand man.

"I did everything for Finley," he related. "I sold tickets, made speeches, answered letters, everything. I got along great with him for eight months, and then I joined his host of enemies. He's an egomaniac. He loved to see his name in the newspaper. He let me live in his apartment in Oakland when he was in Chicago, but he'd call me up at six A.M. every morning and make me read the local papers to him. One day he said, 'You're a lousy reader, aren't you?' so I said, 'Then get somebody else to read your blankety-blank newspapers,' and hung up. But that's not why he fired me."

Piersall paused to sink an eighteen-footer and to scream, "Aweey-aweeyaweeyaw!"

"Finley doesn't like to spend money," he continued. "But I was trying to sell tickets and I had to make these discount deals, which I never told him about. I sold $237,000 worth of tickets that season, but one night I had over one hundred groups in the park on discounts. Sure enough, the next day Finley phoned and told me to meet him in Chicago that afternoon. As soon as I got there, he yelled, 'How dare you spend my money on discounts!' I said, 'Charlie, take the money out of my commission.' So he took the whole commission and there was nothing I could do because we didn't have a contract. Just a handshake. See what I mean about baseball people? But that's not why he fired me, either."

Oakland got into the World Series that year, 1972, and "I taught Charlie about limousines," Piersall said. "I told him, now that you're a winner, you've got to travel in style. So he hired a limousine to go

Courtesy Cleveland Indians

everywhere—to the airport, the ballpark, the hotel, dinner. He loved it until he got the bill. That's when he fired me."

Piersall has been hired and fired many times since. He went from work for the world champion A's to Orangeburg, South Carolina, of the Western Carolina League, where he managed the St. Louis Cardinals' farm team and broke the world record for getting thrown out of games, at least by *his* account. He proceeded from there to the Texas Rangers to serve as top gun for his old adversary Billy Martin.

He was fired by Rangers owner Bob Short and rehired by his successor, Brad Corbett, but to sell plastic pipe. "I knew nothing about plastic pipe," Jimmy conceded, "but I knew how to sell."

During a business trip to Chicago, he was invited on a White Sox broadcast with Harry Caray and did so well that he became a regular. "What did I do right?" said Piersall. "I told Caray he was wrong. I second-guessed him all over the place and the listeners loved it."

But Piersall, as usual, also second-guessed the manager, in this case Chisox manager Tony LaRussa, and he called his players "lazy." When owner Bill Veeck and his wife, Mary Frances, complained on their radio show that Piersall was "too harsh on the players," Jimmy called Mary Frances "a colossal bore." Over the years he said many other outrageous things on the air, some that made your hair turn. Jimmy, being no phony, just couldn't restrain himself. I just wish he showed more discretion. When he tried to choke a visiting Texas sportswriter over his scoring of a past game, the Veecks' son, Mike, clamped Jimmy in a headlock. When WMAQ, the NBC outlet in Chicago, dismissed Piersall in November 1983, he sued the White Sox and NBC for $5.7 million "for firing me without reason."

Once during our round of golf, Piersall said of baseball in general, "They don't want you to talk. They're afraid of people who tell them the truth. They don't want to hear the bad news. So they hire nothing but yes-men, mealymouths. Then they wonder why they have problems."

So, as a consequence, does Jimmy Piersall. But as he proved so many times from the moment he arrived in the major leagues, he's a survivor. And when last sighted, he was a contented man, instructing the Chicago Cubs outfielders in spring training. "What I'd finally like to do is put my knowledge of all aspects of baseball to work," he said.

That remains his goal in baseball, but his priorities have changed since his open-heart surgery in Fort Worth, Texas, in 1976. "That's when you realize what's important and what isn't," he said as we left him on the links. "I feel wonderful. I'm happy to be alive. I can do everything but eat ice cream. Aweeyaweeyaweeyaw!"

Tim Horgan is a sports columnist for the *Boston Herald.*

PETER
GAMMONS
on

LUIS TIANT

It was a weekday afternoon in November 1978. Red Sox pitcher Bill Campbell was relaxing in a whirlpool after playing racquetball in Huntington Beach, California, when he heard the news on the radio. Luis Tiant had left the Boston Red Sox and signed with the New York Yankees. Campbell's eyes filled up, and as he wiped away a tear, he said, "I don't think the Red Sox will ever be the same."

Within hours, at his house in Boca Raton, Florida, Carl Yastrzemski received the same news. "They've torn out the heart and soul of our team," said Yastrzemski. "Either George Steinbrenner thoroughly understood our clubhouse, or our owners didn't understand it at all." Six weeks earlier, the Red Sox had lost a historic playoff game to the Yankees. It took eight seasons before they would again seriously contend in the American League, and by then there were only three players left from that '78 team.

El Tiante was special. No one outside of the Tiant family ever knew how old he was, although it was suspected that he was about halfway between the thirty-seven he claimed he was when he signed with the Yankees and the forty-seven his Boston teammates taunted him as being or the thirty-seven Celsius, as was written. The age thing was part of El Tiante's routine. A Mexican League team contacted him in November 1988 and asked him about trying a comeback. "I'm the Cuban Satchel Paige," said Tiant. He damn near tried it, at an age in the vicinity of the speed limit. He was a powerfully built, barrel-chested, sumo wrestler of a man whose chest and derriere always made him look fat, although he really wasn't, and he

Courtesy Boston Red Sox

had funny little spindly legs that as he whirled and bobbed and hesitated and spun in the midst of his delivery made him resemble one of those bobbing dolls people put in their car rear windows. He was nearly bald, yet his body was a jungle of fur. He had a huge Fu Manchu mustache.

And his cigar. El T loved his cigars, gawdy stogies. He'd sit in front of his locker, nude, reading the paper and smoking his cigar. He smoked them in the whirlpool. He was even known to smoke them while taking a shower.

The only man who could possibly mimic Luis Tiant would be Robin Williams, and even then there'd be a lot lost in the translation. El Tiante has a high-pitched voice, and when he speaks, it sounds as if he's inhaling. No matter what he said, he made his teammates laugh. Practically every day for three years Tiant would go into the can, take his constitutional, and shout, "Good-bye, Tommeeeee," as he flushed the toilet. Everyone in the clubhouse always laughed, especially Tommy Harper. Tiant loved to make jokes about physical appearance; in fact, after putting on his uniform daily, he would always stop in front of the mirror and shout, "Seeeex, too, blond hair, bloooo eye . . . gooood lookin' sonavabeeeetch." He abused Harper for his "leeeeva lips," and when Harper lost a fly in the sun in spring training and was hit square on the mouth, first Tiant—in street clothes—fell to the grass down the right-field line laughing so hard that when trainer Buddy Leroux reached Harper in the outfield, he, too, was laughing so hard Leroux couldn't attend to him. That night, Harper went out with El T as he took a practice drive in a car he was thinking about buying, only to get stopped by a Florida State patrolman. Asked what he thought he was doing going seventy miles an hour, Tiant replied, "Bringing some heeeeet." Brewers outfielder Gorman Thomas sauntered by the Red Sox dugout before a game. Tiant let out a high, piercing shriek, then told Thomas, "You scare people—you could be anything in the jungle but the hunter."

"He was a hero to players because it seemed as if he knew exactly how to orchestrate a team," said Yastrzemski. "He's like a symphony conductor, bringing out the highs and lows and all the things composers have imagined." "You didn't hear much of Luis when we were winning and bus rides were raucous," says Carlton Fisk. "Except sometimes he'd puncture someone who was getting a little big for his britches. But if we'd lose a couple and it would be quiet on the bus or on the plane or in the clubhouse, he had a way of bringing it all back to life." Tiant called Yastrzemski "Polacko," and once tossed Yaz's worn, secondhand Colombo raincoat out a bus window. He called Jim Rice "Mandingo." In spring training, 1978, Mike Torrez had signed as a free agent and had the image of being John Travolta choreographed into baseball. One hot afternoon, as Tiant leaned up against a fence outside the clubhouse, sweaty and in uniform, Torrez swished out the clubhouse door, his hair sprayed perfectly, in white pants, a black shirt opened to the waist, gold jewelry . . . "Hey Taco," Tiant yelled at Torrez. "Just remember—you're just another speeeeeek." At the end of the 1972 season, in which Tiant nearly pitched Boston into first place, rookie pitcher John Curtis wrote a newspaper story in which he recounted trying to explain to his wife what he meant when he said he "loved Luis Tiant."

The Boston fans certainly did. When El Tiante got to Boston in July 1971, he'd twice been released and could no longer dominate hitters the way he could when he was young. Because he was pitching in Cleveland and for some inexplicable reason was in the shadow of the ever-overrated Sam McDowell, Tiant never got his due recognition. Throw hard? Over the three-year span covering the 1966–1968 seasons, Tiant had more strikeouts than innings pitched. Ask anyone about the Year of the Pitcher, 1968 (when Yaz won the batting title at .301 and the offense was so bad they lowered the mounds), and he'll respond with memories of Bob Gibson and Denny McLain. But Tiant was better than McLain. For 30 wins or no 30 wins, if Tiant had pitched for those '68 Tigers, he might have won 35 games. Look at his numbers: 21-9, 152 hits in 258⅓ innings, 264 strikeouts and 73 walks, a 1.60 earned run average. "That year he was the best pitcher I ever saw In the American League, and that includes (Ron) Guidry in '78 and [Roger] Clemens in '86," says Ken Harrelson, who was the American League Player of the Year in 1968.

Two years later, Tiant was traded to Minnesota for four players. He started off 7-3, but cracked a rib. That led to a shoulder injury, and in spring training, 1971, Minnesota owner Calvin Griffith released Tiant so he could be free of his contract, which was $25,000 lower than today's minimum for rookies. The Braves signed him on a one-month tryout basis, but the night that month was up, Boston's Louisville farm club was in Richmond. Tiant walked across the field, met with Pawtucket manager Darrell Johnson, and signed. Fenway Park would be changed for the seventies. Not that it was easy. Tiant came up in July 1971, struggled, and was 1-7. Red Sox manager Eddie Kasko stuck by Tiant's comeback, but after one beating, Clif Keane's lead in the *Boston Globe* was, "Enough is enough." In June 1972, Tiant worked his way out of the bullpen and back into the rotation, where he would lead the league in earned run average at 1.91 (the only other American Leaguer to have two sub-2.00 seasons since World War I was Detroit's Hal Newhouser, and one of his came during World War II when most of the best hitters were in the service). In one stretch, he threw five consecutive shutouts, and armed with a stopper for the first time since Jim Lonborg went skiing with Jill St. John in 1967, the Red Sox crept from last place in the A.L. East into a mad scramble for first. Late in September, Baltimore—winners of the last three pennants—came to Fenway Park for a twinight doubleheader. After Boston won the opener, Tiant walked toward the bullpen in right center field to warm up. The entire crowd rose and began chanting, "Loo-Eee, Loo-Eee." When the gate banged open and he began his walk back toward the dugout to prepare to start, the crowd again rose and began chanting, and thus was born a ritual that would be continued until El Tiante was a Yankee.

El Tiante stoned the Orioles that night, putting the Red Sox temporarily in first place, orchestrating the crowd the way he orchestrated a bus ride. He was the fan's pitcher, spinning and whirling, seemingly acknowledging the kids in the bleachers, then letting go what seemed to be a trick ball attached to a rubber band. Oh-and-two? "No chance," Oakland's great third baseman Sal Bando once said. "You're trying to hit an entire crowd." On a hot August night in 1974 when the Red Sox were 7½ games out in front and El Tiante was rolling to 22 wins, he got Bando 0-and-2, and went into his windup, turned his back, stopped to check the left-field seats, bobbed his head three times, hitched, hesitated . . . and Bando began his swing. Then El T let go of the pitch. On September 16, 1975, he cinched the divisional title by shutting out Jim Palmer and the Orioles with a 2-0 two-hitter on one of the wild nights in Fenway history. That was before the fire laws restricted standing-room-only tickets, and then-club treasurer John Harrington estimated there were 47,000 people in the park, all rising and chanting, "Loo-Eee, Loo-Eee," as he rumba'd through the Orioles. He won 20 games three times in four years, and the year he won 18, 1975, he pitched the Red Sox to the pennant, 3-hit Oakland in the playoff opener, then twice beat Cincinnati in the series. He was not only someone you'd pay to see, he was really good. Most of all, he was good when he had to be.

"As great as Palmer and Catfish Hunter were, if you had to win one game in the seventies, you'd have to have Tiant," said Yastrzemski. "He was the best pitcher with a lead that I ever saw. Get him a 1-0 lead and he defended it as if it were his family. He'd refuse to lose." The Red Sox were heavy underdogs to both the Athletics and Reds in the 1975 postseason, but it never occurred to their players that they would start each series with anything but a victory because of Tiant. He beat Oakland 7-1, and shut out the Reds. In September 1978, when Boston's huge lead over the Yankees had evaporated and a tough loss in Toronto left them 3½ games back, Tiant heard teammate Rick Burleson tell reporters that he felt the race was over. The Red Sox were done. "Bool cheat," Tiant swore as he got into a cab the next morning. "If we lose today, it will be with me facedown on the mound." That afternoon, Tiant allowed fifteen Blue Jay baserunners, but only one scored, and his 3-1 win began a nine-game winning streak that would carry the Red Sox back to within a game of the Yankees entering the last day of the season. Before the Red Sox came to bat, fans in the Fenway bleachers began shouting—the Indians had hit three first-inning homers off Hunter. The Yankees were going to lose. "I turned to Yaz and said, 'We're going to be in the game of our lives,' " said George Scott. "We hadn't even gotten up yet, but El Tiante was pitching, and there was no chance in the world that he would lose." Tiant shut out Toronto 5-0 to set up the playoff. It was, of course, the last game he ever pitched for the Red Sox.

That wasn't Tiant's greatest game, nor was the 2-0 shutout of the Orioles or any of the five straight shutouts in 1972 or any game in

1968. The game that all El Tiante cultists remember was the fourth game of the '75 World Series. He had what he confessed was "bool cheat" that night. He sweated terribly and had none of his swagger. He had a 5-4 lead in the fourth inning and got out of a jam with two runners on base. He had two runners on in the fifth, got out of it, and did the same in the sixth and seventh and eighth. Finally, in the ninth, with runners on first and third and two outs and it still 5-4 Boston in a game the Red Sox had to win to even the series at 2-2, Tiant threw his 172nd pitch. Joe Morgan popped it up. El Tiante was described as John Garfield's boxer in *Body and Soul*, the fisherman in Hemingway's *Old Man and the Sea*, and Washington at Valley Forge, but Fisk said it best: "Luis Tiant proves that all men's hearts are far from created equal."

A decade after he left the Red Sox, El Tiante walked into the Red Sox clubhouse and Rice immediately started laughing. "He's El T," Rice explained. In another corner, Evans told Marty Barrett, "If Don Zimmer had just started El T (instead of Bobby Sprowl) in the final game of that four-game massacre against the Yankees, we'd have won the '78 pennant." Mike Greenwell told a reporter, "That man really must have been great. He's a legend. There are two legends around this clubhouse—Ted Williams and Luis Tiant."

Many athletes are heroes in their towns. But few ever touched as many complex feelings as Luis Tiant. Fans paid to see him, for his showmanship, his appreciation of his audience, and because he was a Larry Bird big-game player. Writers loved him for most of the same reasons, but they also knew him; of all the athletes I have covered in twenty years, El Tiante is unquestionably my personal favorite. Most of all, however, his teammates—as John Curtis wrote—loved El T. He made them laugh, he made them cry with laughter and joy, he made them win, he made them equal, no small feat on a team with a caste history. He also made many of them cry that November 1978 day when he signed with the Yankees. Bill Campbell and Carl Yastrzemski were right. They never were the same.

Peter Gammons writes for *Sports Illustrated* and is a commentator for ESPN. A former sports columnist for the *Boston Globe*, he is the author of *Beyond the Sixth Game* and coauthor of the autobiography *Rocket Man: The Roger Clemens Story*.

LOU PINIELLA

One day in 1977, too lazy to move during a Yankees' rain delay, beer and TV balanced on my stomach, I watched The Hulk telling a story in the dugout. Without hearing any words, I stared at the square jaw, wide gestures, and furious drama. With everyone in the dugout intent upon him, he stalked, stomped, spun, and happened to be facing the camera for the denouement, which featured a clearly shaped obscenity. Having never seen that word on television (almost as good as hearing it), I instantly fell in love, madly, desperately, hopelessly, with Lou Piniella.

He was the first ballplayer who was real to me as a man, not just a uniform. I wasn't the only one, I know that. There were the moans of "Looooooooo, Looooooooo" when he came up to bat, the product endorsements. He received the Joe DiMaggio "Toast of the Town" Award in 1983 as a favorite with New York fans; a year later he copped the Ben Epstein "Good Guy" Award from the NY Baseball Writers Association for cooperation with the press. He's still popular in Kansas City, where he was Rookie of the Year in 1969.

I began to collect Piniella-bilia. There were buttons, baseball cards, baseball stickers, newspaper mentions, and photos, any fragment of anything with his name or face. A shrine soon covered three walls of my bathroom. The best item was a picture of Lou surrounded by three lovely young lady models. I photo-boothed my head to their bodies and added a headline cut from a "You & Lou"isiana travel brochure. I clipped and pasted his picture over and over to create a whole team of Piniellas. Lou was my entire All-Looks team. In those

LOU PINIELLA OF
YANKEES

years it was hard to keep a boyfriend; who wanted to pee surrounded by such devotion?

I meditated on his face. He had a tolerant and yet impatient bearing, the way Einstein must have looked when he could tell no one else got it. Impervious calm followed by explosive frenzy. It was said that Sweet Lou described his clean, compact swing, not his personality.

That was Stage I of my infatuation. I began to watch games to see him, which led to Stage II, a genuine interest in baseball, something I'd dropped in adolescence to be a girl. It turns out, though, that baseball's once-upon-a-time hold hadn't entirely disappeared. Heroin addicts claim the drug is smarter than the junkie; you can quit, but if you start up again you start exactly where you left off. I'm still trying to figure out why Lou Piniella embodies that power.

Yes, he was the one who let (and led) me back into baseball. And because of the kind of ballplayer he was. Not a supernova or an immortal, not a Reggie Jackson whom everyone knew, watched, quoted, but a piece of everyday baseball life. Real baseball life is the names, nicknames, stats, and stances that are as carelessly familiar as my brother's voice on the telephone. Not an immutable presence as much as something you'd miss like a mailbox if it disappeared. A fan's player, separating the connoisseur from World Series Johnny-come-latelies. I began to learn the game, as well as see Lou as more than a man who wore pinstripes.

By his numbers he won't make the Hall of Fame. But what he could do, he did impeccably. He was famous for hitting line drives, singles sleek as shadows. Just as you'd imagine that Einstein awoke mumbling equations, I can see Lou springing out of bed, brandishing an illusory bat with that crystalline swing. His lifetime batting average was .291, with 1,257 of his 1,705 hits singles.

But those line drives didn't come every at-bat, and when they didn't, The Temper appeared, flinging bats and gloves, smashing helmets, watercoolers, and once, the new 100-cup clubhouse coffeepot. This was a big part of Lou's popularity. He can't control himself! But it's okay! He's childish in such a manly way!

A Lou Piniella home run was about as common as a Lou Piniella stolen base. He did have the distinction of getting caught stealing for the cycle when he played for Kansas City, thrown out at every base. In sixteen years in the big leagues, he played in five playoffs, four World Series, and one All-Star game. Piniella wasn't handicapped by his lack of speed and so-so arm, because he could position himself as well as anyone in the game. "The best slow outfielder in baseball," Sparky Lyle called him. Swinging too readily at the first pitch was his main fault as a hitter. Stolid, he didn't seem as though he'd ever been a graceful young man, nor even much of an athlete. Not a fraud, but why could he do what he could do? Hitting to keep the world at bay.

No Yankee or Red Sox fan will forget the Bucky-Bleeping-Dent (aka the Bucky-Fucking-Dent) playoff game in Boston in 1978, when Dent, the No. 9 hitter, put the Yankees ahead with a 3-run homer. The other big play was the fly ball Lou Piniella lost in the sun in the bottom of the ninth. "I saw the ball leave the bat and that was the last time I saw it," he said. Bluffing all the way, he kept his composure. "I just thought, 'Don't panic. Don't wave your damn arms and let the runner know you've lost it.' " He suddenly saw the ball bouncing right in front of him. "I lunged and it slapped into my glove. I whirled to my right and fired a throw to third. It was the best throw I had ever made in my entire career . . . Burleson stopped at second." Jim Rice flied out, which would have scored Burleson if he had gone to third, and Yastrzemski popped up to end the game. The Yankees went on to win the World Series.

There I was, deep in my personal crush and the larger pattern of baseball. With Lou the center of both, it was time to go looking for him. Hence, spring training, Florida, 1981. Lou left the game after a few innings and I ducked out after him. Ohmigod, look how close I am. He was big, but not weirdly big like football or basketball players. While infinite, baseball is still a human game. He wasn't The Hulk, but he was definitely a hunk—tall, tanned, big-jawed, with muscles like emergencies.

Other women may have been Loooooooooo-ing as lustily, but I doubt that anyone else's Lifetime Most Embarassing Moment involves Lou Piniella. Some little boys ran after him too. Without turning around, he flicked his hand and said, "Kids! Go back and watch the game." They split, but I said, "I'm not a kid and I don't want your autograph." At that he stopped. His eyes were blankly tolerant. "I don't want your autograph," I said. "I just want to touch you." Without pausing, I reached out and brushed his forearm with my hand. Eek! His mouth opened but he said nothing, and I scurried off.

I think about it a lot. If I ever meet him again, it has to be on equal terms—he has to know who I am. That'll never happen, so it's best just to have a red face and a full heart. I never did dream about him.

But I did have my synthesis: a crush on someone whose skills I could appreciate. As Lou went the way of age, it turns out it was baseball I needed. Such as: the pleasure of sitting dreamily under the blue and over the green, getting lost into the past and the present. My eyes filling with the hopes of thousands as my ears fill with "Take Me Out to the Ball Game." Baseball, which taught my immigrant father to be an American—he had an accountant's sense of symmetry, and the diamond pleased him, the implications and profusion of numbers impressed him. Baseball, something I've shared with my brother longer and more consistently than I've shared anything with anybody, a passion deep as childhood, urgent as a World Series charivari. Something we linger over, from morning box scores to evening arguments. There's always time for baseball. Not to mention baseball players.

Elinor Nauen is a New York poet who directed the Theater Series at the St. Mark's Poetry Project for three seasons. She is the author of the book *CARS and Other Poems* and has been anthologized in *Up Late: American Poetry Since 1970* and *The Stiffest Corpse.* Her poem "Winfield's Infield Hit" was recently translated into French for the French anthology *Aires.*

MURRAY CHASS on

ROBERTO CLEMENTE

The baseball rests on a shelf in the family room of my home, encased in a plastic holder to keep the name from fading. It is one of three baseballs that reside there, the only balls I have had autographed since I transformed myself too many years ago from baseball fan to baseball writer.

The other two balls have a unique standing in my newspaper career. They are signed by Hank Aaron and Darnell Coles, and they are there because they represent the two times I have been hit by batted balls while sitting in a press box covering a game. (When I asked Coles for his signature on his foul ball, I don't think he understood what I was talking about when I told him about the Hank Aaron baseball.)

The third ball did not hit me. I don't even recall where I picked it up. Nor do I remember when I asked for the autograph. Actually, as my children know all too well, I have a policy against asking players for autographs. But every policy has an exception, and it was a rare exception when I asked Roberto Clemente to sign this particular baseball.

"Best wishes, Roberto Clemente," it says, sitting on my shelf.

The autograph was an exception because Clemente was an exception.

As a boy growing up in Pittsburgh, I was as avid a Pirates fan as old Forbes Field ever held. In my earliest years as a fan, several seasons before Clemente arrived, the players I rooted for the hardest were not of Clemente's stature. But then, the Pirates did not have

many players of that stature. Ralph Kiner was there at the time, hitting home run after home run, but he was not my hero. My heroes were Ted Beard and Tom Saffell, two outfielders about whom no one has written books, chapters, or even paragraphs.

When Clemente joined the Pirates in 1955, I was finishing my junior year in high school. For five years, I watched him, enjoyed him, rooted for him as a fan. Then, I began watching Clemente professionally. I could still enjoy the way he played, but I could no longer root for him. My new status forced me to adopt a different perspective and a different approach to this player who could be so easy for a fan to adore but so difficult for a writer to cover.

There was the summer, for example, when the Pirates were in New York (where I had moved in pursuit of my career) and I went to Shea Stadium to do a story on him. I did not expect him to remember me from my Pittsburgh days so I introduced myself.

As soon as he heard that I was a New York writer, he made it clear he would not speak to me. He did not care for baseball writers generally, but at this time he specifically wanted nothing to do with the New York variety of baseball writers. It seems that one New York writer had written a piece about his celebrated physical ailments, a subject that wasn't his favorite, and had mocked him by suggesting that he was a hypochondriac and had been treated by a witch doctor in Puerto Rico. For this, he was angry with all New York writers.

Faced with a noninterview, I was tempted to say to him, "How

can you do this? I'm from Pittsburgh and I used to root for you."
When I related this story years later to a friend of Clemente's, he
told me that that approach would probably have enabled me to sal-
vage the interview. But, I told myself at the time (and would reiterate
today), that was not the professional thing to do.

A few years later, I approached Clemente in another clubhouse,
this one in Baltimore, and this time he talked freely—to me and
dozens of other writers. The Pirates had just won the 1971 World
Series, and Clemente was the hero, the player who batted .414, compiled a .759 slugging percentage, and made possibly the best throw
in a World Series that didn't get the runner.

All of this and more accomplished by a man who a year and a
half earlier had said that the 1970 season "could be my last year."

Had Clemente quit after the 1970 season, he would not have
become the eleventh player in major league history to amass 3,000
hits in his career, and he would never have attained the fame and
appreciation that truly belonged to him.

As absurd as it seemed then and still seems now, Clemente did
not become a nationally recognized superstar until the 1971 World
Series. It mattered not that he had played for seventeen years, won
four batting championships, eleven Gold Gloves and one Most Valuable Player award, played in fourteen All-Star games and batted
.300 twelve times, including eleven times in a twelve-year span (he
would, in 1972, make that thirteen times and twelve in thirteen
years). Fans throughout the country inexplicably remained ignorant
of just how great a player he was until he showed them in seven
televised games in October 1971.

Fans in Pittsburgh did not need those games to show them how
great Clemente was. They had known for years. His teammates and
opponents did not need those games. They had known, too.

"People in Pittsburgh and people who had to deal with him on
the field knew," says Willie Stargell, Clemente's teammate and fellow
Hall of Fame member. "He commanded their respect. That was the
peace of mind that really made him feel good. He knew in due time
that people would put him up there with the best players who ever
played in the National League. He knew he didn't have to take a
backseat to anybody. You talk about Aaron, Mays, Clemente. They're
all right there."

Stargell would get no argument from Al Campanis, who as a
Brooklyn Dodgers' scout discovered Clemente in 1953 in a tryout
camp in the town of Santurce in Puerto Rico.

"He was rare," Campanis says. "He was the best natural athlete

I had seen. He could run so well, he could field, he could throw, he could hit. When you see a star, you tingle all over."

Clemente, no overwhelming physical presence but a rock-hard 5'11" and 185 pounds, sent chills up and down tingling spines with his flamboyant style of play. He executed his inside out swing with flair, seemingly snatching the baseball out of the catcher's glove and lining it to right field. He ran the bases with flash, his strong legs churning like pistons and his arms pumping in unison. He chased fly balls in the outfield with abandon, sliding across the grass to catch the ball or catching it on the run and throwing it to third or home, where the runner always knew he could be in jeopardy.

His actions were not the work of a player who used his ailments to excuse himself from the lineup. He is No. 1 in Pirates' history in games played, just as he is No. 1 in times at bat, hits, and total bases. He is third in runs scored, runs batted in, doubles, triples, and home runs.

"Most of the time," says Bill Virdon, a former Pittsburgh center-fielder, addressing Clemente's alleged hypochondria, "if we felt he was hurt, he was going to have a good game. That's kind of the way it turned out."

A play he made in the second game of the 1971 World Series epitomized Clemente's dazzling defensive ability. He raced toward the right-field line for a fly ball hit by Frank Robinson, wheeled around counterclockwise as he caught the ball, and whipped it to third, where Richie Hebner just missed getting the sliding Merv Rettenmund.

Bill Virdon, who played next to Clemente and managed him, recalls another unforgettable example of the Clemente style of play.

"In a game at Forbes Field," Virdon relates, "he caught the ball over his shoulder and ran into the concrete wall in right field where the fence angled out. There were some ornaments on the fence that jutted out, and he was going headfirst into it. Somehow he threw his head back and he got cut under the chin instead of getting hit in the throat. It probably saved his life. He caught the ball and hung on to it. When I got there and turned him over, all I could see was the gash under his chin. But other than that, he didn't hurt himself."

There was, obviously, nothing subtle about Clemente's style of play on the field. Nor was there in his actions and words off the field. He was outspoken and he cared about people. The two traits often meshed.

"I am very outspoken," he once acknowledged. "When I hear

something that is unjust to my teammates or somebody else, I'm going to say something about it."

Clemente often railed at writers for the lack of recognition he felt they accorded him. No question exists in my mind that if he had played in New York, he would have rivaled contemporaries Willie Mays and Mickey Mantle for the adulation of fans and the attention generated by newspapers, magazines, and television networks.

But Clemente was as outspoken, if not more so, about the way Latins and blacks were slighted generally. He was in the advance guard of people who criticized the baseball establishment for shunning blacks for managerial jobs. He also spoke out against the reserve system that bound a player to one team until he was traded or released.

He was the first nonwhite player representative on the executive board of the players' union, and he spoke out there, too. Richard Moss, former general counsel of the union, recalls an important meeting in New York that was attended by about 125 players.

"He stood up at that meeting," Moss says, "and talked about why it's important to stick together. He hit everything on the head. He was so influential with the players. It was a very stirring talk."

Marvin Miller, who was the union's executive director, went back even further and remembered a time before Clemente became the Pirates' player representative.

"We were meeting in Mexico City and the Pirates' rep and alternate rep couldn't attend," Miller relates. "I called Roberto. I told him my concerns, that the player reps couldn't come and it was an important meeting. He said, 'You think it's important?' Yes. 'I'll be there.' "

Miller and Moss had a special relationship with Clemente. Like me, they lived in Pittsburgh (working for the steelworkers' union) when he began playing for the Pirates and became ardent fans. The difference was that when they moved to New York, they could not only continue being fans but they could also solicit his cooperation and get it. "He was my favorite player as a fan before I got involved," Moss says, "and he was one of my favorite player reps."

So many people have fond memories of Clemente, but none have fonder ones than Stargell, who became a legend himself in Pittsburgh. Stargell talks of the effect Clemente had on his baseball career and how he touched his life in many ways. "He was like the big brother I never had," says Stargell, prefacing a story about how Clemente gave part of himself to others.

"I remember we were up in Montreal one time," Stargell relates.

"Something happened to my back and I couldn't play. I was left in the clubhouse for treatment. Roberto didn't play the first game. He stayed in the clubhouse through the entire game and gave me an ice rubdown. He put this cold ice in his bare hands and would rub and apply pressure to different areas of my back. He said I would be able to play the next day based on things he had learned. It must have been about forty minutes of constant rubbing with that ice. We all know when you put ice in your hand for any period of time, you must release that ice after about five minutes at the most, but he was so into what he was doing, it didn't faze him at all. That was a lesson, too, of what winners are about. Winners are people who give of themselves and that's what he did in so many ways. A winner to me is not just someone who has great ability. A lot of people have God-given talent, but not many people have the ability to give of themselves and do things for others, bring important issues to the table. It didn't surprise me that that would be the way he would leave this earth because he gave so much of himself."

Clemente, his 3,000th hit attained in his last game of the 1972 season, was killed in a plane crash on New Year's Eve that year. It wasn't just a crash of a commercial plane flying to some exotic vacation spot. Clemente, at the age of thirty-eight, father of three young sons, was killed doing something for someone else. He was chairman of a Puerto Rican relief committee that had chartered the plane to take supplies to Nicaragua, which days before had been devastated by an earthquake. Clemente could have let others deliver the plane-load of supplies, but he personally wanted to make sure the supplies were reaching the right people.

"New Year's Eve is one of the most sacred days in Puerto Rico, where everyone spends time with their families," Stargell says. "For him to do that, it was totally out of character in terms of the tradition of his country. But he said, 'Hey, I'm very fortunate that I have my family, and I want to do something for people less fortunate.' "

In his eighteen years in Pittsburgh, Clemente excited the fans as few players had. He inspired his teammates, too. "They held a memorial service for him in Puerto Rico, and a lot of the players were there," Richard Moss recalls. "Manny Sanguillen was out in the bay diving for his body the whole time. Al Oliver didn't stop crying the two or three days they were there. Usually players don't react to other players like that."

Like everyone else, I was shocked at the news of Clemente's death. Unlike most people, though, I was a participant in the next development, albeit posthumous, in Clemente's career. The Baseball Writers Association of America, whose ten-year members vote for the Hall of Fame, decided to waive the five-year waiting period and have a special election, with Clemente's name the only one on the ballot.

As great as Clemente was and as certain a future Hall of Famer he was, I was reluctant to vote yes on this ballot because I was concerned that it might set an undesirable precedent. After debating with myself, however, I finally marked the yes box. I realized that if I didn't vote for Clemente then, I would never again have the opportunity because, as certain as his talent and his character were, so were his chances for election into the Hall of Fame on his first try.

Murray Chass is a sports writer for the *New York Times.* He is the author of *Pittsburgh's Steelers* and *Power Football.*

MAX
MANNING
on
SATCHEL PAIGE

I began pitching for my high school team in Pleasantville, New Jersey, in 1934, the year he supposedly started 29 games in one month and won 105 games for a team in Bismark, North Dakota. I hadn't yet heard of Leroy "Satchel" Paige, although it had been more than a decade since he had begun his legendary forty-year professional career, during which he'd hurl approximately 8,000 games and 55 no-hitters in the United States, Mexico, and the Caribbean. My coach, Emory "Ty" Helfich, who had played against Paige as he barnstormed through the East, first told me about this tall, lanky pitcher with a blazing fastball that was unhittable and a tireless arm that allowed him annually to pitch 300 games during a twelve-month schedule— even in his late fifties he'd take the mound more than 150 times a year.

Ty also informed me that I could make "good" money in the Negro Leagues, where Satchel had achieved much of his fame. So after I finished high school, I signed with the Newark Eagles. Since I was in the National League of the Negro Leagues and Satchel played several years with the Kansas City Monarchs in the American League, I didn't get to see him a lot until the two teams met up in the 1946 World Series. But I continued to hear stories about him. The players and coaches who had seen Satchel always described him as being "the best" and "the fastest" and "the most cunning." They also told me that he was so confident that at times he called in his outfielders and then struck out the side. I heard how he told major league star Ducky Medwick that he could strike him out on three pitches and then made good on his challenge, getting Medwick to lean lower and lower with every pitch and wave helplessly at the ball. In one of his frequent exhibition games against major-leaguers, Satchel fanned Rogers Hornsby five times! He outpitched Dizzy Dean 1–0 in another classic game. Perhaps there was a little yeast added to Satchel's reputation, but at least 70 percent of everything attributed to him was correct. You can't build legends on nothing. Too many people were eyewitnesses to what he did.

I became an eyewitness when we faced Kansas City in the 1946 World Series. We managed to squeak out a 2–1 win against him in the final game in the Polo Grounds, but before that he beat us twice. I still remember how impressed I was. He lived up to everything I'd heard. Looking at his 6'3½" right-hander with legs so thin that he'd wear two pairs of stockings, you'd never think he could do the things he was doing. He wasn't fluid in his motions as are most great athletes. In fact, his delivery was awkward. We'd follow his pitch from the dugout. It didn't look like anything special until it reached the plate. Then it did something strange. It can best be described as a "phantom pitch." The guys would swing, but they couldn't hit it. It was like magic. We marveled at his talents and wondered, "How did he do that?"

Satchel would challenge hitters, but on his own terms. He'd say, "You can hit a fastball—but I'll throw it where you can't hit it." He wouldn't try to fool the hitter by throwing a ball that would curve or drop way out of the strike zone. Instead, he would throw all his pitches around the knees, where it was hard to hit. His "Be Ball" was a ball that he said would "be" where he wanted it to "be." There may have been pitchers who could throw as hard as Satchel, but none had his combination of speed and pinpoint control. He was just fantastic. And what was amazing is that this was Paige at the age of forty. I wondered how great he must have been in his prime!

It was also evident that Satchel could field his position and swing the bat far better than most pitchers. He was proud of his hitting and no one could take him for granted at the plate. Years later Willie Mays would claim to have doubled off Paige, but Satchel remembered the event as Mays's "robbing me of a double."

I had my best season in 1946, being chosen the National League's pitcher of the year after finishing 15–1 (I lost only my first game). So after the World Series I was invited to be part of that year's edition of Satchel Paige's All-Stars. In October, we toured America, playing fourteen games against Bob Feller's All-Stars, comprised of major-leaguers like Ken Keltner, Phil Rizzuto, Frank Hayes, Bob Lemon,

and Charlie Keller. Since there were no rumors about major league baseball's being integrated the following year, we didn't consider these games to be a showcase for major league scouts. However, while we never talked about the importance of beating a white major league team, we knew it had special meaning. We played those games for keeps. I remember how upset I was when I took a 1–0 lead into the ninth in a game in Dayton, only to walk a batter and give up a two-run homer over the shallow right-field fence to Spud Chandler, a pitcher. I struck out 14 batters that game, including Charlie "King Kong" Keller four times. There wasn't much fraternization between players on the two teams, but I do remember that Keller, who was an unfriendly-looking man with dark hair and dark eyebrows, went out of his way to be friendly. And Phil Rizzuto always had something cheerful to say when he passed me on the field, like "Big Max!" I appreciated that.

It didn't matter much who the players were on the field; Satchel was the main attraction with the racially mixed crowds. He would pitch three innings in the big cities, like New York, Baltimore, and Cincinnati, and we other pitchers would go the distance in the smaller cities. Satchel was all business when he pitched, especially when he went head-to-head against Feller in some tremendous confrontations. He didn't participate in the clowning in the dugout. He just did what he had to do for three innings. When he finished, he showered and instead of returning to the dugout, sat in the stands, signing autographs, telling stories, and watching the rest of the game. He enjoyed crowds.

I remember one time Satchel was pitching. Frank Hayes had reached first against him and was taking a small lead. After a pitch, our catcher Quincy Trouppe returned the ball to the mound. Hayes turned his back on Satchel and casually returned to first. He never made it. No one will believe this: Satchel caught the ball from Trouppe and raced to first, tagging Hayes on the back before he got back to the bag. Everybody was stunned. Then there was laughter. Satchel went on pitching as if nothing had happened. Once in Atlantic City I had seen Rats Henderson almost tag out a guy who had a lead off second, but Satchel actually did it. Seeing him do impossible things like this made me realize that the other extraordinary things attributed to him were in the realm of possibility.

Paige thought he was the greatest, that there was nobody like Satch. I wasn't turned off by his egotism because I thought it was well-founded. But it made him somewhat unapproachable. He wasn't easy to get close to. I knew that he had a high opinion of me as a ballplayer or I wouldn't have been on his team, but I felt that if I'd put a hand on his shoulder, buddy-buddy, and said, "Hey, Satch, how's it going?" he'd resent it. So I stayed away. I don't like to be offended. (Years later I walked up to Elston Howard and reminded him that we'd once played against each other, and he treated me like a snake. I turned on my heels and walked away.)

Satchel wasn't really a loner, but he spent much of his time away from the other, younger players. He was friends with his valet and one or two of the guys. They'd go out to bars for a few rounds. I didn't socialize with Satchel, but I do have a dim memory of going to his home in Kansas City. He wasn't married then so there was no one else around. All I remember is that he had a cabinet filled with an impressive collection of rifles and pistols. I better remember the plane trips with Satchel. While the guys would sing and joke around, I'd often overhear Satchel telling stories, burping the whole time because of a persistent gastronomical problem. He told about taking a 36-inch bat all the way to Puerto Rico for winter ball just so he "could hit those damn curve balls—broke it on the first pitch, first at-bat, on a fastball." He also recalled George Scales, a curve-ball hitter of renown who in his first time up in Puerto Rico made Satchel "jump rope" by hitting it through his legs. Paige promised Scales,

"You won't do that again." Of course, Scales couldn't do it again for the rest of the season.

We won eight of the fourteen games against Feller's All-Stars. Then we went our separate ways. I never met up with Satchel again, but like many players in the black leagues, I kept up with his career. It had started long before mine began, and remarkably, it concluded long after mine ended.

Although Satchel made more money than a lot of major-leaguers by being the original "Travelin' Man," he resented that he was the victim of baseball's Jim Crow tradition. When Jackie Robinson was chosen as the first black since the late 1800s to play in the majors, Satch was bitter about it. "That was my right," he argued. "Watching me made them think about Negroes in the majors. I am the one everybody says should be in the majors." I think he was right, even though Jackie was indeed an excellent choice.

There are many theories as to why Satchel wasn't picked: too old, no future; we have to have the "right" one, we need someone who has the "right" style, class, temperament; Satch was too flamboyant and uncontrollable. Of course, some may have feared that this gangling man might even at his advanced age destroy the myth of white superiority in the national pastime.

Satchel finally arrived in the majors on July 7, 1948, his birthday, a month after he signed with Bill Veeck's Cleveland Indians. He was the oldest rookie in major league history, passing for forty-two. In a devastating editorial, the Sporting News, the so-called baseball bible, attacked the signing for being a publicity stunt and "a travesty on baseball." Satch would prove it wrong. He debuted with two innings of scoreless relief against the St. Louis Browns and won his first major league game six days later, pitching 3⅓ scoreless innings against the Philadelphia Athletics. He continued to do excellent work as a reliever for over a month. On August 13, he made his first start against the Chicago White Sox at a packed Comiskey Park. Using an array of fastballs and hesitation pitches and varying the point of his delivery, he kept the Sox hitters completely off balance, limiting them to 5 singles and walking none in a 5–0 whitewashing. A record crowd of 78,382 turned out in Cleveland to watch Paige's next start. Again his opponent was Chicago, and again he shut them out, 1–0 on a 3-hitter. Paige finished his brief season with a 6–1 record and a 2.48 ERA, and he was a key figure in the Indians' successful drive for the pennant, which they won in a playoff.

Paige returned to the Indians in 1950 and then rejoined Bill Veeck in St. Louis for three seasons with the Browns. In 1952, at the age of forty-seven, he won 12 games, had a stingy 3.07 ERA, and struck out 91 batters in 138 innings.

The Browns moved to Baltimore after the 1953 season and Satchel moved on, pitching in the minors and barnstorming during the off-season. In successive seasons he pitched more than 160 consecutive days. From 1956 to 1958, Satchel played for the Miami Marlins in the International League, a move that was orchestrated, naturally, by Bill Veeck. His record for Miami was a most respectable 30–14 and he attracted huge crowds whenever he pitched, including a minor league record 55,000 people one night at the Orange Bowl. Most memorable, according to Satch, was his helicopter ride into the park, after which he retired to a rocking chair to recover.

In 1965, at the age of fifty-nine, Satchel made his last appearance in the majors, for the Kansas City Athletics. It may have been a publicity stunt to boost attendance, but Paige wasn't fooling around, giving up only a scratch single to Carl Yastrzemski in three scoreless innings against Boston. Two years later, he pitched an inning for the Atlanta Braves in an exhibition game against their AAA Richmond farm team. The sixty-one-year-old struck out two. He spent the year as an Atlanta coach, sitting in a rocking chair with a "nurse" beside him to massage his arm. The Braves were kind to Satchel in that they allowed him to make up his pension time as a coach. It's strange that none of the other organizations he played for felt they owed him as much.

So that was it for Satchel Paige's brief life in the majors, a world that was formerly the white players' exclusive domain. (Cap Anson saw to this in the late 1800s by using his popularity to generate hostility toward black players and force them out of the game.) Had there not been an agreed-upon ban against black ballplayers, imagine what a young Satchel would have done. It is difficult to say what might have happened if Satchel and all his great black contemporaries had spent ten or fifteen years in the majors. Fortunately Satchel is remembered—I'm so saddened that many great players I played with and competed against will never get the recognition they richly deserved. At least his brief, belated major league career caused many skeptics to reconsider their opinion about the quality of Negro League baseball.

Satchel's enshrinement in the Hall of Fame in 1971 was not without incident. Commissioner Bowie Kuhn contended that a "special niche" at Cooperstown would be adequate to honor former Negro League players. At first Satchel was amenable, stating that he "didn't feel segregated," although at the time he must have felt diminished.

To Satchel it must have been confusing to have heard all his life, "If only you were white," and then listened to all the rhetoric about where a plaque should be placed in a large two-story building. After much controversy, Kuhn and others agreed that Paige and all Negro League players enshrined in the future would be inducted as bona fide Hall of Famers. When this decision was reached, Satchel commented on why he hadn't previously raised objections: "I was just going along with the program." A very un-Satchel-like statement. Satchel was always first class in everything he did, and it's hard to believe that he didn't care where he was put in the Hall of Fame. In his heart, he knew where he belonged and that was *beside* all the other baseball immortals.

Finally, Satchel was called upon to be just mortal. Everyone suspected he couldn't pitch forever. He could not and would not live forever. He never did look back, but something was gaining on him just the same. After a bout with emphysema, which confined him to a wheelchair and an air-conditioned environment, Satchel was called out by the umpire upstairs. He died on June 5, 1982, a month away from his seventy-seventh birthday. It was seventy years since he'd picked up his famous nickname by inventing a contraption to carry four satchels at a time through the Mobile, Alabama, railroad station in which he worked.

Leroy Robert "Satchel" Paige was an athlete of his time and all times. A champion with the heart of a lion, a competitive fire unequaled in sports, and unmatched pride and ego—qualities that made Satchel difficult to beat. Satchel is gone, but for me and millions of others his memory will linger on. He was an original, a man who equaled his myth.

Max Manning is a retired New Jersey schoolteacher. He was a star pitcher in the Negro Leagues.

KIM FOWLEY
on
LUKE EASTER

In 1949, I was ten years old. Already "too tall" for my age, I found a role model who also was "too tall" for his peer group. "Too Tall" Lucious Luke Easter was the man of that moment. A former star softball player who didn't even play hardball until 1946, Easter had been one of the most intimidating figures of the Negro Leagues, hitting tape-measure homers with shocking regularity, including the first of three balls ever hit into the center-field bleachers in the Polo Grounds. Acquired by San Diego Padres president William Starr after a brief stint with the Homestead Greys, Luke quickly became the "Black Babe Ruth" of this Navy-damaged border town, an instant legend, and the top draw in the Pacific Coast League.

My dad was the "B" picture actor Douglas Fowley. He was a working actor, but he had an "almost" jinx and a violent temper. At that time, Doug had just acquired wife number four, a Norwegian-American, San Diego–area schoolteacher named Joy Torstrup. Real strict, real stern, a real "typical stepmother": the Wicked Witch of the North meets one of Cinderella's wicked stepsisters! At least that was what I thought as a ten-year-old.

Joy was from Pacific Beach, on Mission Bay, up from Balboa Stadium, the Padres' home base. My B-pix dad parked me there to interact with her family. He left me with various friends and ever-changing family members whenever possible; Doug thought it was the right thing to do. Let the kid get a "dose" of real normal American family life. I had no choice. Horace Heidt's TV show played on the neighbor's Zenith; a popular song was "Don't Cry, Joe, Let Her Go";

I got an English pug dog named Duke; and I discovered "The Loneliness of Luke Easter."

Monte Ivans was a red-faced grandfather type with no grandson.
I filled the bill. The Torstrup family gladly passed me on to Mr.
Ivans, who decided he would take me to my first professional baseball game. We rode the bus, transferred, and rode the bus some more,
till we got to the ballpark to see the San Diego Padres in action.

I had listened to Bill Stearn's re-created baseball broadcasts from
back east. I even watched Chuck Connors play first base for the
Chicago Cubs' farm team at Wrigley Field in Los Angeles. But that
had been on local television. This was something else. A real
crowd—the biggest I'd been in since I'd gone to the circus at Gilmore
Field in Hollywood in 1945, only to learn that show wouldn't go on
because FDR had died that day. A real team. A real hot dog with
mustard. Hot dogs *always* taste better at a baseball game. The "seventh-inning stretch" was the closest thing to a "tribal experience" I
had yet witnessed.

Luke Easter stood 6'4½" and weighed 240 pounds. Paul Bunyan
in a baseball-uniform masquerade. He didn't hang out with the rest
of his team. He was alone with his bat. As alone as I was with my
dog when my dad and his new wife would get intense. The dog and
I would hit the street, lookin' for action: another kid, another dog.

Luke batted lefty. He leaned slightly over the plate, his jaw nearly
touching his right shoulder, his hands held high, his arms coiled,

Courtesy Cleveland Indians

his bat at a sharp angle behind his head. He hit the ball and the "crack" made the crowd moan, groan, and shoot upward. In later years, it would be the power chord of a rhythm guitar that excited me, but that night it was the *splat* as ball reached bat and the ball splashed out in the bay behind the stadium. That's what Monte Ivans said always happened when Luke hit a long ball.

Luke Easter wound up alone again when he crossed home plate. The white players nodded and turned away. The crowd sat down; like in *Spartacus* when a gladiator offed a lion and the crowd turned on to the concept of "where's the next spectacle?" Luke sat in the dugout, away from the other guys. He must have felt the same way veteran blues guitarist Albert King would feel in the late sixties when Jimi Hendrix raved about him, still unknown and unsung: too little, too late. Luke was the only human with style the night I went to that game; the only guy with the "groove"; the only superstar; the only black player on his team.

Luke slugged 25 homers and drove in 92 runs in just 80 games with the Padres before going down with a busted kneecap. When he recovered, he reported to the Cleveland Indians, the Padres' parent club. He claimed to be twenty-eight so the Indians would think he was in his prime, but he was at least thirty-five when he debuted, an age when most major-leaguers were considered over-the-hill. Over the next three seasons with the Indians, Easter wasn't in the starting lineup 78 times, yet still drove in 307 runs and slugged 86 homers, including the longest blast in the history of Municipal Stadium.

Luke got the thrill of the "major league experience." Doug Fowley moved us to Beverly Hills. In 1952, he played the movie director in the MGM classic *Singing in the Rain*. The dog and I hit every magazine stand in Beverly Hills. Duke, my $450 dog, was the decoy while I shoplifted wrestling magazines. My favorites were Killer Kowalski, Ski Hi Lee, and Yukon Eric. I was a member of the Mike & Ben Sharpe World Heavyweight Tag Team Fan Club. I had a picture of Arlene Dahl on my wall.

Luke started only 56 games at first in 1953. He hit .303 but his power stats were down, and the Indians didn't want to give him another chance. In 1954, Cleveland returned him to San Diego. In 1954, Doug Fowley sent fifteen-year-old Kim, the dog, Joy (the soon-to-be-ex-wife), and her new actor-conceived baby back to San Diego. My day job was Catholic school. My night job was at the San Diego Arena. I sold hot dogs; they never tasted the same as the ones at the ballpark. My wrestling idol was Hombre Montana. Luke was in trouble that year; he batted only .278, compared to .363 in 1949.

CULT BASEBALL PLAYERS

Mr. Ivans kept in touch. He introduced me to an "automatic pitcher" concession—a bad version of James Michener's *Fires of Spring*—near the ballpark. The machine threw the ball too fast; the drunk sailors couldn't get a decent hit. Neither could Luke Easter. I also started to follow Earl Brucker, Jr., Luke's teammate on the Padres. He was a chunky guy with rimless glasses who hit the most amazing "towering" foul tips. But he never got consistent hits. Neither did Luke Easter. Neither would Kim Fowley.

Luke Easter played in Charleston in 1955, then spent nine seasons as a tremendous gate attraction with the Buffalo Bisons and Rochester Red Wings in the International League, amassing some of the top slugging statistics in minor league history. He was about fifty when he quit. Luke died in 1979, in Euclid, Ohio. He was chief steward for the Aircraft Workers Alliance at TRW, Inc. when he was fatally shot by two holdup men outside a bank. Doug Fowley had at least four more wives. We last saw each other in 1959. He may be alive. I am; I was fifty on my last birthday. I am 6'4¾" tall, around the same altitude as Luke Easter. Duke's gone, but I have a toy stuffed bulldog in my hotel room as I write this.

I am currently writing songs with Warron Zevon, who once wrote a song about pitcher Bill Lee. But I don't follow baseball anymore. Not since, as Skip Battin lamented in a song we cowrote, "the St. Louis Browns left town and became the Baltimore Orioles."

But baseball's cool. Bo Belinsky got Mamie Van Doren. Ty Cobb got to be great. Bill Veeck, who signed my hero, got to be creative. And Kim Fowley got to learn "The Emptiness," which must be the same as "The Loneliness of Luke Easter."

Kim Fowley has earned a cult following among pop music fans as a producer, composer, publisher, and singer. He has worked with such performers as Kiss, Helen Reddy, Alice Cooper, the Byrds, Skip Battin, the Mermaids, the Beach Boys, Gene Vincent, Joan Jett, and the Runaways, whom he formed, managed, and produced. He cowrote Skip Battin's baseball tribute "The St. Louis Browns."

◆

JOHN KRICH
on

VIDA BLUE

◆

Young people today don't willingly accept orders unless they
know the whys, the whos, and the insides. And I'm part of
the times. I've changed with the times.

—Vida Blue, 1972

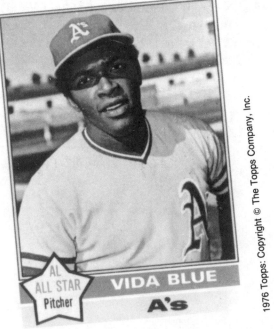

Vida Rochelle Meshach Abednego Blue, Jr., and I go back a long way. Fate brought me to California's promised land at nearly the same time, the same age, and the same moment of national turmoil and questioning. The first time this New York transplant ever cared whether a newly arrived team called the Oakland A's won or lost was in September 1970, when I accidentally turned on the radio broadcast of a no-hitter thrown against Minnesota in only the eighth major league start of this prodigious phenom with the lusciously onomatopoetic name. The first time I went to a game at the Oakland Coliseum was in 1971 to watch twenty-one-year-old Vida win his fourteenth victory of the season and pick up a powder-blue Cadillac purchased by A's owner Charles O. Finley. The first opening day I ever attended was during Vida's celebrated salary dispute in 1972 so that I could hold a banner in the bleachers reading VIDA SI! CHARLEY NO!

This application of a political slogan from my college days to the cause of fandom was hardly accidental. Through Vida Blue, I'd been made to see how an identification with the style and travails of a bubble-gum-card hero could help me identify with larger social concerns. The next time I saw Vida, in his first start after returning to the club, I didn't have to suffer the guilt of adding to Charlie O.'s till because this had been declared "Mustache Day." I was let in free, along with seven thousand other weirdo-beardos, because the hippie revolt had finally been acknowledged by baseball through Oakland's hairy A's. Finley offered A's players cash incentives to grow mustaches for his promotion. I didn't hear until afterward that Vida had shaved his upper lip before the game to show his defiance.

Ever since he was brought up to the Oakland A's in 1971, I found in this brash and respectful, naive and savvy, conciliatory and angry athlete from Mansfield, Louisiana, an external representation of my own groping toward manhood. Together, he and I bartered away and exhausted our youthful gifts, faced outlandish compromises, stared down moral dragons, negotiated through the minefields of adulthood. Luckily for me, I didn't have to do this while anyone was watching. Unfortunately for Vida Blue, he had to do it all out in public—with nothing to aid him but charm and a rising, letter-high fastball. But such are the rewards of being a fan, and the agonies. Through the compressed time frame provided by professional sports, we routinely get to observe talents blossoming and wilting. Though it's no longer in fashion to claim that sport builds character—given the recent results—it's still uncontestable that sport does a damn good job of revealing character. And our fascination with sport lies in the fact that sometimes what gets revealed are things we'd rather not see.

Not much has been seen or heard of Vida Blue since 1987, on the eve of a spring training that was supposed to mark his sentimental return to the team where he'd begun his career. A statement was issued then announcing his sudden retirement from the occupation of major league player, an occupation he'd plied, with some interruption, for seventeen years. The statement claimed that his decision was uncoerced and not caused by a deteroration in physical condition. Like most every public pronouncement ever made by Vida Blue, it was scrupulously truthful in what was stated but painfully dishonest in all that it omitted. Soon enough, leaks would reveal that Blue, already suspended once from baseball for cocaine use, under parole from a 1983 Kansas City conviction for cocaine possession, had tested positive for cocaine several times during his 1986 "comeback" stint with the San Francisco Giants. Caught red-handed at the worst crime currently known to mankind, he was forced to quit before he was fired. Begun with one of the loudest bangs in sporting history, Vida's sporting story-line ended with a whimper. It would have no storybook ending.

After the announcement, the sports pages were full of pontificating and guesswork and long-distance psychoanalysis. The expected cries went up—from "Vida abused our trust!" to "Vida abused himself," to "Vida, get thee to a nunnery!" to "Vida, we hardly knew ye!" Of these, only the last seems beyond cliché and therefore striking. It's true that for a man who had been so accessible, affable, and on display, Vida had remained remarkably shrouded. Is he the phenom who had it all or the victim who never wanted any of this? A well-behaved southern gentleman or a smoldering black militant? The cheerleader or the dope fiend? Try as we might, Vida's lasting image remains out of focus.

I won't attempt to delineate the "real Vida." I can only speak of Vida Blue in terms of what he meant to me and perhaps to Oakland, to flip to the back of the card and review the record of all the blue days and nights. Though it would probably make him cringe and come back with an "Aw gee," I must think of this bashful idol as a symbol—of what the marketplace does with human dignity, of why a period of black self-assertion led directly into a period of black disillusionment, of how success in America is sometimes the greatest failure.

If Vida's final tragedy was failing to complete the circle back to

Oakland, that seems only fitting. Everything that was to befall him may well have stemmed from the trauma inflicted there during his first time around. Though the experience has been repeated often since, no ballplayer before Vida had ever flown so high and then been so swiftly brought crashing back to reality, baseball-style.

In 1971, Vida Blue was the toast of the nation—the youngest man ever to win the Cy Young and Most Valuable Player awards. After being bombed on Opening Day in Washington (before the Mad Bomber, Dick Nixon), Vida went on to fashion one of the most remarkable streaks in baseball history. He won ten games in a row, five with shutouts; all were complete games in which he allowed six hits or less. By the midway point of the season, he'd amassed 17 victories against 3 defeats. With the pure uncoiled heat of the pitch that would become known as the Blue Blazer, this young southpaw embarrassed the most experienced major league hitters. In the words of A's radio announcer Monte Moore, Vida was "so fast he could throw a pork chop past a timber wolf."

After one springtime stretch of glory he was no longer "Junior," the eldest of six children whose father, an iron foundry worker, had died when he was seventeen, whose mother took jobs in a shirt factory and school cafeteria so her son's athletic potential could be realized. Now he wasn't just the easygoing, standout high-school quarterback of a sleepy town along the Mississippi, a kid known for eating six or seven hamburgers at a sitting. He'd become the cover boy of *Newsweek*, *Time*, and *Sports Illustrated*. He packed them in, in every park around the country.

Vida's appeal stemmed from more than statistics. Though he exhibited occasional moodiness, he greeted his success with freshness and wit. He offered a personality that was breezy, open, unstudied. Though his struggle with shyness was endearingly obvious, he also found ways to relish his newfound renown. At an A's team visit to the White House, he stole the show by teaching President Nixon the "powershake," quipping, "This is how we do it." In addition, he was so handsome that whenever his cap flew off on trots to the mound, whole sections of female fans would lean over the railings intently. And he wasn't just the lucky bearer of a singularly luscious moniker. In the words of a popular song of the day, Blue was one of those "people who were darker than blue." Instantly, he became the favorite second cousin of the largely black, largely southern-born population of Oakland. He gave Oaklanders "one of their own" on a team whose militantly midwestern, Irish owner had spent much of his time wooing suburban fans with honky heartland promotions like Farmers' Day. Now everyone came out to the Coliseum to "come see about Vida." He was the town's shining young prince, its living blues idiom.

Reggie Jackson, the A's other black star, offered a jock brashness harnessed to the cause of proving how all-American blacks could really be. Along with his customized cars, Reggie always made a great show of his white girlfriends and white pals, once making the remarkable confession that "I wouldn't know what color I was if whites didn't make me feel black and blacks didn't make me feel blacker." But Vida always seemed like a frail kid off the block trying to plant his feet firmly in a white world. He lived in an Oakland housing project with black teammate Tommy Davis and spent his off-days hanging out with neighborhood kids or helping wait tables at the soul-food restaurant Lois the Pie Queen. For him, his blackness seemed an accepted fact, a source of both strength and consternation. As one of the first black idols in a period of growing black self-awareness, just after the arrival of Muhammad Ali and the "Black Power" Olympians, Blue did not have to posture or rage to show where his heart lay. It came out in every offhanded quip, in every explosively fluid left-handed windup.

If Vida didn't really want to draw attention to his race, A's owner Charles O. Finley's paternalism and insensitivity forced his hand. As a reward for the young star who was earning $14,750, Finley decided to bestow a powder-blue Cadillac with personalized plates, a gasoline credit card, and two thousand bucks spending money for a flashy new wardrobe. Though Vida said he'd prefer to have his contract renegotiated, and that he really "wasn't a Cadillac kind of guy," he had to stomach an evening at the ballpark built around Massa Charlie's beneficence. All that was missing, as sportswriters of the time remarked, were the watermelons. Finley flew in the entire Blue family to witness the great moment—and Sallie Blue ended up taking the car back to Mansfield because her son didn't like the attention it drew. When Finley went even further in his reckless promoting, offering Vida $2,000 to change his first name to True, his young charge could hold back no longer. "Why doesn't he change his name to True Finley?" Vida asked. "I like my name. It was my father's name. It's Spanish. It means life."

In the throes of self-discovery, Vida was revealing in being, as another song of the period put it, "young, gifted, and black." Apparently, Charlie Finley couldn't fathom any of the above. As the miracle season concluded (24–7, 1.82 ERA, 301 Ks), Vida made an Aqua-Velva commercial in which he vowed, "Next year, I'm gonna be makin' a whole lotta money." Maybe Charlie Finley had even agreed. He was, after all, a professed believer in the just rewards of the free enterprise system. But he'd also become a millionaire by measuring "a whole lotta money" differently for his employees than he did for himself. Almost inevitably, Finley's "Blue Boy," as the announcers were instructed to call him, quickly became Finley's Bad Boy. Given the explosion in players' salaries that was soon to follow, the amounts in dispute seem beside the point, but for the record: through Los Angeles attorney Robert Gerst, Vida asked for a second-year stipend of $92,000. Finley offered $50,000 and refused to budge. Both figures were arguably quite reasonable—but were based upon two entirely incomparable scales of estimation. Finley operated within the boundaries of established procedures, which provided for a player's worth to rise slowly over a long career. Like most baseball executives, he also based his calculations on the likelihood that Vida would be unable to reproduce his great season. Vida, on the other hand, asked to be properly compensated for the profits he'd already generated for Finley. Never had a contract negotiation been so frankly based on hard gate receipts, and never did a player have so good a case. The simple fact was that, in 1971, Vida had pulled in $1.5 million in ticket sales for the A's. He drew 43 percent of the A's total attendance. One out of every twelve tickets sold in the American League was on a day he pitched. He was on the mound ten of the thirteen games the A's had attracted 30,000 fans on the road, and all six times they played before more than 40,000. Lawyer Gerst even brought up a remark from the previous year, when Finley admitted that a rain-out of a single one of Vida's starts cost him $30,000.

Even President Nixon, commenting at a Texas barbecue hosted by John Connally, advised, "The young man has so much talent. Maybe Finley ought to pay him." But Finley hadn't chosen a mule as his mascot for nothing. The owner refused to budge. Finley wanted to teach this uppity black kid a lesson he'd never forget. Vida had to learn to be respectful and play by the old rules—even if those rules were collapsing around the irascible Charlie O. But Vida never did anything by anyone's rules. By hiring a slick lawyer like Gerst, he'd broken one rule already. He went even further by insisting on a contract without the dreaded "reserve clause" that tied a player to one team for life, and which at that very moment was being challenged before the Supreme Court by Oakland native Curt Flood. Vida also suggested that he was willing to have the matter settled through arbitration. (Two years later, thanks to the growing strength of the players' union, arbitration on contracts was instituted—with more Oakland A's taking advantage of it in the first year than members of any other team.) He even went so far as to propose that Finley could help Vida earn what he didn't want to pay him by filming a joint television commercial. But Finley, the tireless promoter who gave whole new regions of connotation to the word "crass," turned down this innovative approach because his wife told him it might be demeaning. The truth was that Finley was willing to reward Vida only if he continued to play the humble field hand grateful for any and all crumbs off the master's table. As soon as the pitcher behaved on the assumption that he might be Mr. Finley's equal (in some legal if not cosmological sense), then the owner turned upon him like a father betrayed.

In the A's patriarchal family, the sons with spine, like Blue or Reggie Jackson before him, had to be "broken in" one at a time. And since the father remained suffocatingly close at hand (often reaching right into the dugout during games with his telephonic "hot line"), one eventually had to make a kind of peace with this overbearing authority. But rebellion, even open hostility, did not guarantee expulsion from the clan. As is true with real families, this father secretly admired the charges who bridled at his reins. After Jackson concluded a walkout in 1970, he told reporters that he knew he'd "die in the green-and-gold." But Vida would upstage Reggie—no easy accomplishment. He would scream louder and as a result, last longer as an Athletic. Little did he know that his courage would ensure that he'd be the very last of Finley's prized possessions to be pawned off.

Vida Blue conducted the last and most rancorous protest of the pre-free-agency era. He did it with tremendous flair, as he did everything in his public life, but also with an alternating candor and coyness that proved self-defeating. In the midst of spring training, he actually announced his premature "retirement" from the game. With great fanfare, he accepted an executive vice presidency in a Los Angeles firm making steel cabinets. But the ploy fooled no one, especially when Blue got the giggles at his press conference, and when it turned out the company's main product was a bathroom cabinet called the Over-John. It even played into the hands of Finley, the self-made millionaire. "I'm pleased to see Vida's joined the steel industry," Finley needled, calling the pitcher's bluff. "I personally spent five years with U.S. Steel in Gary, the first four as an apprentice in a machine shop." Later, Vida signed a contract to appear as an actor in one of the *Shaft* black detective movies, declaring, "I'm happy to sign a contract that doesn't have a reserve clause in it."

Transparent as these moves appeared, they emphasized the pro athlete's vulnerability in a way nothing else has, before or since. Without baseball, Vida was just another poor black kid who'd sacrificed a college degree to play ball. Even as an ex-superstar, his opportunities were not limitless. He had to look out for himself. "Beware of backstabbers!" Blue warned his fellows, echoing the soul tune.

Finley was already stabbing away. Drawing upon his wealth of experience at incurring bitterness, the A's owner began strikebreaking by releasing Vida's friend and roommate Tommy Davis. Though Davis had hit .324 (in 219 at-bats) for the club in the preceding season and was having an excellent spring training, he was punished for introducing Blue to attorney Gerst. As usual, the owner tried to portray the agent as the villain in the piece. Though praising Gerst's acumen in private, Finley always referred to him publicly as "the notary." In Finley's scheme, only owners were supposed to have legal help. "I feel that Mr. Gerst has temporarily hurt Vida's wonderful image," Finley would tell the press. Apparently, the image remained wonderful only so long as Vida shut up and pitched.

But those days were rapidly coming to an end. In the midst of Blue's holdout, the major league players went on strike for the first time in history. Blue now found himself a holdout among holdouts, his case lost amidst the larger feud—but he did not break. When Curt Flood's suit before the Supreme Court was rejected (though the "reserve clause" would be set aside eventually through arbitrator Peter Seitz's ruling), Vida stood steadfast. Speaking for all his colleagues, Blue blasphemed against the baseball gospel: "Once a young man would walk through a wall for a boss. Now young people will run through the wall only if it's soft enough. . . . I am man enough to feel justified in my feelings."

At twenty-three, was Vida man enough to swallow those feelings in defeat? Complaints of gate losses due to Blue's continuing absence forced Baseball Commissioner Bowie Kuhn to negotiate a settlement of the contract dispute. Though Finley protested this intrusion into his domain loudly enough to be fined by Kuhn, Blue quickly agreed to terms that were meant to stay secret. But Finley delayed the signing well into the season and rubbed salt in Vida's wounds by making the contract quite public. Vida's base salary was just the $50,000 Finley insisted upon. For his struggle, the pitcher received a paltry $5,000, plus $8,000 for future college tuition—which he never used. The young man's much-publicized gamble ended in national humiliation.

Badly out of shape, morally confused, Blue hardly contributed to Oakland's first championship season. Again, he was the victim of poor timing—his lonely struggle was swamped by the general celebration. Though he rallied himself to fire a dazzling, vengeful performance in relief that wrapped up the A's pennant in the final playoff game against Detroit, Vida was a bitter, scowling odd man out in the locker room afterward. He even baited teammate "Blue Moon" Odom for the jitters that had caused Blue to be brought into the game for the last four innings. In a single year, Vida had learned that baseball was a business in which only the heartless survived. From now on, his demeanor seemed to tell the world he was only a commodity inside a uniform.

It is a testament to his remarkable athletic skills that Blue continued to perform ably under the yoke of Massa Charlie. In the next five seasons, he notched 91 victories. When Finley's attempt to auction Blue outright to the New York Yankees for a million dollars was blocked by Commissioner Kuhn, it seemed that Vida would never be unshackled. Just before the 1978 season, as a failing Finley attempted to run his operations for the least amount of money possible, Blue was finally shipped across the bay in exchange for six available bodies.

With the San Francisco Giants, Vida's verve was temporarily restored. Now, it seemed, he could wind up and throw his Blue Blazer with somewhat less ambivalence. And he was finally rewarded with a lucrative multiyear contract. In return, Vida became the club cheerleader, throwing his considerable charm into whipping up fan support. But I never found his rah-rah act terribly believable. Vida was busily attempting to show the world he could be content with the same old jive as everyone else. And once again, his saving grace was that he was so unconvincing.

The fresh, flippant Vida had definitely fled—and so, apparently, had his fastball. Blue's statistics began to deteriorate, but baseball people blamed it on the fact that he'd failed to make the customary adjustment to age. He would have to find new tricks to make up for his loss in velocity. But Vida, who'd had his youth so prematurely robbed from him, was acting as if he could pitch young forever. Nobody publicly suggested that his performance might have been affected by drugs. But Frank Robinson suspected something when he took over as manager of the team in 1982. Finding Vida listless, overweight, and complaining, he okayed a trade to Kansas City.

Why did Vida turn to drugs? Only he knows for sure. But in this solution, he was certainly not alone. As he said in his younger days, he was, indeed, "part of the times." In the early seventies, he had joined a generation of blacks in celebrating pride and self-determination. By the late seventies, he had learned like a lot of other members of his generation—black and white—to work within the system and had reaped the rewards of success. But he, too, had found that success spiritually hollow. I believe the turn to drugs wasn't, as it's so often painted by the mass media, a celebration of the "good life" gone out of control. I think it was an act of profound despair, boredom, and cynicism. And what more cynical act could there be for an athlete than the disregard of the body?

By the middle of the next season, Blue had been released—though the Royals had to continue paying out the rest of his large salary. He was suddenly, mysteriously, washed up. ("It's happened to the best of 'em," it was said.) The real explanation came in October of 1983 when Blue was indicted for cocaine use along with three teammates. He became the only player to cooperate with the grand jury investigation, apparently because he faced the most serious charges. As a result, he was able to bargain for a guilty plea on a misdemeanor charge of possession of one-tenth of an ounce of cocaine. For this he was sentenced to one year in prison, reduced to three months. Once again, Blue's timing was awful. If he had not been among the first players caught with powder up their noses, and if he hadn't been in a conservative town like Kansas City, he would not have been punished so severely. (At his sentencing, Vida made another of his overly contrite statements, telling the judge that his experience had made him "a person who appreciates the opportunity this great country has given him.") Now the man who'd once been Richard Nixon's—and America's—darling joined Willie Wilson, Willie Aikens, and Jerry Martin as the first active major-leaguers to go to prison on drug charges. As if that weren't enough, he was suspended from earning his livelihood for a year after his release.

A lesser man, or a wiser man, might have run and hid. But Vida, who knew best how to hide amidst public glare, came back for more. His boyish pluck and his fastball carried the day once again. For a second time, the Giants served as the vehicle for his resurrection—setting the stage for what was supposed to be his career-capping stint with the A's. But of course, all was not what it appeared.

At the Giants' Phoenix camp in 1986, I finally got a close-up glimpse of my longtime, long-distance intimate. I was shocked at what I saw. Though Vida was relaxed, articulate, utterly without airs, he was also balding, haggard, and conspicuously paunchy even for an aging ballplayer. What had become of Oakland's handsome prince? I hoped the years had not been as unkind to me as they'd been to my sporting shadow.

That would prove to be Vida's final spring training; he would test positive for cocaine during the season.

And so what? Nobody knew until afterward, so clearly, if Vida did use drugs, they hadn't interfered with the fulfillment of his tasks. If he were an office worker, would he have been banned from his company for life? Maybe Vida Blue hadn't kicked his habit, maybe it was a dangerous one for him to kick. But so long as he and so many other pro athletes do their job, what does it matter? Not one of baseball's compassionate employers care if their employees take a shot of whiskey now and then. In fact, half the vaunted "legends of the game" were flagrant alcoholics. Likewise, it's no big deal to employers if ballplayers are addicted to television or pornography or Jesus or hunting rabbits or abusing their wives.

And even if Vida was guilty the last time with Oakland, which has hardly been proven, does the punishment fit the crime? Did it ever? Did his example really lead thousands of adoring children toward sin and debauchery? Did the man kill somebody? I only saw him strike them out. Embezzle or cheat? I never felt cheated when I went to the park. Was he even culpable, like Charlie O. Finley, for aggrandizing his fortune or ego through the exploitation of others? Was anyone Vida's victim? Nobody had his innocence crushed but him. Nobody went to prison but him. Nobody had his livelihood denied but him. And what's the pain of our having lost some pristine image of a gilded hero compared with his ceasing to be a hero to himself? All he asked was to be himself—and look what he got in return.

Unable to resist a fan's urge to add up the score, I've got to feel that if Vida Blue really "failed" baseball, then it was not until baseball had failed him. Long before it should have, the "Blazer" was made to burn out and fall from the sky. Now there will be no more days and nights with Vida Blue.

Vida. It's Spanish. It means livin' it up. Blue. It's English, in the vernacular. It means just gettin' by.

John Krich won a Pen/Hemingway Citation for *A Totally Free Man, the Unauthorized Autobiography of Fidel Castro*. He is also the author of *Music in Every Room: Around the World in a Bad Mood, One Big Bed, Bump City*, and *El Béisbol*. He contributed the essay on Manny Mota to this volume.

MARK FIDRYCH

Mark "the Bird" Fidrych was the most charismatic ballplayer I ever saw. No one even came close. In my forty-three years of big-league announcing, no player so quickly captured the imagination of the fans and became a cult hero.

Mark Steven Fidrych had been in the Tiger organization three years when spring training rolled around in 1976. He was not even on the Tigers' major league roster. But he made an impression. Then he became a sensation. Although Mark didn't make his first regular-season start until May 15, he went on to win 19 games, including 4 shutouts, strike out 217 batters, lead the American League with 24 complete games and a 2.34 ERA, and be voted Rookie of the Year. Unfortunately, he was to pitch only 27 more times and win only 10 more games for the rest of his career.

But the 1976 baseball season belonged to him. For that one year he was a national hero. And in Detroit, at least, it was the Year of the Bird.

He was admired by all baseball fans for his talent and style, adored by the lunch-pail crowd for his working-class ethic (it helped that he was getting only a rookie's salary and had recently had a job pumping gas), and loved by females because of his boyish good looks. He was a free spirit and fresh breeze in the fetid atmosphere of salary battles, court suits, lawyers, and agents. "I don't need an agent," said Fidrych. "Why should I give somebody ten percent when I do all the work?" Mark was definitely flaky. He'd get down on his hands and knees and clean the pitching rubber. He actually talked to the

Courtesy Detroit Tigers

ball before each pitch (that became his trademark), usually a blazing fastball that he'd deliver with flailing arms. Nineteen times he jumped into the air and raced around the diamond shaking hands with his teammates.

I think the best way to assess a player is by the reaction of his teammates. With the Tiger players Fidrych was tops. He may have been getting all the headlines, but his teammates loved him—just as the fans loved him. They quickly accepted him. He gave his teammates credit for his success and they appreciated his thoughtfulness and generosity. And that he produced. Players on opposing teams admired him, too. Often when he took curtain calls after a victory, they would hang around their dugouts and watch. I think Mark was the first big-leaguer to take curtain calls on a regular basis.

Wherever he pitched he drew big crowds. Rival club owners would pray that Fidrych's pitching turn would come during one of their series with the Tigers. NBC's *Game of the Week* would schedule the Tigers on those Saturdays Fidrych was due to pitch. He was extra money in the bank for everybody.

His fans were everywhere, not just in Detroit. When the California

Angels organization found that Mark would not be in the pitching rotation for an Angels-Tigers series, it staged a "Mark Fidrych Autograph Day" at the Anaheim ballpark. The Bird sat at a table and signed autographs for thousands of fans. He did it cheerfully and was never paid for the tedium.

His apartment in Southgate, a Detroit suburb, was constantly surrounded by young girls who hoped to get a glimpse of their hero. When he went to the barbershop, adoring groupies burst inside, scrambled onto the floor, and fought over his discarded blond curls.

Through it all, he was a picture of animated politeness. He seemed to enjoy the attention and was always pleasant.

My daughter Carolyn was a typical Fidrych fan. She kept a large scrapbook of his exploits. It contained pictures, cartoons, and accounts of his diamond triumphs. I asked him if he'd come out of the clubhouse and take a quick look at her book.

He came and looked for twenty minutes.

"That's a good picture," he told her. "Where did you get it?"

"I like this article," he said. "Hey, you did a great job putting this stuff together. I really appreciate it."

He was great because he was natural. As Bill Veeck told me, "If someone had tried to stage Fidrych, it would have fallen flat. It would have been artificial—too contrived."

Ralph Houk was the Detroit manager in the Year of the Bird. He kept him under wraps for the first six weeks of the season. I think he handled Fidrych well. An early disaster might have been the intro to a different story. Anyway, you can't argue with success. The Major made the right move.

Houk recognized that Fidrych had more than talent. The kid also had excellent baseball instincts. The first two times he handled rundowns, for instance, he followed the fundamentals with clinical perfection. Mark may have seemed hyperactive, but he knew what he was doing out there.

Off the field, he was easy and natural with the media and the fans. He had a delightful way of expressing himself, sprinkling his conversation with one malaprop after another. Early in that first year, Houk had to move the Bird to the far end of the dugout to avoid eardrum damage from Mark's constant cheerleading. Once during a rally Fidrych shouted, "Come on, gang. Remember a hit is as good as a walk."

Later when teammate Mickey Stanley was thrown out attempting to steal third base, Fidrych yelled, "All right, team, let's capitalize on that now."

We were in Oakland in September when I saw an item in a syndicated entertainment column that Fidrych would appear in a baseball TV series. I asked him about it. "I don't know," he said, "maybe my agent will be making a deal. But I'll tell you this, Ernie. No matter what happens, I have the last hearsay."

Another time we were on the team bus headed down Michigan Boulevard, in Chicago. It was the summer that the King Tut exhibition was on display at the Chicago Art Institute. Much publicity had surrounded the event, but apparently Mark hadn't been privy to any of it. Several of the players were talking about the long lines of people who were anxious to see the King Tut artifacts. Overhearing the conversation, Fidrych turned around and asked, "King Tut? What is that? A new rock group?"

Poor Bird. He was a one-year sensation. He hurt his knee in spring training of 1977, then got arm miseries and was never able to reach those heights again. He tried. He tried as much as anybody has ever tried. Therapy, operations, rehabilitation—all of it.

During one of his comeback efforts I interviewed him in the Tiger clubhouse in Kansas City.

"Mark, you're back on the active list now. How is the arm feeling?" I asked.

"Oh, it's feeling real good, Ernie," he said into the mike.

"What does the Tiger team doctor, Dr. Clarence Livingood, say about your arm?"

"Oh, Dr. Livingood. He don't know about arms. He's a skin doctor. One of them gynecologists."

Fidrych continued to struggle with arm problems. Then he seemed to be ready physically. However, even with his arm back in shape, he was never able to regain the ability he showed in that one brilliant season.

Many in the Tiger organization felt that the Bird's comeback was deterred as much by a mental block as by any kind of arm ailment.

"He seemed to be completely confused," one of his coaches said. "He threw as well as he did before. But it just couldn't happen for him again."

The Tigers gave up on him and released him after the 1981 season. The Red Sox signed him the next February, but he never again captured his glory. He would retire and eventually wind up living on a pig farm outside Boston and returning to his working-class roots, paving driveways. In the late eighties he began playing semipro ball and was tempted to be in the new senior baseball league in Florida.

The greatest quality Mark Fidrych showed me was this: Up or

down, on top or on the bottom, he was still the same great, enthusiastic kid.

He was baseball's answer to the challenge put forth by Rudyard Kipling in his poem "If":

If you can meet with Triumph and Disaster
And treat those two imposters just the same . . .
Yours is the Earth and everything that's in it.
And—which is more—you'll be a Man, my son.

Ernie Harwell has been the broadcaster for the Detroit Tigers for forty-three years. His autobiography is *Tuned to Baseball.*

TIM MCCARVER on
BOB UECKER

When Mr. Baseball made the first of his more than eighty appearances on the *Tonight* show, Johnny Carson didn't know what to expect. He had never heard of Bob Uecker. Even if he had known more about baseball, he probably wouldn't have heard of this guest, a rarely used backup catcher for his entire six-year career. And Uecker took advantage of his anonymity, telling improbable—and hilarious—stories about what sounded like the worst career in major league history, and explaining how he cleverly managed to collect his salary from four big-league teams despite not being able to hit or catch. He clearly had a novel approach to the game: "Anybody can play sober—I liked to get out there and play liquored up." This character whom Ueck had created and was playing to perfection seemed to be bragging, yet everything he said made him out to be a fool. The peculiar humor was carefully designed to make the audience laugh *at* the character, rather than with him. Ueck soon had Carson falling out of his chair, laughing uncontrollably. Meanwhile he maintained the chiseled-chin look and matter-of-fact, deadpan delivery that would eventually make him familiar to all America. Afterward, the story goes, Carson congratulated his talent coordinator for finding Uecker, doing stand-up at Al Hirt's club in New Orleans, and eager to have him back on the show as soon as possible, asked incredulously, "Who is this guy? What's his background?" He had no idea. Nobody did.

Well, I could have told him. You see, our careers were interconnected, even before both of us ex-backstops became broadcasters.

Courtesy St. Louis Cardinals

We were even roommates one year. Bob came to the majors in 1962, playing in Milwaukee, his hometown, and backing up Braves catchers Del Crandall and Joe Torre. Gene Oliver was the St. Louis receiver then and I was in the minors waiting my turn. Bob played all of 13 games as Torre's caddie in 1963, the year the Cardinals brought me up to stay. I remember when our manager, Johnny Keane, told me that the Cards were considering trading Oliver and playing me every day. He asked me if I could hit left-handers, as if I could hit them if I said I could hit them. Of course I said I could hit them—I wanted to be the regular. Satisfied, they dispatched Oliver to the Braves. That deal made Uecker expendable in Milwaukee, and a couple of days before the 1964 season, the Cards acquired him to back me up.

At that time, Ueck didn't have a reputation around the league. If he were known as a character, it was confined to Milwaukee. I didn't realize that he was a very funny man. I remember that our initial conversation was not in a humorous vein. It took place two days before spring-training break, right after he came over. I said, "Bob, I don't know how you feel about other catchers, but I've never had a problem. I'm not trying to butter you up, but I'll work with you and do anything I can. If you play, I'll be pulling for you. I don't know you, but if I play, I hope it will be the same." Bob said that Joe Torre had told him the same thing in Milwaukee, and he assured me that he would be rooting for me whenever I caught and he sat. True to his word, Bob was extremely supportive and understanding. If I had a good game, he'd be the first to shake my hand. If I had a bad game, he'd be the first to pat me on the back.

Ironically, when we opened the season in Los Angeles against Sandy Koufax, baseball's dominant lefty, I found myself on the bench cheering as my new backup got the coveted opening-day assignment. I'd been promised I'd play every day, but who could argue with Keane for starting Uecker: for some reason, Koufax was one of the few guys Bob could hit with consistency. As a matter of fact, Ueck's lifetime average against Sandy would be over .400, more than twice what he hit against all other pitchers, and he clubbed 2 of his 14 career homers off him. Who could figure it?

We lost on opening day, and I moved into the starting lineup the next game and Uecker settled down on the bench. He harbored no resentment. He told me he was just going to enjoy the summer since I was going to catch most of the games anyway. So he just enjoyed the summer. He was a great swimmer, and every day, regardless of the weather, he'd go down to the hotel pool. Even in April. Apparently he'd gotten used to swimming in cold weather while growing up in Wisconsin. Curt Simmons began to call Bob "The Lifeguard" because he developed such a great tan, one that George Hamilton or Zonker in *Doonesbury* would envy.

Ueck also had a fun thing to do at the ballpark that took away some of the sting and boredom of not playing. He threw batting practice to the pitchers. He loved it. The pitchers would split into two five-man teams and play a nine-inning game, and Ueck would toss easy pitches to them and judge whether they got hits or made outs. He really looked forward to doing that each day. Another thing Ueck liked to do was spread trade rumors to gullible reporters. Ueck lived on false trade rumors. Jack Herman of the *St. Louis Globe-Democrat* was the easiest to put on, and Ueck would nestle up to him and whisper "Hey, Jack" and give him "inside scoops" on upcoming trades, some involving him. At first Jack would check them out, but later on you'd read something like "The Cardinals are seriously considering trading Bob Uecker for Clay Dalrymple or Alex Johnson." Ueck used to fabricate the trades, but a couple of times they actually came to pass.

People who take Uecker's talk-show character seriously assume he was a George Plimpton type who sneaked into the big leagues just so he could relate funny and colorful anecdotes years later. But Bob was a ballplayer. He may not have been much standing at the plate, but he was marvelous crouching behind it. Few people realize how good a catcher he was. He was terrific defensively and took pride in that. Bob had a strong arm and could throw, he was quick and had great soft hands. We've all heard Ueck joke that the only way he could catch a knuckle ball was to "wait till it stops rolling and pick it up." In truth, Ueck didn't have to chase every knuckler to the screen. He could catch the best knuckle ball—just ask Barney Schultz and Phil Niekro. He could catch anything. Moreover, he was willing to take a beating, stopping balls in the dirt and blocking the plate on close plays at home. He was tough as nails. You don't realize how big Ueck is, but he's a big man, with big bones and broad shoulders.

His weakness was as a hitter. He could hit the high fastball, but he couldn't handle the breaking ball at all. Years later, he would tell Johnny Carson that he practiced hitting the curve off a pitching machine. Only he did it at night with the lights out. He never mastered it, he explained, because of the pain that developed in his left arm after the ball kept hitting him.

Bob was a fierce competitor who wanted to win and to contribute to the effort. He never complained about sitting because he didn't want to be disruptive, but he cared so much that not playing must have been more difficult for him than he let on. I remember a game Ueck started in St. Louis when I needed a day off. He hadn't played in a long time and was rusty. He made a key throwing error and went 0 for 4 and the home crowd booed him. Afterward he stormed into the locker room and attacked the fans, saying, "I hope every fucking one of them has an accident on the way home." It was a vicious remark, which he didn't mean because he truly liked Cards fans, but I mention it to show just how emotional Bob, who wasn't emotional off the field, could be about the game of baseball. He didn't want to make people laugh with slapstick on the diamond. He really did care about how he performed. That's why everyone was going up to him and patting him on the back as if he were a football kicker who had just lost the game with a botched field-goal attempt. I felt a bit awkward. I thought that he might indirectly blame me for having a poor outing because he had been playing so sparingly. But he wasn't like that.

Uecker may not have played a lot in 1964, but he knew he was an integral part of the team. He helped on the field when he had the chance to catch, and all the players respected his defensive talent and the way he called a game. However, if you would have asked me at the end of the year what Bob's greatest contribution had been to our championship season, I would have answered that he kept—and I mean *kept*—everybody loose. I was young and intense in those days, and there's no question that Bob helped me relax with his special brand of humor. And the other players, in the throes of a pressure-packed pennant race, felt indebted to Bob as well. Today you always hear about guys keeping spirits high with foolish pranks. Bob did it just by being funny. I wish I'd had the wherewithal to have written down all the things he said and did because it would have been a hilarious book. I'm familiar with his expressionless talk-show character and that always cheery character in all those commercials who refuses to recognize that everyone around him thinks he's an absolute jerk, because Ueck was already doing similar off-the-wall comedy back then. It was amazing that a professional writer wasn't supplying his material.

My most vivid memories of Bob were of his looking at things or picking up objects in rooms or restaurants and improvising funny stories in which the props figured prominently. I remember he carried around a windup frog that would make a *click-click-click* noise as it hopped around. Bob and Ray Sadecki, a pretty zany guy himself, worked out a ridiculous newsmen routine in which they announced "Dateline New York" and read newspaper headlines and improvised reports while the clicking frog hopped around and served as their ticker. I remember that Bob put a picture of an ugly female, a complete stranger, in his wallet. He'd claim this dog was his wife if anyone wanted to converse about respective families—that face in the photo, which could have stopped a clock, ended all discussions immediately.

All the players loved Bob and they'd always gather around him in the hotel bars or in the backs of buses and planes. Those were the funniest trips I ever had in baseball. Bob did routines that would have been great on FM radio. He had been in the Army for two years and often drew on his own experiences for stories. There was his Army drill sergeant giving orders to a firing squad. And there was the soldier who didn't hold the pin down on a grenade—his name was Lefty. One of Bob's funniest characters was a German U-boat commander with an up-periscope. Bob was of German descent, born and bred in Milwaukee, and he had the German dialect down pat.

CULT BASEBALL PLAYERS

That character's name was Krueger, and our coach Joe Schultz used to love when Bob did him. In fact, Joe nicknamed him Krueger. Herr Krueger. We all knew who Herr Krueger was. But Bob acquired about ten more nicknames, all stemming from new routines he did. It got to the point where we'd ask Bob for encores. Among my favorites was a silent bit in which he'd flush his face red and walk in such a way that he'd convince you he was drunk. Equally impressive was another mime routine in which he pretended to be walking uphill. He'd walk on level ground, but when you saw him pulling, pushing, and straining, you'd swear he was trying to climb a steep incline. He was just a brilliant comic.

Bob wasn't really into practical jokes, but there was one I remember because Sadecki and I helped him out. We used to have a dummy that we'd dress up and stuff pillows inside. It had the mask-face of a Neanderthal man and we used to call him Tom the Werewolf. We'd drag him around to all occasions. Once we took him on the plane. Ray put a pillow under his jacket, added a tie and a hat that covered part of the mask, and attached a piece of cardboard that went from the bottom of the jacket to the floor. Then we added shoes and perched Tom on the toilet in the bathroom. Ueck then told the stewardess that there was a terrible odor coming from the bathroom. So she went to check and opened the door and found this strangely dressed animal sitting there. When we heard her squeal, we knew that our scheme had worked to perfection.

That prank was well planned but most of Uecker's humor was spontaneous. You always sensed that he was about to say or do something funny, but he caught you off guard anyway. I often tell about the day the Cards players had a meeting to divide up shares. At the time there were six games left in the season, but the race was so tight that we still didn't know if we'd finish first, second, third, or fourth. We had to decide how many shares there would be and whether to give money to the grounds crew, equipment man, etc. Ken Boyer, our captain and player rep, conducted the meeting. At the end, everyone was about to leave when pitcher Roger Craig stood up and gave a heartfelt plea on behalf of Bing Devine, who had been fired as Cards general manager on August 5. It was a shock when Devine was dismissed, and Roger was so emotional because everybody on the team and in St. Louis respected him and was unhappy with the situation. Roger said, "We don't know if we're going to finish first or fourth, but if we vote Devine money, that would be kind of tasteless and tacky and would be an insult." Now the entire room was filled with tension and emotion. Building up steam, Roger continued, "But if we do win it, then I think we should at least give him a ring." Suddenly Uecker volunteers from the back of the room, "I'll give him a call." Roger and everyone else in the room just fell down on the floor laughing. You talk about comic relief.

We did clinch the pennant on the last day and everyone on the team was hysterical during the celebration in the clubhouse. If you can believe it, our inspirational song that year was that tired ditty "Pass the Biscuits, Miranda." That was because our trainer Bob Bowman had also been the trainer of the '46 Cards. It was the least-inspiring song that I ever heard in my life. But we sang it just the same. There was champagne all over the place and broken bottles on the floor. It got so bad that the guards told us to keep our shoes on. Ueck was the only guy who was barefoot. He had no clothes on and he was doing a modern dance to "Pass the Biscuits, Miranda," miraculously weaving through the broken glass without cutting himself. That is a beautiful image I'll never forget.

Ueck has always made light of not playing in the 1964 World Series against the Yankees (contending that his absence contributed to our victory). Nevertheless, he made his presence felt. During batting practice before the first game in Busch Stadium, Bob took the tuba from a musician in the left-field band. In addition to tooting the instrument, he used it to scoop up grounders. He stood in the outfield tooting and fielding. Naturally, it's not easy to catch bouncing baseballs with a tuba without denting it, and the Cards later got a bill for damage done. They actually took the money out of Bob's World Series check, which was ridiculous considering all the positive publicity the team got because of Bob's actions. In those days, the baseball establishment frowned on players' screwing around, and it's really remarkable and to Ueck's credit that he got away with some of the stuff he did.

During the 1964 season, some of us who were living in St. Louis without our families stayed at the Bel-Air Hotel. Bob and I paid $12 each to share a room. Everyone always asks me how much fun I used to have in the room with Bob Uecker providing nonstop entertainment. To be honest, Bob was quite different in the room. I had often heard that comedians were serious out of the spotlight, and that was certainly the case with Ueck. It was almost as if he were two different people. Outside the room, which is when I preferred Bob's company, he was always on. Once we got in the car to drive to the ballpark, he opened up and was hilarious. But inside that room he was eerily quiet. He was just in another world, completely unto himself. He wouldn't joke, he wouldn't talk about baseball. He would just sit and watch television and nothing would bother him. You could walk in front of him, the phone could ring. It was like he had tunnel vision. Bob was a stoic in the dugout, too. You might guess that Ueck was a world-class heckler, but he was content just to sit peacefully in the dugout for hours without saying anything.

Maybe that was Bob's way of dealing with family and career pressures. He had a shaky marriage and four kids, so he had to be feeling some pressure. He wouldn't allow others into that part of his life. He kept his privacy. However, he did tell me about his father. Gus. He always called him Gus. He revered Gus. Bob told me that Gus had a circulation problem and had had both his legs amputated. Gus never wore artificial legs. So Bob used to take his dad down to the bar and sit him on a stool and wait for him while he drank with his pals and told stories. And when Gus was through talking and full of beer, Bob would take him home. I was so touched by that story. It reveals the depth of Bob's feelings.

Back then, Uecker never mentioned if he had entertainment aspirations, but he did talk about becoming a broadcaster. Like most everyone who grew up in the Midwest in the forties and fifties, Uecker had been affected by Harry Caray. He used to do Harry Caray to the point where he sounded just like him. Harry tells the story about when Uecker broke into broadcasting in Milwaukee: "I'm driving down the street and I heard this voice on the radio and I said, 'Damn! That sounds like me!' Do you know who it was? It was Bob Uecker! And I called him and told him, 'Hey, Ueck, you sound just like me!' "

Uecker played with the Cards for two years, then in October 1965, he was packaged with Dick Groat and Bill White in a big six-player deal with the Phillies, four years before I'd be traded to them in another six-player deal. Ironically, Alex Johnson was one of the players we got (along with Pat Corrales and Art Mahaffey), but first-string catcher Clay Dalrymple, the other player Uecker used to tell Jack Herman he was about to be traded for, stayed put. Bob wasn't upset about being traded, although he wasn't thrilled about going to Philadelphia. He'd later joke, "The cops picked me up on the street at three A.M. and fined me five hundred dollars for being drunk and one hundred dollars for being with the Phillies." Today some of his funniest stories are about his year playing for Gene Mauch, who had no idea what kind of personality he had gotten in the trade. Gene was so serious about the game and Ueck always saw the funny side to everything. It was in Philadelphia that Uecker really started to build a reputation as a wit. He got along with the press there. They loved him. They hooked onto Ueck's line about the Philadelphia fans being so rough that they boo kids who come up empty in the Easter Sunday egg hunt. Uecker platooned with Dalrymple in 1966, playing against left-handers, and accumulated a career-high 207 at-bats and 7 homers. Unfortunately, his .208 average didn't impress Mauch. He'd later contend that Mauch considered him such a bad hitter that he nailed his bats to the bat rack so he couldn't get them out.

The following January, Uecker was traded again. Ironically, he was swapped straight up for the same Gene Oliver whose acquisition by the Braves from the Cards in 1963 had resulted in Ueck being sent to the Cards. So, for his final season, Bob returned to his first team, the Braves, who were now transplanted in Atlanta, and was again expected to back up Joe Torre. Talk about a circular career! Talk about a dead-end career! But I think Ueck enjoyed his final year in the majors. He got to be a player-coach with Atlanta. That meant he could carry around a pocket watch like all the other coaches did. He just loved that watch and always made a big deal of pulling it out of his pocket. He gloated, "I can act like a coach."

I think Bob would have preferred having a great career, but since he didn't come close to greatness, I assume he's delighted that it was as undistinguished as it was. I'm sure that in retrospect he's glad that he hit a puny .150 in his final season and lowered his career average to exactly .200. As he brags in his book, *Catcher in the Wry*, "Not .201 or .199. A cool .200 lifetime. A lot of retired players joke about being a career .200 hitter, but I was the real article." If Uecker had hit .300, would he be as funny today? I don't know. Surely his self-deprecating humor wouldn't be as effective.

Because Bob and I are broadcasters in different leagues, our paths rarely cross anymore. Which is a shame, because I enjoy seeing him so much. Like most of America, I catch up with Bob by watching him on talk shows and in commercials, especially those popular Miller Lite ads. His character may not know he's making a fool of himself or have any idea what's going on around him—he actually believes that those seats they exile him to at the top of the stadium are as good as those in "the front row"—but you'll notice that he's never in a bad mood and never expresses an ounce of meanness. That's the Bob Uecker I remember from our playing days. He comes across as just a guy going through life having a good time. If you want to hook on and laugh along, that's fine, and if not, that's fine with him, too. He still makes me happy. Bob Uecker makes a lot of people happy.

Tim McCarver is a broadcaster for the New York Mets and CBS's *Game of the Week.* He was the colorman on ABC's *Monday Night Baseball.* His book, *Oh, Baby, I Love It!* (with Ray Robinson), recalls his catching career in the major leagues, from 1959 to 1980.

TOM SEWELL on

MOE BERG

Will the real Moe Berg stand up, please?

There is general stirring among the contestants on the stage. The linguist, clad in tweed sports coat, sweater, and woolen trousers, shifts in his chair, as the major league baseball player, dressed in peaked cap, flannel uniform, catcher's mitt, and cleats, signals he's about to get up, also. The third contestant, the spy, adjusts his dark, wraparound glasses and slowly rises.

A series of gasps ripples through the auditorium . . . all three men have stood up!

Is it possible that they all represent the same man? The mysterious Mr. Moe Berg?

Flashback: Fenway Park, Boston, 1939. Ted Williams—aka The Splendid Splinter, The Kid—is sitting on the dugout bench while Moe Berg, a two-fortyish lifetime batter, cracks a rare line drive off the Green Monster in left field. Later, Moe huffs into the dugout and turns to Williams and instructs, tongue in cheek, "I hope you were watching, Ted. That's the way you're supposed to do it."

Flashback: Tokyo, Japan. 1934. Moe Berg is dressed in a black kimono and carries a bouquet of flowers as he tiptoes to the exit door of St. Luke's International Hospital. He climbs the stairs to the roof, where he sets the flowers down and then lifts his kimono and un-hinges the motion picture camera that is strapped to his hip. While Babe Ruth slams a home run at a nearby ballpark—and the other players on the visiting American all-star team wonder where their third-string catcher is—Moe begins taking shots of Tokyo—pictures

that will later be used in General Jimmy Doolittle's famous raid over Tokyo.

Flashback: A train en route from New York to Princeton. Sometime in the thirties. Moe Berg and *New York Times* sports columnist John Kiernan huddle over a Latin dictionary as they trace words from the original Latin into English. "John," says Moe to the writer, "imagine wasting time and money in a nightclub when you can have fun like this."

Moe Berg was not an ordinary ballplayer. He was the quintessential Renaissance man, perhaps the most cerebral player ever to don a major league baseball uniform. He was Phi Beta Kappa at Princeton University, spoke a dozen languages fluently, spent fifteen years in the majors, and committed espionage against the Japanese while he was a ballplayer.

He also was an enduring enigma, a man obsessed with privacy. Casey Stengel variously described him as a "big question-mark guy," the "mystery catcher," and the "strangest fella who ever put on a uniform."

His mysterious nature followed him through Princeton, baseball, World War II, and in later life. "Moe was a man of mystery. No one could quite account for all the things he did and the places he went," recalls Don Griffin, a Princeton classmate. "He traveled alone most of the time and you never saw him with anyone."

"Moe was absolutely ideal for undercover work," noted Michael

Burke, former president of the New York Yankees. "Not by design; just by nature."

But being a major league baseball player thrust him into the public eye, whether he liked it or not. And his celebrated status as baseball's most intelligent player made him an oddity next to his mostly un-lettered teammates.

Morris "Moe" Berg was born in New York City, in 1902, but grew up in Newark, New Jersey, where his father opened a drugstore. Moe's parents were Russian Jews who had fled czarist pogroms in the late 1800s. They emphasized hard work, scholarship, and love for their new country. But Moe's first and foremost love was baseball. "Ever since he was two years old it was, 'Hey, Sam, let's play catch.' It could be with a ball, an orange, anything," recalls Dr. Samuel Berg, Moe's older brother.

Moe excelled at baseball in high school and at Princeton, becom-ing the most illustrious ballplayer in Old Nassau's history. When Moe got an offer to join the Brooklyn Dodgers after graduating from the university, his father vehemently opposed the move. He wanted his son to become a professional, such as a teacher or a lawyer. Moe, in fact, had been offered a teaching post at Princeton's renowned Romance Languages Department but he opted for baseball instead—creating a chasm between father and son that never healed. Moe tried to appease his disappointed father by attending the Sorbonne in Paris, where he studied philology, and Columbia Law School during off-season periods. He obtained his law degree and gained admit-tance to the New York State bar, but his father remained implacable and never attended any of the major league games in which Moe appeared.

As he moved from one team to another—playing for the Brooklyn Dodgers, Chicago White Sox, Cleveland Indians, Washington Sena-tors, the Indians again, and the Boston Red Sox—Moe provided sportswriters with a different kind of copy to write. One popular anecdote involved a player who complained to Moe about having an upset stomach. "You're suffering from intestinal fortitude," Moe told his worried teammate, who scratched his head and said, "In-testinal fortitude? What can I do to cure it?" Moe recommended taking two aspirin and getting to bed early. The next morning the teammate rushed toward Moe. "You ought to be a doctor, Moe. I did what you said and the intestinal fortitude is all gone."

Moe's reading habits generated humorous stories for sportswrit-ers. He read many foreign-language newspapers, as well as four or five different U.S. dailies every day. But he had an idiosyncrasy about his newspapers: No one could touch them before he was finished reading them. "It's alive," he'd caution teammates about his freshly bought paper. "When it's dead, you can read it." If anyone violated his edict, Moe would rush out—even in a storm—and buy a new copy.

While he was with the Washington Senators, it was reported that Moe always kept a neatly pressed tuxedo in his locker, just in case he got an invite to some foreign-embassy party in the nation's capital. At such functions, Moe would regale his hosts with his knowledge of their language, customs, and politics.

Joe Cronin, who managed the Red Sox and was later president of the American League, recalled, "Moe was the only man I know who could sit on the bench for two months, then be brought into a game and catch perfectly." Much praised for his defensive play, Moe did suffer an occasional lapse. In a tie game with a runner on third and only one out, he caught a pop foul and believing there were two out, mistakenly flipped the ball over his shoulder toward the unattended mound. The runner on third tagged up and scored the winning run. Sportswriters and players never let Moe forget that gaffe, reminding him that despite his intellectual prowess he still hadn't learned to count beyond two.

Moe batted a mediocre .242 lifetime and had only 6 home runs in fifteen years in the majors. His longevity was largely attributed to his astute perception of the game. His wide knowledge was evidenced in 1941 when Moe penned "Pitchers and Catchers" for *Atlantic Monthly*. The lengthy article was noted for its sublime insights into the intricacies and strategies of the game of baseball. The piece is considered a classic of its genre.

Moe's intellectual persona prompted an invitation to appear on the popular radio show *Information Please*. He was asked a series of esoteric questions and provided correct answers for all of them, including the meaning of the word *loi* (French for law) and a description of the "Willie-Nicky exchange" (pre–World War I telegrams between the kaiser and the czar).

His success on *Information Please* served as both a blessing and a curse: it elevated public opinion of ballplayers' IQs, but it haunted Moe wherever he appeared—even in the bullpen.

As he warmed up a pitcher, fans would shout down at the catcher: "Moe, recite the Book of Leviticus!" "Moe, is it walruses or walrii for the plural?" "Moe, what color were Martha's bloomers at the inauguration?"

In 1932, Moe, Frank "Lefty" O'Doul, and Ted Lyons were invited to Japan to teach Japanese youth the rudiments of baseball. Moe quickly fell in love with the country and its people and eventually mastered the Japanese language. That proved helpful in 1934 when Moe was named to a Japan-bound American League all-star team consisting of Babe Ruth, Lou Gehrig, Vernon "Lefty" Gomez, Charlie Gehringer, Earl Averill, Clint Brown, Jimmie Foxx, Eric McNair, Frank "Gabby" Hayes, Hal Warstler, Joe Cascarella, Edmund J. Miller, and Earl Whitehill. The all-stars were managed by the fabled Connie Mack.

It was on this trip that Moe took the secret films of Tokyo from the rooftop of St. Luke's International Hospital, an assignment whose disclosure years later would separate the catcher from his teammates and raise questions about why he did it and who ordered him to do it.

During World War II, Moe was recruited into the OSS, the spy organization led by General William "Wild Bill" Donovan. He carried out a number of crucial missions before being chosen for the biggest assignment of his life: spying on Hitler's atomic bomb project. Moe was one of the few people aware of the life-and-death struggle for the bomb; not even Vice President Harry Truman knew of it.

In a letter to Moe dated August 9, 1945, Whitney Shepardson, head of OSS Secret Intelligence, asked the catcher to recount in writing his wartime atomic bomb espionage missions. "We [OSS] are entitled to claim credit at the appropriate time for our contribution [in spying on the German A-bomb project] and that contribution has been very largely through you," Shepardson stated. "I don't believe there is anyone in the organization who can make this record correctly and in detail except yourself . . ."

After the war, Moe was preoccupied with books and the accumulation of knowledge. He learned Sanskrit. He toured Russia and China before that was the fashionable thing to do. While researching and coauthoring his biography, I was constantly amazed by his wide range of interests. However, baseball would remain a top priority— he once told New York Times sports columnist Arthur Daley that baseball was his "theater"—and invariably he appeared at ballparks throughout the country for All-Star and World Series contests. And like the mystery man that he was, he always dressed in dark clothes. And fittingly, his last words to a nurse from his hospital deathbed were, "How did the Mets do today?"

Moe was dead by the time I began to work on his biography. I have always felt cheated that I never had the chance to meet him in

Courtesy Samuel Berg

person. I would have liked the opportunity to have gotten to know the real Moe Berg.

But did anybody ever get to know the real Moe Berg?

I often wonder. He was friendly with Nelson Rockefeller; General Leslie Groves, the head of the Manhattan Project; General William "Wild Bill" Donovan; and Babe Ruth and Lou Gehrig, among scores of big-league ballplayers. He was also a friend of the great sportswriters of his day, including Red Smith, Arthur Daley, John Kiernan, Jerome Holtzman, Bill Cunningham, Shirley Povich, and Jimmy Cannon.

But I doubt that any of them ever really knew Moe Berg. That was part of the man's special charm. He was the Mona Lisa smile of the baseball diamond.

Tom Sewell is a Massachusetts-based correspondent for the *Providence Journal*. He is the coauthor of *Moe Berg: Athlete, Scholar, Spy* (with Louis Kaufman and Barbara Fitzgerald).

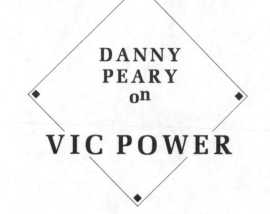

DANNY
PEARY
on
VIC POWER

Victor Pellot, a baseball idol in Puerto Rico since debuting for Caguas in 1947, recently accepted an invitation to play in an old-timers game in the States, where in twelve major league seasons (1954–65), he also made a name for himself—using another name. "Vic Power!" exclaimed the elated Ted Lepcio when he recognized his teammate for the game. "I . . . I thought you were dead!" Then Lepcio burst out crying.

Victor Pellot Power, making an infrequent return to the mainland, was taken aback by the tears because Lepcio had barely known him during the eight years their careers overlapped and had played mostly with Boston, a team on which "the only player who liked me was Ted Williams." But I can understand Lepcio's reaction. For the nostalgic former utility infielder, Vic Power's unexpected appearance proved that his memory of fifties baseball was not, as he feared, just a glorious fantasy. There really had been a Spanish-speaking black from Puerto Rico who stood menacingly at the plate in a weird stance, swinging his bat in his left hand like a pendulum, with the barrel repeatedly pointing directly at the pitcher (who must have felt like William Tell's son); who ripped high fastballs through the box or wherever he pleased; who played first base with joy, cunning, the grace of a ballet dancer, and unmatchable skill, popping bubble gum, clowning with baserunners, and deftly snaring wild throws, hot liners, and high pop-ups with just one sweeping hand,

VIC POWER
outfield PHILADELPHIA ATHLETICS

1954 Topps: Copyright © The Topps Company, Inc.

as if he were a lepidopterist netting the most delicate prized butterfly; who refused to take a ninety mph beanball thrown by a white pitcher and ordered by a white manager as a joke; and who played the game the way it was meant to be played but wouldn't "play the game." And if there is and was a Vic Power, then there really was that peculiar and wonderful decade of baseball.

As Lepcio realized, this native of Arecibo, Puerto Rico, with a lovely smile but fists at the ready, became a true symbol of American baseball in the fifties as it further emerged from the Light Ages into the more enlightened Dark Ages. With a defiantly independent attitude and an unbridled flamboyance that hadn't been so openly displayed by a black sports figure since Jack Johnson, Power outraged owners, antagonized sportswriters (who unfairly labeled him a "showboat" and "clubhouse lawyer"), scared opponents, excited fans, and came to represent the tension, entertainment, and color (in more ways than one), if not the false innocence, of fifties baseball. The Yankees owned his contract but foolishly traded their top minor league prospect because he didn't project the wholesome image they demanded of their players, especially their first black player (instead his mild-mannered roommate Elston Howard was designated a year later), and he was forced to play his prime years out of the spotlight;

nevertheless, he stood out from the 400 major-leaguers of the time and for those who followed his career, transcended the sport. As Brendan C. Boyd and Fred C. Harris wrote, "With the possible exception of Jonas Salk, John Foster Dulles, and Annette Funicello, no one public figure so personified the fifties as did Vic Power."

I believe my hero was truly synonymous with fifties baseball, but I'm grateful he waited until the midsixties and I'd sufficiently grown up before he retired. Because in the years between a toddler named Suzy and a teenager named Donna, Vic Power was the love of my life, the adopted member of my family. Calvin has his Hobbes and I had my Vic Power; and everyone who got to know me got to know all about my favorite player, even if they were completely indifferent to baseball. If he wasn't the reason I woke up each morning, then he was the reason I got up as early as I did and frantically raced barefoot across our dew-chilled lawn to grab the paper and beat my older brother to the box scores. He was also the reason I stayed up so late, with a transistor radio clutched in my hand on the pillow, especially at the end of his career when I lived on the East Coast and he played in California and I'd listen to the faraway, drowned-in-static stations of the other American League teams long past midnight, just in case he'd pinch-hit against them or come in for late-inning defense. I spent most of my youth in need of a nap.

I also spent most of my youth moving, as my father took different teaching jobs and summer positions. I went to seven schools during Power's career and lived in two apartments and four houses in three states, plus another place each summer. Friends came and went, but Vic Power remained loyal, the most stable element in my life. No matter where I was, I could open up the daily sports page and find his name in a box score—usually doing me proud. So when he started moving around with increasing frequency, I remained loyal, too. I was passionate about his first team, the lowly Athletics of Philadelphia (1954) and Kansas City (1955), but when he was traded to the colorful Indians (in 1958), powerful Twins (1962), infectious Angels (1964), doomed Phillies (for the September swoon in 1964), and Angels again (1965), I instantly became devoted to his new team, picking the club that desired him rather than the one that had discarded him. The only team I never forgave, however, was the Yankees. They hadn't the guts to put him on their major league roster, although his flashy style would have made him a surefire sensation in New York, especially with black and Puerto Rican fans. It pleased me that throughout his career he hit the Yankees better than any other team.

I wanted to play like Vic Power so I copied his pendulum batting stance, though I had no idea why he used it, and tried to nonchalantly catch everything one-handed, a dangerous endeavor with my permanently squashed Green Stamps–purchased Joe Adcock mitt. Because I was always new in school or the neighborhood, I identified with Power's outcast-outsider status. Once I moved from the South to the Northeast, I began to realize how uncomfortable he must have felt with his strong "foreign" accent. Being timid, I admired his aggressiveness and showy style. And just as I sensed I was a neat kid who, being painfully shy, had to be "discovered" so that my talents (football stars usually weigh more than eleven pounds) and best qualities (I knew a lot of movie and rock 'n' roll titles) would be revealed, I thought Power was properly appreciated only by the few savvy fans and sportswriters who had "discovered" him playing in Kansas City and Cleveland. (He should have been elected the All-Star first baseman, not the backup.) I also liked that he retained his strength, spirit, and sense of humor despite the racial incidents I read about (and would years later talk to him about); certainly my knowledge of what Vic Power went through in order to play professional baseball in America fueled my rebelliousness and heightened my social consciousness—and helped prepare me for the sixties.

My fanaticism for Vic Power began during his rookie year, 1954, when I was four years old or, as I like to think, directly on my fifth birthday. That year we were living in Upper Darby, Pennsylvania, outside Philadelphia, but were visiting relatives in New York when my great-uncle Israel earned a permanent place in my heart by buying me several packs of baseball cards. My brother had a large card collection that I'd gone through carefully with my red crayon, but I had none of my own despite being a budding baseball maniac (by the time I turned six, I not only knew all the current players but had memorized every one of their stats). So I was thrilled by the present. A pivotal moment in my life: I opened my first wrapper and there was my first card, that of a Philadelphia Athletic. I still distinctly remember the impact. Vic Power! What a name for a ballplayer! There was a dramatic background shot of him leaping into the air to make a catch with arms and legs outstretched (he spent a long day jumping for the cameraman), and a large close-up of a face that was matinee-idol handsome, confident, friendly, and youthful. And he was exhibiting his soon-to-be-familiar cheery smile with "teeth," wrote Larry Merchant years later, "that gleamed like visual castanets." And he was black, very black, which definitely contributed to his appeal. At that age, I wouldn't allow my parents to take me to a movie that didn't have Indians, so it made sense that I'd be attracted to a striking-looking nonwhite baseball player.

Now skeptics would argue that I would have fallen madly in love with whatever player I found on my first card, especially one who played in Philadelphia, but no player other than Vic Power could have been behind that wrapper. It would have been equally impossible for Romeo to have run into Juliet's gorgeous older sister Peggy before he had his love-at-first-sight encounter with Juliet. Vic Power was destined to have this scrawny, three-foot-tall white boy as his biggest fan in the world, and I was destined to have the greatest baseball hero.

My oldest possession today, that 1954 Topps baseball card, with the marvelous pictures on the front and superstats on the back (in 1953, he'd led the American Association with a .349 average), promised me years of excitement, and my player delivered. I no longer have my Vic Power scrapbook, but my memories are vivid. For instance, I remember the night in 1958 when he became the only player since Herbert Hoover was president to steal home twice in one game, tying the score with his first steal and then ending it with his second. A kid passed me on the street and told me the news, and even I thought it was a ruse because Power stole only one other base all season. I remember his slinging bats into the stands—a tradition that would pass on to his pupil, Tony Oliva. I remember his struggling with his English during media interviews, but that he'd keep smiling and laughing and make odd, hilarious remarks. I remember his arguing with umps and pitchers. I also remember seeing his picture in the paper, soaking his hand in an ice bucket after a brawl and saying, "I don't know who I hit, but whoever it was has the blackest eye." I remember a television game in which he jumped on the back of his good friend and Cleveland teammate Jimmy Piersall to prevent him from tearing into the umpire who thumbed him for distracting batter Ted Williams (by racing back and forth in the outfield). I remember him on television hitting a broken-bat, one-handed homer against Detroit; and an inside-the-park homer in Yankee Stadium that had Mickey Mantle (ha! ha!) chasing the ball around the monuments in center field like a slapstick comic. I remember listening to him homer in extra innings to give the Twins a key victory over the Yankees; and in the only time I saw him in person, at Yankee Stadium, single up the middle his first time up (!) to key a 2-run rally that led to a 5–4 Minnesota victory. And I remember buying the Greatest-Hits album of Ritchie Valens, and choosing to forever bond my favorite baseball player and my favorite singer, writing on the back cover, "Acquired on August 29, 1963, the same day Vic Power hit 2 homers and had 4 RBIs as the Twins set a record of 8 homers in a 14–2 win over Washington."

How I remember his hitting. A contact hitter with superior bat control, he seldom walked and struck out even less (just 14 times in 590 at-bats in 1958). He was a bad-ball, first-pitch hitter, yet managed to surpass .300 in three of his first five seasons (while winning two batting titles in the winter leagues in Puerto Rico), hit around .290 three other times, and wind up with a solid .284 career average. He had the ability to hit homers (126 lifetime), leading the winter league one year and clubbing 19 in his sophomore season in the majors, but he was more adept at slashing doubles and triples (leading the league in 1958), dragging bunts, and slapping seeing-eye singles to right (only Dick Groat was better at the hit-and-run). He was at his most effective batting second for the Twins, but he had success as a leadoff man for the Athletics and cleanup hitter for the Indians when Rocky Colavito wasn't around. In fact, he batted everywhere in the lineup from first to seventh, showing the same adaptability that he had in the field, where he started at every position but pitcher and catcher.

Of course, I remember his fielding most of all. Although he was an outfielder his first year and would later play extensively and most impressively at third and second, Power was primarily a first baseman. As great as Keith Hernandez is, Vic Power was better (despite being right-handed). He was the best. He had finesse and flair, stunning reflexes, uncanny anticipation, and tremendous range—he stayed deep and played the ball like a shortstop. And he could catch anything . . . with, to the consternation of baseball coaches across America, one hand in an era when other first basemen had trouble catching with two. He repeatedly lead the league in assists and double plays, and those years he wasn't league leader in putouts, total chances per game, and fielding average, he was near the top. He deservedly was awarded the Gold Glove the first seven years it was given. Vic Power's legendary fielding was both an art and a weapon.

In spring 1966, I learned how Charlie Brown felt when his favorite player, Joe Schlabotnik, was demoted to the minors. I read in the paper that "the Angels have tendered Vic Power his release." I have never before or after seen the word "tendered" used in connection to a player's release, and ever since I have detested that word like no other.

For a brief time, he unsuccessfully tried to break into motion pictures. (Having gained weight and lost hair, he resembled, I thought, likable forties' black character actor Sam "Deacon" Mc-Daniel, but I couldn't see Power in any of those porter and butler roles McDaniel played.) Power then returned to Puerto Rico and into mythology as far as I was concerned. Baseball would never be the same. He would manage occasionally in the winter leagues and eventually began working as a scout for the Angels and running free baseball clinics for teenagers. He had married for a second time and had a fourth son—Victor, a teenager with baseball aspirations. Naturally, I always regretted that I'd never met him and that he didn't know about me, his greatest fan. I did dream I met him once and he had blue lips—but that was totally unsatisfying.

This book gave me a reason (actually an excuse) to contact Vic Power. I called him long distance. Imagine calling up Davy Crockett or Indiana Jones and having him answer the phone. That's how unreal it seemed. I could barely talk, but he agreed to meet me if I came to Puerto Rico. So on my birthday, my wife, Suzanne, and I flew to San Juan, and a third of a century after I got my Vic Power card, I met Vic Power! I knew how Stanley felt when he tracked down Livingston. Meeting a childhood idol and being disappointed can be a traumatic experience, but I didn't worry. I knew Vic Power even before I got to know him. He signed that cherished baseball card, which after years in my wallet looked worn but loved, putting his autograph above the printed signature. Then he told me that instead of the three hours I had requested for the interview, he would give me three days. A dream come true: For three days, our warm, congenial host drove us around the island. He took us to Old San Juan, to the beach (I went for a dip with Vic Power!), to visit his tiny granddaughter, to the interior. Although I was with my idol, I wasn't nervous because it felt just like being with a dear friend, yet every night when I'd return to the hotel, I'd come to my senses and gasp, "I can't believe it!" This was the reaction I had wanted: Vic Power the ballplayer was still my hero.

Perhaps the highlight of the visit began at Luquillo Beach. We were swimming when he started talking to a teenage boy from Boston. The teenager was visiting the island for the first time with his Puerto Rican father, who had left the island in 1952 and hadn't returned until then. Power told the boy, "Boston! I used to hit a lot of homers against Boston!" When asked by the confused boy if he played baseball, he joked, "I'm Vic Power, the best first baseman ever!" The boy admitted he hadn't heard of him but said his father, a baseball fan, probably had. But when he went to shore, the name Vic Power wasn't enough to convince his father to enter the water. An hour later, we drove to an out-of-the-way fish restaurant. Soon, another car pulled up carrying, coincidentally, the boy, his father, and grandfather. We sat at nearby tables, and Power ventured into a conversation in Spanish with the grandfather. The boy's father seemed uninterested, even when the name Vic Power was spoken. But then Vic Power mentioned the name he had played under in Puerto Rico. Suddenly the father's eyes widened in disbelief. He jumped up and raced across the restaurant, breathlessly calling, "Victor Pellot! Victor Pellot! Victor Pellot!" and merrily embraced his idol of many years ago, an idol he assumed was as dead as his lamented Puerto Rico of 1952. After having his picture taken with Victor Pellot Power, he crumbled in his chair, his eyes closed and his shaking head in his hands, weeping without tears and muttering over and over again, "Victor Pellot! Victor Pellot!" A glorious part of his past had come back—alive. Ted Lepcio would have known how he felt. I certainly did.

Danny Peary is the editor of this book.

Interview
with Vic Power

DANNY PEARY: I'm fortunate you turned out to be exactly as I expected. But many people are afraid to meet their childhood sports idols because they don't want to discover they rooted for the wrong guy all those years.

VIC POWER: I know how they feel. I recently spoke at a tribute honoring a Puerto Rican pitcher who was one of my heroes as a youngster. I said I had liked him so much because he was an upstanding guy who never drank. Then I glanced over at him and he was so drunk that he was falling out of his chair. I had to cover my eyes with my hand for the rest of the evening and hope no one heard what I said.

DP: Did you know about American baseball as a youngster in Arecibo?

VP: The first uniform I put on as a young boy was a Yankee uniform they sold in the drugstore. Everybody in Puerto Rico heard of the Yankees. But we didn't know who they were. Nobody knew the American players or what the major leagues was.

DP: So your goal was just to play professionally in Puerto Rico?

VP: I painted and a lot of people thought I had the talent to be an artist, but I wanted to be a lawyer. When I was thirteen, my father died from tetanus after cutting his finger in a factory accident. My mother was a real hero—she raised three boys and three girls by sewing dresses. Meanwhile, she was expecting to get $10,000 compensation from the factory, but as we later found out, her lawyer took money from the factory to drop the case. I wanted to be a lawyer so I could reopen the case and get my mother that money she lost.

   In 1947, I signed a contract to play with Caguas in the winter leagues. Everyone said I wouldn't play because they already had the

CULT BASEBALL PLAYERS

Victor Pellot at 19.

best first baseman in Puerto Rico. But he was around thirty-five and I was sixteen and full of life. In the first day of infield practice, I scooped up some bad throws with one hand and everyone went crazy. The next day he retired! I got $250 a month during the four-month season and managed to keep the family together. My salary doubled my second year, and I bought a house in San Juan and moved my family there. I was able to support my mother and put my brothers and sisters through high school and take care of them until they were married. I also finished high school, but I gave up plans to go to college or law school.

DP: How did you end up in the Yankee organization?

VP: In 1949, Quincy Trouppe, who had been a catcher in the Negro Leagues, signed me to play in Canada in the independent Provincial League, with Drummondville. I took my first plane and got airsick. Then I got homesick because I'd never been away from my family and didn't know how to speak English or French. But the people were friendly and Quincy took care of me like a father. I played right field and hit .329, two points from the top. My salary increased my second year from $800 to $1,000 a month, which I got on top of my winter leagues salary. Then I played first, hit .334, and won the batting title [and drove in 105 runs in 105 games]. The Yankees sent Tom Greenwade, who signed Mickey Mantle, to watch me at the Provincial League All-Star Game. I made an error so he reported that I was a good hitter, an average runner, and a poor fielder. The Yankees then bought my contract from Drummondville for $7,500. I didn't care about the Yankees, so I threatened not to sign unless the Drummondville general manager gave me some of that money. He got so nervous and handed me a lot of Canadian paper money. It turned out to be only $500. I didn't know that I could have sold myself and kept all the money.

DP: Were you known as Vic Power yet?

VP: Some people got mad at me because they thought that the moment I went to the States I changed my name from Pellot because I didn't want to be known as a Puerto Rican. But let me explain. My mother's father's name was Pové, but when she went to school for the first time, her English teacher told her that she got her name wrong, and that Pové was a French name. And the teacher changed the v to a w and added the r and told my mother that her name was Power. My mother didn't say anything. Well, in Puerto Rico, we used two names, my father's name, Pellot, followed by my mother's family name. So I used to write Victor Pellot Power. At Drummondville, I was called Victor Pellot. But the French Canadians would say "La Pellot" with an l sound, rather than a y sound. That sounded similar to a French sexual term and everyone would laugh. So they started calling me Victor Power instead. Finally, it was cut to Vic Power. But when I went back to play in the winter leagues, I was still Victor Pellot.

DP: You hit .294 with Syracuse in the International League in 1951; then a .331 average, with the Kansas City Blues of the American Association in 1952. You deserved to be the Yankees first black player, but they kept you at Kansas City for another year. When you responded by hitting a league-leading .349, they sent you to the lowly Philadelphia Athletics in a thirteen-player deal.

VP: People wonder if I regret that I didn't play another couple of years at the end of my career, but I wish I had come to the majors two years earlier than I did. I tried to just do my job in the minors and be patient. But for some reason the Yankees weren't ready for a black ballplayer. Years later sportswriters would ask me why the Yankees kept me in the minors when they were bringing up my white teammates, and I'd answer, "They were waiting to see if I could turn white, but I couldn't do it." You see, I had to make fun and joke so I could survive in the game. Blacks and Puerto Ricans picketed Yankee Stadium so they would bring me up, and the Yankees got mad at me. They kept making excuses. They'd say, "Vic Power didn't prove to us that he can hit a major league pitcher." Well, how could I when I'd never seen a major league pitcher? The Yankees wouldn't even invite me to spring training. They'd say, we want a "decent" black. That's why everyone started thinking, "What's wrong with Vic Power?"

DP: You had a reputation that frightened the Yankees.

VP: I wasn't outspoken. I never had any trouble with my managers or my white teammates. I was never drunk or late to the ballpark. I never missed a sign. And when hecklers would shout, "Hey, Vic Power, you're black!" I knew that so it didn't bother me. But I did respond when guys started throwing beanballs. I was the only black on the team, and every time Bill Skowron or Bill Renna homered, the pitcher would throw at my head. There weren't helmets then so I had to rely on my reflexes and my fists. I had to protect myself. How can you have a bad reputation when you fight for your life? I had a temper and got into some brutal fights. Being a Puerto Rican, I'd fight anybody. Maybe the Yankees didn't want a player like that. Because I soon learned it was just as bad in the majors. For instance, one pitcher threatened to throw a ball in one ear and make it come out the other ear; I said, "This guy's pretty rough."

DP: In those years in the Yankee chain and in your early years with the Athletics, weren't you developing a reputation off the field as well?

VP: I played in Kansas City in 1952 and 1953 in the minors for the Blues and from 1955 to 1958 in the majors for the Athletics, after we spent a year in Philadelphia. I never got into an argument with a sportswriter there, but those guys had it in for me. They called me a showboat because I caught everything with one hand and had that pendulum swing. But what really bothered them was my conduct off the field. They thought, "You field good, you hit good, you are intelligent, but you like white girls and drive a Cadillac." Maybe if I had driven a Volkswagen and told them I was after a big, fat colored girl, they would have said, "Oh, he's a nice guy, see how beautiful he is."

In Puerto Rico there is no such thing as color, there is no discrimination, everyone is together. So I couldn't understand why everyone got so upset when I went out with light-skinned women in Kansas City. In baseball, there were many black players like Willie Mays and Roberto Clemente who dated white women, just as there were white players who went out with black women, and it would get me mad that they had better reputations than me because they did it secretly. For instance, if they went to a motel, they would each get a room and get together later. If I wanted to go out with a white girl, I'd just go. We'd sit down and listen to music, in public. I'd drive around in a Cadillac with the top down. I didn't hide that my closest friend was a white woman. She also appreciated art and liked to watch baseball. I was having problems in Kansas City with restaurants that didn't serve blacks, so we'd stop in front of a restaurant and she'd go inside and get the food. They didn't like that kind of behavior. When the manager said I could bring a white friend to a team picnic, they didn't like it when I brought a woman.

DP: Did the police give you trouble in Kansas City?

VP: Oh, baby. I'd be driving my Cadillac twenty-five miles per hour, and they'd pull me over and ask, "Where did you get that car?" So I'd tell them I bought it and give them the name of the dealer. Then they'd ask, "Who are you?" I'd say, "Vic Power, the ballplayer." They'd say, "Okay, we were just making a routine investigation." The editor of the black paper in Kansas City wrote that he saw fifty policemen while driving by the ballpark; two blocks later he spotted a man beating his screaming wife, but there were no police around, he wrote, because they were at the ballpark "waiting for Vic Power so they could make a routine investigation." I remember once a policeman said he thought I had stolen my car. I got mad because I had just received a certificate for being the best-dressed player in the major leagues and I was well dressed in a hat and tie. I told him, "You look more like a thief than me." When I married for the first time, I brought my wife from Puerto Rico. She was light-skinned, with dyed blond hair. The police always pulled us over. They'd ask her rude questions about her race and get angry when she didn't answer. When I tried to tell them that she didn't speak English, they'd snap, "We didn't ask you!" So it wasn't easy. When I played baseball, I was neither white nor black, and the white fans loved me, but after the game I was just another colored guy in town.

DP: I know you had troubles outside Kansas City as well, particularly when you were in spring training and traveling through the South. Were you surprised?

VP: No one warned me about segregation in the South. No one told me why black players couldn't date light-skinned women, or stay in the same hotel as white players, or eat in the same restaurant. I went into a restaurant in Little Rock, Arkansas, and the waitress said, "We don't serve Negroes," and I said, "That's okay, I don't eat Negroes. I want rice and beans." I would get mad, because they were pushing me. My mother couldn't believe it when I wrote her that a restaurant wouldn't serve a hungry person who had money. I wish someone would have explained to me about the racial problem because it was confusing. They just let me find out for myself. I gained so much respect for Jackie Robinson, Willie Mays, and the other blacks who came before me.

The first time I went to spring training in Florida, I knew something was strange. The other players stayed in a hotel near the ballpark, but without explanation, I was sent to the "colored section" to stay. I had to walk two miles to and from practice every day because blacks weren't allowed to take taxis. They'd pick the best house in the colored section for me, and for one period I had to stay with a funeral director. I tell you, it's scary sleeping upstairs with those corpses downstairs. Eventually, they let blacks stay in the same hotels as whites, but they still told us not to use the pool, look at white women, or eat in the hotel restaurant. I had trouble adjusting to the way blacks ate in America; I wasn't used to greasy foods or grits. So I'd go to a supermarket and buy salami, ham, and bananas and take that to my room. One night I walked to a store and was stopped by police because there was a municipal law that said blacks weren't allowed downtown after six P.M. There were all kinds of municipal laws. For instance, I wasn't allowed to drink the cold water in the dugout—I was supposed to drink hot water from a fountain behind the center-field billboard.

I got arrested for jaywalking in Orlando, for crossing the street on a red light. I explained to the judge, "I'm a Puerto Rican and on my island, a Negro and white go to school together, dance together, and get married. But here I try to go to a restaurant and there's a sign that says 'For Whites Only.' And I try to go to a bar or a movie house, or drink from a water fountain or use a bathroom, but I see that sign, 'For Whites Only.' So when I saw white people crossing the street when the green light came on, I figured that colored people could only cross when the light was red." He dismissed the case.

The worst experience I had was in Lake Okeechobee when we were returning from Fort Meyers to West Palm Beach. We stopped at a gas station for what they called "piss call." All the players got off the bus to use the bathroom, but the attendant wouldn't let me go in because I was black. I had to go so badly but couldn't go behind the bus with that guy watching me. So I bought a Coke from his soda machine and planned to use the empty bottle. When it was time to get on the bus, the guy ordered me to return the bottle although I hadn't finished the Coke. I offered to give him a quarter deposit but he insisted I give him the bottle. So I pushed it at him. He then ran and called the sheriff and told him to arrest "that black bastard in the back of the bus." But the players wouldn't let him on. The sheriff talked to the attendant and then told me I could have the bottle for a $500 deposit. I had to borrow the money from my teammates so we could leave. I was so afraid that I never used the bottle. So I paid $500 for a Coke. But I was lucky. After that the team left me home when we went to little towns to play. I thought that was nice, but I wish they had forced the issue more.

DP: Were your white teammates always supportive?

VP: When I belonged to the Yankees, we were friendly on the field, but I wondered why they'd drive past me when I was walking two miles to the colored section. I thought they were afraid of breaking a municipal law. We'd stop at restaurants and I'd have to stay on the bus, which I didn't mind because it gave me the chance to read and learn English, but not once did a teammate or the manager or the driver offer to bring me something to eat. I didn't want to force those guys to accept me. If they didn't like me or the Yankees didn't like me, it was their problem.

DP: Did the blacks who saw you play in the South cheer for you?

VP: As a Puerto Rican, I didn't think of myself as any color, but when the blacks in the South saw me playing with whites, they thought it was good for their people. I remember playing an exhibition game in Mobile, Alabama. The white fans were in the good seats behind the plate. The blacks sat in a little area in the right-field bleachers that had no shade from the sun. I was the only black in the game and felt funny because they cheered everything I did. They made me feel special. Now there was a wood sign out in right field that said, "Yellow Taxis for Whites Only." And I hit a fly that knocked that sign down. Those people went wild. It was a big party! I'll never forget that!

DP: Were you friendly with your Blues roommate, Elston Howard, or did you compete to become the Yankees first black?

VP: We were friendly, but I thought he was too much of a yes-man. He was like a lot of blacks in those days—like Larry Doby, Monte Irvin, and my good friend Junior Gilliam—who would never speak out about anything. He wasn't my competition because he wasn't a star. He was a conservative player and his numbers weren't too good. If the Yankees wanted to bring up a black player, they couldn't justify picking him as long as I was in the organization. But I was traded in 1954, and they brought him up in 1955.

DP: Did you always do so well against the Yankees because you were angry they traded you?

VP: I was in New Orleans, trying to ship my car to Puerto Rico, when I looked down on the floor and saw an old newspaper that said the Yankees had traded me to Philadelphia. That's how I found out, but I didn't care too much, because I just wanted to play somewhere. I would hit the Yankees better than other teams because I got excited being in Yankee Stadium where Babe Ruth and Lou Gehrig used to play, and being cheered by Puerto Rican fans. The Puerto Ricans in New York got madder at the Yankees than me. They wanted me to play in New York, and in the midfifties, they held a day for me at Yankee Stadium. They had a trophy to give me before the game, but the Yankees wouldn't let them do it at home plate, so the ceremony was held in the stands. I'll always remember that day. After the presentation, we played a fourteen-inning game and the Puerto Rican fans kept yelling, "Vic, the rice and beans are getting cold—we gotta go." I hit two homers, one against the right-field pole, and the other against the left-field pole, and we won.

I remember that my rookie season started on the road against the Indians. I batted against Mike Garcia, Bob Lemon, Bob Feller, who was still so fast, and Early Wynn, the toughest pitcher I ever faced—

I read that he said he'd knock down his grandmother if she got a hit off him, and since I wasn't family, I worried he might kill me. I went 0 for 16 against those guys. If I'd been with the Yankees, I might have been sent down, but I was still in the Athletics' lineup when we came to New York. I was playing center field and either Mickey Mantle was on third or he was the one who hit a deep, deep ball to center that I caught and threw in to double up the runner at home. That was the first play I made in Yankee Stadium, and it was the best play I made in my entire career, and it wasn't as a first baseman. If I'd been a visiting player in a Puerto Rican game, I probably would have been hit by an orange, but everyone in Yankee Stadium gave me a standing ovation. That was such a thrill.

DP: The Philadelphia Atheltics of 1954 were the first team I rooted for. But they were terrible and you had a disappointing rookie season.

VP: We had such a depressing team. We won only 51 games and no pitcher had 10 victories. And they couldn't strike anybody out. I'd move to my left and they'd hit it to my right, I'd move to my right and they'd hit it to my left—I'd get so tired. Our best hitter, Gus Zernial, broke his collarbone making a shoestring catch, and the Philadelphia fans were so mean they booed him as he was carried off the field. I was supposed to be a Rookie-of-the-Year candidate and got a lot of attention, but I hit only .255. I don't want to make excuses, but the batting coach, Wally Moses, took away my 36-ounce bat and made me use a light bat.

The next year we moved to Kansas City; Lou Boudreau, a beautiful man, became my manager; I played first base; and I got my heavy bat back. I hit .319, second to Al Kaline's .340. We were close until the last month, but he was too much. When I'd get two hits, he'd get three, and when I'd get three hits, he'd get four. So I just said to hell with it and had more fun than he did. When he was sleeping, I was out listening to jazz or classical music.

That year I became the first Puerto Rican to play in the All-Star Game—I'm very proud of that and still wear that 1955 All-Star ring. I had such a good year [second in batting average, third in hits, second in doubles, third in triples, third in total bases, fifth in slugging average, first among first basemen in putouts, assists, double plays, and total chances per game]. So I expected to win a contest the sportswriters were holding for the most popular player in Kansas City and be given a new Chrysler. But those writers gave it to Enos Slaughter, who batted about 250 times and wasn't even with us all season. I recently saw Enos at an old-timers game and he complained that when he drove that car away, he got a ticket. Well, he got a ticket, but he also got the car.

DP: There was another interesting veteran on that team, Elmer Valo, the only Czechoslovakian-born major-leaguer.

VP: He used to be my English teacher on the bench. Only he learned my accent and when the umpire made a bad call, Valo yelled out in my accent, "You son of a bitch." The umpire would see me in the dugout and throw me out of the game. Anytime the umpire made a bad call, I'd have to run into the clubhouse before Valo cursed at him.

DP: Did you have a really good friend on that team?

VP: Except for Bill Tuttle, who I could sense didn't like blacks, I got along with my teammates—even Slaughter, who was a tough guy. I was friends with Valo, and Jim Finigan, a nice, intelligent man . . . But my best friend was Cletis Boyer. He came to the team in 1955 and got $35,000 as a rookie, three times what I got as a rookie and just $3,000 less than the top salary I'd get in the majors. We were just like a couple of kids together. He had come from a small town in Missouri and he'd tell me that if he ever brought me home, I'd be hanged or tarred and feathered. My black teammates, Harry Simpson and Hector Lopez, got mad at me because they thought that blacks should stick together. I was Puerto Rican and didn't know why I couldn't be friends with a white player. Simpson called me an Uncle Tom, but I pretended I didn't know what that meant. Cletis used to tease Simpson by singing, "Eenie Meenie Minie Moe, I got Simpson by the toe." But Simpson wouldn't want to fight him—he'd want to fight me.

DP: Was there camaraderie among blacks throughout the league?

VP: We'd get together when our teams would play each other. Of course, Minnie Minoso and the other Latin blacks would talk because we all spoke Spanish. I remember that in 1957, when I played against Chicago, I started calling Minoso "Mau Mau" and he had no idea I was referring to those black terrorists in Kenya. And when I went to New York, I'd call Howard "Mau Mau." Soon, all the blacks in the league were calling each other Mau Mau. Then the white players started calling the black players Mau Mau. You know the Copacabana incident? Well, what happened is that Sammy Davis, Jr., was performing and Billy Martin called him Mau Mau. The black people at the next table didn't like that and there was a fight, which resulted in the Yankees trading Martin to Kansas City.

DP: Did you like Billy Martin?

VP: Oh, yes. I worried before we met because I had read that he had fought with black players on the Dodgers. I told myself to be ready for him. But the first time I played against the Yankees he came over and shook hands. Maybe he knew I used to be in the organization. Later, we would play together in Kansas City, Cleveland, and Minnesota and get along beautifully.

DP: Did you get along with the other Yankees, too?

VP: Most of them. Phil Rizzuto, Yogi—when I'd come to bat, he would ask me all about my family, and by the time I finished answering, I'd have three strikes. They all respected me, but some of them didn't like my style of playing. Hank Bauer used to deliberately step on my heel when he crossed first base—he broke six pairs of my shoes. Jim Coates used to throw at me all the time. He was a bad guy. But I got back at him—I hit four homers off him, and I know he'll never forget them because they came on Memorial Day, Mother's Day, Father's Day . . . Mickey Mantle didn't like me, either. He thought he deserved special treatment because he was Mickey Mantle, and when I picked him off first, he didn't think I was supposed to do that. And when I took an extra base on him because I read he had a bad hand, he'd curse me for taking advantage of him. I told him I didn't like that he made all that money and wouldn't run to first on a grounder. So I pretended to accidentally miss the bag with my foot. Then all the Yankees would yell for Mantle to run down the line and he'd have to do it—only to see me tag the base just before he got there. Oh, that made him mad. You know, I have two photographs that show Mantle and me at first base. In the first, he is lying on the ground injured and I'm leaning over trying to help him; in the second, I am lying on the ground injured after he ran into me, and he's standing on the bag, looking the other way.

DP: What did you think of Casey Stengel?

VP: I loved Casey! And he was a fan of mine. He always told me that he wished I had been a Yankee. Because I would drive him crazy by doing anything it took to win: break up a double play, bunt, steal, be hit by a pitch, hit-and-run, hit a sacrifice fly, go for the long ball. And in the field I always guessed when he was going to bunt or hit-and-run and would be in perfect position. I used to hit his pitchers pretty good, so they'd often throw at me, which got me mad—I'd go crazy—and made me more aggressive at the plate and on the base-paths, so he'd shout to them, "Don't wake him up!" He also knew that I was a bad-ball hitter, so he'd tell his pitchers, "Just throw him strikes!" I remember a game in the late fifties. I was at bat. There were dark shadows late in the seventh inning, and Casey brought in Ryne Duren, who wore dark sunglasses and was an alcoholic. He threw the first warm-up pitch into the stands and my legs started shaking. After some more wild throws, I nervously got ready for my first official pitch. But Duren started squinting, trying to make out Yogi's sign. Then he took off his glasses and cleaned them off. My anxiety increased. Finally, he threw a fastball behind my back. I got off the ground and took my bat and walked over to the Yankee bench, where everyone was laughing. I told Casey, "Listen, old man, if he hits me, I'm not going to fight him, I'm going to fight *you!*" Of course, I didn't want to fight him, I was just so nervous I had to say something. Casey just kept laughing.

DP: Did you have feuds with any opposing manager?

VP: I had problems with Al Lopez. Minnie Minoso told me that Lopez had trouble with black players. He also didn't like Latin players and wouldn't let them speak Spanish. Both times he managed Minoso, he traded him. I once asked Mike Garcia why he threw at my shins all the time when Lopez was his manager, and he told me that Lopez told him never to throw at black players' heads because they have good reflexes. In my career I was hit in the head and the face, but the most frightened I ever got was when I was hit in the back by Dick Donovan, who was pitching for Lopez. Oh, baby, I still feel that one. I stayed in that game and later homered, but I was so mad. I called Lopez a lot of names and challenged him to come out.

A couple of weeks later, I was picked for the All-Star team, which would be managed by Lopez. I told a sportswriter, "I'll bet I don't play." On the day of the game, I had a cold and bad fever. Lopez told me that after introductions, I should just go into the clubhouse for the rest of the game. So I went inside and took off all my clothes and listened to the game on radio. But around the sixth inning, with two men on base, Lopez sent the trainer in to get me to pinch-hit. I was so scared because I didn't have any clothes. And I was so sick. I couldn't do it. The next day, there was a big headline in the Chicago papers, "Vic Power Didn't Want to Play in the All-Star Game Because He Had a Bet." I had to fly to New York to talk to the commissioner and explain that the bet wasn't serious. The next day there was another big headline. It didn't say, "Vic Power Is Clear." It said, "The Boy Is Clear." You see; that's my story.

DP: Did you get along with your own managers?

VP: Yes. I liked playing for guys like Lou Boudreau of the Athletics, Joe Gordon of the Indians, Sam Mele of the Twins, and Bill Rigney of the Angels because they appreciated my style. In fact, I only argued one time with a manager, Jimmy Dykes. Frank Lane, Cleveland's general manager, brought Dykes to Cleveland in exchange for Joe Gordon. Gordon was a funny, easygoing manager and Dykes was like an army sergeant. Once at a rest stop I thought we had stopped to eat and I ordered food—Dykes got furious because we'd stopped only to use the bathroom. So we yelled at each other. He always tried to intimidate me. He once fined me for missing midnight curfew when all I did was step outside the hotel at three A.M. to watch a lunar eclipse. He fined Minoso, Woody Held, Tito Francona, Billy Martin, and me for trying to sneak in at one A.M., after bowling—he got the elevator operator to ask everyone who came in past curfew to autograph a baseball.

DP: When the Athletics sent you to the Indians during the 1958 season, I remember reading speculation that you were traded because you were a clubhouse lawyer.

VP: Listen, one time they tried to interview me on radio and I had a lot of trouble because of my accent. When I was asked about American League pitchers, I started to say "some of the pitches," but it sounded like "son of a bitches" and they shut off the program. How could I be a clubhouse lawyer when I couldn't even speak English? I was a funny guy in the clubhouse, I never caused problems, I never held out, I respected the manager, general manager, and owner. I didn't try to challenge the system.

DP: Were you unhappy to be traded, although you would get a chance to play on a contender?

VP: I didn't have a bad reaction. Frank Lane told me that if I could make it to Cleveland in time for a series against the Yankees, he would give me $3,000. So I started packing like crazy. But it took me three days to drive there, and I never did get that money. Still, I liked being on a good team.

The one who had a bad reaction was Roger Maris, who went to the Athletics. Maybe he didn't like going to Kansas City or maybe he didn't like being traded for a black player, but I could tell he was mad at me. One time when I was playing second for the Indians, Maris slid very hard with his spikes high and caught me in the ribs. I warned him that the next time he slid like that I was going to give him an eye for an eye. I had watched how Jackie Robinson jumped over a sliding runner and came down on top him with his spikes, and that's what I planned for Maris. And the next time he slid hard into the base I jumped up into the air. But he slid past the base and I realized that I was about to come down directly on his face. It would have looked like an accident if I came straight down, but I quickly split my legs and landed with my spikes on both sides of his face. I didn't hurt him, but I did teach him a lesson.

DP: I know you roomed with Minoso for part of the time in Cleveland. Was he a nice guy?

VP: Well, we don't want to say he was a nice guy. He was a good ballplayer. My best roommate was Mudcat Grant because we had a lot in common. He would dress up, he liked music, and if I invited him to my sister's to eat rice and beans, he would be happy to come. He also got along with white players as well as black players. Minoso was a roommate, but he never stayed in the room. He liked girls and he liked to dance. Once we were in New Orleans to play an exhibition game and went to a nightclub. He found this 6'3" girl and danced with her all night. He kept telling me how beautiful she was. Oh, he was proud of his beautiful girlfriend. But I knew something was wrong because she had the head of a first baseman and the neck of a football player. At four o'clock, the lights came on and it was a guy—oh, Minnie wanted to kill him.

DP: You were great friends with Jimmy Piersall . . .

VP: It didn't start out that way. When I was on Kansas City and he was on Boston, he got mad when I caught his line drive to first and he shouted, "You black son of a bitch!" from the dugout. The next time he got on first, I told Bobby Shantz to throw over. Shantz didn't want to do it because we were way ahead and Piersall wasn't going to run, but I insisted. So he threw to first and I gave Piersall a hard tag on the back of the neck. He got mad and yelled at me for hitting him so hard, and I told him I would hit him as hard as I wanted. I told him I was going to kill him and dropped my glove, and the umpires ran up and it looked like we were going to fight. Then he took a deep breath and said, "You don't' want to kill me. I've got a big family." And everyone started laughing. When we played together in Cleveland, he gave me his book *Fear Strikes Out* to read and it was a very sad story. He wasn't crazy anymore he said, but he still was sick and I tried to protect him. Joe Cronin, the American League president, kept sending him telegrams telling him to behave. I'll never forget when Jimmy got into an argument with an umpire and took a water pistol from his pocket and shot water into the umpire's face—that was awful. He once asked for time when batting against Detroit and ran into the clubhouse. He came back with something hidden in his hand. It turned out to be a mosquito spray. When the ball was pitched, he whipped it out and sprayed the ball. There was smoke all over and everyone was laughing.

Then there was the time he took a home run ball that bounced back on the field and threw it at Bill Veeck's expensive new scoreboard, which was blaring music and explosive noises—and it broke. I remember that he hit a home run against Jim Bunning in a key game in front of 40,000 people. He bowed to all the people, but wouldn't run. Suddenly he took off as if he was beating out an inside-the-park homer and he slid into home plate. And then he just lay there sleeping. That caused a big fight. We had to run out there and save him. One day, they let about 8,000 kids into the ballpark free and they sat in the stands together. When Jimmy was in the outfield, they yelled for him to come over and sign autographs. Well, he waved them to come onto the field and they climbed over the fence and ran over to him—and during the middle of the game, he started signing autographs. But it was more dangerous in Yankee Stadium when some tough young guys started calling him names and he challenged one to a fight and a bunch of them went onto the field after him. They started kicking him. So our second baseman—Johnny Temple—and I ran out to rescue him. Temple, who was a tough guy, really hit those guys. Jimmy wasn't a fighter. He would just throw tantrums like a little boy. We used to love to drive him crazy. He didn't like smoke and every time he got on the bus, Barry Latman and the others would light up cigars and blow smoke at him, and he'd go wild and make the driver stop the bus so he could take a taxi. I think I enjoyed playing with him more than anyone because he would do something different every day—and that kept me relaxed.

DP: What about Rocky Colavito?

VP: He was a nice guy and very religious. He'd get mad at me for eating fish on Friday and sleeping late on Sunday instead of going to church. He was a leader on the team. I felt that if Rocky used his power, the pitcher had control, and I had my glove, the Indians would win. It's too bad Frank Lane traded Rocky to Detroit in 1960 because we counted on him for home runs. In fact, when I stole home to win that game against Detroit in 1958, a sportswriter didn't congratulate me—he questioned what I did when Colavito was at bat and could have homered.

DP: When you stole home twice in one game, to tie it at 8–8 and win it 9–8, you became the only player in the last fifty years to equal that unbreakable record. Considering that you stole only three bases the entire 1958 season, what made you do it?

VP: I did it because those guys on Detroit used to hit me with pitches all the time. I remember on the first steal my strategy was go and come back, go and come back. And I heard Leo Durocher, who was a Tiger coach, yell to Frank Lary, "Don't look at that monkey. He wants to make you nervous." I hated that he called me a monkey and I later told him I could understand why Laraine Day divorced him.

DP: Was the second steal a close play?

VP: Neither play was close. If it had been close, I would probably have been called out. Black players didn't get many close calls. I know I didn't. In fact, the reason I swung at the first pitch and at so many bad pitches was that some umpires would call anything a strike on me. In the winter leagues I was a patient hitter, but not in the majors with umpires like Ed Runge. Just a couple of years ago, Moe Drabowsky, who was a crazy-eyed pitcher, confided that an umpire told him that all he had to do was pitch the ball to me and he'd call it a strike—not because I was black but because I was Vic Power. I remember a game against Boston when the plate umpire called a strike on an obvious ball. So I stepped out to argue. Then I called time. But the umpire told the pitcher to throw the ball so he could call a strike. He threw it and I jumped back into the batter's box and tripled. There was a big argument—they were mad at the umpire.

DP: You had a quick bat despite your pendulum batting stance, where it seemed you were preparing to hit a golf ball off a tee.

VP: The best pitchers threw the ball low. I swung the bat low so they would think I wanted a low pitch. Then they would throw it high, at eye level, where I liked it, not thinking I had time to pull my bat up and back and swing up there. But I pulled out of the pendulum just in time for the pitch.

DP: Even more than your pendulum swing, you were famous for your fielding. I just wish there were films of you at first base.

VP: Oh, I'm proud of my fielding. I won seven Gold Gloves at first, but I was also good at other positions and played them, not because of a promotion, but because they needed me there. I don't want to get people mad by saying I was the closest to Brooks Robinson as a third baseman, because I love Brooksie, but I don't remember making an error there. Once I made the All-Star team as a utility infielder. No matter what position I played, I caught everything one-handed. I was happy it entertained people because I believed in giving fans their money's worth, but I did it only because it gave me more flexibility and range. Catching with two hands made me feel tight—anyway, if the guy who invented baseball had wanted fielders to use two hands, he would have had them wear two gloves. At first, I would play extremely deep so I could cover a lot of territory. I had to convince my infielders to throw to the empty base rather than to throw once I got there—they were reluctant to do this until I proved I would always get there in time to catch the ball. Early in my career, I began to learn about the hitters and I knew where a Ted Williams or a Nellie Fox would hit the ball, how hard they would hit it, and how fast they could run—they'd always get so mad because I'd catch it and just beat them to the base. I also knew when a player would bunt against me and would race from the edge of the outfield and pounce on it. I was always in the game. I didn't have a great arm, but I had a quick release; I wasn't fast, but I was quick and got a tremendous jump; I had great reflexes and great instincts, even a sixth sense. I did things at first that were ahead of their time, that Keith Hernandez does now. When I held a man on, I would keep my right foot on the base and my left in foul territory; if, with a man on second, I caught a grounder, rather than going to first for the sure out, I would throw to third. And of course, no one caught one-handed then—and even today, no one uses my special little "move" with the glove.

It began to upset me that when I caught one-handed, a Mickey Mantle would scream I was a "hot dog," "clown," and "son of a bitch." I told Jimmy Dykes that I was going to try to change my style and catch everything with two hands so people wouldn't be mad at me. And Dykes told me something I never forgot; he said: "Don't argue with success." He explained that the only reason those guys hated my style is that I'd beat them with it. So because of what he said, I kept using one hand, despite that sportswriters wrote I was a showboat and opposing players and their fans cursed at me. Sometimes it even made my own fans nervous. I still get letters from people in Minnesota who remember how I caught the final pop-up of Jack Kralick's no-hitter: they say they almost had a heart attack because I used only one hand. But I never dropped a ball.

DP: In 1962, you were traded to the Twins, who had finished seventh the previous year. They finished second, only five games behind the Yankees, and despite the excellent pitching and 185 team home runs, you were voted the team's MVP.

VP: Sam Mele said that I stabilized his young infield. Zoilo Versalles at short, Bernie Allen at second, and Rich Rollins at third made some interesting throws. They estimated I saved Versalles 47 errors. We were voted the best infield in the league. The defense was so good that Camilo Pascual thanked me for letting him win 20 games for the first time.

Versalles was crazy, and Bob Allison didn't seem to like black players, but otherwise I liked playing with those guys. Billy Martin, Earl Battey . . . Jimmy Kaat was a smart guy, Harmon Killebrew was a beautiful guy.

DP: At the end of the 1963 season, Tony Oliva joined the Twins. He barely spoke English and I know you took him under your wing.

VP: I rarely socialized with my teammates during my major league career because very few of them liked to go to art museums, shop for clothes, eat at good restaurants, or see classical music or jazz. They wanted to play cards and drink beer. But Tony would follow me everywhere. In fact, he would do everything I did. If I bought a shirt, he would buy the same shirt, in the same color. Whatever I ordered on a menu, he would do the same. He would have eaten snake. He wasn't too sophisticated. When I told him we'd be facing Whitey Ford, he asked me if Whitey was a black guy. He thought Floyd Robinson on the White Sox was Jackie Robinson. He couldn't read English, so when he saw his name in the paper, he'd ask me to translate. I'd say that Fidel Castro had passed a law saying all Cuban ballplayers, including Oliva, would have to pay him 50 percent of their salaries—and Tony would get so upset. I loved to tease him. I hated shoveling snow, so I told Oliva that Ted Williams became such a good hitter because he spent a lot of time shoveling snow. On the morning of the next big snow, I looked out the window and Tony was outside with a shovel. He shoveled our sidewalk and driveway all winter. He led the league in hitting and always believed it was because he shoveled snow. I remember the time I caught him walking through a hotel lobby with an ugly girl. I said, "Tony, this is the big leagues, you can't go out with women who look like Willie Mays." He told me, "Every time I go out with her, I go five for five." So I said, "Okay, you go out with her, but you gotta use the fire escape." Soon after, I introduced Tony to his wife. I also taught Tony how to drive, but he was hopeless, like my wife. When I had to renew my license, I took them both to take their driving tests—I flunked and they both passed. I was afraid to go home with them.

DP: Oliva's arrival in Minnesota resulted in Bob Allison's being switched to first and your being traded to the Angels.

VP: Everyone knew I was a better player than Allison, but he had more power. That trade really frustrated me. When I had bought a house in Kansas City I was traded, when I bought a house in Cleveland I was traded, and now when I bought a house in Minnesota I was traded. You see why I respect Curt Flood so much for challenging the reserve clause—everyone makes money and has security because of what he did, but no one remembers him.

When I went to the Angels I lived in an apartment in Hollywood, when the hippies were coming in. There weren't too many sports fans; I'd say I was a player and people would think I was a musician.

But I enjoyed my stay. I loved Gene Autry. We used to stay at the Melody Ranch in Palm Springs. Late at night, he used to get drunk at the bar and want to sing in Spanish, so he'd tell the bartender, "Call Vic Power!" So they'd wake me up to come sing with Gene Autry.

I was reunited with Jimmy Piersall. I also spent a lot of time with Dean Chance and Bo Belinsky, the playboy. I got to go to their parties. Until I saw Chance, I thought Bobby Shantz was the best pitcher I ever played behind. Dean would say, get me one run and I'll win. And he always did it. In 1964, he pitched 11 shutouts! He was also a lot of fun off the field. He was almost as wild as Belinsky. I remember one party. Bo was supposed to show up any minute and one of his girlfriends was drunk and in a dark bedroom. A player would knock on the door. She'd call out, "Who is it?" He'd answer, "Bo Belinsky." And she'd say, "Come in." So he'd go inside. About ten players knocked on the door and went inside, claiming to be Bo Belinsky. Bo never did come to that party.

DP: In September, you joined the Philadelphia Phillies, who seemed on their way to a pennant. Instead they blew it . . .

VP: Frank Thomas broke his finger so the Phillies acquired me. They were in first place and had a good team: Johnny Callison, Jim Bunning, Tony Gonzalez, Richie Allen, Chris Short, Tony Taylor, Alex Johnson, who was a nice guy but no one would leave him alone—they kept giving him deodorant and he'd get furious. I thought I had a chance to appear in my first World Series. But every day, we'd lose a close game. The pitchers were too tired. Gene Mauch was nervous because he even asked me, "What are we gonna do?" He wasn't very professional. And I couldn't help. We were playing the Dodgers and Willie Davis was up. I was positioned where I wanted, but Mauch thought he'd bunt and kept calling me in. Instead Davis smashed the ball at me and it hurt my finger for the rest of the season. It was so disappointing.

DP: You returned to the Angels in 1965, your final year.

VP: I wish I could have had a better year, but I just couldn't produce. At the end of the season, the Angels wanted to sell my contract to Japan, but I didn't want to go. I didn't want to play anymore—I'd played eleven years in the majors and about the same in the winter leagues. Instead I decided to break into motion pictures. I was given a screen test for a film about the history of the United States. They liked me until they heard my accent. Then, early in the morning, they had me ride a horse for two or three hours. I didn't like it—I wanted to play Superman.

In 1967, my mother got cancer and I returned to Puerto Rico. I thought it would only be temporary, but I ended up staying, managing, scouting for the Angels, conducting baseball clinics with teenagers to keep them off drugs and out of trouble.

DP: Tell me about Roberto Clemente.

VP: I was three years older than Clemente and started playing in Puerto Rico several years before him. We became friends and would go out together, and I managed him at Caguas in the midfifties, although he played mostly for other teams. I had a better career than him in the winter leagues. He won a batting title, but he didn't play too much because he had a sore back. We did play together in Cuba, in a Caribbean series. He became a hero in Puerto Rico because of his play in America. The Puerto Ricans would read the papers to find out about Clemente, Orlando Cepeda, and me. We remained close, though we had little chance to see each other during the major league season because he was in the National League. But he was one of the players who came when I organized a Latin players all-star game, the final game ever played in the Polo Grounds. He was a very proud ballplayer. He hated to lose. He was a great hitter but he also could run and field. He would make circus catches. Of course, the sportswriters called him a showboat, too—why didn't they ever call a white player a showboat?

I was very sad when he died. He left his wife and children. I have pictures of him and his son. We were together in Nicaragua two weeks before his death with the Puerto Rican National Amateur Team. Then there was the earthquake in Nicaragua and he wanted to go back there. Some people think he wanted to go back because of a girlfriend, but I don't think so.

He tried to go back with provisions. The pilot was drunk. It was an old plane and it was overloaded and wouldn't start the first three times. It was black, windy, and rainy. He didn't make it. The next day when they found the plane, I knew he'd been in it because I recognized among the debris a small suitcase that he'd bought in Nicaragua. He was so worried about it because it had a little alligator head on it—he wanted to cut it off because he thought it looked feminine. I said to leave it like that. . . .

DP: Looking back on your career, do you have any regrets?

VP: I didn't play in a World Series or hit enough homers to make the Hall of Fame, but I'm very proud of my accomplishments, especially the seven Gold Gloves, seven All-Star appearances, and being the first Puerto Rican to play in an All-Star game. I got to travel and meet all kinds of people in and out of baseball: John Kennedy, Fidel Castro, Ty Cobb—when I bragged I was hitting .331, he asked if I were in a slump—Satchel Paige, Connie Mack, Jackie Robinson, Jimmy Piersall, Bo Belinsky. I got to play with the best players: Ted Williams, the greatest hitter ever, Bob Feller, Sandy Koufax, Willie Mays, Brooks Robinson, Luis Aparicio, Nellie Fox, Henry Aaron, Roberto Clemente, Mickey Vernon, Rocky Colavito, Harmon Killebrew . . . I got to see the Boston Pops in Boston, Tito Puente at the Paladium in New York, Lionel Hampton, Duke Ellington, Count Basie, even Billie Holliday and the Beatles. So you see, baseball was never everything. I got to combine work with pleasure. I had marvelous careers in Puerto Rico and in the major leagues. I played enough. People remember me . . . you remember me.

Index

About the Editor

Danny Peary is a film and television critic, sportswriter, and script-writer. He has a B.A. in history from the University of Wisconsin and an M.A. in cinema from the University of Southern California. He was the sports editor of *L.A. Panorama* and writes the annual *365 Sports-Facts-A-Year-Calendar*. He is the author of *Cult Movies, Cult Movies 2, Cult Movies 3,* and *Guide for the Film Fanatic*. His wife, Suzanne, is a book editor and their daughter, Zoë, attends the University of Michigan.